Alternative Assets and Cryptocurrencies

Alternative Assets and Cryptocurrencies

Special Issue Editor

Christian Hafner

MDPI • Basel • Beijing • Wuhan • Barcelona • Belgrade

MDPI

Special Issue Editor
Christian Hafner
Université catholique de Louvain
Belgium

Editorial Office
MDPI
St. Alban-Anlage 66
4052 Basel, Switzerland

This is a reprint of articles from the Special Issue published online in the open access journal *Journal of Risk and Financial Management* (ISSN 1911-8074) from 2017 to 2018 (available at: https://www.mdpi.com/journal/jrfm/special_issues/alternative_assets_and_cryptocurrencies)

For citation purposes, cite each article independently as indicated on the article page online and as indicated below:

LastName, A.A.; LastName, B.B.; LastName, C.C. Article Title. *Journal Name* **Year**, *Article Number*, Page Range.

ISBN 978-3-03897-978-4 (Pbk)
ISBN 978-3-03897-979-1 (PDF)

Contents

About the Special Issue Editor

Christian Hafner is a professor of econometrics at the Louvain Institute of Data Analysis and Modeling of the Université Catholique de Louvain, Belgium. He previously served as an assistant professor at Erasmus University Rotterdam, Netherlands. He holds a Ph.D. in economics from Humboldt University Berlin, Germany, and is a Distinguished Fellow of the International Engineering and Technology Institute. In 2018 he received the Econometric Theory Award in Recognition of Research Contributions to the Science of Econometrics, *Multa Scripsit*. His main research interests are financial econometrics, time series analysis, and empirical finance. He is currently the associate editor of the journals *Digital Finance, Studies in Nonlinear Dynamics and Econometrics, Journal of Business and Economic Statistics, Econometrics*, and *Journal of Risk and Financial Management*. He is a co-author of the book *Statistics of Financial Markets* and has published widely in peer-reviewed international journals in finance, econometrics and statistics.

Preface to "Alternative Assets and Cryptocurrencies"

This book collects high profile research papers on the innovative topic of alternative assets and cryptocurrencies. It aims at providing a guideline and inspiration for both researchers and practitioners in financial technology. Alternative assets such as fine art, wine or diamonds have become popular investment vehicles in the aftermath of the global financial crisis. Triggered by low correlation with classical financial markets, diversification benefits arise for portfolio allocation and risk management. Cryptocurrencies share many features of alternative assets, but are hampered by high volatility, sluggish commercial acceptance, and regulatory uncertainties.

The papers comprised in this special issue address alternative assets and cryptocurrencies from economic, financial, statistical, and technical points of view. It gives an overview of the current state of the art and helps to understand their properties and prospects using innovative approaches and methodologies. The timeliness of this collection is apparent from the view and download statistics of the journal's website, where at the time of this writing most of the papers are in the top ten over the last year or more, which highlights the general interest in the topic.

A first challenge is the analysis of time series properties such as volatility, including financial applications. Conrad, Custovic and Ghysels study long and short term volatility components and find that Bitcoin volatility is closely linked to indicators of global economic activity. Henriques and Sadorsky use multivariate GARCH-type models to show that there is an economic value for risk averse investors to replace gold by Bitcoin in investment portfolios. Kjaerland, Khazal, Krogstad, Nordstrøm and Oust identify dynamic pricing factors for Bitcoin using autoregressive distributed lags (ADL) and GARCH. They find that the Google search indicator and returns on the S&P 500 stock index are significant pricing factors.

A second block of papers deals with high frequency data for cryptocurrencies, meaning minute-stamped or transaction data. A common theme is predictability, which is confirmed in several papers, and which would violate classical concepts of market efficiency. Fischer, Krauss and Deinert use a specific trading strategy to show that there are statistical arbitrage opportunities in the cross-section of cryptocurrencies. In a deep learning framework, Shintate and Pichl propose a so-called random sampling method for trend prediction classification, applied to high frequency Bitcoin prices. Catania and Sandholdt find predictability at high frequencies up to six hours, but not at higher aggregation levels, while realized volatility is characterized by long memory and leverage effects. Schnaubelt, Rende and Krauss study the properties of Bitcoin limit order books. Their findings suggest that, while many features are similar to classical financial markets, the distributions of trade sizes and limit order prices are rather distinct, and liquidity costs are relatively high.

Third, a few papers deal with peculiarities of cryptocurrencies such as initial coin offerings, proof-of-work protocols and sentiment indices. Ante, Sandner, Fiedler investigate blockchain-based initial coin offerings (ICOs) and find that they exhibit similarities to classical crowdfunding and venture capital markets, including the determinants of success factors. Bocart proposes a new proof-of-work protocol to establish consensus about transactions to be added to the blockchain, arguing that the availability of alternatives to the classical SHA256 algorithm used by Bitcoin reduces the risk of attacks against particular proof-of-work protocols. Finally, Chen and Hafner use a publicly available crypto-market sentiment index as an explanatory variable for locally explosive behavior of crypto prices and volatility. In a smooth transition autoregressive model, they identify bubble periods for Bitcoin and the CRIX, a crypto market index.

Last, but not least, we have indeed a paper that deals with a "classical" alternative asset, that is, diamonds. Jotanovic and D'Ecclesia show that, perhaps counterintuitively, investing in diamond mining stocks is not a valid alternative to investing in diamonds commodity directly. Moreover, diamond stock returns are not driven by diamond price dynamics, but rather by local market stock indices.

All of the above papers cover many diverse aspects of alternative assets and cryptocurrencies that we hope will contribute to the already rich literature and become useful resources and inspirations for anyone working in the exciting new field of financial technology.

Christian Hafner
Special Issue Editor

Journal of
Risk and Financial Management

MDPI

Article

Long- and Short-Term Cryptocurrency Volatility Components: A GARCH-MIDAS Analysis

Christian Conrad [1,*], Anessa Custovic [2] and Eric Ghysels [2,3]

[1] Department of Economics, Heidelberg University, Bergheimer Strasse 58, 69115 Heidelberg, Germany
[2] Department of Economics, University of North Carolina, Chapel Hill, NC 27599, USA;
    anessa1@live.unc.edu (A.C.); eghysels@gmail.com (E.G.)
[3] CEPR, Department of Finance, Kenan-Flagler School of Business, University of North Carolina,
    Chapel Hill, NC 27599, USA
* Correspondence: christian.conrad@awi.uni-heidelberg.de; Tel.: +49-6221-54-3173

Received: 10 April 2018; Accepted: 8 May 2018; Published: 10 May 2018

Abstract: We use the GARCH-MIDAS model to extract the long- and short-term volatility components of cryptocurrencies. As potential drivers of Bitcoin volatility, we consider measures of volatility and risk in the US stock market as well as a measure of global economic activity. We find that S&P 500 realized volatility has a negative and highly significant effect on long-term Bitcoin volatility. The finding is atypical for volatility co-movements across financial markets. Moreover, we find that the S&P 500 volatility risk premium has a significantly positive effect on long-term Bitcoin volatility. Finally, we find a strong positive association between the Baltic dry index and long-term Bitcoin volatility. This result shows that Bitcoin volatility is closely linked to global economic activity. Overall, our findings can be used to construct improved forecasts of long-term Bitcoin volatility.

Keywords: Baltic dry index; Bitcoin volatility; digital currency; GARCH-MIDAS; pro-cyclical volatility; volume

JEL Classification: C53; C58; F31; G15

"After Lehman Brothers toppled in September 2008, it took 24 days for US stocks to slide more than 20 per cent into official bear market territory. Bitcoin, the new age cryptocurrency that has been breaking bull market records, did the same on Wednesday in just under six hours"

Financial Times—30 November 2017—*Bitcoin swings from bull to bear and back in one day*

1. Introduction

Bitcoin is surely not short on publicity as its rise, subsequent decline and volatile swings have drawn the attention from academics and business leaders alike. There are many critics. For example, Nobel laureate Joseph Stiglitz said that Bitcoin ought to be outlawed whereas fellow Nobel laureate Robert Shiller said the currency appeals to some investors because it has an anti-government, anti-regulation feel. Many business leaders, including Carl Icahn and Warren Buffett, characterized its spectacular price increases as a bubble. Jamie Dimon, CEO of JP Morgan called it a fraud, and implicitly alluding to bubbles that ultimately burst, predicted that it eventually would blow up. Along similar lines, Goldman Sachs CEO Lloyd Blankfein is on the record for saying that the currency serves as a vehicle for perpetrating fraud, although he acknowledged that the currency could have potential if volatility drops.

Cryptocurrencies has its defenders and enthusiasts as well. The CME Group listed Bitcoin futures in mid-December 2017 and Nasdaq plans to launch Bitcoin futures this year. The currency also has many supporters in Silicon Valley. The listing of Bitcoin futures and the proliferation of cryptocurrencies in general has generated a growing literature on the topic.

Most of the existing studies focus on Bitcoin returns. For example, Baur et al. (2017) show that Bitcoin returns are essentially uncorrelated with traditional asset classes such as stocks or bonds, which points to diversification possibilities. Others investigate the determinants of Bitcoin returns. The findings of Li and Wang (2017), among others, suggest that measures of financial and macroeconomic activity are drivers of Bitcoin returns. Kristoufek (2015) considers financial uncertainty, Bitcoin trading volume in Chinese Yuan and Google trends as potential drivers of Bitcoin returns. The inclusion of Google trends as some sort of proxy for sentiment or interest is fairly common within the literature (see, for example, Polasik et al. (2015)). A recurrent theme in the literature is the question to which asset class Bitcoin belongs, with many comparing it to gold, others to precious metals or to speculative assets (see, among others, Baur et al. (2017); or Bouri et al. (2017)). Some have classified Bitcoin as something in between a currency and a commodity (see, for example, Dyhrberg (2016)). For other recent contributions, see Cheah et al. (2018); Khuntia and Pattanayak (2018); and Koutmos (2018).

A second strand of literature tries to model Bitcoin volatility. Among the first papers is Balcilar et al. (2017), who analyze the causal relation between trading volume and Bitcoin returns and volatility. They find that volume cannot help predict the volatility of Bitcoin returns. Dyhrberg (2016) explores Bitcoin volatility using GARCH models. The models estimated in Dyhrberg (2016) suggest that Bitcoin has several similarities with both gold and the dollar. Bouri et al. (2017) find no evidence for asymmetry in the conditional volatility of Bitcoins when considering the post December 2013 period and investigate the relation between the VIX index and Bitcoin volatility. Al-Khazali et al. (2018) consider a model for daily Bitcoin returns and show that Bitcoin volatility tends to decrease in response to positive news about the US economy. Finally, Katsiampa (2017) explores the applicability of several ARCH-type specifications to model Bitcoin volatility and selects an AR-CGARCH model as the preferred specification. Although Katsiampa (2017) suggests that Bitcoin volatility consists of long- and short-term components, he does not investigate the determinants of Bitcoin volatility.

We use the GARCH-MIDAS model of Engle et al. (2013) for investigating the economic determinants of long-term Bitcoin volatility. While all the previous studies considered Bitcoin returns/volatility as well as their potential determinants at the same (daily) frequency, the MIxed Data Sampling (MIDAS) technique offers a unique framework to investigate macroeconomic and financial variables that are sampled at a lower (monthly) frequency than the Bitcoin returns as potential drivers of Bitcoin volatility. Specifically, the two-component GARCH-MIDAS model consists of a short-term GARCH component and a long-term component. The model allows explanatory variables to enter directly into the specification of the long-term component.

As potential drivers of Bitcoin volatility, we consider macroeconomic and financial variables, such as the Baltic dry index and the VIX, but also Bitcoin specific variables, such as trading volume. In addition, we analyze the drivers of the volatility of the S&P 500, the Nikkei 225, gold and copper. This allows for a comparison of the effects on the different assets and provides further useful insights for a classification of Bitcoin as an asset class.

Our main findings can be summarized as follows: First, Bitcoin volatility is negatively related to US stock market volatility. This observation is consistent with investors who consider Bitcoin as a safe-haven. Second, in contrast to stock market volatility, Bitcoin volatility behaves pro-cyclical, i.e., increases with higher levels of global economic activity. Third, the response of Bitcoin volatility to higher levels of US stock market volatility is the opposite of the response of gold volatility. This questions the meaningfulness of comparisons between Bitcoin and gold. Finally, while most previous studies focused on short-term relationships using exclusively daily data, our results highlight the importance of also investigating the relationship between long-term Bitcoin volatility and its economic drivers.

In Section 2, we introduce the GARCH-MIDAS model as it is applied in the current setting. Section 3 describes the data. The empirical results are presented in Section 4. Section 5 concludes the paper.

2. Model

We model Bitcoin volatility as a GARCH-MIDAS processs. Engle et al. (2013) discuss the technical details of this class of models where the conditional variance is multiplicatively decomposed into a short-term (high-frequency) and a long-term (low-frequency) component. The long-term component is expressed as a function of observable explanatory variables. This allows us to investigate the financial and macroeconomic determinants of Bitcoin volatility. In the empirical application, we consider daily Bitcoin returns and monthly explanatory variables.

We define daily Bitcoin returns as $r_{i,t} = 100 \cdot (\ln(P_{i,t} - \ln(P_{i-1,t}))$, where $t = 1, \ldots, T$ denotes the monthly frequency and $i = 1, \ldots, N_t$ the number of days within month t. We assume that the conditional mean of Bitcoin returns is constant, i.e.,

$$r_{i,t} = \mu + \varepsilon_{i,t}, \tag{1}$$

with

$$\varepsilon_{i,t} = \sqrt{h_{i,t}\tau_t}Z_{i,t}. \tag{2}$$

The innovation $Z_{i,t}$ is assumed to be i.i.d. with mean zero and variance one. $h_{i,t}$ and τ_t denote the short- and long-term component of the conditional variance, respectively. The short-term component $h_{i,t}$ varies at the daily frequency and follows a unit-variance GARCH(1,1) process

$$h_{i,t} = (1 - \alpha - \beta) + \alpha\frac{\varepsilon_{i-1,t}^2}{\tau_t} + \beta h_{i-1,t}, \tag{3}$$

where $\alpha > 0$, $\beta \geq 0$ and $\alpha + \beta < 1$. The long-term component varies at the monthly frequency and is given by

$$\tau_t = m + \sum_{k=1}^{K} \varphi_k(\omega_1, \omega_2)X_{t-k}, \tag{4}$$

where X_t denotes the explanatory variable and $\varphi_k(\omega_1, \omega_2)$ a certain weighting scheme. We opt for the Beta weighting scheme, which is given by

$$\varphi_k(\omega_1, \omega_2) = \frac{(k/(K+1))^{\omega_1-1} \cdot (1 - k/(K+1))^{\omega_2-1}}{\sum_{j=1}^{K} (j/(K+1))^{\omega_1-1} \cdot (1 - j/(K+1))^{\omega_2-1}}. \tag{5}$$

By construction, the weights $\varphi_k(\omega_1, \omega_2) \geq 0, k = 1, \ldots, K$, sum to one. In the empirical application, we impose the restriction that $\omega_1 = 1$, which implies that the weights are monotonically declining. Following Conrad and Loch (2015), we employ three MIDAS lag years, i.e., we choose $K = 36$ for the monthly explanatory variables. Our empirical results show that this choice is appropriate in the sense that the estimated weights approach zero before lag 36. As in Engle et al. (2013), we estimate the GARCH-MIDAS models by quasi-maximum likelihood and construct heteroscedasticity and autocorrelation consistent (HAC) standard errors.

3. Data

Our analysis utilizes cryptocurrency specific data, measures of financial conditions, and measures of macroeconomic activity from May 2013 to December 2017. Data are collected from a number of sources and are described in more detail in what follows.

3.1. Data Descriptions

Daily Bitcoin prices and trading volumes were taken from bitcoinity.[1] The monthly realized volatility for Bitcoin was constructed using daily squared returns. The Bitcoin (BTC) trading volume by currency is simply the sum of all BTC traded in a selected period in specific currencies. It is worth noting, however, that traders are able to trade in any currency they choose, regardless of geographic location.

The financial measures used consist of the following: commodity ETFs, a luxury goods index, monthly realized volatility and daily returns for the S&P 500 and the Nikkei 225, the VIX index, and the Variance Risk Premium. For the luxury goods index, we use the S&P Global Luxury Index (Glux). This offers exposure to over 80 luxury brands in a number of countries. For our commodities, we use SPDR Gold Shares ETF (GLD) and iPath Bloomberg Copper ETF (JJC).

The S&P 500 monthly realized volatility is constructed using the daily realized variances, $RVar_{i,t}^{SP}$, based on 5-min intra-day returns from the Oxford-Man Institute of Quantitative Finance. The daily realized variances are then used to construct annualized monthly realized volatility as $RVol_t^{SP} = \sqrt{12 \cdot \sum_{i=1}^{N_t} RVar_{i,t}^{SP}}$. The Nikkei 225 monthly realized volatility is constructed analogously. The VIX index, from the Chicago Board of Options Exchange (Cboe), is computed from a panel of options prices and is a "risk-neutral" implied volatility measure of the stock market. It is frequently referred to as a "fear index" and is a gauge of perceived volatility, in both directions. The Variance Risk Premium, VRP_t, is calculated as the difference between the squared VIX and the expected realized variance. Assuming the realized variance is a random walk, this is then a purely data-driven measure of the risk premium.

The measure of macroeconomic activity used consists of the Baltic dry index (BDI), retrieved from Quandl.[2] BDI is an economic indicator issued by the Baltic Exchange based in London and was first released in January 1985. The BDI is a composite of the following four different Baltic indices: the Capesize, Handysize, Panamax, and Supramax. Everyday, a panel submits current freight cost estimates on various routes. These rates are then weighted by size to create the BDI. The index covers a range of carriers who transport a number of commodities and provides a cost assessment of moving raw materials by water. It is frequently thought of as a good indicator of future economic growth and production.

Since Bitcoin has been receiving more attention in the news, we follow Kristoufek (2015) and utilize Google Trend data to see how this may contribute to the volatility of Bitcoin. We use monthly indexes constructed by Google Trends for all web searches and monthly indexes for news searches only. The spikes in the indices coincide with big events, both positive and negative. Moreover, we were able to match large weekly swings in the index to specific events throughout the sample period. Periods in the sample where Bitcoin did not have any major events take place had low, constant interest index values. Hence, we believe that the Google Trends index is a fair proxy for large events, both positive and negative, that may affect the volatility of Bitcoin.

3.2. Summary Statistics

Table 1 provides summary statistics. Panel A presents descriptive statistics for the Bitcoin returns as well as returns on the S&P 500, Nikkei 225, Gold and Copper. The average daily Bitcoin return is 0.271% during our sample period. On an annualized basis, this corresponds to a return of approximately 68%, which is much higher than for the other assets (e.g., 11.34% for the S&P 500). However, the minimum and maximum of daily Bitcoin returns are also much more extreme than for the other assets. This is also reflected in a kurtosis of 11.93 (vs. 5.99 for the S&P 500). Note that

---

[1]   All data on data.bitcoinity.org is retrieved directly from exchanges through their APIs and is regularly updated for accuracy.
[2]   Note, Quandl's data source for the BDI is Lloyd's List.

Bitcoins are traded seven days per week while the other assets are not traded over the weekend or on bank holidays, which explains the variation in the number of observations across the assets. The extraordinary price development of the Bitcoin is depicted in Figure 1. In particular, the price action in 2017 is dramatic: from January 2017 to December 2017 the Bitcoin price increased by 1318%!

Table 1. Descriptive statistics.

Variable	Mean	Min	Max	SD	Skew.	Kurt.	Obs.
Panel A: Daily return data							
Bitcoin	0.271	−26.620	35.745	4.400	−0.139	11.929	1706
S&P 500	0.045	−4.044	3.801	0.748	−0.423	5.985	1176
Nikkei 225	0.043	−8.253	7.426	1.389	−0.391	7.817	1145
Gold	−0.012	−5.479	4.832	0.967	0.022	5.873	1177
Copper	−0.004	−5.126	6.594	1.323	0.018	4.812	1177
Panel B: Monthly realized volatilities (annualized)							
RV-Bitcoin	73.063	21.519	224.690	42.349	1.414	5.472	56
RV-S&P 500	10.879	4.219	28.435	4.825	1.263	4.909	56
RV-Nikkei 225	19.701	6.336	41.969	9.328	0.981	3.039	56
RV-Gold	14.519	8.026	30.734	5.014	1.052	3.735	56
RV-Copper	20.132	8.265	36.396	6.037	0.493	2.930	56
RV-Glux	12.469	4.087	31.537	5.114	1.359	5.536	56
Panel C: Monthly explanatory variables							
VIX	14.684	9.510	28.430	3.602	1.424	5.832	56
VRP	9.819	−8.337	20.299	5.837	−0.463	4.538	56
Baltic dry index	983.150	306.905	2178.059	383.597	0.774	3.613	56
RV-Glux	12.469	4.087	31.537	5.114	1.359	5.536	56
Panel D: Monthly Bitcoin specific explanatory variables							
Google Trends (all)	7.661	2.000	100.000	14.395	5.156	32.147	56
Google Trends (news)	10.625	2.000	100.000	15.304	4.056	22.532	56
US-TV	2,308,314	603,946	4,947,777	1,047,524	0.573	2.686	56
CNY-TV	24,897,595	4693	173,047,579	42,509,087	2.180	7.056	56

Notes: The sample covers the 2013M05–2017M12 period. The reported statistics include the mean, the minimum (Min) and maximum (Max), standard deviation (SD), Skewness (Skew.), Kurtosis (Kurt.), and the number of observations (Obs.).

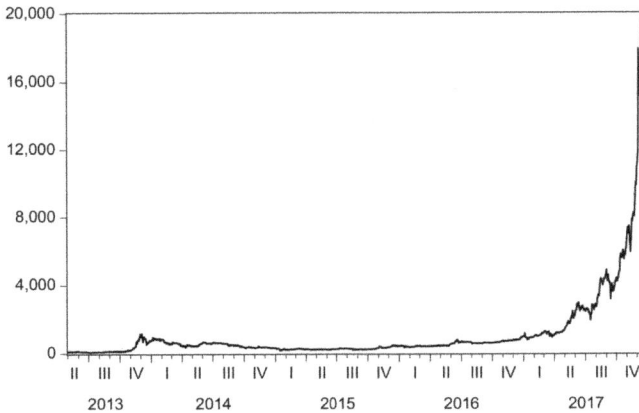

Figure 1. Bitcoin price development in the 2013:M5 to 2017:M12 period.

The monthly realized volatilities (RV) are presented in Panel B. Clearly, Bitcoin realized volatility stands out as by far the highest. The average annualized Bitcoin RV is 73% as compared to 11% for the S&P 500. Figure 2 shows the times series of annualized monthly realized volatilities. During the entire sample period Bitcoin realized volatility by far exceeds realized volatility in all other assets. Specifically, the year 2017 was characterized by unusually low volatility in stock markets: in 2017, the Cboe's volatility index, VIX, fell to the lowest level during the last 23 years and realized volatility in US stock markets was the lowest since the mid-1990s. In sharp contrast, Bitcoin volatility was increasing over almost the entire year.

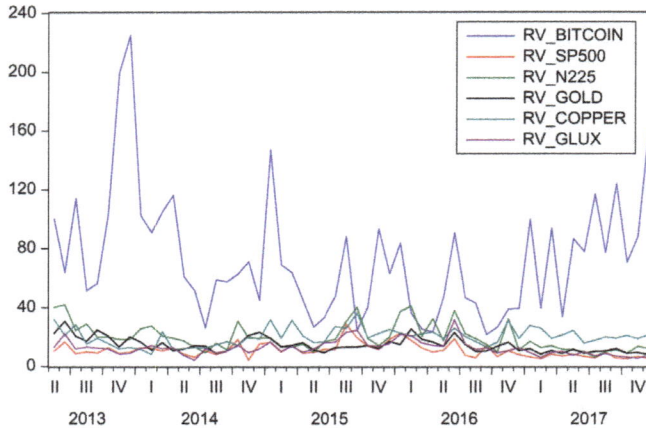

Figure 2. Annualized monthly realized volatilities.

Panels C and D provide summary statistics for the macro/financial and Bitcoin specific explanatory variables. Prior to the estimation, all explanatory variables are standardized.

Table 2 presents the contemporaneous correlations between the realized volatilities of the different assets. While there is a strong co-movement between the realized volatilities of the S&P 500 and the Nikkei 225 as well as a very strong correlation of both RVs with the realized volatility of the luxury goods index, Bitcoin realized volatility is only weakly correlated with the RV of all other assets. Although the contemporaneous correlations are close to zero, the correlation between $RVol_t^{Bit}$ and $RVol_{t-1}^{SP}$ is -0.1236 and between $RVol_t^{Bit}$ and $RVol_{t-2}^{SP}$ is -0.2623. This suggests that lagged S&P 500 realized volatility may be a useful predictor for future Bitcoin volatility.

In the empirical analysis, we use the explanatory variables in levels. This is justified because the persistence of the explanatory variables is not too strong at the monthly frequency. For example, the first order autocorrelation of the Baltic dry index and trading volume in US dollars is 0.79 and 0.48, respectively. Nevertheless, we also estimated GARCH-MIDAS models using the first difference of the explanatory variables. All our results were robust to this modification.

Table 2. Contemporaneous correlations between monthly realized volatilities.

	RV-Bitcoin	RV-S&P 500	RV-Nikkei 225	RV-Gold	RV-Copper	RV-Glux
RV-Bitcoin	1.000	−0.074	−0.048	0.059	−0.080	−0.179
RV-S&P 500		1.000	0.636	0.369	0.252	0.818
RV-Nikkei 255			1.000	0.634	0.333	0.743
RV-Gold				1.000	0.220	0.469
RV-Copper					1.000	0.367
RV-Glux						1.000

Notes: The sample covers the 2013M05-2017M12 period. The table reports the contemporaneous correlations between the various realized volatilities.

4. Empirical Results

4.1. Macro and Financial Drivers of Long-Term Bitcoin Volatility

In this section, we analyze the determinants of long-term Bitcoin volatility. In general, once the long-term component is accounted for, the short-term volatility component is well described by a GARCH(1,1) process. As potential drivers of Bitcoin volatility, we consider measures of volatility and risk in the US stock market as well as a measure of global economic activity. These measures have been shown to be important drivers of US stock market volatility in previous studies (see, among others, (Engle et al. 2013; Conrad and Loch 2015; and Conrad and Kleen 2018)). Bouri et al. (2017) found only weak evidence for a relation between US stock market volatility and Bitcoin volatility. However, their analysis was based on daily data and focused on short-term effects. In contrast, the GARCH-MIDAS model allows us to investigate whether US stock market volatility has an effect on long-term Bitcoin volatility. For comparison, we also present how these measures are related to the volatility of the S&P 500, the Nikkei 225 and the volatility of gold and copper.[3]

As a benchmark model, we estimate a simple GARCH(1,1) for the Bitcoin returns. The parameter estimates are presented in the first line of Table 3. The constant in the mean as well as the two GARCH parameters are highly significant. The sum of the estimates of α and β is slightly above one. Therefore, the estimated GARCH model does not satisfy the condition for covariance stationarity. This result is likely to be driven by the extreme swings in Bitcoin volatility and suggests that a two-component model may be more appropriate.[4] We also estimated a GJR-GARCH and—in line with Bouri et al. (2017)—found no evidence for asymmetry in the conditional volatility.

The remainder of Table 3 presents the parameter estimates for the GARCH-MIDAS models. For those models, the estimates of α and β satisfy the condition for covariance stationarity, i.e., accounting for long-term volatility reduces persistence in the short-term component. First, we use S&P 500 realized volatility as an explanatory variable for long-term Bitcoin volatility. Interestingly, we find that $RVol_t^{SP}$ has a negative and highly significant effect on long-term Bitcoin volatility. Since the estimated weighting scheme puts a weight of 0.09 on the first lag, our parameter estimates imply that a one standard deviation increase in $RVol_t^{SP}$ this month predicts a decline of 17% in long-term Bitcoin volatility next month. The finding that $RVol_t^{SP}$ is negatively related to Bitcoin volatility is in contrast to the usual findings for other markets. For comparison, Tables 4 and 5 present parameters estimates for GARCH-MIDAS models applied to the S&P 500 and the Nikkei 225. As expected, higher levels of $RVol_t^{SP}$ predict increases in S&P 500 long-term volatility as well as increases in the long-term volatility of the Nikkei 225.

Second, we find that the VIX and RV-Glux are negatively related to long-term Bitcoin volatility. Since both measures are positively related to $RVol_t^{SP}$ (see Table 2), this finding is not surprising. Again, Tables 4 and 5 show that the opposite effect is true for the two stock markets.

Third, Table 3 implies that the VRP has a significantly positive effect on long-term Bitcoin volatility. A high VRP is typically interpreted either as a sign of high aggregate risk aversion (Bekaert et al. (2009)) or high economic uncertainty (Bollerslev et al. (2009)). We observe the same effect for the Nikkei 225 (see Table 5) but no such effect for the S&P 500 (see Table 4).

Fourth, we find a strong positive association between the Baltic dry index and long-term Bitcoin volatility. The finding of a pro-cyclical behavior of Bitcoin volatility is noteworthy, since it contrasts with the counter-cyclical behavior usually observed for financial volatility (see Schwert (1989); or Engle et al. (2013)).

---

[3] Fang et al. (2018) investigate whether global economic policy uncertainty predicts long-term gold volatility. We are not aware of any applications of the GARCH-MIDAS to copper returns.

[4] Similarly, Katsiampa (2017) estimates a non-stationary GARCH(1,1) for Bitcoin returns (see his Table 1). See also Chen et al. (2018) for GARCH estimates of Bitcoin volatility.

Table 3. GARCH-MIDAS for Bitcoin: financial and macroeconomic explanatory variables.

Variable	μ	α	β	m	θ	ω_2	LLF	AIC	BIC
GARCH(1,1)	0.1730*** (0.0674)	0.1470*** (0.0472)	0.8560*** (0.0507)	0.3319*** (0.2643)	-	-	−4738.71	5.4608	5.4734
RV-S&P 500	0.1656** (0.0661)	0.1607*** (0.0445)	0.8087*** (0.0550)	2.7211*** (0.3775)	−2.1114*** (0.7576)	3.4269*** (0.8575)	−4618.47	5.4182	5.4374
VIX	0.1734*** (0.0670)	0.1526*** (0.0540)	0.8236*** (0.0691)	2.4882*** (0.4579)	−2.3137* (1.2905)	3.5195*** (1.0696)	−4627.25	5.4285	5.4477
RV-Glux	0.1813*** (0.0648)	0.1688*** (0.0428)	0.7951*** (0.0530)	2.5390*** (0.3701)	−1.7776*** (0.5208)	5.2603*** (1.5561)	−4620.62	5.4208	5.4399
VRP	0.1205* (0.0669)	0.1939*** (0.0390)	0.7710*** (0.0432)	4.8269*** (0.5759)	6.6860*** (1.9478)	5.3861*** (0.8519)	−4613.61	5.4126	5.4317
Baltic	0.1946*** (0.0354)	0.1707*** (0.0431)	0.7464*** (0.0431)	3.4942*** (0.2503)	1.5342*** (0.3257)	18.3834** (7.8759)	−4597.37	5.3935	5.4127

Notes: The table reports estimation results for the GARCH-MIDAS-X models including 3 MIDAS lag years ($K = 36$) of a monthly explanatory variable X. The sample period is 2013M05-2017M12. The conditional variance of the GARCH(1,1) is specified as $h_{i,t} = m + \alpha\varepsilon_{i-1,t}^2 + \beta h_{i-1,t}$. The numbers in parentheses are HAC standard errors. ***, **, * indicate significance at the 1%, 5%, and 10% level. LLF is the value of the maximized log-likelihood function. AIC and BIC are the Akaike and Bayesian information criteria.

Table 4. GARCH-MIDAS for S&P 500.

Variable	μ	α	β	m	θ	ω_2	LLF	AIC	BIC
RV-S&P 500	0.0673*** (0.0171)	0.1835*** (0.0396)	0.6818*** (0.0552)	−0.4549*** (0.1493)	0.8907*** (0.3283)	6.9532*** (2.6901)	−1191.81	2.0371	2.0630
VIX	0.0647*** (0.0169)	0.1717*** (0.0381)	0.6663*** (0.0560)	−0.2394 (0.1554)	1.1889*** (0.3138)	8.7747*** (3.3672)	−1185.90	2.0270	2.0529
RV-Glux	0.0675*** (0.0171)	0.1897*** (0.0418)	0.7046*** (0.0560)	−0.3969* (0.1985)	0.6072* (0.3308)	9.1559*** (2.2863)	−1194.99	2.0425	2.0684
VRP	0.0625*** (0.0169)	0.1763*** (0.0460)	0.7376*** (0.0620)	−0.3678 (0.3327)	0.8226 (1.0205)	42.9597 (103.8718)	−1193.83	2.0405	2.0664
Baltic	0.0662*** (0.0174)	0.1876*** (0.0435)	0.7275*** (0.0548)	−0.7358*** (0.2314)	−0.3833 (0.3218)	34.5626 (40.4420)	−1196.75	2.0455	2.0714

Notes: See Table 3.

Table 5. GARCH-MIDAS for Nikkei 225.

Variable	μ	α	β	m	θ	ω_2	LLF	AIC	BIC
RV-N225	0.0733** (0.0319)	0.1435*** (0.0287)	0.8118*** (0.0407)	0.6529 (0.4419)	0.5956*** (0.2388)	8.5433*** (2.3603)	−1854.00	3.2489	3.2753
RV-S&P 500	0.0804*** (0.0307)	0.1256*** (0.0270)	0.8120*** (0.0387)	0.9172*** (0.2233)	2.6059*** (1.1214)	2.5956** (1.1835)	−1845.16	3.2335	3.2599
VIX	0.0823*** (0.0306)	0.1194*** (0.0266)	0.8058*** (0.0408)	1.2615*** (0.2406)	2.6210*** (0.6460)	3.1827*** (0.7872)	−1841.19	3.2265	3.2530
RV-Glux	0.0775** (0.0307)	0.1314*** (0.0269)	0.8240*** (0.0364)	1.1043*** (0.3341)	1.4996* (0.8430)	4.7827 (4.2353)	−1850.32	3.2425	3.2689
VRP	0.0772** (0.0310)	0.1259*** (0.0308)	0.8494*** (0.0379)	1.6757** (0.7000)	4.1277** (1.7917)	2.7717** (1.2418)	−1851.00	3.2437	3.2701
Baltic	0.0741** (0.0301)	0.1398*** (0.0282)	0.8522*** (0.0356)	1.0786 (3.0334)	−1.0354 (0.8642)	10.4773** (5.2701)	−1853.51	3.2480	3.2745

Notes: See Table 3.

According to the Akaike and Bayesian information criteria, the preferred GARCH-MIDAS model for Bitcoin volatility is based on the Baltic dry index (see Table 3). The left panel of Figure 3 shows the estimated long- and short-term components from this specification. About 65% percent of the variation in the monthly conditional volatility can be explained by movements in long-term volatility. For comparison, the right panel shows the long- and short-term components for the model based on the volatility of the luxury goods index. Clearly, the comparison of graphs confirms that the Baltic dry index has more explanatory power for Bitcoin volatility than RV-Glux.

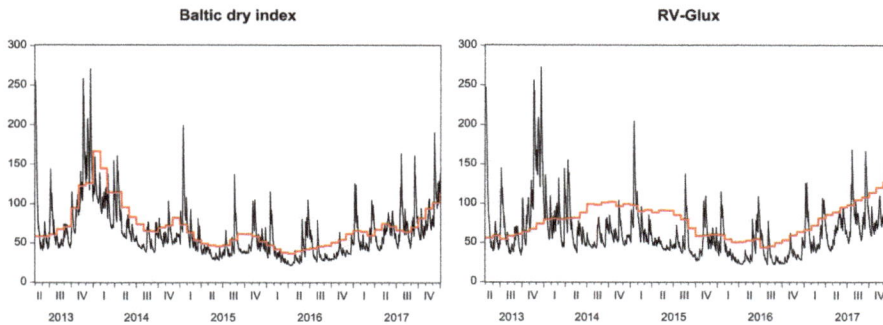

Figure 3. The figure shows the annualized long-term (bold red line) and short-term (black line) volatility components as estimated by the GARCH-MIDAS models with the Baltic dry index (**left**) and the realized volatility of the luxury goods index (**right**) as explanatory variables.

Finally, Table 6 presents the GARCH-MIDAS estimates for gold and copper. In the table, we include only explanatory variables for which the estimate of θ is significant. We find that the GARCH persistence parameter, β, is high for both Gold and Copper across all models. Long-term gold volatility is positively related to realized volatility in the S&P 500, the VIX and realized volatility in the luxury goods index. Interestingly, there is a strongly negative relation between long-term copper volatility and the baltic dry index. Elevated levels of global economic activity go along with high demand for copper and, hence, an increasing copper price and low volatility.

Table 6. GARCH-MIDAS for Gold and Copper.

Variable	μ	α	β	m	θ	ω_2	LLF	AIC	BIC
				Panel A: Gold					
RV-S&P 500	−0.0079 (0.0251)	0.0217 ** (0.0085)	0.9653 *** (0.0169)	0.1068 (0.1900)	2.1937 *** (0.7128)	1.9838 *** (0.6000)	−1567.17	2.6732	2.6990
VIX	−0.0078 (0.0250)	0.0214 ** (0.0091)	0.9551 *** (0.0217)	0.3289 ** (0.1672)	1.9879 *** (0.4169)	2.3936 *** (0.5787)	−1564.76	2.6691	2.6949
RV-Glux	−0.0072 (0.0251)	0.0234 *** (0.0083)	0.9689 *** (0.0136)	0.1612 (0.3205)	1.4024 ** (0.5529)	2.0356* (1.1250)	−1570.45	2.6788	2.7046
				Panel B: Copper					
RV-S&P 500	−0.0038 (0.0349)	0.0247 *** (0.0083)	0.9640 *** (0.0113)	0.5844 *** (0.1753)	0.2444** (0.0998)	386.9946 *** (0.0165)	−1965.14	3.3494	3.3753
Baltic	−0.0086 (0.0353)	0.0262 ** (0.0119)	0.9369 *** (0.0384)	0.1945 (0.1732)	−0.7006 *** (0.2647)	8.1959 ** (3.4636)	−1965.09	3.3493	3.3752

Notes: See Table 3.

In summary, we find that the behavior of long-term Bitcoin volatility is rather unusual. Unlike volatility in the two stock markets and volatility of gold/copper, Bitcoin volatility decreases in response to higher realized or expected volatility in the US stock market. A potential explanation might be that Bitcoin investors may have lost faith in institutions such as governments and central banks and consider Bitcoin as a safe-haven.[5] Furthermore, while stock market volatility and copper volatility behave counter-cyclically, Bitcoin volatility appears to behave strongly pro-cyclically. This is an interesting result that distinguishes Bitcoin from stocks but also from commodities or precious metals. Since Bitcoin neither has an income stream (as compared to stocks) nor an intrinsic value (as compared to commodities), it is often compared to precious metals such as gold. However, our results

---

5   For example, in a Reuters article from 11 April 2013, it is argued that the Bitcoin "currency has gained in prominence amid the euro zone sovereign debt crisis as more people start to question the safety of holding their cash in the bank. Bitcoins shot up in value in March when investors took fright at Cyprus' plans to impose losses on bank deposits."

suggest that the link between Bitcoin volatility and macro/financial variables is very different from the link between those variables and stocks/copper/gold.

4.2. Bitcoin Specific Explanatory Variables

Next, we consider Bitcoin specific explanatory variables. The parameter estimates are presented in Table 7. As expected, we find that both Google Trend measures (all web searches and monthly news searches) are significantly positively related to Bitcoin volatility. That is, more attention in terms of Google searches predicts higher levels of long-term volatility.[6] Finally, we estimate two models that include Bitcoin trading volume in US dollar (US-TV) and Chinese yuan (CNY-TV), respectively. In both cases, we find a significantly negative effect of trading volume. We conjecture that increasing trading volume goes along with higher levels of "trust" or "confidence" in Bitcoin as a payment system and, hence, predicts lower Bitcoin volatility. Recall that Balcilar et al. (2017) analyze the causal relation between trading volume and Bitcoin returns and volatility. They find that volume cannot help predict the volatility of Bitcoin returns. It appears therefore that separating out long-term components is important in finding significant patterns between volatility and trading volume.

Table 7. GARCH-MIDAS for Bitcoin specific explanatory variables

Variable	μ	α	β	m	θ	ω_2	LLF	AIC	BIC
Google Trends (all)	0.1833 *** (0.0665)	0.1691 *** (0.0357)	0.7863 *** (0.0450)	2.5337 *** (0.3240)	0.0927 ** (0.0422)	17.7833 (14.9715)	−4628.06	5.4295	5.4486
Google Trends (news)	0.1924 *** (0.0666)	0.1870 *** (0.0367)	0.7558 *** (0.0428)	2.4217 *** (0.3154)	0.0622 *** (0.0207)	53.9053 (42.3308)	−4614.86	5.4140	5.4331
US-TV	0.1804 *** (0.0685)	0.1598 *** (0.0365)	0.8079 *** (0.0429)	3.4516 *** (0.3102)	−1.9630 ** (0.8046)	2.1127 *** (0.6752)	−4457.43	5.4234	5.4431
CNY-TV	0.1651 ** (0.0721)	0.1840 *** (0.0321)	0.7731 *** (0.0386)	2.9714 *** (0.3101)	−0.4701 * (0.2677)	11.0465 *** (3.5819)	−3387.81	5.1774	5.2011

Notes: See Table 3.

5. Conclusions

Cryptocurrency is a relatively unexplored area of research and the fluctuations of Bitcoin prices are still poorly understood. As cryptocurrencies appear to gain interest and legitimacy, particularly with the establishment of derivatives markets, it is important to understand the driving forces behind market movements. We tried to tease out what are the drivers of long-term volatility in Bitcoin. We find that S&P 500 realized volatility has a negative and highly significant effect on long-term Bitcoin volatility and that the S&P 500 volatility risk premium has a significantly positive effect on long-term Bitcoin volatility. Moreover, we find a strong positive association between the Baltic dry index and long-term Bitcoin volatility and report a significantly negative effect of Bitcoin trading volume.

It is worth noting that there are a number of series we considered—such as crime-related statistics—which did not really seem to explain Bitcoin volatility, despite the popular press coverage on the topic. We also experimented with a flight-to-safety indictor suggested in Engle et al. (2012) and found that long-term Bitcoin volatility tends to decrease during flight-to-safety periods. This result squares with our finding of a negative relation between Bitcoin volatility and risks in the US stock market.

Since our findings suggest that Bitcoin volatility forecasts based on the GARCH-MIDAS model are superior to forecasts based on simple GARCH models, our results can be used, for example, to construct improved time-varying portfolio weights when building portfolios of Bitcoins and other assets such as stocks and bonds. Our results may also be useful for the pricing of Bitcoin futures, since they allow us to anticipate changes in Bitcoin volatility at longer horizons. Finally, the GARCH-MIDAS model can be

---

[6] There is already some evidence that Google searches can be used to forecast macroeconomic variables such as the unemployment rate (see D'Amuri and Marcucci (2017)).

used to simulate Bitcoin volatility based on alternative scenarios for the development of the US stock market or global economic activity. We look forward to sort out these possibilities in future research.

Nevertheless, we would like to emphasize that all our results are based on a relatively short sample period. It will be interesting to see whether our results still hold in longer samples and when the Bitcoin currency has become more mature.

Author Contributions: C.C., A.C. and E.G. have contributed jointly to all of the sections of the paper. The authors analyzed the data and wrote the paper jointly.

Acknowledgments: We thank Christian Hafner for inviting us to write on the topic of cryptocurrency. We thank Peter Hansen and Steve Raymond for helpful comments.

Conflicts of Interest: The authors declare no conflict of interest.

References

Al-Khazali, Osamah, Bouri Elie, and David Roubaud. 2018. The impact of positive and negative macroeconomic news surprises: Gold versus Bitcoin. *Economics Bulletin* 38: 373–82.

Balcilar, Mehmet, Elie Bouri, Rangan Gupta, and David Roubaud. 2017. Can volume predict Bitcoin returns and volatility? A quantiles-based approach. *Economic Modelling* 64: 74–81. [CrossRef]

Baur, Dirk G., Kihoon Hong, and Adrian D. Lee. 2017. Bitcoin: Medium of Exchange or Speculative Assets? Available online: https://ssrn.com/abstract=2561183 (accessed on 25 April 2018). [CrossRef]

Bekaert, Geert, Eric Engstrom, and Yuhang Xing. 2009. Risk, uncertainty, and asset prices. *Journal of Financial Economics* 91: 59–82. [CrossRef]

Bollerslev, Tim, George Tauchen, and Hao Zhou. 2009. Expected stock returns and variance risk premia. *Review of Financial Studies* 22: 4463–92. [CrossRef]

Bouri, Elie, Georges Azzi, and Anne Haubo Dyhrberg. 2017. On the return-volatility relationship in the Bitcoin market around the price crash of 2013. *Economics* 11: 1–16. [CrossRef]

Chen, Cathy Y. H., Wolfgang Karl Härdle, Ai Jun Hou, and Weining Wang. 2018. *Pricing Cryptocurrency Options: The Case of CRIX and Bitcoin*. IRTG 1792 Discussion Paper 2018-004. Berlin: Humboldt-Universität zu Berlin.

Cheah, Eng-Tuck, Tapas Mishra, Mamata Parhi, and Zhuang Zhang. 2018. Long memory interdependency and inefficiency in Bitcoin markets. *Economics Letters* 167: 18–25. [CrossRef]

Conrad, Christian, and Onno Kleen. 2018. Two Are Better Than One: Volatility Forecasting Using Multiplicative Component GARCH Models. Available online: https://ssrn.com/abstract=2752354 (accessed on 15 October 2017).

Conrad, Christian, and Karin Loch. 2015. Anticipating long-term stock market volatility. *Journal of Applied Econometrics* 30: 1090–114. [CrossRef]

D'Amuri, Francesco, and Juri Marcucci. 2017. The predictive power of Google searches in forecasting US unemployment. *International Journal of Forecasting* 33: 801–16. [CrossRef]

Dyhrberg, Anne Haubo. 2016. Bitcoin, gold and the dollar—A GARCH volatility analysis. *Finance Research Letters* 16: 85–92. [CrossRef]

Engle, Robert, Michael Fleming, Eric Ghysels, and Giang Nguyen. 2012. *Liquidity, Volatility, and Flights to Safety in the U.S. Treasury Market: Evidence from a New Class of Dynamic Order Book Models*. FRB of New York Staff Report No. 590. Available online: http://dx.doi.org/10.2139/ssrn.2195655 (accessed on 9 October 2017).

Engle, Robert F., Eric Ghysels, and Bumjean Sohn. 2013. Stock market volatility and macroeconomic fundamentals. *Review of Economics and Statistics* 95: 776–97. [CrossRef]

Fang, Libing, Baizhu Chen, Honghai Yu, and Yichuo Qian. 2018. The importance of global economic policy uncertainty in predicting gold futures market volatility: A GARCH-MIDAS approach. *Journal of Futures Markets* 38: 413–22. [CrossRef]

Katsiampa, Paraskevi. 2017. Volatility estimation for Bitcoin: A comparison of GARCH models. *Economics Letters* 158: 3–6. [CrossRef]

Kristoufek, Ladislav. 2015. What are the main drivers of the Bitcoin price? Evidence from Wavelet coherence analysis. *PLoS ONE* 10: e0123923. [CrossRef] [PubMed]

Khuntia, Sashikanta, and J. K. Pattanayak. 2018. Adaptive market hypothesis and evolving predictability of Bitcoin. *Economics Letters* 167: 26–28. [CrossRef]

Koutmos, Dimitrios. 2018. Bitcoin returns and transaction activity. *Economics Letters* 167: 81–85. [CrossRef]

Li, Xin, and Chong Alex Wang. 2017. The technology and economic determinants of cryptocurrency exchange rates: The case of Bitcoin. *Decision Support Systems* 95: 49–60. [CrossRef]

Polasik, Michal, Anna Iwona Piotrowska, Tomasz Piotr Wisniewski, Radoslaw Kotkowski, and Geoffrey Lightfoot. 2015. Price Fluctuations and the Use of Bitcoin: An Empirical Inquiry. *International Journal of Electronic Commerce* 20: 9–49. [CrossRef]

Schwert, G. William. 1989. Why does stock market volatility change over time? *The Journal of Finance* 44: 1115–53. [CrossRef]

Journal of
Risk and Financial Management

MDPI

Article

Can Bitcoin Replace Gold in an Investment Portfolio?

Irene Henriques and Perry Sadorsky *

Schulich School of Business, York University, Toronto, ON M3J 1P3, Canada; ihenriqu@schulich.yorku.ca
* Correspondence: psadorsk@schulich.yorku.ca; Tel.: +1-416-736-5067

Received: 2 July 2018; Accepted: 13 August 2018; Published: 14 August 2018

Abstract: Bitcoin is an exciting new financial product that may be useful for inclusion in investment portfolios. This paper investigates the implications of replacing gold in an investment portfolio with bitcoin ("digital gold"). Our approach is to use several different multivariate GARCH models (dynamic conditional correlation (DCC), asymmetric DCC (ADCC), generalized orthogonal GARCH (GO-GARCH)) to estimate minimum variance equity portfolios. Both long and short portfolios are considered. An analysis of the economic value shows that risk-averse investors will be willing to pay a high performance fee to switch from a portfolio with gold to a portfolio with bitcoin. These results are robust to the inclusion of trading costs.

Keywords: Bitcoin; gold; GARCH; portfolio modelling; risk management

JEL Classification: G11; G17; G32

1. Introduction

Bitcoin is an exciting new financial product that has the potential to disrupt existing economic payment systems. Bitcoin is a peer-to-peer digital cryptocurrency that was launched in 2009 based on an open source project developed by Nakamoto (2008). As of 15 March 2018, a single bitcoin was worth $8014.92, the daily transaction volume was approximately 165,142 and the supply of bitcoins on the network (i.e., have been "mined") was 16,923,238.[1] As a decentralized protocol, Bitcoin is not controlled by any organization or government, but its supply has been set in advance at 21 million bitcoins. The total supply of bitcoin in circulation grows at a predictable rate and is set to reach 21 million by September 2140 (Zohar 2015; Hendrickson et al. 2016).

Bitcoin has on occasion been called digital gold (Popper 2015a, 2015b). Gold is often advocated as a hedge against inflation, a safe haven investment and a way to increase portfolio diversification (Eichengreen 1992). Gold, a mined asset, has been used as a form of currency for much of the history of civilization (Michaud et al. 2006). Interestingly, Bitcoin also uses the mining terminology to describe what "miners" receive once they provide proof-of-work associated with the verification of a transaction and the completion of a block in blockchain (i.e., the decentralized ledger). Bitcoin is possible due to blockchain technology which enables secure electronic transactions without needing a centralized ledger and preventing users from replicating the payment for other uses, also known as the double spending problem (Kiviat 2015; Zohar 2015). The units awarded can be used to make a transaction or invest.

The notion that Bitcoin can replace gold as a hedge against inflation has especially interested people in countries where governments were struggling with hyperinflation. In the mid-2000s for example, Argentine businesses, entrepreneurs and citizens seeking to protect the value of their currency

---

[1]   Daily data are available at https://blockchain.info/charts. By convention, we use Bitcoin with a capital "B" to denote the Bitcoin network and "bitcoin" with a small "b" to denote the unit of account.

were helpless as inflation rose and the government imposed greater and greater currency controls on the Argentine peso. Although Bitcoin adoption was slow in North America, the same could not be said for Latin America where currency controls were impeding transactions and Bitcoin adoption was growing as people sought both a cheaper way of moving money across international borders and a safe store of value (Popper 2015b). In fact, in a comparison of 16 different currencies, Kim (2017) found bitcoin currency exchange transaction costs to be lower than the retail foreign exchange transaction costs. As a result, Bitcoin has experienced a rapid rise in popularity over the past several years and in December 2017, the CME Group launched bitcoin futures contracts.

Our objective is to examine the impact that replacing gold with bitcoin would have on investment portfolio characteristics and returns. Eliminating a safe haven asset such as gold from an investment portfolio will have implications for risk and return trade-offs, because it reduces diversification. In fact, there is a large literature showing the effectiveness of gold in diversifying portfolio risk (Baur and Lucey 2010; Hillier et al. 2006; Jaffe 1989; Reboredo 2013a, 2013b; Baur and McDermott 2010; Ciner et al. 2013; Beckmann et al. 2015). Gold divestment, therefore, may reduce returns and increase risk. Substituting bitcoin for gold, however, may increase returns and reduce risk. To address whether this is the case, a rigorous empirical analysis using modern portfolio theory is required.

This paper makes three important contributions to the literature. First, we investigate the financial implications of replacing gold in an investment portfolio with bitcoin, using modern portfolio theory. We compare two portfolios: (1) A portfolio that includes gold, and (2) a portfolio that replaces gold with bitcoin. Second, to compare optimal weights for minimum variance equity portfolios subject to a target return, we use three different multivariate GARCH models: dynamic conditional correlation (DCC), asymmetric dynamic conditional correlation (ADCC), and generalized orthogonal GARCH (GO-GARCH). While many papers use DCC and ADCC to estimate optimal portfolio weights, few use GO-GARCH. Given the volatile nature of bitcoin, an analysis that provides more accurate volatility estimates is needed. GO-GARCH not only incorporates persistence in volatility and correlation, as well as time-varying correlation (as do DCC and ADCC), but also allows for spill-over effects in volatility and is closed under linear transformation. Comparing weights computed from three different models demonstrates the robustness of our portfolio results to the choice of GARCH model. Third, we calculate optimal portfolio weights using a fixed-width rolling window, which mitigates the effects of changing dynamics, parameter heterogeneity, and structural change.

The paper is organized as follows. We first present a brief literature review of Bitcoin and its investment potential. We then present our modern portfolio model followed by the methodology, description of the data, empirical results and some robustness analyses. We conclude the paper with some important implications for investors who seek to include bitcoin in their investment portfolios.

2. What Is Bitcoin—Currency or Asset?

The core of Bitcoin's innovation is blockchain, which forms "an incremental log of all transactions that have ever occurred since the creation of Bitcoin, starting with the "Genesis Block"—the first block in the chain" (Zohar 2015, p. 107). This allows transactions to be processed over a distributed network using public-private key technology, where the sender and the receiver of a transaction use a private key and everyone else on the network uses a public key to verify the legitimacy of the transaction. The public verification system is known as "mining". Böhme et al. (2015) view the verification system in which users are encouraged to keep the transaction record operational and updated as a public good. Unfortunately, public goods are underprovided unless there are incentives (McNutt 2002). To encourage user participation, users who solve a computationally intensive and random mathematical puzzle associated with the pre-existing contents of a block, known as proof-of-work, are awarded newly minted bitcoins (Böhme et al. 2015). As there is a finite number of bitcoins, the puzzles become more computationally difficult over time.

The advantages of using bitcoin are: (1) as a purely digital currency, Bitcoin allows payments to be sent nearly instantly over the internet for very low fees (Zohar 2015), (2) like cash, bitcoin is nearly anonymous and irreversible once committed, and (3) as there is no controlling organization (private or public), Bitcoin is less open to regulatory oversight (Böhme et al. 2015). The disadvantages of Bitcoin are associated with the fact that it functions outside the purview of financial institutions, governments and without regard to national borders; users of the system are identifiable only by their virtual addresses (Hendrickson et al. 2016). Early adopters of Bitcoin were individuals and businesses who were attracted to the anonymity of the system and the lack of government oversight. Böhme et al. (2015) cite the online sale of narcotics, and gambling as the two of the largest adopters of Bitcoin.

Today, however, businesses are beginning to view Bitcoin as a method to reduce their credit card transaction fees. Such fees can range from 1.65 to 2.71% of transaction sales (Canadian Federation of Independent Business 2018). As of January 2018, companies and organizations such as Overstock.com, KFC Canada, Microsoft, CheapAir.com, Newegg.com, Zynga, Save the Children, and Universidad de las Americas Puebla—just to name a few—accept bitcoin.[2] As more and more merchants adjust their payment systems to accept bitcoin, Bitcoin as a method of payment will grow. Consumers, however, may be less inclined to use bitcoin as traditional financial accounts payments can be reversed if an error were to occur whereas it cannot be reversed with bitcoin due to the pseudonymous exchange (Hendrickson et al. 2016).

The question remains as to whether Bitcoin should be considered a currency. Lo and Wang (2014) examine whether Bitcoin can serve as an alternative form of money by evaluating Bitcoin against the three properties of money, namely its ability to act as a medium of exchange, a unit of account and a store of value. In the case of Bitcoin's ability to act as a medium of exchange, the authors note that bitcoin is not backed by any sovereign entity and therefore its success will be based on its acceptance by private agents. As Bitcoin's transaction confirmation times decrease (it now takes less than 10 min) and its fees are less than those of other financial intermediaries such as banks and credit card companies, more agents will view this as potential medium of exchange.

Using bitcoin as a unit of account, however, appears to be a problem due to its remarkable volatility. Lo and Wang (2014) argue that despite merchants accepting bitcoin as payment, they continue to post their prices in standard currencies due to bitcoin's volatility. The store of value function of money, on the other hand, is based on agents' acceptance that bitcoin's value will be accepted in the future. Volatility and speculative holdings in bitcoin have suggested that bitcoin may be in a state of speculative play (Glaser et al. 2014). This volatility is catching the attention of market participants who seek to profit from such volatility. This has led to the discussion of the creation of Bitcoin futures contracts (Hopkins 2017) and in December 2017 The CME Group launched bitcoin futures contracts.

Although Bitcoin is seen as a digital currency that can provide a secure, low-cost platform for digital payments (Hendrickson et al. 2016), Glaser et al. (2014) argue that most users of Bitcoin treat their bitcoin investment as a speculative asset rather than as a means of payment. Financial assets allow an investor to diversify her portfolio. An asset can act as a safe haven, a hedge, and/or a diversifier. Bitcoin is highly volatile and (Dyhrberg 2016a) found that bitcoin can be classified somewhere between a currency and a commodity with the associated financial advantages. Dyhrberg (2016b) also suggests that Bitcoin can act as a hedge between UK equities and the US dollar.

Bouri et al. (2017) examine whether bitcoin can be used as a safe haven, diversifier or hedge using daily and weekly data. From a risk perspective, including an asset that is negatively correlated with another decreases risk; the authors, using dynamic conditional correlation models, find that bitcoin can be used as an effective diversifier for most of the cases examined. Using bitcoin as a safe haven, however, was not evidenced in daily movements due perhaps to bitcoin's speculative nature (Ciaian et al. 2016; Bouri et al. 2017). Zhu et al. (2017) use a vector error correction model to study the dynamic interaction between bitcoin and important economic variables like the US dollar index, stock prices, the

---

2   See https://99bitcoins.com/who-accepts-bitcoins-payment-companies-stores-take-bitcoins/.

Federal Funds Rate, and gold prices. They find that all variables have a long-term influence on bitcoin prices, but the US dollar index has the largest impact, while gold prices have the least. These authors recommend that bitcoin should be treated as a speculative asset rather than a credit currency. Guesmi et al. (2018) use GARCH models to study the usefulness of using Bitcoin to hedge investments in gold, oil and emerging market stocks. All portfolios are two-asset portfolios that include Bitcoin and one other asset. For an emerging market (global market) portfolio, the average optimal portfolio weight for Bitcoin is 0.051 (0.033). Evidence is also presented showing that Bitcoin is a useful hedging instrument.

The question remains as to bitcoin's contribution to an investor's portfolio. Is bitcoin an asset that should be added to an investor's portfolio? Does bitcoin live up to its name as digital gold (Popper 2015b) and can it be a good gold replacement? These are some of the questions we wish to address.

3. Empirical Model

Using modern portfolio theory (Elton and Gruber 1997), we consider an investor who wants to determine the optimal portfolio weights for a minimum variance equity portfolio subject to a target return of μ_{TR}. The optimal portfolio weights are found by solving the following optimization problem:

$$\min_{w_t} \quad w_t' \sum_t w_t \quad s.t. \ w_t' \iota = 1, w_t' \mu = \mu_{TR} \tag{1}$$

In Equation (1), $\sum_t$ is the variance-covariance matrix, μ is a vector of mean returns and w_t are the portfolio weights. There are no restrictions on short sales. The solution to Equation (1) gives the expression for the optimal portfolio weights:

$$w_t = \frac{\mu_{TR} \sum_t^{-1} \mu}{\mu' \sum_t^{-1} \mu} \tag{2}$$

The optimal portfolio weights depend upon the covariance matrix and the mean returns. The covariance matrix is estimated using three types of multivariate GARCH models. Sample mean returns are used to estimate μ (Fleming et al. 2001).

A GARCH model consists of a mean equation and a variance equation. A vector of $n \times 1$ asset returns is denoted r_t. An AR(1) process for the asset returns, r_t, conditional on the information set I_{t-1} is written as:

$$r_t = \mu + a r_{t-1} + \varepsilon_t \tag{3}$$

The residuals are modelled as:

$$\varepsilon_t = H_t^{1/2} z_t \tag{4}$$

where H_t is the conditional covariance matrix of r_t and z_t is a $n \times 1$ i.i.d. random vector of errors.

One popular and easy approach to estimating optimal portfolio weights is to use a DCC GARCH model to estimate the variance-covariance matrix. Engle (2002) proposed a two-step methodology to estimate dynamic conditional correlations. In the first step, the GARCH parameters are estimated using single equation GARCH models. In the second step, the conditional correlations are estimated using:

$$H_t = D_t R_t D_t \tag{5}$$

H_t is a $n \times n$ conditional covariance matrix, R_t is the conditional correlation matrix, and D_t is a diagonal matrix with time-varying standard deviations on the diagonal.

$$D_t = diag\left(h_{1,t}^{1/2}, \ldots h_{n,t}^{1/2}\right) \tag{6}$$

$$R_t = diag\left(q_{1,t}^{-1/2}, \ldots q_{n,t}^{-1/2}\right) Q_t \ diag\left(q_{1,t}^{-1/2}, \ldots q_{n,t}^{-1/2}\right) \tag{7}$$

The expressions for h are univariate GARCH models (H is a diagonal matrix). For the GARCH(1,1) model, the elements of H_t can be written as:

$$h_{i,t} = \omega_i + \alpha_i \varepsilon_{i,t-1}^2 + \beta_i h_{i,t-1} \tag{8}$$

Q_t is a symmetric positive definite matrix.

$$Q_t = (1 - \theta_1 - \theta_2)\overline{Q} + \theta_1 z_{t-1} z_{t-1}' + \theta_2 Q_{t-1} \tag{9}$$

$\overline{Q}$ is the n × n unconditional correlation matrix of the standardized residuals $z_{i,t}$ ($z_{i,t} = \varepsilon_{i,t}/\sqrt{h_{i,t}}$). The parameters θ_1 and θ_2 are non-negative. These parameters are associated with the exponential smoothing process that is used to construct the dynamic conditional correlations. The DCC model is mean reverting as long as $\theta_1 + \theta_2 < 1$. The correlation estimator is:

$$\rho_{i,j,t} = \frac{q_{i,j,t}}{\sqrt{q_{i,i,t} q_{j,j,t}}} \tag{10}$$

The second approach to is to use the ADCC GARCH model of Cappiello et al. (2006) to estimate the variance-covariance matrix. This approach, building upon the work of Glosten et al. (1993), contains an asymmetric term in the variance equation.

$$h_{i,t} = \omega_i + \alpha_i \varepsilon_{i,t-1}^2 + \beta_i h_{i,t-1} + d_i \varepsilon_{i,t-1}^2 I(\varepsilon_{i,t-1}) \tag{11}$$

The indicator function $I(\varepsilon_{i,t-1})$ is equal to one if $\varepsilon_{i,t-1} < 0$ and 0 otherwise. A positive value for d means that negative residuals tend to increase the variance more than positive returns. The asymmetric effect, which is sometimes referred to as the "leverage effect", is designed to capture an often-observed characteristic of financial assets that an unexpected drop in asset prices tends to increase volatility more than an unexpected increase in asset prices of the same magnitude. This can be interpreted as bad news increasing volatility more than good news.

For the ADCC model, the dynamics of Q are given by:

$$Q_t = \left(\overline{Q} - A'\overline{Q}A - B'\overline{Q}B - G'\overline{Q}^- G \right) + A'z_{t-1} z_{t-1}' A + B'Q_{t-1} B + G'z_t^- z_t^{-'} G \tag{12}$$

In the above equation, A, B and G are $n \times n$ parameter matrices and z_t^- are zero-threshold standardized errors, which are equal to z_t when less than zero and zero otherwise. The matrices $\overline{Q}$ and $\overline{Q}^-$ are the unconditional matrices of z_t and z_t^-, respectively.

The third approach to estimating optimal portfolio weights is to use a GO-GARCH model to estimate the variance-covariance matrix (Van Der Weide 2002). The GO-GARCH model maps a set of asset returns, r_t, onto a set of uncorrelated components, z_t, using a mapping Z.

$$r_t = Zy_t \tag{13}$$

The unobserved components, y_t, are normalized to have unit variance. Each component of y_t can be described by a GARCH process. For example, consider a standard GARCH(1,1) process with a normal distribution.

$$y_t \sim N(0, H_t) \tag{14}$$

$$H_t = diag(h_{1,t}, \dots, h_{n,t}) \tag{15}$$

$$h_{i,t} = \omega_i + \alpha_i y_{i,t-1}^2 + \beta_i h_{i,t-1}^2 \tag{16}$$

The index i runs from 1 to n. The unconditional covariance matrix of y_t is $H_0 = I$. The conditional covariance matrix of r_t is:

$$V_t = ZH_tZ' \tag{17}$$

The matrix Z maps the uncorrelated components y_t to the observed returns r_t. There exists an orthogonal matrix U such that:

$$Z = P\Lambda^{1/2}U' \tag{18}$$

The matrices P and Λ can be obtained from singular value decomposition on the unconditional variance matrix V. For example, P contains the orthonormal eigenvectors of $ZZ' = V$ and Λ contains the eigenvalues. The matrix U can be obtained from the conditional variance matrix V_t. Recent work on GO-GARCH is concentrated on finding different ways to parameterize and estimate the matrix U. Boswijk and van der Weide (2006) provide a more detailed discussion of these efforts.

The GO-GARCH model assumes that (1) Z is time invariant, and (2) H_t is a diagonal matrix. An orthogonal GARCH (OGARCH) model is the result when Z is restricted to be orthogonal (Alexander 2001). The OGARCH model can be estimated using principle components on the normalized data and GARCH models estimated on the principle components. This corresponds to U being an identity matrix. In the original formation of the GO-GARCH model, Van Der Weide (2002) uses a 1-step maximum likelihood approach to jointly estimate the rotation matrix and the dynamics. This method, however, is impractical for many assets because the maximum likelihood estimation procedure may fail to converge. The matrix U can also be estimated using nonlinear least squares (Boswijk and van der Weide 2006) and method of moments (Boswijk and van der Weide 2011), both of which involve two-step and three-step estimation procedures. More recently, it has been proposed that U can be estimated by independent component analysis (ICA) (Broda and Paolella 2009; Zhang and Chan 2009) and is the method employed in this paper[3].

Asset returns are characterized by autocorrelation, volatility clustering and distributions that are asymmetric and have fat tails. This suggests an AR(1) mean equation for each GARCH model and a distribution that takes into account fat tails. In particular, the DCC and ADCC are each estimated with multivariate Student t (MVT) distributions. The GO-GARCH is estimated with the multivariate affine normal inverse Gaussian (MANIG) distribution. These distributions are useful for modelling data with heavy tails. All estimation is done in R (R Core Team 2015; Ghalanos 2015).

The use of DCC warrants some additional comments. DCC is a very popular multivariate GARCH model. Typing "Dynamic conditional correlation" into Google Scholar on 1 August 2018 returned about 8200 results. Despite the popularity of DCC, there is criticism that DCC is not a true model because it lacks specific technical details (Caporin and McAleer 2013; Aielli 2013). DCC is stated rather than derived, has no moments, does not have testable regularity conditions, and has no asymptotic properties. Caporin and McAleer (2013) argue against the use of DCC as a model because of the lack of moment conditions and asymptotic properties but recommend that DCC may be used as a filter, like EWMA, or as a diagnostic check. Viewed in the context of a filter, DCC may be useful for forecasting dynamic conditional covariances and correlations. We caution, however, that in the absence of any valid moment conditions or asymptotic properties, DCC forecasts may be imprecise and this may affect the estimates of the portfolio returns and any resulting statistical analysis.

Rolling window estimation is used to estimate the GARCH models and construct the portfolio weights. One period ahead conditional expected return and volatility forecasts are required to compute the optimal portfolio weights. For example, consider the case of a fixed window length of 1200 observations. The first 1200 observations are used to estimate the GARCH models and make one period forecasts of the variance-covariance matrix. One period ahead mean values for the returns are calculated from 1200 sample observations. The in sample mean values are used as a naïve forecast for the next period (Fleming et al. 2001). The mean values and covariance matrix are used to construct the one period ahead portfolio weights. Then the process is rolled forward one period by adding on

---

[3] The rotation matrix U needs to be estimated. For all but a few factors, maximum likelihood is not feasible. For a larger number of factors, alternative estimation methods must be used. ICA is a fast statistical technique for estimating hidden factors in relation to observable data.

observation and dropping the first observation so that the next estimation period is for observations 2 to 1201. This process is rolled through the data set producing a sequence of one period forecasts for the GARCH variance-covariance matrices, mean values, and portfolio weights. The portfolio weights are used in the construction of equity portfolios.

Equity portfolios are compared using standard risk-return measures like Sharpe Ratios, Omega Ratios, Sortino Ratios, and Information Ratios (Feibel 2003). The Sharpe Ratio measures excess returns relative to risk when risk is measured as the standard deviation. Excess returns are measured relative to a time-independent benchmark. Sharpe value at risk (VaR) and Sharpe expected shortfall (ES) are calculated at 5%. The Sortino Ratio measures excess returns relative to downside semi-variance. The Omega Ratio measures the ratio of probability weighted gains to losses relative to a threshold or benchmark value. Unlike the Sharpe Ratio, which only takes into account the first two moments of a distribution (mean, variance), the Omega Ratio includes information on the mean, variance, skewness, and kurtosis and is therefore well suited for investments with non-normal distribution. The Sharpe Ratio, Sortino Ratio and Omega ratio are estimated using a benchmark value of 1% on an annualized basis. The Information Ratio is similar to the Sharpe Ratio but is calculated as the ratio of the active premium to the tracking error relative to a time-dependent benchmark, which in this paper is the yield on a three-month US T-bill. Statistical significance of Sharpe Ratios are tested using the block bootstrap method of by Ledoit and Wolf (2008).

The performance fee (Δ) approach is used to estimate the economic value of switching between portfolios (Fleming et al. 2001). This approach measures the economic value of different asset allocations. The performance fee, Δ, represents the management fee an investor with a mean variance utility function would be willing to pay to switch from a benchmark portfolio that includes gold to an alternative portfolio that replaces gold for bitcoin without being made worse off in terms of utility. The performance fee is found by solving the following nonlinear equation:

$$\sum_{t=0}^{T-1}\left[\left(r_{p,t+1}^a - \Delta\right) - \frac{\gamma}{2(1+\gamma)}\left(r_{p,t+1}^a - \Delta\right)^2\right] = \sum_{t=0}^{T-1}\left[\left(r_{p,t+1}^b\right) - \frac{\gamma}{2(1+\gamma)}\left(r_{p,t+1}^b\right)^2\right] \qquad (19)$$

The sample size is T, the portfolio return is r_p, the superscripts a and b denote the alternative portfolio and the benchmark portfolio, respectively, and γ denotes the degree of risk relative risk aversion.

Portfolio turnover is used to measure the number of trades per time period and calculate trading costs. Following DeMiguel et al. (2009), the portfolio turnover is calculated as:

$$Turnover = \frac{1}{T - \tau - 1}\sum_{t=\tau}^{T-1}\sum_{j=1}^{N}\left(\mid w_{j,t+1}^i - w_{j,t}^i \mid\right) \qquad (20)$$

where $w_{j,t}^i$ is the portfolio weight in asset j chosen at time t using strategy i and $w_{j,t+1}^i$ is the portfolio weight in asset j chosen at time $t + 1$ after rebalancing using strategy i. The portfolio turnover is equal to the sum of the absolute value of the rebalancing trades across the N assets and over the $T - \tau - 1$ trades, normalized by the total number of trading days.

4. Data

Daily stock price data are collected on five exchange traded funds (ETFs) and the price of bitcoin. The ETFs consist of US equities (SPY), US bonds (TLT), US real estate (VNQ), Europe and Far East equities (EFA), and gold (GLD). Ticker symbols are listed in parentheses. These are widely traded ETFs and form the basis of many portfolio allocation strategies. GLD is an ETF backed by physical gold and movements in the price of GLD are meant to reflect movements in the price of gold bullion. ETF data is downloaded from Yahoo Finance and bitcoin prices (BIT) are downloaded from Coindesk.

The daily data cover the period of 4 January 2011 to 31 October 2017[4]. The starting period is chosen based on the start of bitcoin trading. Time series plots clearly show that VNQ, TLT, SPY, and EFA display similar upward trending patterns, while GLD has been trending down and BIT displays an exponential growth pattern (Figure 1).

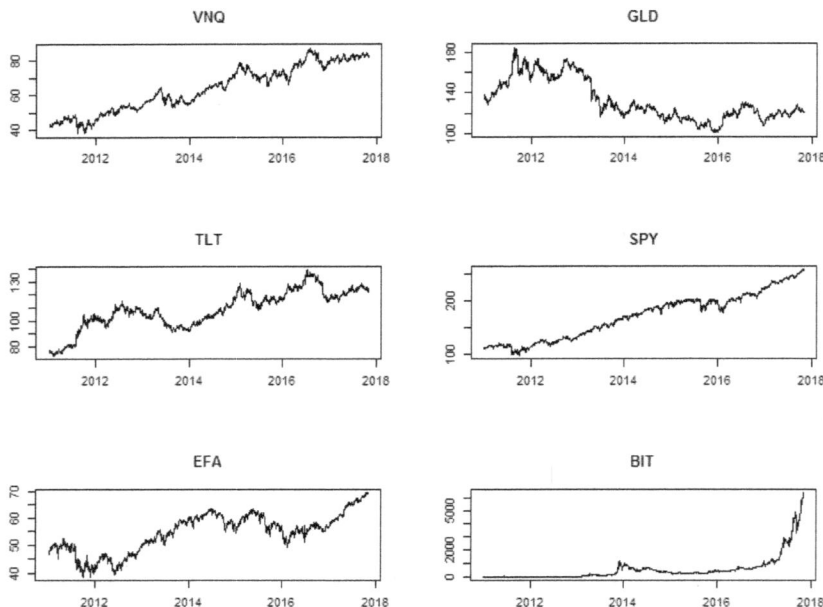

Figure 1. Time series plots of assets.

Summary statistics for daily returns indicate that, except for GLD, each series has a positive mean and median value (Table 1)[5]. BIT has the highest average return, while GLD has the lowest. Consistent with the findings of Fry and Cheah (2016), BIT has the highest standard deviation. The coefficient of variation, which is meaningful for positive values, shows that BIT has the least variation, while EFA has the most. Each series has skewness and kurtosis and rejects the null hypothesis of normality, indicating that distributions that take into account fat tails are likely to provide a better fit than a normal distribution. Unit root tests (not reported) indicate that each series is stationary. Correlation coefficients show that SPY, VNQ, and EFA correlate highly with each other (Table 2). TLT correlates negatively with VNQ, SPY, EFA, and BIT, but positively with GLD. Notice that BIT has very low correlation with the other assets, indicating the possible usefulness of bitcoin in diversifying risk. QQ plots show that each series has fat tails, which is common with asset price returns (Figure 2). In Figure 2, the black line is the theoretical quantiles and the circle line is the sample quantiles.

---

[4] Bitcoin price data was from 18 July 2010, but there was not much price variability over the first few months.
[5] Summary statistics are computed using continuously compounded daily returns. Portfolio weights are estimated using discrete returns because discrete returns are additive across assets. The resulting portfolio returns are then converted to continuous returns for the calculation of portfolio summary statistics.

Table 1. Summary statistics for daily percent returns.

	VNQ	GLD	TLT	SPY	EFA	BIT
median	0.083	0.024	0.076	0.061	0.052	0.247
mean	0.037	−0.008	0.028	0.049	0.022	0.582
SE.mean	0.026	0.025	0.022	0.022	0.028	0.154
CI.mean.0.95	0.052	0.050	0.042	0.042	0.054	0.301
var	1.193	1.100	0.799	0.805	1.316	40.537
std.dev	1.092	1.049	0.894	0.897	1.147	6.367
coef.var	29.151	−134.32	32.012	18.296	53.190	10.934
skewness	−0.364	−0.610	−0.121	−0.572	−0.778	0.148
skew.2SE	−3.080	−5.165	−1.023	−4.843	−6.591	1.251
kurtosis	7.349	5.915	1.696	5.182	6.711	9.633
kurt.2SE	31.142	25.066	7.188	21.961	28.439	40.822
normtest.W	0.934	0.948	0.986	0.938	0.930	0.843
normtest.p	0.000	0.000	0.000	0.000	0.000	0.000

Daily data from 4 January 2011 to 31 October 2017 (1719 observations). Ticker symbols: VNQ (US REITs), GLD (gold), TLT (US long bonds), SPY (US equities), EFA (Europe and Far East equities), BIT (bitcoin).

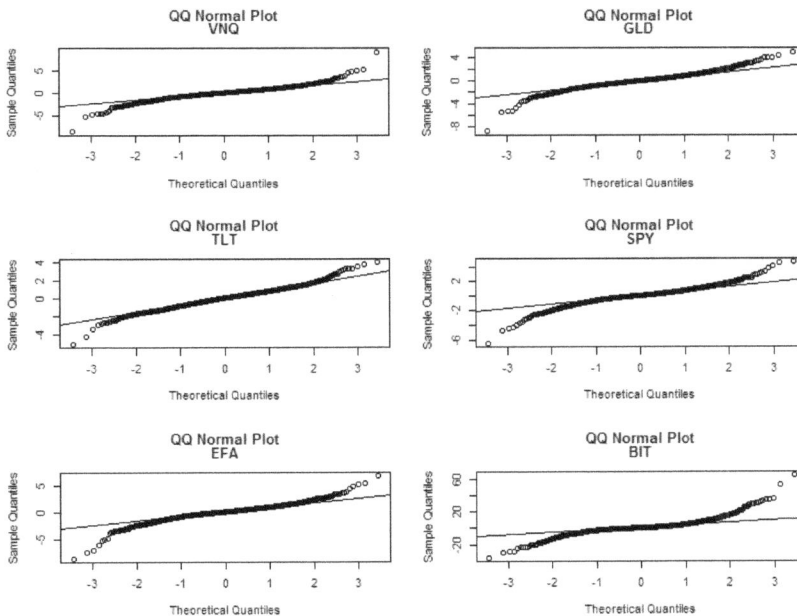

Figure 2. QQ plots of asset returns.

Table 2. Correlation coefficients for daily percent returns.

	VNQ	GLD	TLT	SPY	EFA	BIT
VNQ	1	0.07 *	−0.19 *	0.73 *	0.66 *	0.07 *
GLD	0.07 *	1	0.2 *	−0.03	0.06 *	0.02
TLT	−0.19 *	0.2 *	1	−0.5 *	−0.47 *	−0.02
SPY	0.73 *	−0.03	−0.5 *	1	0.88 *	0.04
EFA	0.66 *	0.06 *	−0.47 *	0.88 *	1	0.03
BIT	0.07 *	0.02	−0.02	0.04	0.03	1

Pairwise Pearson correlations. * Denotes significant at the 5% level of significance.

5. Results

Table 3 shows the average value and standard deviation of the optimal portfolio weights calculated from the BIT and GLD portfolio[6]. The BIT portfolio consists of SPY, TLT, VNQ, EFA and BIT. The GLD portfolio consists of SPY, TLT, VNQ, EFA and GLD. Portfolio weights are constructed using three GARCH models (DCC, ADCC, and GO). There are no restrictions on short sales. For each GARCH model, portfolios are estimated for a global minimum variance portfolio and annual target returns of 13%, 15%, and 17%. For most assets, portfolio weights calculated from GO have lower standard deviation than those of DCC or ADCC.

Table 3. Optimal portfolio weights.

BIT	Mean					Sd				
	VNQ	TLT	SPY	EFA	BIT	VNQ	TLT	SPY	EFA	BIT
DCC–13	−0.073	0.457	0.602	−0.003	0.017	0.067	0.074	0.204	0.119	0.009
DCC–15	−0.073	0.441	0.653	−0.050	0.028	0.068	0.079	0.224	0.133	0.010
DCC–17	−0.072	0.425	0.704	−0.096	0.039	0.069	0.084	0.248	0.152	0.011
DCC-GMV	−0.071	0.464	0.570	0.022	0.015	0.066	0.071	0.192	0.114	0.012
ADCC-13	−0.061	0.439	0.629	−0.022	0.015	0.084	0.081	0.238	0.132	0.010
ADCC-15	−0.061	0.423	0.680	−0.068	0.026	0.086	0.085	0.255	0.145	0.011
ADCC-17	−0.060	0.407	0.731	−0.115	0.037	0.088	0.090	0.277	0.162	0.012
ADCC-GMV	−0.059	0.446	0.595	0.006	0.012	0.084	0.081	0.235	0.134	0.012
GO-13	−0.126	0.483	0.654	−0.028	0.017	0.087	0.055	0.122	0.064	0.007
GO-15	−0.127	0.468	0.702	−0.072	0.028	0.086	0.063	0.141	0.087	0.008
GO-17	−0.128	0.453	0.751	−0.116	0.040	0.087	0.072	0.167	0.113	0.010
GO-GMV	−0.124	0.495	0.606	0.011	0.012	0.087	0.048	0.120	0.048	0.013

GOLD	Mean					Sd				
	VNQ	GLD	TLT	SPY	EFA	VNQ	GLD	TLT	SPY	EFA
DCC−13	−0.058	−0.021	0.432	0.890	−0.244	0.089	0.066	0.100	0.187	0.078
DCC−15	−0.047	−0.089	0.447	1.049	−0.360	0.103	0.081	0.116	0.208	0.088
DCC−17	−0.036	−0.157	0.461	1.208	−0.476	0.119	0.097	0.132	0.231	0.105
DCC−GMV	−0.074	0.123	0.393	0.580	−0.021	0.065	0.044	0.063	0.192	0.105
ADCC−13	−0.045	−0.024	0.422	0.875	−0.228	0.107	0.082	0.120	0.214	0.091
ADCC−15	−0.033	−0.093	0.435	1.033	−0.343	0.123	0.099	0.139	0.245	0.107
ADCC−17	−0.020	−0.161	0.449	1.190	−0.458	0.141	0.116	0.158	0.277	0.129
ADCC−GMV	−0.064	0.115	0.381	0.597	−0.030	0.073	0.047	0.068	0.228	0.120
GO−13	−0.087	−0.004	0.436	0.948	−0.293	0.075	0.044	0.058	0.177	0.066
GO−15	−0.076	−0.076	0.456	1.104	−0.408	0.082	0.055	0.063	0.191	0.072
GO−17	−0.065	−0.149	0.476	1.260	−0.523	0.092	0.067	0.071	0.207	0.081
GO−GMV	−0.103	0.168	0.383	0.591	−0.038	0.078	0.052	0.070	0.118	0.049

Summary statistics on optimal portfolio weights calculated for various target returns (13%, 15%, and 17%) and global minimum variance (GMV).

Table 4 provides a comparison between the BIT portfolio and the GLD portfolio. For the bitcoin portfolio, and a particular target return, ADCC portfolios have higher risk adjusted measures. For example, for a target return of 15%, DCC-15, ADCC-15, and GO-15 produce Sharpe ratios of 2.089, 2.246, and 2.239, respectively. A similar pattern is observed for the gold portfolio.

One of the strongest results from Table 4 is that for a particular target return and GARCH model, the highest risk adjusted returns are observed for the BIT portfolio, indicating that on a risk adjusted basis, the BIT portfolio is preferred over the GLD portfolio. For example, consider the case of estimating

---

[6] GARCH models are estimated using 1200 observations, and 519 one step forecasts are generated using rolling window estimation. The estimation window of 1200 observations is chosen based on a Monte Carlo comparison of RMSE. GARCH models are refitted every 60 observations. The portfolio results are robust to refits between 40 and 120 observations.

portfolio weights using DCC-13. The BIT portfolio has Sortino, Omega, and Information values of 0.170, 0.365, and 1.849, respectively. These values are larger than their corresponding values for the GLD portfolio of 0.156, 0.346, and 1.683, respectively. The results in Table 4 are important in showing that for a particular target return (or minimum variance portfolio) and using a GARCH estimation technique, the bitcoin portfolio is preferred over the gold portfolio.

Equity curves are shown in Figure 3a,b. The bitcoin equity curves for target return portfolios look very similar. Notice that, as expected, portfolios calculated using a target return of 17% have larger final values then portfolios calculated using other target returns. Global minimum variance portfolios have larger drawdowns, which is consistent with the drawdown statistics in Table 4. A similar pattern is observed for the gold portfolio equity curves.

A statistical comparison between the Sharpe Ratio for the BIT portfolio and the GLD portfolio reveals no statistically significant difference between the Sharpe Ratios (Table 5). Sharpe Ratios, however, focus on the first two moments of the portfolio return distribution and do not take into account other factors like performance fees.

The performance fees indicate that the economic value an investor places on switching from a GLD portfolio to the BIT portfolio is substantial (Table 6). For example, in the case of a relative risk aversion of 5, the performance fees for GARCH models range between slightly above 28 basis points (DCC-13) to over 400 (GO-17). Performance fees are higher for portfolios with higher target returns.

In order to make the portfolio comparison more realistic, values for portfolio turnover are constructed (Table 7). Turnover is expressed as the average number of trades per day. For example, for the bitcoin portfolio estimated using DCC-13, a turnover of 0.125 indicates that on average 0.125 trades are made per day. The GO portfolios produce the least turnover. Turnover can be used to estimate trading costs. The turnover values can be annualized by multiplying by 252 to get the number of trades per year and the result multiplied by the trading costs in dollars per trade. These costs are expressed as a percentage of a $1,000,000 portfolio and converted to basis points. As the results in Table 7 show, even with relatively high trading costs of $20 per trade, the total trading costs are less than the performance fee, indicating the benefits of switching to a bitcoin-based portfolio. Notice that portfolios constructed using GO have less transaction costs, which is consistent with GO optimal portfolio weights, for most assets, having a lower standard deviation compared to optimal portfolio weights constructed using either DCC or ADCC.

Table 4. Portfolio comparisons.

Bitcoin Portfolio

	DCC-13	DCC-15	DCC-17	DCC-GMV	ADCC-13	ADCC-15	ADCC-17	ADCC-GMV	GO-13	GO-15	GO-17	GO-GMV
Mean	11.737	13.684	15.623	10.899	12.277	14.244	16.204	11.483	12.954	14.934	16.906	11.881
Sd	6.340	6.462	6.694	6.325	6.139	6.261	6.497	6.115	6.463	6.589	6.830	6.427
Sharp	1.823	2.089	2.307	1.694	1.970	2.246	2.466	1.848	1.976	2.239	2.449	1.820
Sharpe VaR	1.194	1.384	1.542	1.104	1.298	1.497	1.659	1.212	1.303	1.492	1.646	1.192
Sharpe ES	0.937	1.084	1.205	0.868	1.018	1.171	1.295	0.951	1.021	1.167	1.285	0.936
Sortino	0.170	0.198	0.222	0.156	0.189	0.218	0.243	0.175	0.190	0.218	0.241	0.173
Omega	0.365	0.427	0.475	0.338	0.400	0.464	0.514	0.372	0.393	0.452	0.499	0.359
Information	1.849	2.153	2.411	1.705	2.010	2.328	2.591	1.872	2.024	2.329	2.582	1.847
Drawdown	0.074	0.069	0.064	0.077	0.062	0.057	0.051	0.065	0.055	0.050	0.044	0.054

Gold Portfolio

	DCC-13	DCC-15	DCC-17	DCC-GMV	ADCC-13	ADCC-15	ADCC-17	ADCC-GMV	GO-13	GO-15	GO-17	GO-GMV
Mean	11.589	12.594	13.578	8.774	11.827	12.941	14.035	9.888	11.565	12.368	13.151	9.644
Sd	6.843	7.610	8.554	6.098	6.613	7.377	8.324	5.907	6.813	7.561	8.478	6.112
Sharp	1.667	1.631	1.566	1.409	1.761	1.729	1.664	1.643	1.671	1.612	1.530	1.548
Sharpe VaR	1.085	1.060	1.015	0.907	1.150	1.128	1.083	1.068	1.087	1.046	0.990	1.003
Sharpe ES	0.853	0.834	0.799	0.715	0.904	0.887	0.851	0.840	0.855	0.823	0.779	0.789
Sortino	0.156	0.152	0.146	0.130	0.166	0.162	0.156	0.156	0.158	0.151	0.142	0.149
Omega	0.346	0.338	0.318	0.274	0.362	0.356	0.337	0.323	0.339	0.324	0.303	0.297
Information	1.683	1.653	1.592	1.387	1.784	1.762	1.701	1.641	1.686	1.631	1.549	1.540
Drawdown	0.063	0.058	0.063	0.086	0.059	0.062	0.069	0.073	0.046	0.050	0.054	0.065

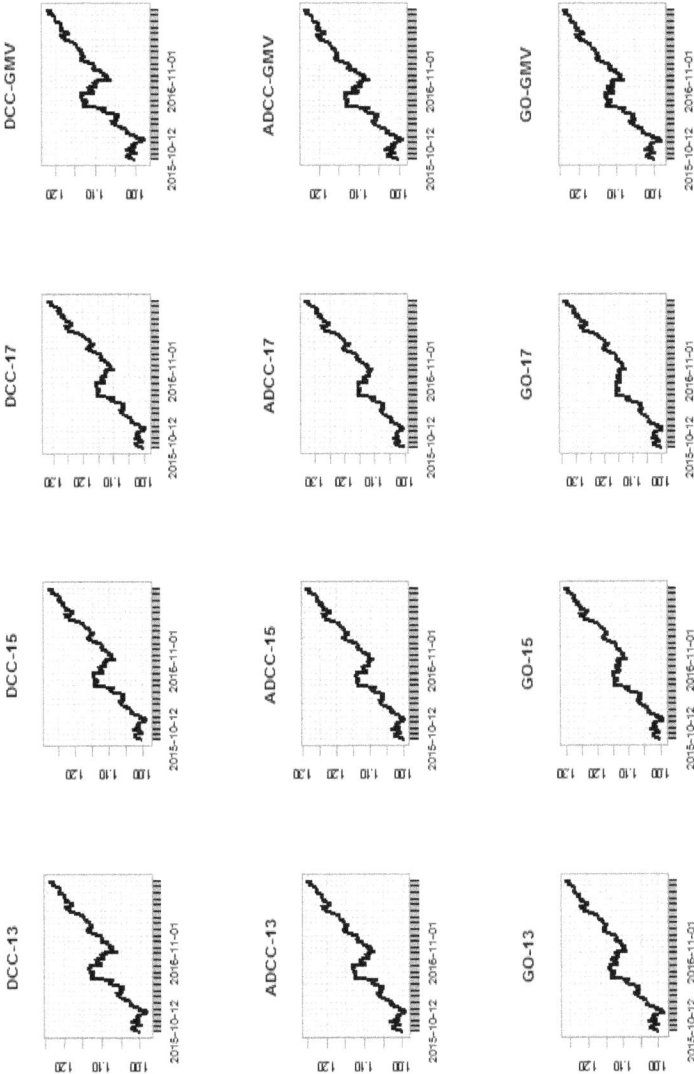

(a)

Figure 3. *Cont.*

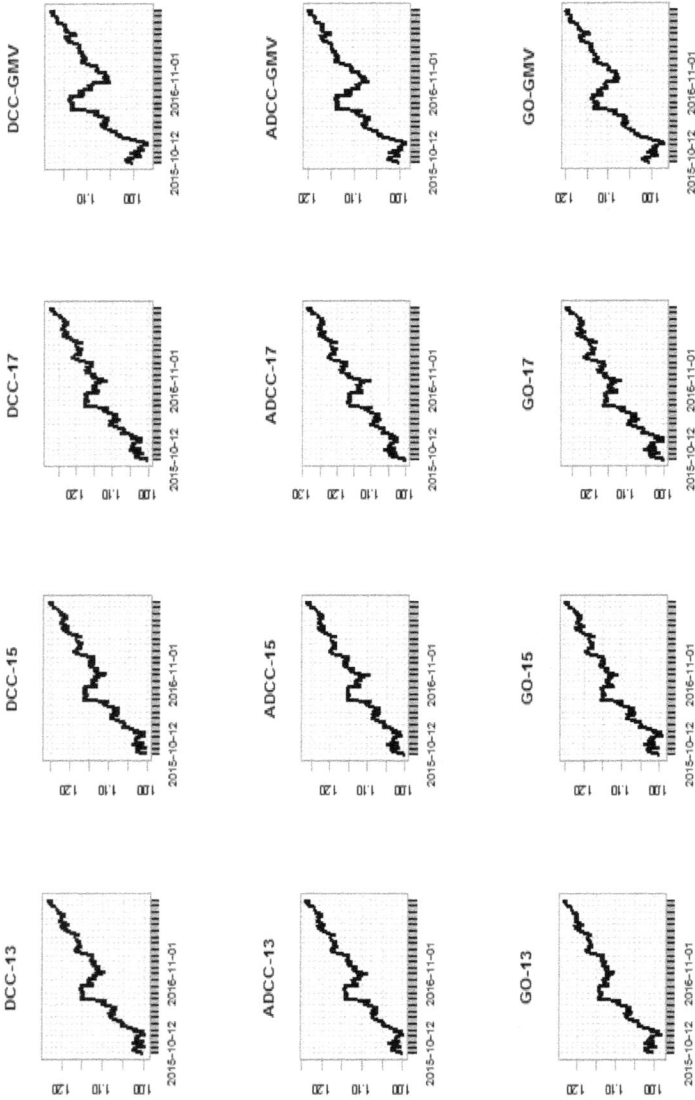

(b)

Figure 3. (a) Equity curves for bitcoin portfolio. (b) Equity curves for gold portfolio.

Table 5. Comparison of Sharpe Ratios.

	DCC-13	DCC-15	DCC-17	DCC-GMV	ADCC-13	ADCC-15	ADCC-17	ADCC-GMV	GO-13	GO-15	GO-17	GO-GMV
Diff	0.010	0.028	0.046	0.018	0.013	0.032	0.050	0.013	0.019	0.039	0.057	0.017
p value	0.611	0.257	0.146	0.230	0.476	0.192	0.115	0.389	0.351	0.142	0.070	0.345

The variable diff represents the difference between the portfolio with bitcoin Sharpe Ratio and the portfolio with gold Sharpe Ratio. Sharpe Ratios are calculated using returns in excess of a 3-month T bill. The p values are computed using block bootstrapping with 5000 replications.

Table 6. Performance fees.

	DCC-13	DCC-15	DCC-17	DCC-GMV	ADCC-13	ADCC-15	ADCC-17	ADCC-GMV	GO-13	GO-15	GO-17	GO-GMV
$\gamma = 1$	14.873	109.067	204.591	212.566	45.007	130.366	217.066	159.585	139.024	256.772	375.691	223.790
$\gamma = 5$	28.161	141.374	261.263	206.981	57.096	160.762	271.158	154.603	148.323	284.251	426.049	215.929
$\gamma = 10$	44.840	181.937	332.429	199.976	72.271	198.929	339.095	148.353	159.995	318.748	489.280	206.067

The values represent the management fee, in annualized basis points, an investor would be willing to pay to switch from a portfolio with gold to a portfolio with bitcoin. The γ values represent the degree of relative risk aversion.

Table 7. Turnover and trading costs.

	DCC-13	DCC-15	DCC-17	DCC-GMV	ADCC-13	ADCC-15	ADCC-17	ADCC-GMV	GO-13	GO-15	GO-17	GO-GMV
BIT	0.125	0.136	0.148	0.129	0.129	0.140	0.153	0.133	0.078	0.093	0.109	0.074
Gold	0.128	0.148	0.172	0.129	0.136	0.157	0.182	0.133	0.063	0.073	0.085	0.065
TC = $5												
BIT	1.576	1.708	1.870	1.623	1.620	1.759	1.931	1.673	0.979	1.169	1.378	0.927
Gold	1.618	1.870	2.163	1.624	1.716	1.977	2.288	1.678	0.788	0.916	1.069	0.821
TC = $10												
BIT	3.151	3.417	3.741	3.247	3.239	3.518	3.862	3.347	1.959	2.338	2.756	1.854
Gold	3.236	3.741	4.326	3.247	3.432	3.954	4.576	3.355	1.576	1.832	2.138	1.641
TC = $20												
BIT	6.303	6.833	7.481	6.493	6.479	7.035	7.725	6.693	3.917	4.676	5.511	3.707
Gold	6.472	7.481	8.652	6.495	6.864	7.908	9.151	6.710	3.152	3.663	4.276	3.282

Turnover is the average number of trades per day. Trading costs in annual basis points based on a $1,000,000 portfolio with trading costs (TC) in dollars per trade.

6. Robust Analysis: Long Only Portfolios

The preceding analysis has been conducted assuming short sales are allowed. This section reports on results obtained by assuming long portfolios only. Since the average returns of gold and bitcoin are so different, we only present results on global minimum variance portfolios.

For a particular type of GARCH model, the portfolio with bitcoin produces higher risk-adjusted returns compared to the portfolio with gold (Table 8). Performance fees, the amount an investor would be willing to pay to switch from a portfolio with gold to one with bitcoin are positive and fairly large (Table 9). Transaction costs are smaller than performance fees, indicating that even after adjusting for transaction costs, a risk adverse investor would be willing to pay a fee to switch from a portfolio with gold to one with bitcoin (Table 10). These results for long only portfolios are consistent with our results that allow for short sales.

Table 8. Portfolio comparisons: Long only.

	BIT			GLD		
	DCC-GMV	ADCC-GMV	GO-GMV	DCC-GMV	ADCC-GMV	GO-GMV
Mean	10.557	10.475	11.088	8.316	8.778	8.785
Sd	6.405	6.231	6.440	6.191	6.056	6.146
Sharp	1.620	1.652	1.693	1.314	1.419	1.400
SharpeVaR	1.052	1.074	1.103	0.843	0.914	0.901
SharpeES	0.828	0.845	0.867	0.665	0.721	0.710
Sortino	0.146	0.152	0.156	0.119	0.131	0.131
Omega	0.324	0.329	0.337	0.257	0.277	0.269
Information	1.623	1.656	1.706	1.285	1.398	1.378
Drawdown	0.081	0.071	0.065	0.093	0.082	0.077

Table 9. Performance fees: Long only.

	DCC-GMV	ADCC-GMV	GO-GMV
$\gamma = 1$	224.177	169.771	230.425
$\gamma = 5$	218.885	165.505	223.109
$\gamma = 10$	212.250	160.155	213.935

The values represent the management fee, in annualized basis points, an investor would be willing to pay to switch from a portfolio with gold to a portfolio with bitcoin. The γ values represent the degree of relative risk aversion.

Table 10. Turnover and trading costs: Long only.

	DCC-GMV	ADCC-GMV	GO-GMV
BIT	0.088	0.086	0.037
Gold	0.081	0.084	0.033
TC = $5			
BIT	1.104	1.088	0.465
Gold	1.019	1.055	0.410
TC = $10			
BIT	2.208	2.177	0.930
Gold	2.037	2.111	0.819
TC = $20			
BIT	4.415	4.353	1.860
Gold	4.075	4.221	1.638

Turnover is the average number of trades per day. Trading costs in annual basis points based on a $1,000,000 portfolio with trading costs (TC) in dollars per trade.

7. Conclusions and Implications

Bitcoin is an exciting new financial product that may be useful for inclusion in investment portfolios. There has been discussion that bitcoin may even by a useful substitute for gold. The purpose of this paper is to investigate the portfolio implications of switching from a portfolio with gold to a portfolio with bitcoin. Given the current interest in Bitcoin investing, this is an important and timely topic to study. Our approach is to use multivariate GARCH models to estimate minimum variance equity portfolios subject to a target return for a US benchmark portfolio that includes gold and a portfolio that substitutes gold for bitcoin. The benchmark portfolio includes US equities, US bonds, US real estate, EAFE equities, and gold. A comparison between these portfolios helps to gain a better understanding of the economic value of substituting bitcoin for gold in an investment portfolio.

Three different multivariable GARCH models (DCC, ADCC, and GO) are used to estimate the optimal portfolio weights. Comparing weights computed from different models demonstrates the robustness of the portfolio results to the choice of GARCH model. Optimal portfolio weights are estimated using rolling window analysis. This mitigates the effects of changing dynamics, parameter heterogeneity, and structural change. For most assets, the optimal portfolio weights estimated from GO have lower standard deviation than those from DCC or ADCC.

Our results show that portfolios with bitcoin rank highest according to risk-adjusted measures such as the Sharpe, Sortino, Omega, and Information ratios. This result is robust to the choice of GARCH model (DCC, ADCC, or GO) used to compute optimal portfolio weights. An analysis of the economic value shows that risk-averse investors will be willing to pay a high performance fee to switch from a portfolio with gold to a portfolio with bitcoin. These results are robust to the inclusion of trading costs. We find that it is possible for an investor to substitute bitcoin for gold in an investment portfolio and achieve a higher risk adjusted return.

While our results on bitcoin investing are encouraging, there are certain limitations that require future research. First, we only have six years of data and more data will be required to test the voracity of our results. Second, in the absence of any valid moment conditions or asymptotic properties DCC forecasts may be imprecise and this may affect the estimates of the portfolio returns and any resulting statistical analysis. Third, as with any new financial asset, the level of widespread adoption will be crucial to its acceptance. Currently, bitcoin is viewed by many investors as a speculative asset and this limits its widespread acceptability. Fourth, bitcoin is in its infancy and the choice of cryptocurrencies is growing. It is not clear if bitcoin will be the preferred cryptocurrency in the future.

Author Contributions: Both authors contributed equally in the preparation of the manuscript.

Funding: This research received no funding.

Acknowledgments: We thank the Editor and two anonymous reviewers for helpful comments.

Conflicts of Interest: The authors declare no conflict of interest.

References

Aielli, Gian Piero. 2013. Dynamic Conditional Correlation: On Properties and Estimation. *Journal of Business & Economic Statistics* 31: 282–99. [CrossRef]

Alexander, Carol. 2001. *Market Models: A Guide to Financial Data Analysis.* Chichester: John Wiley & Sons.

Baur, Dirk G., and Brian M. Lucey. 2010. Is Gold a Hedge or a Safe Haven? An Analysis of Stocks, Bonds and Gold. *Financial Review* 45: 217–29. [CrossRef]

Baur, Dirk G., and Thomas K. McDermott. 2010. Is Gold a Safe Haven? International Evidence. *Journal of Banking & Finance* 34: 1886–98. [CrossRef]

Beckmann, Joscha, Theo Berger, and Robert Czudaj. 2015. Does Gold Act as a Hedge or a Safe Haven for Stocks? A Smooth Transition Approach. *Economic Modelling* 48: 16–24. [CrossRef]

Böhme, Rainer, Nicolas Christin, Benjamin Edelman, and Tyler Moore. 2015. Bitcoin: Economics, Technology, and Governance. *Journal of Economic Perspectives* 29: 213–38. [CrossRef]

Boswijk, H. Peter, and Roy van der Weide. 2006. Wake Me up before You GO-GARCH. 2006/3. Amsterdam School of Economics. Available online: http://dare.uva.nl/record/390623%5Cnpapers2://publication/uuid/A8691D04-AD04-42B6-8F98-34FD4CA86521 (accessed on 15 March 2018).

Boswijk, H. Peter, and Roy van der Weide. 2011. Method of Moments Estimation of GO-GARCH Models. *Journal of Econometrics* 163: 118–26. [CrossRef]

Bouri, Elie, Peter Molnár, Georges Azzi, David Roubaud, and Lars Ivar Hagfors. 2017. On the Hedge and Safe Haven Properties of Bitcoin: Is It Really More than a Diversifier? *Finance Research Letters* 20: 192–98. [CrossRef]

Broda, Simon A., and Marc S. Paolella. 2009. CHICAGO: A Fast and Accurate Method for Portfolio Risk Calculation. *Journal of Financial Econometrics* 7: 412–36. [CrossRef]

Canadian Federation of Independent Business. 2018. *Regular vs. Premium Credit Card Rate Chart for Small Business*. Toronto: CFIB.

Caporin, Massimiliano, and Michael McAleer. 2013. Ten Things You Should Know about the Dynamic Conditional Correlation Representation. *Econometrics* 1: 115–26. [CrossRef]

Cappiello, Lorenzo, Robert F. Engle, and Kevin Sheppard. 2006. Asymmetric Dynamics in the Correlations of Global Equity and Bond Returns. *Journal of Financial Econometrics* 4: 537–72. [CrossRef]

Ciaian, Pavel, Miroslava Rajcaniova, and D'Artis Kancs. 2016. The Economics of BitCoin Price Formation. *Applied Economics* 48: 1799–815. [CrossRef]

Ciner, Cetin, Constantin Gurdgiev, and Brian M. Lucey. 2013. Hedges and Safe Havens: An Examination of Stocks, Bonds, Gold, Oil and Exchange Rates. *International Review of Financial Analysis* 29: 202–11. [CrossRef]

DeMiguel, Victor, Lorenzo Garlappi, Francisco J. Nogales, and Raman Uppal. 2009. A Generalized Approach to Portfolio Optimization: Improving Performance by Constraining Portfolio Norms. *Management Science* 55: 798–812. [CrossRef]

Dyhrberg, Anne Haubo. 2016a. Bitcoin, Gold and the Dollar—A GARCH Volatility Analysis. *Finance Research Letters* 16: 85–92. [CrossRef]

Dyhrberg, Anne Haubo. 2016b. Hedging Capabilities of Bitcoin. Is It the Virtual Gold? *Finance Research Letters* 16: 139–44. [CrossRef]

Eichengreen, Barry. 1992. *Golden Fetters: The Gold Standard and the Great Depression, 1919–1939*. New York: Oxford University Press.

Elton, Edwin J., and Martin J. Gruber. 1997. Modern Portfolio Theory, 1950 to Date. *Journal of Banking and Finance* 21: 1743–59. [CrossRef]

Engle, Robert F. 2002. Dynamic Conditional Correlation: A simple class of multivariate generalized autoregressive conditional heteroskedasticity models. *Journal of Business & Economic Statistics* 20: 339–50. [CrossRef]

Feibel, Bruce J. 2003. *Investment Performance Measurement*. Hoboken: John Wiley & Sons.

Fleming, Jeff, Chris Kirby, and Barbara Ostdiek. 2001. The Economic Value of Volatility Timing. *The Journal of Finance* 56: 329–52. [CrossRef]

Fry, John, and Eng-Tuck Cheah. 2016. Negative Bubbles and Shocks in Cryptocurrency Markets. *International Review of Financial Analysis* 47: 343–52. [CrossRef]

Ghalanos, Alexios. 2015. Rmgarch: Multivariate GARCH Models. R Package Version 1.2-8. Available online: https://cran.r-project.org/web/packages/rmgarch/index.html (accessed on 15 March 2018).

Glaser, Florian, Kai Zimmerman, Martin Haferkorn, Moritz Christian Weber, and Michael Siering. 2014. Bitcoin—Asset or Currency? Revealing Users' Hidden Intentions. Paper presented at Twenty Second European Conference on Information Systems, Tel Aviv, Israel, June 9–14; pp. 1–14. [CrossRef]

Glosten, Lawrence R., Ravi Jagannathan, and David E. Runkle. 1993. On the Relation between the Expected Value and the Volatility of the Nominal Excess Return on Stocks. *The Journal of Finance* 48: 1779–801. [CrossRef]

Guesmi, Khaled, Samir Saadi, Ilyes Abid, and Zied Ftiti. 2018. Portfolio Diversification with Virtual Currency: Evidence from Bitcoin. *International Review of Financial Analysis*. [CrossRef]

Hendrickson, Joshua R., Thomas L. Hogan, and William J. Luther. 2016. The Political Economy of Bitcoin. *Economic Inquiry* 54: 925–39. [CrossRef]

Hillier, David, Paul Draper, and Robert Faff. 2006. Do Precious Metals Shine? An Investment Perspective. *Financial Analysts Journal* 62: 98–106. [CrossRef]

Hopkins, Jamie. 2017. Bitcoin Might Be A 'Bubble' But Digital Currencies Are Not. *Forbes*, November 29.

Jaffe, Jeffrey F. 1989. Gold and Gold Stocks as Investments for Institutional Portfolios. *Financial Analysts Journal* 45: 53–59. [CrossRef]

Kim, Thomas. 2017. On the Transaction Cost of Bitcoin. *Finance Research Letters* 23: 300–5. [CrossRef]

Kiviat, Trevor I. 2015. Beyond Bitcoin: Issues in Regulating Blockchain Transactions. *Duke Law Journal* 65: 569–608. [CrossRef]

Ledoit, Oliver, and Michael Wolf. 2008. Robust Performance Hypothesis Testing with the Sharpe Ratio. *Journal of Empirical Finance* 15: 850–59. [CrossRef]

Lo, Stephanie, and J. Christina Wang. 2014. Bitcoin as Money? *Federal Reserve Bank of Boston* 14: 1–28.

McNutt, Patrick. 2002. *The Economics of Public Choice II*. Cheltenham: Edward Elgar Publishing.

Michaud, By Richard, Robert Michaud, and Katharine Pulvermacher. 2006. *Gold as a Strategic Asset*. London: World Gold Council.

Nakamoto, Satoshi. 2008. Bitcoin: A Peer-to-Peer Electronic Cash System. Available online: https://bitcoin.org/en/bitcoin-paper (accessed on 15 March 2018).

Popper, Nathaniel. 2015a. Can Bitcoin Conquer Argentina? *The New York Times*, April 29.

Popper, Nathaniel. 2015b. Digital Gold: Bitcoin and the Inside Story of Misfits and Millionaires Trying to Reinvent Money. New York: HarperCollins.

R Core Team. 2015. R: A Language and Environment for Statistical Computing. R Foundation for Statistical Computing, Vienna, Austria. Available online: http://www.r-project.org/ (accessed on 15 March 2018).

Reboredo, Juan C. 2013a. Is Gold a Hedge or Safe Haven against Oil Price Movements? *Resources Policy* 38: 130–37. [CrossRef]

Reboredo, Juan C. 2013b. Is Gold a Safe Haven or a Hedge for the US Dollar? Implications for Risk Management. *Journal of Banking & Finance* 37: 2665–76. [CrossRef]

Van Der Weide, Roy. 2002. GO-GARCH: A Multivariate Generalized Orthogonal GARCH Model. *Journal of Applied Econometrics* 17: 549–64. [CrossRef]

Zhang, Kun, and Laiwan Chan. 2009. Efficient Factor GARCH Models and Factor-DCC Models. *Quantitative Finance* 9: 71–91. [CrossRef]

Zhu, Yechen, David Dickinson, and Jianjun Li. 2017. Analysis on the Influence Factors of Bitcoin's Price Based on VEC Model. *Financial Innovation* 3: 3. [CrossRef]

Zohar, Aviv. 2015. Bitcoin. *Communications of the ACM* 58: 104–13. [CrossRef]

Journal of
Risk and Financial Management

MDPI

Article

An Analysis of Bitcoin's Price Dynamics

Frode Kjærland [1,2,*]**, Aras Khazal** [1]**, Erlend A. Krogstad** [1]**, Frans B. G. Nordstrøm** [1] **and Are Oust** [1]

[1] NTNU Business School, Norwegian University of Science and Technology, 7491 Trondheim, Norway;
    aras.kj@ntnu.no (A.K.); erlekrog@gmail.com (E.A.K.); fransbgn@gmail.com (F.B.G.N.);
    are.oust@ntnu.no (A.O.)
[2] Nord University Business School, Nord University, 8049 Bodø, Norway
* Correspondence: frode.kjarland@ntnu.no

Received: 20 September 2018; Accepted: 11 October 2018; Published: 15 October 2018

Abstract: This paper aims to enhance the understanding of which factors affect the price development of Bitcoin in order for investors to make sound investment decisions. Previous literature has covered only a small extent of the highly volatile period during the last months of 2017 and the beginning of 2018. To examine the potential price drivers, we use the Autoregressive Distributed Lag and Generalized Autoregressive Conditional Heteroscedasticity approach. Our study identifies the technological factor Hashrate as irrelevant for modeling Bitcoin price dynamics. This irrelevance is due to the underlying code that makes the supply of Bitcoins deterministic, and it stands in contrast to previous literature that has included Hashrate as a crucial independent variable. Moreover, the empirical findings indicate that the price of Bitcoin is affected by returns on the S&P 500 and Google searches, showing consistency with results from previous literature. In contrast to previous literature, we find the CBOE volatility index (VIX), oil, gold, and Bitcoin transaction volume to be insignificant.

Keywords: Bitcoin; cryptocurrency; Hashrate

JEL Classification: C10; G15

1. Introduction

The purpose of this study is to identify the factors that have an impact on the price of Bitcoin. The market value of Bitcoin has grown tremendously in 2017. As the market values of cryptocurrencies grow, it is reasonable to assume that they will start having an effect on certain economies. By estimating the price drivers during the period ranging from 2013 to 2018, this paper will assist investors in making sound investment decisions and aid in the understanding of what drives this phenomenon's price fluctuations.

Cryptocurrencies are decentralized digital currencies that use encryption to verify transactions. In 2008, Nakamoto (2008) released his paper describing Bitcoin. In January of the following year, Nakamoto released the software that launched the Bitcoin network. As of 2018, Bitcoin is the most commonly known and used cryptocurrency. Since its founding in 2009, the price of Bitcoin has risen from USD 0.07 to an all-time high of USD 20,089 on 17 December 2017 (Quandl.com). At this point in time, its market capitalization was approximately USD 336.4 Billion.

From January 2017 through December, Bitcoin increased by 1270%, and the total cryptocurrency trading volume passed USD 5 billion a day. Interest from the mainstream media, regulators, and the public and financial markets accelerated so much that some call this period Bitcoin's "IPO moment" (Forbes.com 2017). During 2017, Bitcoin garnered more focus from institutional money, hedge funds, and public funds. Its success culminated with the approval and introduction of Bitcoin derivatives. Due to the exponential rise in attention, we have included two sub-periods to test if the factors have been the same before and after 2017.

We believe that it is important to understand the underlying factors affecting the price of such a highly volatile financial phenomenon. Just as the price of Bitcoins has had an exponential rise in the past year, the academic literature on Bitcoin and cryptocurrencies has experienced a similar increase. Previous literature has used macro-economic, technological, and publicity factors in Bitcoin models (Aalborg et al. 2018; Bouoiyour and Selmi 2016; Ciaian et al. 2016; Garcia et al. 2014; Kristoufek 2013, 2015; Kjærland et al. 2018). However, few academic studies include data that reflect the price fluctuations that Bitcoin experienced in 2017 and 2018. This paper addresses this gap in the literature by assessing what variables drive the price of Bitcoin. As Kristoufek (2015) noted, *"because of the dynamic nature of Bitcoin and its rapid price fluctuations, it is logical that the drivers behind the price will vary over time."* Therefore, we have chosen to analyze the drivers yet again.

To estimate the short- and long-term effects of potential price drivers on Bitcoin, an Autoregressive Distributed Lag (ARDL) and Generalized Autoregressive Conditional Heteroscedasticity (GARCH) model is estimated. We find Hashrate to be an irrelevant variable due to the deterministic feature of the Bitcoin supply. The supply of Bitcoins are not dependent on price, as a normal good, but instead the supply of Bitcoins are given by the Bitcoin code and solely dependent on time. Consistent with the previous literature, we find that the S&P 500, Google searches and last week's return on Bitcoin to be significant explanatory variables, while gold, oil, CBOE volatility index (VIX), and Bitcoin transaction volume are found to be insignificant in the estimation period.

This paper is organized as follows. Section 2 contains a literature review, Section 3 includes a description of the data and econometric methods, Section 4 presents the results, and Section 5 includes a discussion of the results and provides the conclusions.

2. Background and Literature Review

2.1. Introduction to Cryptocurrencies and Bitcoin

Several studies focus on the key concepts of cryptocurrencies and particularly Bitcoin (Becker et al. 2013; Brandvold et al. 2015; Dwyer 2015; Nica et al. 2017; Segendorf 2014). According to Dwyer (2015), the major innovation in Bitcoin is its decentralized technology. Instead of storing transactions on a single or set of servers, the database is distributed across a network of participating computers (Böhme et al. 2015). This database is what is called a Blockchain. Blocks are added to the chain in the process of mining Bitcoins. The process of mining revolves around solving complex computational puzzles, and the incentive for miners to participate are transaction fees and Bitcoin rewards. To solve these puzzles, miners need computational power, which is measured by the Hashrate. The Hashrate is the speed at which a computer can complete an operation in the Bitcoin code, while the mining difficulty refers to the level of complexity in the computational puzzles and is directly correlated with the Hashrate. As the Hashrate, either increases or decreases, the underlying Bitcoin algorithm adjusts the mining difficulty so that the supply of Bitcoins follows a predetermined path.[1] New coins are generated approximately every 10 min independent of the current price, meaning that the Bitcoin supply is inelastic and time-dependent, as shown in Figure 1. Since the supply is solely dependent on time, we choose to classify the Bitcoin supply as deterministic.

---

[1] Bitcoin rewards are currently at 12.5 coins per block, but the protocol requires that the reward is halved every 210,000 mined blocks. Mining 210,000 blocks takes approximately four years. Given the current level of network processing power, the next halving will take place around early June 2020, bringing the mining reward down to 6.25 coins.

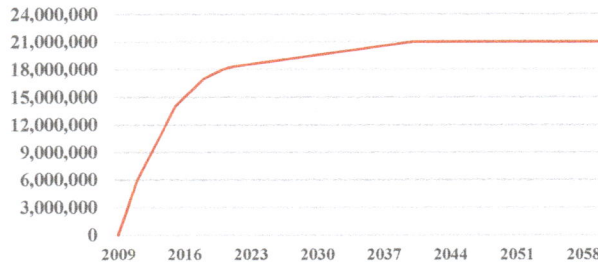

Figure 1. Bitcoin deterministic supply.

2.2. Literature Review

Several authors have attempted to describe Bitcoin as a currency, stock, or asset. Yermack (2013) argues that Bitcoin appears to behave more similar to a speculative store of value rather than a currency. Dwyer (2015), on the other hand, describes Bitcoin as an electronic currency that can be used to trade and store in a personal balance sheet. Dwyer's argument is supported by Polasik et al. (2015), who adds that Bitcoin can operate as a medium of exchange alongside other payment technologies.

An increasing number of researchers have focused on the existence of a fundamental value of Bitcoin, and some have studied whether or not it is a bubble. Garcia et al. (2014) finds that Bitcoin is a financial bubble because of the difference between the exchange rate and fundamental value of Bitcoin. He argues for a fundamental value given the cost of mining. Similarly, Hayes (2015, 2018) proposed a specific cost of production model for valuating Bitcoin. Additionally, Cheah and Fry (2015) conclude that Bitcoin is a speculative bubble and that the fundamental value of Bitcoin is zero. Unlike earlier studies, Corbet et al. (2017) found that there is no clear evidence of a bubble in Bitcoin. While these authors discuss if Bitcoin is a bubble or not, Bouri et al. (2017b) found that Bitcoin could be used as an effective diversifier and, in some periods, also display safe-haven and hedge properties.

Some studies have been dedicated to determining the factors that drive the price of Bitcoin. Bouoiyour and Selmi (2015) argue that long-term fundamentals are likely to be major contributors to Bitcoin price variations. Among others, they also found technical factors to be a positive driver of Bitcoin prices (Bouoiyour and Selmi 2015; Ciaian et al. 2016; Garcia et al. 2014; Georgoula et al. 2015; Hayes 2015; Kristoufek 2015). Specifically, Georgoula et al. (2015) and Hayes (2015) found the technical factor Hashrate to be a significant positive price driver. Bouoiyour and Selmi (2016), Garcia et al. (2014), Kristoufek (2015), Kjærland et al. (2018), and Sovbetov (2018) have all used Hashrate as a variable in their respective models.

Other scholars also argue for the significance of fundamental factors such as exchange-trade, equity market indices, currency exchange rates, commodity prices, and transaction volume (Balcilar et al. 2017; Bouri et al. 2018a; Bouoiyour and Selmi 2016; Bouoiyour et al. 2016; Ciaian et al. 2016; Dyhrberg 2016; Kristoufek 2013; Yermack 2013). In contrast to Bouoiyour and Selmi (2015), Polasik et al. (2015) states that an increase in the transaction volume will lead to higher prices and that global economic factors do not seem to be an important driver. Ciaian et al. (2016) also found that supply and demand factors have strong impacts on price and that standard economic currency models can partly explain price fluctuations.

Kristoufek (2013, 2015) analyzed the frequency of online searches on Bitcoin, found them to be a good proxy for interest and popularity, and discovered that the relationship between the price of Bitcoin and online popularity is bidirectional. Ciaian et al. (2016) also found a positive relationship between Wikipedia searches and Bitcoin. Others argue along the same lines as Kristoufek in that it is primarily popularity and investor attractiveness that drive price movements (Bouoiyour et al. 2016).

2.3. Theoretical Foundation

2.3.1. Stock Price Theories and Momentum Theory

Santoni (1987) considers two theories that potentially explain stock prices: the Efficient Market Hypothesis and the Greater Fool theory. The efficient market hypothesis tells us that all relevant information is contained in current stock prices and that prices only change when investors receive new information about fundamentals (Fama 1976). If this theory holds, past price changes contain no useful information about future price changes. The Greater Fool theory says that investors regard fundamental information as irrelevant. An investor buys shares on the belief that some bigger fool will buy them from him at a higher price in the future. This scheme is all about speculation and anticipation of continuing price increases due only to the fact that it has increased in the past.

Momentum in the financial market is an empirically observed trend for rising asset prices to rise further and that decreasing asset prices lead to further decreases. Momentum theory shows that stocks with strong past performance will outperform stocks that have a weak past performance (Jegadeesh and Titman 1993, 2001). This theory relies on short-term movements rather than fundamentals. In financial theory, the cause of momentum is known to be cognitive bias and investors behaving irrationally.[2]

2.3.2. Volatility

Global financial turmoil impacts economies, assets, and currencies around the world. Financial turmoil also affects the market participants and their investment decisions. During periods of crisis, investors are more inclined to redistribute their investments to assets that are considered to be safe-havens, including currencies. A currency is considered a safe-haven asset if international investors invest in it to minimize losses during periods of financial turmoil. Because of its impact on the development of currency exchange rates, financial turmoil, measured in volatility, is important to include in an exchange rate model.

While there is evidence of negative shocks to equities generating more volatility than positive shocks (Glosten et al. 1993), Baur and McDermott (2012) found that the volatility of gold returns reacts inversely to negative shocks. According to Baur and McDermott (2012), this volatility relation is due to the safe-haven properties of gold. Investors interpret rising gold prices as an increase in macroeconomic uncertainty. Rising uncertainty increases the volatility of gold prices. However, a study by Bouri et al. (2016) find no evidence of an asymmetric return-volatility relation in the Bitcoin market—which in contrast support a safe haven property of Bitcoin. On the other side, Kjærland et al. (2018) have the opposite finding.

3. Research Design

3.1. Data

The dependent variable to be explained by the models is the exchange rate between Bitcoin and the US dollar. The original data are daily spot rates for BTC/USD for the period between 1 January 2013 and 20 February 2018.

To avoid potential issues related to autocorrelation, the daily data are modified into weekly averages. As Bitcoin is traded every day of the week, we filter the data so that only common observations are used. Days when some of the variables have missing values have been removed. The data are gathered from various sources on 21 February 2018. The dependent variable and independent explanatory variables are summarized in Table 1. These are chosen based on previous literature and what we believe affects the price of Bitcoin.

---

2   Cognitive biases are errors in thinking that affect the decisions and judgments that people make.

Table 1. Variable Overview.

Variable	Description	Source
BTC	exchange rate between Bitcoin and the US Dollar	Quandl
Hashrate	the estimated number of giga hashes per second the Bitcoin network is performing	Quandl
Volume	total output volume of Bitcoin	Quandl
S&P 500	S&P 500 is an index of the 500 largest US listed Corporations	Thomson Reuters Eikon
Gold	Goldman Sachs Commodity Index Gold	Thomson Reuters Eikon
Oil	WTI Crude Oil Spot Price in USD per barrel	Thomson Reuters Eikon
VIX	implicit volatility of options on the S&P 500, a measure of the expected market volatility the next 30 days	Thomson Reuters Eikon
Google	normalized weekly statistics on the search term "Bitcoin", corrected for trends	Google Trend

In accordance with the previous literature, we have included the S&P 500 and CBOE Volatility Index (VIX). The S&P 500 is a good indicator of how financial markets are doing, and the VIX is intended to provide an instantaneous measure regarding how much the market believes that the S&P 500 will fluctuate in the next 30 days. By including these two variables, we consider both the numerical returns and risks in the financial markets. Furthermore, we have included the prices of WTI Oil and Gold in our model. Both are considered to be important global commodities whose prices have impacts on almost all economies around the world. These variables are all weekly observations obtained from Thomson Reuters.

To test if publicity and attention given to Bitcoin has an impact on price changes, we include Google Trends. Google search data show normalized weekly statistics that are corrected for trends on searches mentioning the term "Bitcoin" (Google Trends Help) [3]. We also test for traditional supply and demand effects by including Bitcoin transaction volume as a variable in this study. Finally, the technological factor Hashrate is included. Volume and Hashrate are weekly data obtained from Quandl.com.

3.2. Descriptive Statistics

Table 2 shows the descriptive statistics of the variables. Figures 2–9 display the changes in selected variables over the estimated period.

Table 2. Descriptive statistics.

Variable	Obs.	Mean	Std. Dev.	Min.	Max.
BTC	267	1372.9	2836.016	13.47221	17,612.51
Hashrate	267	2,132,903	3,936,302	20.80583	2.26×10^7
Volume	267	238,664.5	85,023.81	73,429.4	558,364.4
S&P 500	267	2053.9	296.3	1462.5	2844.4
Gold	267	1270.8	114.3	1063.0	1685.2
Oil	267	66.7	24.7	28.5	108.9
VIX	267	14.4	3.6	9.3	31.5
Google	267	7.3	13.4	1	100

---

[3] Google does not differentiate between the upper- and lowercase letters, meaning that searches made on "Bitcoin" or "bitcoin" are considered the same.

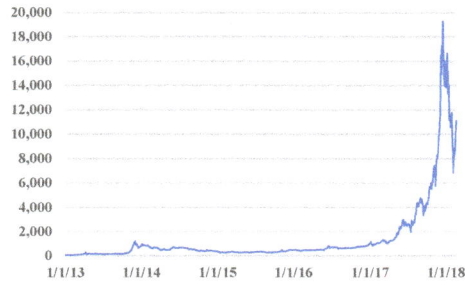

Figure 2. Bitcoin Market Price (USD), Quandl.

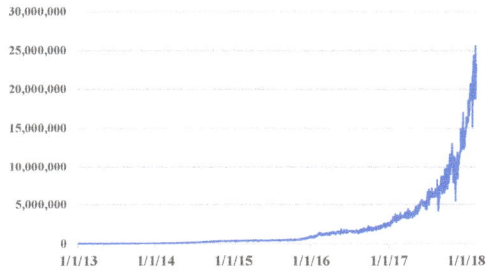

Figure 3. Bitcoin Hashrate, Quandl.

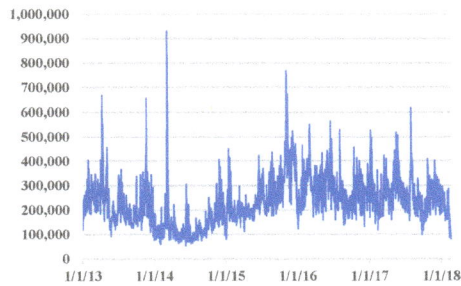

Figure 4. Bitcoin Transaction Volume, Quandl.

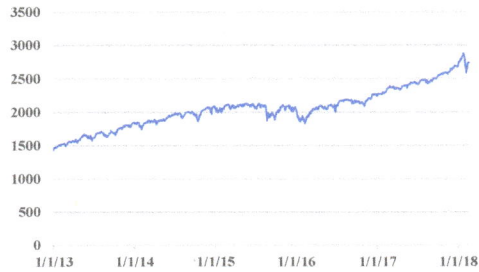

Figure 5. S&P 500 Index, Thomson Reuters.

Figure 6. Gold Index (USD), Thomson Reuters.

Figure 7. Crude Oil-WTI Spot, Thomson Reuters.

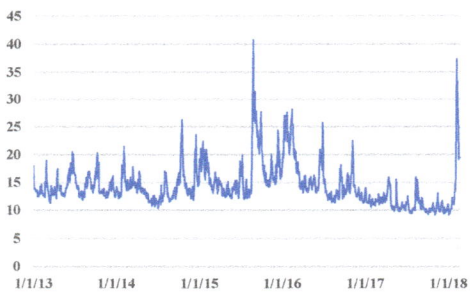

Figure 8. CBOE Volatility Index, Thomson Reuters.

Figure 9. Google Search "Bitcoin," Google Trends.

3.3. Econometric Method

3.3.1. Autoregressive Distributed Lag Model

According to Im et al. (2003), the ARDL technique is used to estimate short- and long-term relationships between a group of variables by including lags for both the dependent and independent variables. The ARDL model is estimated using ordinary least squares (OLS), where the only difference is the inclusion of lags. As long as the OLS assumptions are fulfilled, the ARDL approach will yield consistent estimates. This procedure is also followed by Ciaian et al. (2016) and Bouri et al. (2018b).

To find the appropriate lag length for each of the underlying variables in the ARDL model, we used the modified Akaike information criteria (AIC), since this criterion is known for having a theoretical advantage over other information criteria (Enders 2009). The model with the lowest AIC and highest R-squared is considered the best. We put in dummy variables for the minimum and maximum observations, in order to tackle the outliers. Using these dummy variables in the regression enhances the reliability of the model (Hansen 2001).

To test for stationarity in a single time series, we use an augmented Dickey–Fuller (ADF) test. If the ADF test shows signs of non-stationarity, the variables can be transformed into first differences, and the test is reapplied. To address possible structural breaks in the time series, we combine the ADF test with a Zivot–Andrews (ZA) test. If structural breaks are identified, the ZA test can be used since it takes structural breaks into account (Vogelsang and Perron 1998).

3.3.2. The Generalized Autoregressive Conditional Heteroscedasticity Model

Regarding the GARCH, in order to control for homoscedasticity, we test the unconditional variance of the regression. Breaking this assumption means that the Gauss–Markov theorem does not hold and that the OLS estimators are not BLUE. Even though the unconditional variance is stable, the conditional variance may not be constant over time. Engle (1982) developed the Autoregressive Conditional Heteroskedasticity (ARCH) model that recognizes the difference between unconditional and conditional variance and lets the conditional variance change over time as a function of previous periods' error terms. This technique has the ability to capture the effect of volatility clustering, but it requires a model with a relatively long lag structure, which makes estimation difficult. To make this task easier, Bollerslev (1986) proposed the GARCH model that enables a reduction in the number of parameters by imposing nonlinear restrictions. The GARCH model can predict unconditional variance and requires fewer parameters. In a GARCH model, the most recent observations have greater impacts on the predicted volatility.

3.4. Model Estimation

By using OLS, we present three ARDL models. The testing of the models has also been done over different in-sample periods, from 2013, Week 1, to 2016, Week 52, and from 2017, Week 1, to 2018, Week 7. These periods have been chosen to assess the potential changes in what variables affects the price of Bitcoins. The extreme price development in 2017 is also the background for this choice.

Model 1:

$$\Delta lnBTC_t = \alpha + \beta 1 \Delta lnBTC_{t-1} + \beta 2 \Delta lnVolume_t + \beta 3 \Delta lnSP500_t + \sum_{p=1}^{n} \beta 4 \Delta lnOil_{t-p}$$
$$+ \sum_{p=1}^{n} \beta 5 \Delta lnGold_{t-p} + \beta 6 \Delta lnVIX_t + \sum_{p=2}^{n} \beta 7 \Delta lnGoogle_{t-p} + Trend + \varepsilon_t. \tag{1}$$

Model 2:

$$\Delta lnBTC_t = \alpha + \beta 1 \Delta lnBTC_{t-1} + \beta 2 \Delta lnVolume_t + \beta 3 \Delta lnSP500_t + \sum_{p=2}^{n} \beta 5 \Delta lnGoogle_{t-p}$$
$$+ Trend + \varepsilon_t. \tag{2}$$

Model 3:

$$\Delta lnBTC_t = \alpha + \beta1\Delta lnBTC_{t-1} + \beta2\Delta lnHashrate_t + \beta3\Delta lnVolume_t + \beta4\Delta lnSP500_t$$
$$+ \sum_{p=1}^{n} \beta5\Delta lnOil_{t-p} + \sum_{p=1}^{n} \beta6\Delta lnGold_{t-p} + \beta7\Delta lnVIX_t \qquad (3)$$
$$+ \sum_{p=2}^{n} \beta8\Delta lnGoogle_{t-p} + Trend + \varepsilon_t.$$

A number of post-estimation tests were performed to consider if all the assumptions of OLS are fulfilled. The data set contains of 267 observations. OLS prerequisites were handled by the logarithmic transformation of the data. The post-estimation test results for both the ARDL- and GARCH model can be found in Tables A3–A5.[4]

4. Empirical Results

4.1. Main Model (Model 1)

Tables 3 and 4 present the results of the ARDL and GARCH models. The first model is our main model that includes all variables, while the second model is a reduced version of Model 1 that includes only the significant variables of Model 1 for both the ARDL and GARCH. Table 5 presents the third regression model that includes the variable Hashrate. In the following sections, we will present the results from the main period 2013, Week 1, to 2018, Week 7.

Table 3. Results of ARDL & GARCH models (Model 1).

Time Period	ARDL			GARCH		
	(1)	(2)	(3)	(1)	(2)	(3)
$\Delta lnBTC_{t-1}$	0.19 (2.23) **	0.222 (2.14) **	0.206 (1.04)	0.225 (5.43) ***	0.329 (6.44) ***	0.293 (4.98) ***
$\Delta lnVolume_t$	−0.042 (1.41)	−0.027 (0.79)	−0.134 (2.33) **	−0.046 (2.61) ***	−0.022 (1.26)	−0.15 (0.62)
$\Delta lnSP500_t$	1.772 (2.16) **	2.55 (2.69) ***	−1.707 (1.04)	1.038 (1.59)	1.272 (1.85) *	1.318 (1.90) *
$\Delta lnOil_t$	−0.072 (0.50)	−0.075 (0.47)	−0.141 (0.40)	−0.001 (0.00)	0.021 (0.17)	0.005 (0.04)
$\Delta lnOil_{t-1}$	0.142 (0.95)	0.147 (0.87)	0.341 (0.77)	0.023 (0.18)	0.027 (0.22)	0.005 (0.04)
$\Delta lnGold_t$	0.552 (1.06)	0.546 (0.92)	1.135 (1.08)	−0.013 (0.06)	−0.006 (0.003)	−0.063 (0.27)
$\Delta lnGold_{t-1}$	−0.415 (0.62)	−0384 (0.49)	−0.337 (0.35)	0.049 (0.18)	0.068 (0.24)	0.048 (0.17)
$\Delta lnVIX_t$	0.029 (0.34)	0.126 (1.34)	−0.279 (1.92) *	0.008 (0.12)	−0.039 (0.56)	−0.186 (0.93)
$\Delta lnGoogle_t$	0.109 (3.60) ***	0.102 (2.84) ***	0.140 (3.16) ***	0.045 (2.85) ***	0.030 (1.61)	0.022 (1.18)
$\Delta lnGoogle_{t-1}$	0.105 (3.46) ***	0.093 (2.58) **	0.176 (4.04) ***	0.088 (4.27) ***	0.081 (4.34) ***	0.076 (3.86) ***

---

[4] The following post-estimation tests have been conducted for OLS-assumptions: Ramsey RESET test, Durbin–Watson, Variance Inflation Factors (VIF), and Adjusted Dickey–Fuller. For GARCH: Ljung Box Q-statistics.

Table 3. *Cont.*

	ARDL			GARCH		
Time Period	**(1)**	**(2)**	**(3)**	**(1)**	**(2)**	**(3)**
$\Delta lnGoogle_{t-2}$	0.082 (2.18) **	0.088 (1.98) **	0.022 (0.39)	0.053 (2.76) ***	0.062 (3.35) ***	0.057 (3.00) ***
ARCH Effect				0.562 (3.52) ***	0.771 (3.42) ***	0.599 (3.62) ***
GARCH Effect				0.315 (2.42) **	0.214 (1.61)	0.374 (3.00) ***
Adjusted R^2	0.29	0.23	0.54			
Observations	264	205	56	264	205	56

Note: * $p < 0.10$, ** $p < 0.05$, *** $p < 0.01$. (1) = 2013w1–2018w7, (2) = 2013w1–2016w25, and (3) = 2017w1–2018w7.

Table 4. Results of ARDL & GARCH models (Model 2).

	ARDL			GARCH		
Time Period	**(1)**	**(2)**	**(3)**	**(1)**	**(2)**	**(3)**
$\Delta lnBTC_{t-1}$	0.187 (2.05) **	0.226 (2.05) **	0.065 (0.46)	0.215 (5.24) ***	0.318 (6.05) ***	0.293 (5.01) ***
$\Delta lnSP500_t$	1.411 (3.45) ***	1.364 (2.99) ***	1.59 (1.62)	0.926 (2.76) ***	0.873 (2.62) ***	0.779 (2.27) **
$\Delta lnGoogle_t$	0.105 (3.50) ***	0.099 (2.79) ***	0.100 (1.82) *	0.033 (2.43) **	0.023 (1.5)	0.09 (0.99)
$\Delta lnGoogle_{t-1}$	0.097 (3.18) ***	0.089 (2.43) **	0.122 (2.82)	0.083 (4.66) ***	0.08 (4.68) ***	0.075 (3.91) ***
$\Delta lnGoogle_{t-2}$	0.077 (2.01) **	0.084 (1.88) *	0.061 (1.06)	0.047 (2.63) ***	0.06 (3.35) ***	0.055 (2.84) ***
ARCH Effect				0.581 (3.58) ***	0.696 (3.59) ***	0.497 (3.59) ***
GARCH Effect				0.324 (2.64) ***	0.269 (2.05) **	0.426 (3.53) ***
Adjusted R^2	0.29	0.23	0.50			
Observations	264	205	56	264	205	56

Note: * $p < 0.10$, ** $p < 0.05$, *** $p < 0.01$. (1) = 2013w1–2018w7, (2) = 2013w1–2016w25, and (3) = 2017w1–2018w7.

Table 5. Results of ARDL and GARCH models including Hashrate (Model 3).

	ARDL			GARCH		
Time Period	**(1)**	**(2)**	**(3)**	**(1)**	**(2)**	**(3)**
$\Delta lnBTC_{t-1}$	0.19 (2.25) **	0.222 (2.10) **	0.206 (1.66)	0.225 (5.28) ***	0.329 (6.28) ***	0.258 (3.89) ***
$\Delta lnHashrate_t$	0.067 (0.96)	0.22 (0.26)	0.274 (2.51) ***	0.031 (0.50)	−0.005 (0.08)	−0.039 (0.57)
$\Delta lnVolume_t$	−0.041 (1.36)	−0.027 (0.78)	−0.139 (2.51) **	0.04 (2.64) ***	−0.022 (1.27)	−0.139 (0.34)
$\Delta lnSP500_t$	1.725 (2.11) **	2.532 (2.68) ***	−1.952 (1.33)	1.023 (1.55)	1.274 (1.86) *	1.472 (1.98) **
$\Delta lnOil_t$	−0.069 (2.11) **	−0.075 (0.47)	−0.073 (0.22)	0.008 (0.06)	0.02 (0.16)	−0.012 (0.10)
$\Delta lnOil_{t-1}$	0.137 (0.92)	0.145 (0.85)	0.324 (0.77)	0.019 (0.15)	0.028 (0.22)	0.067 (0.53)
$\Delta lnGold_t$	0.53 (1.01)	0.537 (0.90)	0.918 (0.87)	−0.03 (0.13)	−0.004 (0.02)	−0.061 (0.24)

Table 5. *Cont.*

Time Period	ARDL			GARCH		
	(1)	**(2)**	**(3)**	**(1)**	**(2)**	**(3)**
$\Delta lnGold_{t-1}$	−0.404	−0.38	−0.393	0.04	0.068	0.020
	(0.60)	(0.49)	(0.41)	(0.15)	(0.23)	(0.08)
$\Delta lnVIX_t$	0.023	0.123	−0.294	0.004	0.04	−0.234
	(0.27)	(1.32)	(2.19) **	(0.07)	(0.57)	(1.17)
$\Delta lnGoogle_t$	0.108	0.102	0.118	0.046	0.03	0.021
	(3.58) ***	(2.84) ***	(2.53) **	(2.83) ***	(1.57)	(1.09)
$\Delta lnGoogle_{t-1}$	0.104	0.093	0.165	0.088	0.081	0.076
	(3.41) ***	(2.56) **	(3.96) ***	(4.68) ***	(4.32) ***	(3.41) ***
$\Delta lnGoogle_{t-2}$	0.081	0.088	0.014	0.056	0.062	0.055
	(2.17) **	(1.98) **	−0.25	(2.87) ***	(3.35) ***	(2.87) ***
ARCH Effect				0.547	0.768	0.436
				(3.64) ***	(3.41) ***	(3.72) ***
GARCH Effect				0.345	0.214	0.538
				(2.76) ***	(1.6)	(5.43) ***
Adjusted R^2	0.29	0.23	0.54			
Observations	264	205	56	264	205	56

Note: * $p < 0.10$, ** $p < 0.05$, *** $p < 0.01$. (1) = 2013w1–2018w7, (2) = 2013w1–2016w25, and (3) = 2017w1–2018w7.

4.1.1. ARDL (1)

As shown in Table 3, the lag of Bitcoin seems to have a significant positive effect on the price of Bitcoin at the 5% level. If last week's return of Bitcoin is higher by 1%, it is estimated that the return of Bitcoin this week will be higher by 0.19%.

The first difference of S&P 500 is significant at the 5% level and has a positive sign. When the S&P 500 increases by 1%, the price of Bitcoins increases by 1.77%. In contrast, VIX, Oil, Gold, and Volume do not seem to have any significant impact on the price of Bitcoin in the estimated period.

The first difference in the Google Trends variable and its lag are significant at the 1% level. The short-term effects show that, when Google trends increases by 1%, the Bitcoin price is expected to increase by 0.11%. By including the lag of Google, the short-term effect that Google search has on Bitcoin price is 0.22%. Additionally, by including the second lag of Google, which is significant at the 5% level, the total short-term effect that Google search has on Bitcoin price is 0.30%. Lastly, the long-term effect of Google trends on Bitcoin price is 0.37%.[5]

4.1.2. GARCH (1)

In the GARCH model, the lag of Bitcoin has an almost identical effect as in the ARDL model and is significant at the 1% level. Google and its two lags are significant at the 1% level, which is almost the same as in the ARDL model, although the coefficient for both the first difference and the two lags has decreased. Furthermore, the S&P 500 is found to be insignificant, while it was found significant in the ARDL model. Similar to the ARDL model, VIX, oil, and gold are insignificant. Volume is significant at the 1% level, which is inconsistent with the ARDL model.

The ARCH effects are positive and significant at the 1% level, which indicates that a shock in the variance two weeks ago will have an impact of approximately 56.2% on the volatility in the following week. The GARCH effects are significant at the 5% level. This significance indicates that 31.5% of the volatility last week has an impact on volatility this week. The sum of the ARCH and GARCH effects is approximately 87.7%, which shows the persistence of all volatility and shocks last week, and the impact it has on this week.

---

[5]   The long-term effect of a variable is calculated in following way: $ß_t + ß_{t-1} + ... + ß_{t-n}/(1 - ß_1 \Delta lnBTC_{t-1})$.

4.2. Reduced Model (Model 2)

4.2.1. ARDL (1)

As shown in Table 4, the relationship between the lag and price of Bitcoin is almost the same as in Model 1 and is significant at the 5% level. If the price of Bitcoin last week increased by 1%, the effect is an increase in price this week of 0.19%. Moreover, the S&P 500 seems to have a significant impact on the price of Bitcoin, similar to Model 1. This variable is significant at the 1% level. When the S&P 500 increases by 1%, Bitcoin is estimated to increase by 1.41%.

Google trends has the same significance level as Model 1 and almost equal coefficients. The short-term effect of Google searches is 0.11%, and the total short-term effect is 0.21%. The total long-term effect is 0.34%.

4.2.2. GARCH (1)

The lag of Bitcoin has an almost identical effect as in the ARDL model and is significant at the 1% level. The S&P 500 index is also found to be significant in the GARCH model, just as the ARDL model, but with a slightly lower coefficient.

Google and its two lags are significant at the 5% and 1% levels, respectively, which is almost consistent with the ARDL model. However, the coefficient for both the first difference and the lags has decreased.

The ARCH effects are positive and significant at the 1% level and has an impact of approximately 58.1% on the volatility in the following week. The GARCH effects are positive and significant at the 1% level. About a third (32.4%) of the volatility last week has an impact on the volatility this week. The sum of the ARCH and GARCH effects is approximately 90.5%.

4.3. Model Including Hashrate (Model 3)

The model presented in Table 5 includes the variable Hashrate but is otherwise similar to Model 1. The properties displayed by the variables and their results are also similar to the results of Model 1. However, the first difference of Hashrate has a positive sign in all the estimated periods but is only significant in the third period, from 2017, Week 1, to 2018, Week 7.

4.4. Model Assessment

The weekly log-transformed ARDL models have adjusted R-square values of 29% and 31% for Models 1 and 2, respectively. The ADF test for stationarity indicates that all the variables' residuals are stationary.[6] Other diagnostic tests are run to examine the models' goodness of fit, and they are fulfilled.[7] Lastly, to check for misspecification of the models, a Ramsey RESET test was performed. This test indicates that the models may be misspecified.

5. Discussion and Conclusions

5.1. Discussion

In Model 3, which includes the Hashrate, we observe that the Hashrate has a positive sign in both the estimated period and in-sample periods. The positive sign is contrary to the law of supply and demand, considering that increasing the processing power should in theory lead to an increased supply, which would exert a downward pressure on prices. Due to the deterministic supply of Bitcoins, adding more processing capacity to mining will not lead to an increase in output. However, this variable is only significant in the period from Week 1 of 2017 to Week 7 of 2018, a period of

---

[6] For a complete overview of the ADF and ZA tests, see Tables A1 and A2.
[7] For a complete overview of diagnostic tests for all models, see Tables A3–A6.

exponential growth in both Bitcoin and Hashrate. Therefore, we believe that the causality between Bitcoin and Hashrate is such that it is the Bitcoin price that drives Hashrate, not the other way around. This outcome is consistent with economic theory since an increase in price will naturally result in the increased profitability of mining. As profitability increases, new actors will enter the mining business, and current miners will increase computational power to the point where excess profits are zero. A price drop will naturally lead to computational power being pulled out of Bitcoin mining. Thus, we consider it irrelevant to include Hashrate as an explanatory variable in a model describing Bitcoin's price drivers or in calculations of fundamental values of Bitcoin. This outcome is in contrast to previous research that included Hashrate as a variable (Bouoiyour and Selmi 2015; Garcia et al. 2014; Georgoula et al. 2015; Hayes 2015; Kristoufek 2013, 2015; Kjærland et al. 2018; Sovbetov 2018).

The results from the reported regression models indicate that publicity measured in Google Trends has a positive impact on the price of Bitcoin. According to our findings, when people's curiosity and attention to Bitcoin increase, the demand for Bitcoins also increases. This outcome is consistent with Kristoufek (2013, 2015) and Ciaian et al. (2016), who found that when Google searches on Bitcoin increase, the price of Bitcoin also increases.

We find that the S&P 500 has a positive impact on the price of Bitcoin. This is also the independent variable with the largest coefficient, so it exerts the most influence on the price of Bitcoin in this regression. The interpretation may be as follows: when optimism in financial markets increases, investors also display optimism in Bitcoins. Since risk measured in standard deviation is higher in Bitcoin than that in the S&P 500, Bitcoin investors are likely risk-seeking investors. These findings are also supported by Yermack (2013) and Dyhrberg (2016) studies in which stock markets have an impact on the price of Bitcoin. Interestingly, Bouri et al. (2018c) find moderate integration between Bitcoin and most of the asset classes studied, included MSCI World and gold.

Our results indicate a positive relationship between the Bitcoin price and its lag, which indicates that the efficient market hypothesis seemingly does not hold. Past returns should be uncorrelated with present returns, and an investment strategy based on past returns should not be profitable. However, it is known that the efficient market hypothesis is widely disputed. Some behavioral economists blame imperfections in financial markets on errors in human reasoning and information processing. Since most investors probably have limited experience with Bitcoins, the context around it is confusing, and there is too much new information to consider in too little time; investors must make quick decisions whether or not to invest. Thus, it is reasonable to assume that investors are affected by the momentum effect of rising prices and vice versa. Observing the price increase last week fuels demand and creates a momentum in price. Combined with Momentum theory, one can think along the lines of the Greater Fool theory in which as the price rapidly increases, investors see get-rich-quick potential by buying now and selling to a greater fool next week.

The estimated regression shows that fear in financial markets, as measured in VIX, does not have a significant impact on the price of Bitcoin. However, in the sub-period between 2017 and 2018, we find a significant negative relationship between VIX and Bitcoin price. During this period, the results indicate that increasing fear of financial turmoil reduces demand for Bitcoins. Since a currency is considered a safe-haven if demand rises during periods of financial stress, the abovementioned results indicate that Bitcoin does not inhibit safe-haven properties, which is inconsistent with the findings of Bouri et al. (2017a, 2017b) and to some extent, with Bouri et al. (2016).

Additionally, both oil and gold were found to be insignificant in the estimated regression period. These findings are in contrast to Kristoufek (2015) and Ciaian et al. (2016), who found that gold and oil have significant positive impacts on Bitcoin prices. This outcome indicates that Bitcoin does not inhibit commodity properties. In addition, the volatility in the price of Bitcoin is unlike any of the two commodities, making it difficult to compare. However, our findings are much in line with the recent study of Bouri et al. (2018b), who find no effects of an aggregate commodity index and gold prices on the price of Bitcoin.

Volume seems to have an insignificant impact on the price of Bitcoin in the estimated period, reflecting Kristoufek (2013) findings, which state that the price of Bitcoin cannot be explained by standard economic theory. However, in the GARCH model, volume seems to be a significant variable with a negative sign. The reason may be our use of average daily prices or this outcome may be explained by traditional economic theory regarding supply and demand. When volume increases and demand is met, the price naturally drops, confirming the findings of Ciaian et al. (2016) and Polasik et al. (2015) in which volume exerts an impact on the price of Bitcoin.

In the estimated GARCH model, we find that many of the included variables describe both the return on Bitcoin and volatility. The results of the GARCH model show that the price of Bitcoin is greatly affected by its own historical volatility. The results of the GARCH model are approximately the same as those of the ARDL model, indicating that the ARDL model is robust. Similarly, we observe that our model has approximately the same significant variables during an in-sample period, from Week 1 of 2013 to Week 52 of 2016, the period leading up to the volatile 2017. Although the in-sample period from Week 1 of 2017 to Week 7 of 2018 exhibits different results, it is questionable whether these results are reliable given the low number of observations, the high spike and subsequent fall in price during the period.

5.2. Conclusions

Because of the increase in volatility and the dramatic price fluctuations in 2017, this paper aims to help investors understand the price dynamics of Bitcoin. The results from the empirical analysis provide compelling findings, and the estimated model has strong explanatory power with a high degree of robustness. The primary contribution to Bitcoin research that this study provides is the conclusion that the technological factor Hashrate should not be included in modeling price dynamics or fundamental values since it does not affect Bitcoin supply. Based on our full and reduced model, past price performance, optimism, and Google search volume all play significant roles in explaining Bitcoin prices. When both optimism in financial markets and attention to Bitcoin increase, investors' willingness to allocate funds to more risky assets, such as Bitcoin, increases. Lastly, we observe that price fluctuations in Bitcoin can be associated with investment theories such as The Greater Fool and Momentum theory.

Appendix A

Table A1. Results from Adjusted Dickey–Fuller test and Zivot–Andrews on log-transformed variables.

Variable	ADF-Test					Zivot–Andrews			
	Lag	C, T	t-Statistic	Result	Structural Break	Lag	t-Statistic		Result
BTC	4	C, T	−2.095	I(1)	2016w26	2	−3.983		I(1)
Hashrate	8	C, T	−3.425	I(0)	2013w49	4	−5.142	**	I(0)
Volume	10	C, T	−1.991	I(1)	2014w38	1	−6.059	***	I(0)
S&P 500	6	C, T	−2.043	I(1)	2015w34	1	−5.299	**	I(0)
Gold	2	C, T	−2.974	I(1)	2016w4	2	−4.748		I(1)
Oil	1	C, T	−1.173	I(1)	2014w40	1	−3.767		I(1)
VIX	15	C, T	−2.119	I(1)	2015w34	0	−6.133	***	I(0)
Google	1	C, T	−2.481	I(1)	2016w25	0	−4.709		I(1)

Note: ** $p < 0.05$, *** $p < 0.01$. All variables are in logarithmic form, C = Constant, T = trend, I(1) = unit root (non-stationarity), and I(0) = no unit root (stationary). The Zivot–Andrews structural break is defined as the lowest (most negative) t-statistic in the ADF test. Structural breaks are allowed for both the incline and the level of trend. The Zivot–Andrews critical values are 1% (−5.57), 5% (−5.08), and 10% (−4.82).

Table A2. Results from Adjusted Dickey–Fuller test and Zivot–Andrews on the first difference log-transformed variables.

			ADF-Test					Zivot–Andrews		
Variable	Lag	C, T	t-Statistic		Result	Structural Break	Lag	t-Statistic		Result
BTC	2	C, T	−6.899	***	I(0)	2013w50	2	−6.670	***	I(0)
Hashrate	9	C, T	−1.812		I(1)	2014w39	4	−6.299	***	I(0)
Volume	15	C, T	−5.105	***	I(0)	2014w6	1	−11.382	***	I(0)
S&P 500	3	C, T	−8.091	***	I(0)	2016w7	1	−15.302	***	I(0)
Gold	4	C, T	−7.399	***	I(0)	2014w12	2	−12.356	***	I(0)
Oil	7	C, T	−4.421	***	I(0)	2016w7	1	−12.900	***	I(0)
VIX	15	C, T	−5.267	***	I(0)	2017w17	0	−14.305	***	I(0)
Google	1	C, T	−12.17	***	I(0)	2013w48	0	−18.273	***	I(0)

Note: *** $p < 0.01$. All variables are first difference on the logarithmic form; otherwise, see the note to Table A1.

Table A3. Model 1 assessment.

	ARDL			GARCH		
Period	(1)	(2)	(3)	(1)	(2)	(3)
Outliers	Yes	Yes	No	Yes	Yes	No
Dummies	Yes	Yes	No	Yes	Yes	No
Observations	264	205	56	264	205	56
R^2	0.32	0.27	0.65			
Adjusted R^2	0.29	0.23	0.54			
AIC	−483.83	−359.30	−117.63	−545.39	−432.77	−548.31
Ramsey RESET, *p*-value	0.0000	0.0000	0.911			
Durbin–Watson	2.07	2.13	2.01			
Ljung-Box Q Stat				0.4265	0.5193	0.5088
ADF, residual value	0.0002	0.0017	0.0000	0.0000	0.0004	0.0000

Note: (1) = 2013w1–2018w7, (2) = 2013w1–2016w52, and (3) = 2017w1–2018w7.

Table A4. Model 2 assessment.

	ARDL			GARCH		
Period	(1)	(2)	(3)	(1)	(2)	(3)
Outliers	Yes	Yes	No	Yes	Yes	No
Dummies	Yes	Yes	No	Yes	Yes	No
Observations	264	205	56	264	205	56
R^2	0.31	0.25	0.56			
Adjusted R^2	0.29	0.23	0.50			
AIC	−489.41	−366.10	−117.35	−552.80	−442.78	−554.30
Ramsey RESET, *p*-value	0.0000	0.0000	0.765			
Durbin–Watson	2.08	2.14	1.85			
Ljung-Box Q Stat				0.4155	0.5127	0.5041
ADF, residual value	0.0003	0.0024	0.0008	0.0000	0.0005	0.0000

Note: (1) = 2013w1–2018w7, (2) = 2013w1–2016w52, and (3) = 2017w1–2018w7.

Table A5. Model 3 assessment.

	ARDL			GARCH		
Period	**(1)**	**(2)**	**(3)**	**(1)**	**(2)**	**(3)**
Outliers	Yes	Yes	No	Yes	Yes	No
Dummies	Yes	Yes	No	Yes	Yes	No
Observations	264	205	56	264	205	56
R^2	0.33	0.27	0.68			
Adjusted R^2	0.29	0.22	0.57			
AIC	−482.70	−357.37	−120.47	−543.71	−430.78	−548.59
Ramsey RESET, *p*-value	0.0000	0.0000	0.817			
Durbin–Watson	2.06	2.13	1.87			
Ljung-Box Q Stat				0.4265	0.5187	0.5075
ADF, residual value	0.0001	0.0014	0.0004	0.0000	0.0005	0.0000

Note: (1) = 2013w1–2018w7, (2) = 2013w1–2016w52, and (3) = 2017w1–2018w7.

Table A6. Results of the variance inflation factors: test for autocorrelation.

Model 1		Model 2		Model 3	
Variable	**VIF-Value**	**Variable**	**VIF-Value**	**Variable**	**VIF-Value**
$lnBTC_{t-1}$	1.29	$lnBTC_{t-1}$	1.26	$lnBTC_{t-1}$	1.29
$lnVolume_t$	1.11	$lnSP500_{t-1}$	1.04	$lnVolume_t$	1.11
$lnSP500_{t-1}$	4	$lnGoogle_t$	1.09	$lnSP500_{t-1}$	4.01
$lnOil_t$	1.24	$lnGoogle_{t-1}$	1.17	$lnOil_t$	1.24
$lnGold_t$	1.15	$lnGoogle_{t-2}$	1.16	$lnGold_t$	1.16
$lnVIX_t$	4.03			$lnVIX_t$	4.06
$lnGoogle_t$	1.13			$lnGoogle_t$	1.14
$lnGoogle_{t-1}$	1.25			$lnGoogle_{t-1}$	1.25
$lnGoogle_{t-2}$	1.18			$lnGoogle_{t-2}$	1.18
				$lnHashrate_t$	1.02

References

Aalborg, Halvor Aarhus, Peter Molnár, and Jon Erik de Vries. 2018. What can explain the price, volatility and trading volume of Bitcoin? *Finance Research Letters.* forthcoming. [CrossRef]

Balcilar, Mehmet, Elie Bouri, Rangan Gupta, and David Roubaud. 2017. Can volume predict Bitcoin returns and volatility? A quantiles-based approach. *Economic Modelling* 64: 74–81. [CrossRef]

Baur, Dirk G., and Thomas K.J. McDermott. 2012. Safe haven assets and investor behavior under uncertainty. Institute for International Integration Studies. Available online: https://rbnz.govt.nz/-/media/ReserveBank/Files/Publications/Seminars%20and%20workshops/feb2012/4682207.pdf (accessed on 14 January 2018).

Becker, Jörg, Dominic Breuker, Tobias Heide, Justus Holler, Hans Peter Rauer, and Rainer Böhme. 2013. Can We Afford Integrity by Proof-of-Work? Scenarios Inspired by the Bitcoin Currency. In *The Economics of Information Security and Privacy*. Berlin and Heidelberg: Springer Heidelberg, pp. 135–56.

Böhme, Rainer, Nicolas Christin, Benjamin Edelman, and Tyler Moore. 2015. Bitcoin: Economics, Technology, and Governance. *Journal of Economic Perspectives* 29: 213–38. [CrossRef]

Bollerslev, Tim. 1986. Generalized autoregressive conditional heteroskedasticity. *Journal of Econometrics* 31: 307–27. [CrossRef]

Bouoiyour, Jamal, and Refk Selmi. 2015. What Does Bitcoin Look Like? *Annals of Economics and Finance* 16: 449–92.

Bouoiyour, Jamal, and Refk Selmi. 2016. Bitcoin: A beginning of a new phase? *Economics Bulletin* 36: 1430–40.

Bouoiyour, Jamal, Refk Selmi, Aviral Kumar Tiwari, and Olaolu Richard Olayeni. 2016. What drives Bitcoin price? *Economics Bulletin* 36: 843–50.

Bouri, Elie, Georges Azzi, and Anne Haubo Dyhrberg. 2016. On the Return-Volatility Relationship in the Bitcoin Market around the Price Crash of 2013. Available online: https://ssrn.com/abstract=2869855 or http://dx.doi.org/10.2139/ssrn.2869855 (accessed on 5 February 2018).

Bouri, Elie, Naji Jalkh, Peter Molnár, and David Roubaud. 2017a. Bitcoin for energy commodities before and after the December 2013 crash: Diversifier, hedge or safe haven? In *Applied Economics*. vol. 49, pp. 5063–73. [CrossRef]

Bouri, Elie, Peter Molnár, Georges Azzi, David Roubaud, and Lars Ivar Hagfors. 2017b. On the hedge and safe haven properties of Bitcoin: Is it really more than a diversifier? *Finance Research Letters* 20: 192–8. [CrossRef]

Bouri, Elie, Chi Keung Marco Lau, Brian Lucey, and David Roubaud. 2018a. Trading volume and the predictability of return and volatility in the cryptocurrency market. In *Finance Research Letters*. forthcoming. [CrossRef]

Bouri, Elie, Rangan Gupta, Amine Lahiani, and Muhammad Shahbaz. 2018b. Testing for asymmetric nonlinear short- and long-run relationships between bitcoin, aggregate commodity and gold prices. *Resources Policy* 57: 224–35. [CrossRef]

Bouri, Elie, Mahamitra Das, Rangan Gupta, and David Roubaud. 2018c. Spillovers between Bitcoin and other assets during bear and bull markets. *Applied Economics* 50: 5935–49. [CrossRef]

Brandvold, Morten, Peter Molnár, Kristian Vagstad, and Ole Christian Andreas Valstad. 2015. Price discovery on Bitcoin exchanges. *Journal of International Financial Markets, Institutions and Money* 36: 18–35. [CrossRef]

Cheah, Eng-Tuck, and John Fry. 2015. Speculative bubbles in Bitcoin markets? An empirical investigation into the fundamental value of Bitcoin. *Economics Letters* 130: 32–36. [CrossRef]

Ciaian, Pavel, Miroslava Rajcaniova, and d'Artis Kancs. 2016. The economics of BitCoin price formation. *Applied Economics* 48: 1799–815. [CrossRef]

Corbet, Shaen, Brian Lucey, and Larisa Yarovaya. 2017. Datestamping the Bitcoin and Ethereum bubbles. *Finance Research Letters* 26: 81–88. [CrossRef]

Dwyer, Gerald P. 2015. The economics of Bitcoin and similar private digital currencies. *Journal of Financial Stability* 17: 81–91. [CrossRef]

Dyhrberg, Anne Haubo. 2016. Bitcoin, gold and the dollar—A GARCH volatility analysis. *Finance Research Letters* 16: 85–92. [CrossRef]

Enders, Walter. 2009. *Applied Economic Time Series*, 3rd ed. Hoboken: John Wiley & Sons.

Engle, Robert F. 1982. Autoregressive conditional heteroscedasticity with estimates of the variance of United Kingdom inflation. *Econometrica: Journal of the Econometric Society* 50: 987–1007. [CrossRef]

Fama, Eugene F. 1976. Efficient capital markets: Reply. *The Journal of Finance* 31: 143–45. [CrossRef]

Garcia, David, Claudio J. Tessone, Pavlin Mavrodiev, and Nicolas Perony. 2014. The digital traces of bubbles: Feedback cycles between socio-economics signals in the Bitcoin economy. *Journal of the Royal Society Interface* 11: 1–28. [CrossRef] [PubMed]

Georgoula, Ifigeneia, Demitrios Pournarakis, Christos Bilanakos, Dionisios Sotiropoulos, and George M. Giaglis. 2015. Using Time-Series and Sentiment Analysis to Detect the Determinants of Bitcoin Prices. Available online: http://ssrn.com/abstract=2607167 (accessed on 30 January 2018).

Glosten, Lawrence R., Ravi Jagannathan, and David E. Runkle. 1993. On the relation between the expected value and the volatility of the nominal excess return on stocks. *The Journal of Finance* 48: 1779–801. [CrossRef]

Google Trends Help. 2018. Available online: https://support.google.com/trends/?hl=en#topic=6248052 (accessed on 15 February 2018).

Hansen, Bruce E. 2001. The New Econometrics of Structural Change: Dating Breaks in U.S. Labour Productivity. *Journal of Economic Perspectives* 15: 117–28. [CrossRef]

Hayes, Adam S. 2015. Cryptocurrency value formation: An empirical study leading to a cost of production model for valuing bitcoin. *Telematics and Informatics* 34: 1308–21. [CrossRef]

Hayes, Adam S. 2018. Bitcoin price and its marginal cost of production: Support for a fundamental value. *Applied Economics Letters* 5: 1–7. [CrossRef]

Im, Kyung So, M. Hashem Pesaran, and Yongcheol Shin. 2003. Testing for unit roots in heterogeneous panels. *Journal of Econometrics* 115: 53–74. [CrossRef]

Jegadeesh, Narasimhan, and Sheridan Titman. 1993. Returns to Buying Winners and Selling Losers: Implications for Stock Market Efficiency. *The Journal of Finance* 48: 65–91. [CrossRef]

Jegadeesh, Narasimhan, and Sheridan Titman. 2001. Profitability of momentum strategies: An evaluation of alternative explanations. *The Journal of Finance* 56: 699–720. [CrossRef]

Kjærland, Frode, Maria Meland, Are Oust, and Vilde Øyen. 2018. How can Bitcoin Price Fluctuations be Explained? *International Journal of Economics and Financial Issues* 8: 323–32.

Kristoufek, Ladislav. 2013. BitCoin meets Google Trends and Wikipedia: Quantifying the relationship between phenomena of the Internet era. *Scientific Reports* 3: 3415. [CrossRef] [PubMed]

Kristoufek, Ladislav. 2015. What Are the Main Drivers of the Bitcoin Price? Evidence from Wavelet Coherence Analysis. *PLoS ONE* 10: e0123923. [CrossRef] [PubMed]

Nakamoto, Satoshi. 2008. Bitcoin: A Peer-to-Peer Electronic Cash System. Available online: http://bitcoin.org/bitcoin.pdf (accessed on 9 January 2018).

Nica, Octavian, Karolina Piotrowska, and Klaus Reiner Schenk-Hoppé. 2017. *Cryptocurrencies: Economic Benefits and Risks*. FinTech Working Paper. Manchester: University of Manchester. Available online: https://ssrn.com/abstract=3059856 (accessed on 10 March 2018).

Polasik, Michal, Anna Iwona Piotrowska, Tomasz Piotr Wisniewski, Radoslaw Kotkowski, and Geoffrey Lightfoot. 2015. Price Fluctuations and the Use of Bitcoin: An Empirical Inquiry. *International Journal of Electronic Commerce* 20: 9–49. [CrossRef]

Santoni, Gary J. 1987. The great bull markets 1924–29 and 1982–87: Speculative bubbles or economic fundamentals? *Federal Reserve Bank of St. Louis Review* 69: 16–29. [CrossRef]

Segendorf, Björn. 2014. What is bitcoin? *Sveriges Riksbank Economic Review* 2: 71–87.

Sovbetov, Yhlas. 2018. Factors Influencing Cryptocurrency Prices: Evidence from Bitcoin, Ethereum, Dash, Litcoin, and Monero. *Journal of Economics and Financial Analysis* 2: 1–27.

Vogelsang, Timothy J., and Pierre Perron. 1998. Additional Tests for a Unit Root Allowing for a Break in the Trend Function at an Unknown Time. *International Economic Review* 39: 1073–100. [CrossRef]

Yermack, David. 2013. Is Bitcoin a Real Currency? An economic appraisal. National Bureau of Economic Research Working Paper Series No. 19747. Available online: http://www.nber.org/papers/w19747 (accessed on 18 January 2018).

Journal of
Risk and Financial Management

MDPI

Article

Blockchain-Based ICOs: Pure Hype or the Dawn of a New Era of Startup Financing?

Lennart Ante [1,2,*], Philipp Sandner [3] and Ingo Fiedler [1,2]

[1] Faculty of Business, Economics and Social Sciences, University of Hamburg, Von-Melle-Park 5, 20146 Hamburg, Germany; ingo.fiedler@uni-hamburg.de
[2] Blockchain Research Lab gGmbH, 20354 Hamburg, Germany
[3] Frankfurt School of Finance & Management, Adickesallee 32-34, 60322 Frankfurt am Main, Germany; email@philipp-sandner.de
* Correspondence: lennart.ante@uni-hamburg.de; Tel.: +49-40-42838-6454

Received: 23 October 2018; Accepted: 13 November 2018; Published: 21 November 2018

Abstract: This study explores the determinants of initial coin offering (ICO) success, where success is defined as the amount of capital a project could raise. ICOs are a tool for startups in the blockchain ecosystem to raise early capital with relative ease. The market for ICOs has grown at a rapid pace since its start in 2013. We analyze a unique dataset of 278 projects that finished their ICOs by August 2017 to assess determinants of funding success that we derive from the crowdfunding and venture capital literature. Our results show that ICOs exhibit similarities to classical crowdfunding and venture capital markets. Specifically, we identify resemblances in determinants of funding success regarding human capital characteristics, business model quality, project elaboration, and social media activity.

Keywords: initial coin offering; blockchain; venture capital; crowdfunding

1. Introduction

Understanding the role of blockchain-based initial coin offerings (ICOs), which are claimed to provide startups with a new form of financing, is of increasing importance both from a practical (Clayton 2017) and a scholarly perspective (Conley 2017). Raising funds via ICOs is a very recent phenomenon, with the first such offering having taken place in 2013. Especially over the last two years, the number of ICO projects and the amount of funding raised have grown at a rapid pace and attracted a lot of investors, with over $15 billion raised so far.

The ICO market has so far been characterized by very high yields for investors and, at the same time, a lack of proper regulation. It could be argued that the ICO market has developed into a bubble that could burst, like the dot com bubble (Wheale and Amin 2003), or that the exponential growth of ICOs can solely be explained by the dawn of a new era of corporate financing. While certain return rates for investors are at an abnormal level that is unlikely to be sustained in the future, there are also good arguments why the current hype about ICOs is at least somewhat justified. One major reason is that via the use of the underlying blockchain technology, ICOs enable startups to raise funds from investors around the globe without the need for minimal contribution levels. Another reason is that the tokens sold can usually be transferred immediately and traded on global cryptocurrency exchanges that provide liquid secondary markets and operate 24 h a day and seven days a week.

There are three ways of looking at ICO financing: From the perspective of (1) startups; (2) individual investors[1]; and (3) social welfare. When approaching the topic from the perspective

---

[1] Legally, the term 'investor' may not be universally applicable, as ICO contributions, strictly speaking, often constitute donations.

of startups, the main questions are how ICOs can help finance business ventures and how they are best applied. Individual investors focus on success rates and on the return on their invested capital. From the social welfare perspective, the angle of analysis is on the benefits and costs that ICOs entail for society, how much market value they help create, and how they could be regulated.

Adhami et al. (2018) analyzed success determinants of 253 ICO campaigns and find that code availability, presales, and specific services (like profit sharing) increase the probability of campaign success. Fisch (2019) used a sample of 238 ICOs campaigns between 2016 and 2017 and found that the underlying technology of a project determines the amount of funding, while venture characteristics are less relevant. Amsden and Schweizer (2018) showed in their sample of 1009 projects between 2015 and 2017 that venture uncertainty is negatively correlated and venture quality is positively correlated to ICO success. The term "success" is somewhat misleading, as it can be applied to funding success, venture success, secondary market access, or return on investment. From the perspective of a startup, the initial funding has the highest relevance, which is why we define success as the amount of funding that a project is able to gather.

In this paper, we tackle the question of whether ICOs are pure hype or whether they represent the dawn of a new era of financing from the perspective of startups and investors by analyzing whether investors in ICOs behave similarly to investors in traditional crowdfunding. Signaling theory (Spence 1973) can be used to explain the relevance of specific information for investments into companies (Ahlstrom and Bruton 2006; Coleman and Robb 2014; Robb and Robinson 2014; Ahlers et al. 2015). Ahlers et al. (2015) point to a research gap regarding the signaling of start-ups towards smaller investments in the context of equity crowdfunding. As ICOs are a very new phenomenon, the same research gap can be found for this specific kind of crowdfunding. For this purpose, we examine the determinants of ICO funding using a unique dataset that includes data on the amount of funds raised in 278 ICO projects through the 3 August 2017 (see Supplementary Materials), and a variety of additional variables for each project. We hypothesize that if ICO participants invest their money based on the expected fundamental value, this constitutes evidence of ICOs being a new form of startup financing; otherwise, the current success of ICOs is perhaps more appropriately described as a hype. We argue that we may speak of rational (i.e., fundamentals-based) investment if the amount of funds raised per project is driven by similar variables as in traditional startup financing, such as team size, project quality in terms of the business model, and project elaboration, or social media activity.

Analyzing investor behavior in ICOs allows us to further add to the current stream of literature on venture capital in two ways: We provide both a descriptive overview of the phenomenon of ICOs and an insight into the variables that startups looking for ICO investments should focus on by analyzing how ICO success depends on a range of factors.

2. Literature and Hypotheses

2.1. Startup Financing

When starting a venture, the entrepreneur will eventually face the question of how to fund the business. Sources of external finance will often have to be tapped. While debt funding is not always available, there are several options of equity funding. An angel investor, or business angel (BA), is one such source of capital for early-stage startups. Deakins and Freel (2003) describe BAs as wealthy individuals without any family connection to the entrepreneur who invest their money and experience in the venture. Macht and Robinson (2009) find that BAs help the investees to close funding and knowledge gaps, provide them with business contacts, and facilitate future funding. Harrison and Mason (1996) suggest that most BAs do not participate in follow-up funding, which has, however, been disputed in the literature.

Another form of equity financing is venture capital (VC). Venture capitalists collect funding from larger investors and allocate it to startups based on a sophisticated screening process. VC traditionally covers the larger and more developed stages of startup funding and does not play a role in deals below three or four million dollars (Kim and Wagman 2016). However, to support young ventures for later deals, many VC funds have started to also engage in seed stage financing, i.e., the early-stage funding typically covered by BAs. According to Kim and Wagman (2016), entrepreneurs will typically lose more of their ownership in the startup if they accept VC as compared to angel capital.

The attraction of outside capital constitutes an inherent problem for startups, as the desired amount of collateral or cash flows simply do not exist and there is a significant amount of information asymmetry (Cosh et al. 2009; Schwienbacher and Larralde 2010; Busenitz et al. 2005) or information cascades (Vismara 2016) with investors. Startups face the problem of signaling their quality at an early stage of development. Baum and Silverman (2004) list three major factors that investors may use to assess the quality of a project: Human capital, social (alliance) capital, and intellectual capital. Crowdfunding offers a way for members of the general public to pool their resources to fund a particular project via the internet (Ahlers et al. 2015), and has become a commonplace way for early stage companies to attract financing in recent years (Hornuf and Schwienbacher 2017). As Griffin (2012) states, the existing forms of crowdfunding can be distinguished by the type of rewards that contributors get in return: Crowdfunding campaigns can be (1) donation-based, without any actual rewards; (2) rewards-based, with non-financial rewards in the form of promotion or services; (3) lending-based, with a financial return like interest payments; or (4) equity-based, with financial return in the form of equity or dividends. Crowdfunding campaigns offer a signal regarding the market potential of a product (Schwienbacher and Larralde 2010; Cholakova and Clarysse 2015). In comparison to investments from angels or VC, crowdfunding must attract investors who are small both in terms of their financial contributions and in terms of their stake in the target company (Malmendier and Shanthikumar 2007). Smaller investors are less experienced than VCs and face higher information costs—a relatively small investment does not warrant weeks of researching the target project (Ahlers et al. 2015).

In the following, we will deduce the group of characteristics that will be used to compare blockchain-based ICOs to the traditional markets of VC and crowdfunding. We build upon results obtained in previous studies for these markets, which are most similar to ICOs in terms of the existing literature and procedures.

Human Capital. In line with existing research on VC (e.g., Hsu 2007; Gimmon and Levie 2010), we posit that the human capital of ICO teams will act as a signal for potential investors, assuming that investors gauge the future success of new ventures on the basis of the team's human capital, which is an important resource for organizational success (Becker 1993; Lee et al. 2001). While larger teams have more human capital, as argued above, team size is also a future cost factor, as the team will be paid from the proceeds of the crowdfunding. Previous research has found that venture capitalists value human capital criteria, such as previous startup experience, education, and managerial leadership experience (Hall and Hofer 1993; Muzyka et al. 1996; Zacharakis and Shepherd 2005). Such criteria serve venture capitalists as team quality indicators in the face of uncertain prospects (Gimmon and Levie 2010). In a similar vein, research has shown that investors also value the founders' social capital (Florin et al. 2003; Stuart et al. 1999). Hsu (2007) showed that the effect of human capital on VC valuations positively depends on the novelty of an industry. This result is particularly relevant to our context, blockchain technology, which is also an emerging technology at the moment, much like the Internet was in the 1990s and 2000s (Iansiti and Lakhani 2017). Ahlers et al. (2015) show that human capital is an important factor for the investment decision of small investors in crowdfunding campaigns. Overall, in line with existing research, we posit that a team's human capital endowment will be positively related to the funds raised during an ICO.

Quality of the business model. A business model connects an idea or technology with its potential revenue stream. As methods to define a business model, Chesbrough (2010) suggests the value and revenue proposition, market segment, structure of the value chain, cost structure and profit potential, value network, and competitive strategy. Zott et al. (2011) showed that the literature provides no general and consistent definition of a business model and thus also of its quality. Various determinants of the quality of business models can be identified across the literature, such as the presence of information and communication technologies in the e-commerce literature (Timmers 1998; Dubosson-Torbay et al. 2002), value drivers (Amit and Zott 2001), actual choices by the project (Shafer et al. 2005; Casadesus-Masanell and Ricart 2010), regulatory pressure (Tankhiwale 2009), and discovery-driven experimentation in the strategic literature (McGrath 2010). Technology itself (Chesbrough and Rosenbloom 2002) and technological development and innovation (Calia et al. 2007; Björkdahl 2009) are identified as determinants of quality in the technology and innovation management literature (Zott et al. 2011). Hellmann and Puri (2002) suggest that companies with innovative marketing strategies are more likely to be funded by VC as their products will penetrate the market more quickly. As a successful business model unlocks the realization of economic value from a technical basis (Chesbrough and Rosenbloom 2002), we expect that its quality will be positively related to the funds raised during an ICO.

Project elaboration (whitepaper). We suggest that the availability and quality of a whitepaper, which elaborates on the business project for the information of potential investors, will have a positive impact on the amount of funds that a project is able to raise. A whitepaper for ICOs, which 52% of the companies in our sample provide, can be compared to the business plan or pitch of traditional projects, as it usually contains all the information that may be relevant for investors. Barrow et al. (2001) describe the business plan as the potentially most relevant aspect for the successful creation of a business. Business plans, or the whitepaper of an ICO, represent the first detailed information that a funding team shares with its investors (Shepherd and Douglas 1999). Cumming et al. (2016) showed that fraudulent crowdfunding projects, a recurring phenomenon, are often characterized by badly drafted pitches. Findings by Ahlers et al. (2015) suggest that the provision of detailed information about risks can increase the likelihood of a successful crowdfunding campaign. Du et al. (2015) show that crowdfunding success can be explained by the amount of information that is disclosed in project descriptions. Chen et al. (2009) investigated to what extent entrepreneurial passion influences VC investment decisions. The authors found that funding success is driven not by the founders' passion, but by their level of preparedness. This suggests that ICO projects with very detailed whitepapers will be more successful. We therefore posit a positive relationship between project elaboration and funds raised.

Social media. Based on existing research in crowdfunding and venture capital, we posit that social media activity, as proxied by the number of followers and the number of postings, will positively influence funds raised at ICOs. At least two transmission mechanisms for this expected effect come to mind (Jin et al. 2017; Yang and Berger 2017): First, social media activity may serve as a marketing channel for announcing ICOs and distributing information about the underlying new tokens. Thus, in line with the "salience view" (Solomon et al. 2012), increased social media activity will lead to increased salience of an ICO, directing potential investors to the upcoming investment opportunity (Sprenger et al. 2014). Second, social media activity may also serve as a positive signal of endorsement from others and act as a mechanism to grow a (social) network and future user base (Lechner et al. 2006; Witt 2004). According to this view, ICO projects with more followers on social media will raise more funds because the positive signal to investors indicates higher levels of social network resources. Indeed, recent research has shown that the amount of funds raised by startups is associated both with the number of social messages and with the number of followers. For instance, Jin et al. (2017) show that Twitter influence (a composite score consisting of the number of followers, mentions, impressions, and sentiment on Twitter) is positively related to the funds raised by early-stage startups. Moreover, they find a quadratic relationship between the number of Twitter posts and funds raised, such that more posts initially increase funding while too many posts harm the outcome. In a similar vein, Yang and Berger (2017) have recently shown a positive relationship between the number of followers and the amount of startup funding. Likewise, Nevin et al. (2017) show that the number of social media posts has a positive effect on funds raised through crowdfunding.

Cumming et al. (2016) provide evidence that fraudulent crowdfunding projects are less likely to use social media channels. Colombo et al. (2015) suggest that communication between a project and its potential backers has a positive influence on the success of the campaign. Overall, based on this evidence in the context of startup funding, we expect a positive relationship between social media activity and funds raised at ICOs.

2.2. Hypotheses

Our general hypothesis is that ICO participants invest rationally based on fundamental value expectations. We break this general hypothesis down into four hypotheses that can be tested empirically. Each hypothesis is based on findings from the traditional VC funding and crowdfunding literature, which we discussed above, and which we expect to confirm with respect to ICO funding if investor decisions are driven by fundamental value expectations.

Hypothesis 1 (H1). *There is a positive relationship between the amount of funds raised and the company's human capital characteristics, which we operationalize as (a) team size, (b) team network size, and (c) the number of advisors.*

Hypothesis 2 (H2). *There is a positive relationship between the amount of funds raised and business model quality, which we operationalize as a score variable determined by an industry expert for each project for the respective form of the projects token-based business model (infrastructure, financial, or utility model).*

Hypothesis 3 (H3). *There is a positive relationship between the amount of funds raised and project elaboration, which we operationalize as (a) whitepaper availability and (b) a whitepaper score based on a whitepaper's number of pages and citations.*

Hypothesis 4 (H4). *There is a positive relationship between the amount of funds raised and social media presence, which we operationalize as a score based on the number of Twitter messages and the number of Twitter followers, as Twitter is the most widely used social media channel across the projects covered by our sample. Activity levels on Facebook, Reddit, and Bitcointalk are used as control variables.*

2.3. Blockchain Technology

Blockchain represents an emerging technology that is among the most promising and potentially most disruptive technologies in the future. It was first introduced in October 2008 by an unknown person or entity using the name Satoshi Nakamoto, who presented it as part of the proposal for Bitcoin, its first suggested application (Nakamoto 2008).

A blockchain is a distributed register to store static records and/or dynamic transaction data without central coordination by using a consensus-based mechanism to check the validity of transactions. In simple words, it is a database in which transactions are recorded and which is simultaneously shared among all parties in a participating network. Data is stored in fixed structures, "blocks", which are always linked to the latest block that has been added to the database. As all blocks are linked together in a chain, the entire history of transactions can be accessed and retraced. The verification of each transaction results from the consensus of the majority of participants in the network, without the involvement of any intermediary. In the Bitcoin world, for example, transactions are validated by so-called miners, which are network members with high-level computing power. In order to validate transaction blocks, complex coded problems must be solved. The miners' efforts are then rewarded with Bitcoins (Nakamoto 2008).

The main goal of the technology is to create a decentralized environment where no third party is in control of the transactions and data. Simultaneously, it allows for transaction platforms that are highly secure, cheap, fast, and less prone to error. This innovation will change not only the interaction between individuals and organizations, but also business-to-business (B2B) collaboration, raising the overall productivity of the economy. The potential benefits of blockchain are not restricted to economic matters, but extend to offering solutions to social, political, legal, and health issues (Linn and Koo 2016; Scott 2016; Osgood 2016; De Filippi and Hassan 2018).

While blockchain is much acclaimed for its potential to deliver solutions to a wide range of issues, the adoption of the technology entails significant risks and challenges that require awareness. One of the most significant risks arises from future government regulation, a factor that is crucial to the success of the blockchain industry. We may expect the new technology to be much more heavily monitored and regulated in the future, and these new regulations may either facilitate or slow down the adoption process. Furthermore, several technical challenges and limitations have been identified and must eventually be addressed (Puthal et al. 2018; Joshi et al. 2018). Among them are the limited throughput, the time required to complete a transaction, and high data volumes. Moreover, users worry about a number of security threats. Especially, in financial contexts, there is concern about hackers, identity theft, and money laundering (Ante 2018). All in all, the technology is still evolving and maturing. As ever, more individuals and organizations are investigating and experimenting with it, and new recommendations on how to solve the current issues are made each day.

2.4. Blockchain-Based Startup Financing

An increasing number of startups in the blockchain ecosystem use ICOs to raise early-stage financing. Instead of going for initial public offerings (IPOs), which are expensive and highly regulated, startups often issue a blockchain-based token and distribute it across investors in proportion to their respective investment. So far, ICOs are regulated only very lightly, if at all. This allows for fast processes and low operational cost.

In order to conduct an ICO, a token-based economy must be generated in which the blockchain token has some form of value for investors. Figure 1 provides an example of a token-based economy and the initial distribution of tokens. A company builds a product or a service around a token. The token is used as a project-specific currency, some form of utility (utility token), or a security (security token) that can provide some form of profit participation to investors. Utility tokens are the most widely used token structure for ICOs. They possess some form of utility to token holders, like a software license, which enables startups to bypass security regulations for their token sale. Security token sales are less common, as they entail much higher legal costs and preparation and most cryptocurrency exchanges do not hold the relevant licenses to trade securities, while regulated stock exchanges cannot accommodate tokens yet. This paper focuses on utility tokens, as our sample mainly consists of utility tokens. In order to access the product or service of the ICO project, users will need to possess the specific token. The project simply generates the tokens and offers them to investors for purchase in the ICO. Utility tokens do not represent equity or dividend rights, so they allow startups to obtain finance while retaining full ownership of the company. ICOs are usually carried out at a very early stage of the development process. Investors expect the tokens to increase in value as they speculate that demand for the tokens will increase given the fixed or limited supply.

With the introduction of Ethereum and smart contracts, decentralized computer protocol can automatically be executed upon predefined terms. This enables crowdsale-specific smart contracts that are deployed on the blockchain and contain all crowdfunding details in the form of computer protocol. Newly created tokens on the Ethereum blockchain are automatically distributed to investors upon the successful deposit of funds (in the form of cryptocurrency), and once the crowdfunding goal is reached, all additional payments are automatically returned. Blockchain technology enables various technological innovations in the field of crowdfunding, as the decentralized architecture in combination with low transaction fees permits individuals from anywhere to participate in an ICO with as small an amount as they desire.

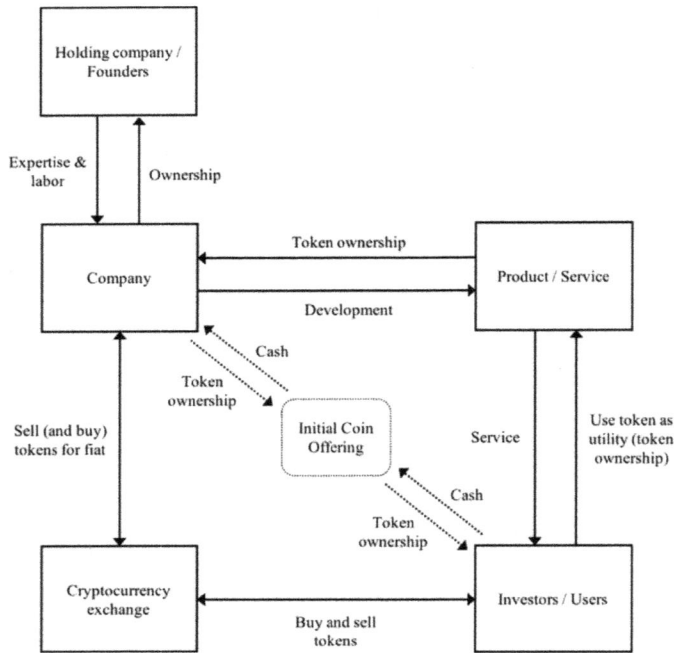

Figure 1. Token-based economy and initial coin offering (ICO).

3. Data and Methodology

3.1. Data Sources

To identify blockchain-based crowdfunding projects, an explorative analysis of the ecosystem was conducted. The online forum, Bitcointalk[2], serves as a platform to announce new projects and to communicate with potential investors. Project details, like crowdfunding date, team information, amount of funding, or token distribution, were sourced from Bitcointalk, where available, or the official web presence of each project. To this day, there is no comprehensive knowledge base that lists information on all ICOs, so most information had to be retrieved manually. Social media statistics, such as likes, followers, or subscribers, for the platforms of Twitter, Facebook, and Reddit were imported directly from the application programming interfaces (APIs) of each social media website.

Our dataset consists of 278 projects that finished their ICO between July 2013 and August 2017. The sample comprises all ICOs during that period for which we were able to collect information on all the variables. Due to a lack of transparency and public data, a number of ICOs had to be omitted from the sample.

3.2. Operationalization of the Variables

Dependent variable. This paper relies on the amount of *funds raised* (in USD) as the dependent variable, i.e., as our measure of ICO success. Since the variable is highly skewed, in the regressions, we use the natural logarithm, in line with existing research (Alexy et al. 2012; Sandner and Block 2011). As projects that finance themselves via an ICO are usually funded in the form of cryptocurrency,

---

[2]   https://bitcointalk.org.

the actual fiat value of the funding depends on the exact point in time at which the prices of the cryptocurrencies, which fluctuate strongly (Yermack 2013), are determined. For comparability, we calculate the fiat equivalent that applied at the time when the crowdfunding process closed.[3]

Independent variables. *Team size* signifies the number of team members listed on the official website of each project. *Team network* represents the adjusted LinkedIn network reach of the team. We calculate the average LinkedIn network of all team members in relation to the number of team members who actually have a LinkedIn account. *Advisors* means the number of project advisors who are listed on the project website.

We use three different score variables (*business model: Infrastructure; business model: Financial;* and *business model: Utility*) to assess the quality of the business model of each project. For this purpose, we had an expert evaluate each project. The expert assigned a score of zero, one, or two for the three business model categories for each project. More specifically, the expert was asked to rate the quality of the projects' tokenized business model with regard to the (1) creation of infrastructure, like protocols that other projects can build on or networks where users can interact with each other; (2) the financial value that a tokenized business model unlocks, like a payment token or cryptocurrency-backed debit card system; and (3) the utility of the underlying token model. Utility represents the overall value that a token brings to a service, an ecosystem, or a network.

Whitepaper: Exists is a dummy variable that indicates the availability of a whitepaper for each project. There is no business standard for the actual contents of a whitepaper, which is why the overall quality can vary greatly. The use of whitepapers in the ICO ecosystem is based on the fact that Bitcoin was introduced in a whitepaper and very successful ICO projects, like Ethereum, also issued whitepapers (Nakamoto 2008; Buterin 2014; Wood 2014). The variable *Whitepaper: Score*, our proxy of whitepaper quality, equals the sum of the number of pages and citations in the document.

Twitter score summarizes the level of activity of a project's Twitter account as the sum of the number of tweets and the number of followers of the project divided by 1000.

Control variables. The variable *ICO duration* represents the number of days between the start and the end of the ICO. Mollick (2013) shows that the duration of a crowdfunding campaign can have a negative effect, as longer duration could be due to a lack of market confidence.

We assigned each project to one of six industry dummy variables: *Financial* (financial sector), *Blocknet* (blockchain network/infrastructure project), *Media* (media and communications sector), *Gambling* (gambling and casino projects), *Gaming* (gaming projects), and *Cloud computing* (cloud computing and cloud storage projects).

Team dispersion captures the number of different home countries represented among the team. This way, we can access the effects of centralized processes in project decisions (Mollick 2013) and the decentralized collaboration approach favored by open-source software projects (Belleflamme et al. 2014).

The *Facebook score* is calculated as the number of likes of the project's Facebook page divided by 1000. Reddit is an online forum where projects can start sub forums to discuss and rate articles and posts. ICO projects usually have their own Reddit page to interact with their community. The variable, *Reddit score*, consists of the number of subscribers to a project's subpage divided by 1000. Bitcointalk is a forum for projects related to cryptocurrencies where most ICO projects have an announcement thread. The *Bitcointalk score* is calculated as the number of total reads and the average number of posts per day of the full project's sub forum divided by 1000.

---

[3]   The example of the project, Digix Global, illustrates the effects of cryptocurrency price fluctuations. The project raised 462,719 Ether in March 2016, worth around $5.5 million at the time. Thanks to the cryptocurrency price increase, the projects' funds were worth around $132 million only two years later (https://etherscan.io/address/0xf0160428a8552ac9bb7e050d90eeade4ddd52843).

4. Results

4.1. Descriptive Statistics

To show the evolution of ICOs and ICO funding, the projects were classified in quarters based on the end date of their ICO (see Figure 2). As the last ICO recorded ended on 3 August 2017, the numbers for the third quarter of that year were extrapolated linearly from the first 33 days of the quarter. The data exhibits a strong upward trend, driven especially by the 2017 ICOs. This trend holds both for the number of ICOs and the average amount raised. Before 2017, the funding amount was dominated by a few large projects, especially *The DAO* in Q2/2016. We thus see evidence of skewness, as also indicated by the large discrepancy between the average ($6.5 million) and median ($0.4 million) amount raised per ICO and the large standard deviation of $23.6 million. A Gini coefficient of 86.7% also suggests that the distribution is strongly concentrated. We respond to this skewness by using the log of funds as our dependent variable (Manning and Mullahy 2001).

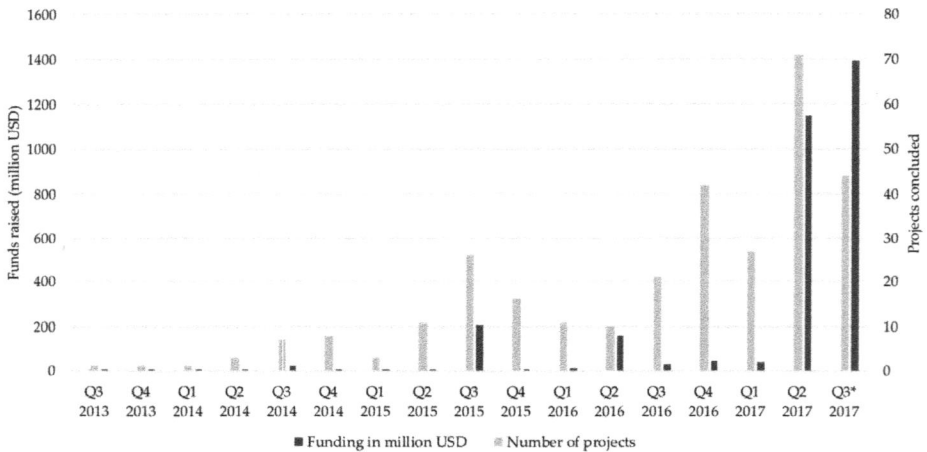

Figure 2. Number of ICOs and ICO funding in million US-dollars over time. Q3* 2017 has been interpolated for the remaining part of the quarter.

In terms of industries, most of the projects in our dataset can be assigned to the financial sector (43.5%), followed by blockchain network and infrastructure projects (13.6%), media and communications (12.5%), gambling (5%), and gaming (4.3%). The classification by industries was conducted manually and is clearly open to debate as many projects could be allocated to multiple sectors. For example, gaming and gambling often overlap, and the sector of cloud computing and storage (2.9%) is not much different from blockchain network or infrastructure projects.

Table 1 provides an overview of the descriptive statistics. The mean amount of funds raised was $6.5 million, with a minimum of $25 and a maximum of about $228 million. The biggest project team had 46 members, while the average across all projects was 3.91. Team members possessed just below 100 LinkedIn contacts on average, while keeping in mind that 500 contacts is the maximal publicly shown amount. The average ICO duration was 26 days and the longest ICO took 906 days to complete. We were able to obtain whitepapers for 52% of all projects.

Table 1. Descriptive statistics.

Variables	Obs.	Mean	Std. Dev.	Median	Min.	Max.
Funds raised	278	6,515,099	23,241,612	436,316	25	227,817,556
Log(Funds raised)	278	5.471	1.315	5.64	1.4	8.36
Team size	278	3.910	6.141	0	0	46
Team network	278	97.477	147.021	0	0	500
Advisors	278	1.162	2.804	0	0	17
Business model: infrastructure	278	0.662	0.779	0	0	2
Business model: financial	278	0.644	0.69	1	0	2
Business model: utility	278	0.651	0.72	1	0	2
ICO duration	276	26.070	62.817	15	0	906
Log(ICO duration) [1]	276	0.996	0.647	1.48	0	2.957
Whitepaper: score	278	13.230	17.601	2.5	0	131
Whitepaper: exists	277	0.520	0.501	1	0	1
Twitter score	278	4.750	9.714	2.025	0	115.21
Facebook score	278	3.332	13.755	0	0	143.213
Reddit Score	278	1.211	8.062	0.002	0	98.033
Bitcointalk Score	278	117.681	266.287	25.85	0	2379.9
Financial	278	0.414	0.493	0	0	1
Blocknet	278	0.133	0.340	0	0	1
Media	278	0.112	0.315	0	0	1
Gambling	278	0.054	0.226	0	0	1
Gaming	278	0.054	0.226	0	0	1
Cloud Computing	278	0.216	0.146	0	0	1
Team dispersion	278	1.040	1.628	0	0	9

[1] If ICO duration > 0, then log(ICO duration), else 0.

4.2. Multivariate Results

The multivariate results are based on four models, which we estimate by ordinary least squares (OLS. The results are reported in Table 2. In models 1 and 2, we added the variable, *ICO duration*, as a control variable to all independent variables to observe any effects of the length of the campaigns, while in model 2, we additionally added the six industry dummies to control for any influence of business sectors. In model 3, we added the variable log(ICO duration) to account for any heteroscedasticity, as there is substantial variation in ICO duration. The social media control variables are introduced in model 4, as is *team dispersion*, to check for any effects of the degree of business centralization. Models 1 and 3 have F values of 39.48 and 39.01 and adjusted R^2 values of 0.5857 and 0.5831, respectively, suggesting a reasonable fit. The fourth model has a lesser fit, at F = 30.79 and adjusted R^2 = 0.5854. The second model has the highest adjusted R^2 (0.6021) and, being based on the largest number of different variables, the lowest F value (26.8).

In models 1, 3, and 4, we find a significant, but small, positive influence of *team size*, while all four models predict a highly significant, but small, positive influence of the team network and a highly significant positive influence of the number of advisors on the funds raised. The existence of the whitepaper has a highly significant positive impact across all models, while for *whitepaper: Score* we find a positive but insignificant coefficient.

Regarding the quality of the business idea, we find highly significant positive results for Business model: Financial in all fours models. For Business model: Utility, we find positive results that are significant at the 1%-level in models 1, 3, and 4. Model 2 returns a weaker association ($p < 0.1$). We also find a marginally significant positive effect of ICO duration in model 1. Interestingly, social media has no significant impact, with the coefficient signs being variously positive (Twitter and Facebook) and negative (Bitcointalk and Reddit). We find a negative impact of Team dispersion in model 4. Regarding the industry dummies in model 4, the only significant result is a strongly negative one for financial projects.

Table 2. Results of OLS regression models.

Variables	Model 1	Model 2	Model 3	Model 4
Team size	0.019 *	0.016	0.018 *	0.032 ***
	(0.075)	(0.123)	(0.089)	(0.009)
Team network	0.009 **	0.001 ***	0.001 *	0.001 **
	(0.047)	(0.008)	(0.045)	(0.014)
Advisors	0.061 ***	0.061 ***	0.063 ***	0.055 **
	(0.007)	(0.008)	(0.006)	(0.016)
Business model: Infrastructure	0.043	−0.034	0.048	0.093
	(0.614)	(0.696)	(0.573)	(0.288)
Business model: Financial	0.358 ***	0.395 ***	0.364 ***	0.391 ***
	(0.000)	(0.000)	(0.000)	(0.000)
Business model: Utility	0.265 ***	0.178 *	0.252 ***	0.266 ***
	(0.005)	(0.065)	(0.008)	(0.005)
Whitepaper: Score	0.005	0.004	0.005	0.004
	(0.291)	(0.321)	(0.279)	(0.367)
Whitepaper: Exists	0.806 ***	0.811 ***	0.783 ***	0.829 ***
	(0.000)	(0.000)	(0.000)	(0.000)
Twitter score	0.008	0.005	0.008	0.011
	(0.169)	(0.410)	(0.200)	(0.148)
Bitcointalk score	-	-	-	−0.000
				(0.446)
Facebook score	-	-	-	0.001
				(0.776)
Reddit score	-	-	-	−0.001
				(0.850)
ICO duration	0.001 *	0.001	-	-
	(0.083)	(0.208)		
Log(ICO duration)	-	-	0.093	-
			(0.274)	
Team dispersion	-	-	-	−0.105 **
				(0.039)
Blocknet	-	0.046	-	-
		(0.801)		
Financial	-	−0.462 ***	-	-
		(0.000)		
Media	-	−0.275	-	-
		(0.149)		
Gambling	-	−0.097	-	-
		(0.696)		
Gaming	-	0.041	-	-
		(0.869)		
Cloud computing	-	0.455	-	-
		(0.227)		
F	39.48	26.8	39.01	30.79
Adj. R^2	0.5857	0.6021	0.5831	0.5854

*, **, *** indicates significance at 0.05, 0.01 and 0.00 respectively.

5. Discussion

5.1. Implications for Theory

The exponential growth in ICO funding may be due to the "free money effect" or "house money effect" (Thaler and Johnson 1990). Early investors in Bitcoin or Ethereum reaped very large gains of many thousands of percent (depending on their entry, of course) that allowed them to invest large sums into ICOs. According to Zelizer (1994) Social Meaning of Money theory, money is treated differently depending on its context. This would imply that money won by investing in cryptocurrencies is not seen as neutral, but as tied to the same market. Compared to money gained in other markets, early cryptocurrency winners are more likely to invest large sums in ICOs. Another reason might reinforce this house money effect: Compared to gambling, early cryptocurrency investors might not perceive their gains as pure luck, but rather as the fruits of investing in a technological breakthrough. As early supporters, they are likely to reuse their funds to foster this technology. The analysis has shown that most funds are raised in a few very large ICOs that appear to attract most investor interest.

The results of the multivariate analysis support some of our hypotheses. Especially, H1, the conjectured positive relationship between human capital and funds raised, is supported by all four models in the form of significant positive effects of team size, team network size, and the number of advisors. This confirms our hypothesis that a larger network and thus greater human capital supports ICO success, in line with the corresponding literature on venture capital (Florin et al. 2003; Stuart et al. 1999), crowdfunding (Ahlers et al. 2015), and ICOs (Fisch 2019).

We also found support for H2 regarding the quality of a project in all four models, as there are significant correlations between funds raised on the business model in regards to financial and utility aspects. This finding suggests that investors, at least to some extent, rationally pick those ICOs which signal strong quality, rather than blindly distributing their funds across the available ICOs. This finding is in line with existing research on ICOs (Fisch 2019; Amsden and Schweizer 2018). Interestingly, we did not find significant results for the third variable, infrastructure. We suggest that investors may possess some form of knowledge to evaluate the quality of a business model.

Furthermore, we found a strong influence of whitepaper existence and thus some support for H3 of a positive relationship between project elaboration and funds raised. Yet, no significant effect was found for the whitepaper score. This suggests that what ICO investors value is not so much a convincing (technical) whitepaper, but rather the quality of the business model in general. This could be a sign that investors expect a whitepaper to be available, but do not actually read it. Our research confirms that the actual level of preparedness in form of a well-structured business plan promotes ICO success, as shown by Chen et al. (2009) for VC investment decisions.

Our hypothesis, H4, a positive relationship between social media presence and funds raised, failed to find any significant support across all social media variables. Twitter has a very small positive impact in all four models, as does Facebook, when included in model 4. Both Bitcointalk and Reddit yield insignificant and negative results. There are two reasons why a negative sign on these two variables is actually not surprising: (1) Whenever a project is exposed to rumors about illegitimacy or fraud, a lot of additional posts are generated, resulting in a high score; (2) projects that occurred towards the start of our sample period tend to raise less capital (by virtue of the growth trend we found), but have had more time to accumulate posts and thus have a higher score.[4] If for these reasons we disregard Bitcointalk and Reddit and thus only interpret it as a proxy for social media attention the Twitter score, as it only comprises followers and project tweets, but not community posts, our result confirms the finding from the venture capital and crowdfunding literature that social media presence has a positive impact on financing campaigns. The finding furthermore suggests that entrepreneurs looking for funding via an ICO should devote attention to social media (Solomon et al. 2012; Sprenger et al. 2014).

In general, we show that investor behavior in ICOs shows similarities to the VC and crowdfunding markets. This suggests that ICOs may need to be integrated into the research on corporate finance. Our research adds to the literature of signaling theory by showing that ICO startups use certain types of information, like human capital characteristics, business model quality, and project elaboration, to signal their quality to campaign contributors.

---

[4] Instead, the number of posts until the end of the ICO phase should have been used to determine the social media scores. Yet, this data is virtually impossible to retrieve automatically for past years.

5.2. Implications for Practice

The blockchain technology is said to hold massive disruptive power for various industries, and to entail groundbreaking changes to numerous aspects of our lives. Startup funding is clearly among the affected fields. If the relevant players, including VC funds, startups, and business angels, are aware of the technology's disruptive potential and learn to harness it to improve current processes or to develop new business models, it can be a highly valuable tool for raising funds.

Furthermore, blockchain can potentially change the way in which businesses are managed and organized. Yet, before concrete action can be taken, companies need to familiarize themselves with the challenges and risks of the technology. In the financial industry, a broad utilization of blockchain is expected in no more than three to five years, so other industries need to start preparing for it.

The fact that companies are able to raise money without the need to offer any form of equity, voting rights, or profit participation in return could herald a new era of corporate financing. If ICO funding keeps growing, traditional methods of corporate finance may have to adapt in some form.

Several aspects of the ICO market suggest that a bubble is emerging. Blockchain-based ICOs and their underlying decentralized approach represent an innovative technology, and innovation lay at the root of the financial bubbles in new economy stocks (Pastor and Veronesi 2009), the Mississippi Bubble, the South Sea Bubble, and the Dutch Windhandel (Frehen et al. 2013). Pástor and Veronesi (2006) show that stock prices in innovative industries grow irrationally high and predict that their price falls once the uncertainty about the technology is resolved. The market for ICOs does fit clientele models as it features both arbitrageurs (informed investors) and noise traders (uninformed investors) (Frehen et al. 2013). Very high returns and rapid market growth constitute additional evidence of a price bubble emerging, which asset managers need to account for in their risk analysis (Lee and Phillips 2016).

5.3. Limitations

Regardless of the strengths of our study (e.g., the comprehensive data set of a wide range of ICOs starting from the very beginning in 2013), the following limitations should be mentioned. First, the ICO tokens issued by various projects represent very different things (Conley 2017). For instance, there are donation tokens, utility tokens (for different sorts of services and products), dividend tokens, and equity tokens. Moreover, a token can also provide two sorts of benefits at the same time. This variation may have unobserved effects on the amount of funds raised. We therefore encourage future studies to explicitly control for token characteristics and to compare the investment consequences of different kinds of tokens.

Second, the regulatory situation and legal status of the ICOs in our sample varied across countries and across time, potentially leading to uncontrolled effects on our observations. ICOs are such a novel phenomenon that there was and still is great regulatory uncertainty in many countries, allowing projects to sell tokens for large sums to investors without conducting Know-Your-Customer (KYC) procedures (Ante 2018). In 2017, the U.S. Securities and Exchange Commission (SEC) stated that the tokens sold in an ICO by the project The DAO (Jentzsch 2016) were indeed securities whose issuance in a crowdfunding campaign would have required a prospectus (SEC 2017a). The SEC additionally issued an investor bulletin that provides potential ICO investors with numerous warnings of investment fraud and a list of challenges that law enforcement face when investigating ICOs, including difficulties in tracing money flows, the international scope, the lack of central authority, and the risks and obstacles of freezing or securing virtual currency (SEC 2017b). On 11 December 2017, the SEC issued a cease-and-desist order to the Delaware-based company, Munchee Inc., that offered securities in their token sale, forcing the company to refund all investments and to abort its campaign. Munchee promised that the value of their offered MUN token would increase because of the company's work and that tokens would be traded on secondary markets. The token did not involve any profit participation mechanisms, such as buybacks or dividends (SEC 2017c). In other countries, ICO tokens may also represent securities or can alternatively also be considered currencies with or without securities characteristics (e.g., Germany). This unclear status may also have had an unobserved effect on our results. However, there is no reason to assume a systematic effect, so the results are unlikely to be biased.

As a mostly unregulated ecosystem, the ICO market is only beginning to mature. The first ICOs were carried out without incorporation or legal protection, which is why only limited information on these projects is available. Our dataset is likely missing a number of failed and abandoned ICO projects, so there is some selection bias in favor of successful projects. It is unclear whether and to what extent our results are influenced by this fact. As the market continues to grow rapidly, the relevant information is becoming much more accessible, so future research along these lines should not face the same problem.

Presales of tokens are a standard process used by many projects. Various different approaches, such as multi-stage presales and undisclosed presales, are used, which further reduces transparency in the market. More and more funds and venture capitalists are entering the ICO market and try to gain access to presale deals. Up until 2017, ICOs usually employed time-based bonus systems to incentivize investors to invest early, a practice that has now been replaced by presales. Our variable funds raised equals the sum of presale and main sale funding. Yet, we may not have captured all presale funding for some projects. As a limitation, we cannot observe whether presale success had any effect on the amount of funding raised in the ICO.

Some projects set minimum and maximum funding caps, while others try to raise as much capital as possible. Our study defined ICO success as the amount of capital that a project was able to raise, yet numerous projects met their funding targets in less than a day, so very likely they could have raised more capital. In these cases, our dependent variable may not adequately capture the true funding potential of a project or, in other words, the cap prevented our explanatory variables from taking full effect. For our dataset, we were unable to identify enough funding caps across all projects due to a lack of transparent data for historic campaigns. By implementing funding caps, the actual success of a project could potentially be defined more clearly. Still, most projects implement funding goals today, so their effects can be tested in future studies.

We have identified a small positive impact of the variable whitepaper score on funding success, while the existence of a whitepaper had a strong effect. Agrawal et al. (2014) show that crowdfunding campaigns tend to be more successful if a unique product or service can be easily explained. Therefore, whitepaper complexity could also impede funding success. Future research should therefore additionally control for the availability of a less complex version of the whitepaper, like a pitch deck.

Our model 4 yielded a negative connection between the funds raised and the geographical dispersion of a project's team members. This finding is at odds with the decentralized approach of the ICO ecosystem. Yet, the effect we found may really be driven by the existence of a collocated or virtual team (Powell et al. 2006) or by cultural differences (Burtch et al. 2013). To check for the second possibility, we conducted alternative calculations using geographical data, such as classifying projects according to cultural dimensions theory (Hofstede 1984) or evaluating whether the presence of a team member from China or eastern countries, like Russia, had any impact on ICO success. No significant results were found. We therefore encourage future research to look into this issue as the data quality continues to improve rapidly.

6. Conclusions

This study of the ICO phenomenon adds to existing research by evaluating how this new ecosystem compares to existing processes in VC and crowdfunding financing. We investigate this question from the perspective of the startups that are looking to raise money for their venture. Our findings suggest that the ICO market indeed exhibits close similarities to the classical markets of VC and crowdfunding: ICO success, as measured by the amount of capital raised, is positively related to human capital characteristics, business model quality, project elaboration, and social media presence. ICO contributors seem to invest rationally based on publicly available data. Yet, our findings regarding the relevance that investors assign to project elaboration and social media presence are to some extent inconclusive and require further research. The market for ICO is still underregulated and intransparent, with large information asymmetries between startups, contributors, and society. ICO success is subject to the same causalities and signals as classic VC and crowdfunding financing. We thus conclude that though ICOs are a new way of financing startups, they do constitute a new form of crowdfunding financing that will technically and legally move closer to traditional mechanisms as markets mature and regulators step in. It still remains to be seen to what extent the other markets will adapt towards the ICO market. By 2018, over $15 billion has been raised in ICOs, so unless regulation puts a stop to it, the phenomenon is here to stay.

Our study adds to research in the field of ICOs as a novel form of fundraising for startups and paves the way for future research in this growing, but as yet under-researched area. Several questions warrant further research. First, longitudinal research is needed to examine ICOs over time and track their long-term development. A panel data set could yield more fine-grained insights into how the predictors influence ICO success and into the mechanisms behind each of the variables. Such research could also reveal the dynamics for certain variables, such as the influence of social media, advisors, or team composition. For instance, it can be assumed that social media may create a hype around certain ICOs. Longitudinal analyses of social media sentiment and funds raised over time could uncover the dynamics underlying the influence of social media. Future research should comprise time-series data on the social media channels of ICO projects to detect information cascades, under- or overpricing, and announcement effects.

Second, while our study has been conducted from a startup's perspective, looking at the determinants of the amount of funds raised, future research may investigate ICOs from an investor's perspective and focus on variables, such as returns, dividends, and market capitalization. For instance, our knowledge of investor strategies and the associated outcomes is very limited. In this regard, it would be interesting to investigate how investors allocate their funds in terms of, for example, industries, geography, and diversification, and what returns these strategies yield.

Third, we see a need to examine ICOs from a regulator's and a legal perspective, and the status of ICOs in society more generally. For instance, since tokens have different characteristics in different countries (being treated for example as securities, as a currency etc.), comparative research on the impact of such differential treatment is needed.

Fourth, given the amount of money at stake, we need to know how this form of funding can be institutionalized in a way that benefits society as a whole. We hope that our study will spark interest in these and related questions and trust that future research will address many of the as yet unresolved puzzles in the emerging token economy.

Supplementary Materials: The following are available online at http://www.mdpi.com/1911-8074/11/4/80/s1, Datensatz ICO bereinigt.

Author Contributions: Conceptualization, L.A., P.S., I.F.; Data curation, L.A.; Formal analysis, L.A., P.S., I.F.; Investigation, L.A., I.F.; Methodology, L.A., P.S., I.F.; Project administration, L.A.; Resources, L.A.; Supervision, L.A. and I.F.; Validation, L.A., P.S., I.F.; Visualization, L.A.; Writing—original draft, L.A., P.S., I.F.; Writing—review and editing, L.A., I.F.

Funding: This research received no external funding.

Conflicts of Interest: The authors declare no conflict of interest.

References

Adhami, Saman, Giancarlo Giudici, and Stefano Martinazzi. 2018. Why do businesses go crypto? An empirical analysis of Initial Coin Offerings. *Journal of Economics and Business*, in press. [CrossRef]

Agrawal, Ajay, Christian Catalini, and Avi Goldfarb. 2014. Some simple economics of crowdfunding. *Innovation Policy and the Economy* 14: 63–97. [CrossRef]

Ahlers, Gerrit K. C., Douglas Cumming, Christina Günther, and Denis Schweizer. 2015. Signaling in equity crowdfunding. *Entrepreneurship Theory and Practice* 39: 955–80. [CrossRef]

Ahlstrom, David, and Garry D. Bruton. 2006. Venture capital in emerging economies: Networks and institutional change. *Entrepreneurship Theory and Practice* 30: 299–320. [CrossRef]

Alexy, Oliver T., Joern H. Block, Philipp Sandner, and Anne L. J. Ter Wal. 2012. Social capital of venture capitalists and start-up funding. *Small Business Economics* 39: 835–51. [CrossRef]

Amit, Raphael, and Christoph Zott. 2001. Value creation in e-business. *Strategic Management Journal* 22: 493–520. [CrossRef]

Amsden, Ryan, and Denis Schweizer. 2018. Are Blockchain Crowdsales the New 'Gold Rush'? Success Determinants of Initial Coin Offerings. Available online: https://ssrn.com/abstract=3163849 (accessed on 1 August 2018).

Ante, Lennart. 2018. Cryptocurrency and crime. In *The Money Laundering Market: Regulating the Criminal Economy*. Edited by Killian J. McCarthy. London: Agenda Publishing.

Barrow, Colin, Paul Barrow, and Robert Brown. 2001. *The Business Plan Workbook*, 4th ed. London: Kogan Page.

Baum, Joel A. C., and Brian S. Silverman. 2004. Picking winners or building them? Alliance, intellectual, and human capital as selection criteria in venture financing and performance of biotechnology startups. *Journal of Business Venturing* 19: 411–36. [CrossRef]

Becker, Gary S. 1993. Nobel lecture: The economic way of looking at behavior. *Journal of Political Economy* 101: 385–409. [CrossRef]

Belleflamme, Paul, Thomas Lambert, and Armin Schwienbacher. 2014. Crowdfunding: Tapping the right crowd. *Journal of Business Venturing* 29: 585–609. [CrossRef]

Björkdahl, Joakim. 2009. Technology cross fertilization and the business model: The case of integrating ICTs in mechanical engineering products. *Research Policy* 38: 1468–77. [CrossRef]

Burtch, Gordon, Anindya Ghose, and Sunil Wattal. 2013. Cultural differences and geography as determinants of online pro-social lending. *Business Research Paper*, November 21.

Busenitz, Lowell W., James O. Fiet, and Douglas D. Moesel. 2005. Signaling in venture capitalists—New venture team funding decisions: Does it indicate long-term venture outcomes? *Entrepreneurship Theory and Practice* 29: 1–12. [CrossRef]

Buterin, Vitalik. 2014. Ethereum: A Next-Generation Smart Contract and Decentralized Application Platform. Available online: https://github.com/ethereum/wiki/wiki/White-Paper (accessed on 20 September 2018).

Calia, Rogerio C., Fabio M. Guerrini, and Gilnei L. Moura. 2007. Innovation networks: From technological development to business model reconfiguration. *Technovation* 27: 426–32. [CrossRef]

Casadesus-Masanell, Ramon, and Joan Enric Ricart. 2010. From strategy to business models and to tactics. *Long Range Planning* 43: 195–215. [CrossRef]

Chen, Xiao-Ping, Xin Yao, and Suresh Kotha. 2009. Entrepreneur passion and preparedness in business plan presentations: A persuasion analysis of venture capitalists' funding decisions. *Academy of Management Journal* 52: 199–214. [CrossRef]

Chesbrough, Henry. 2010. Business model innovation: opportunities and barriers. *Long Range Planning* 43: 354–63. [CrossRef]

Chesbrough, Henry, and Richard S. Rosenbloom. 2002. The role of the business model in capturing value from innovation: Evidence from Xerox Corporation's technology spin-off companies. *Industrial and Corporate Change* 11: 529–55. [CrossRef]

Cholakova, Magdalena, and Bart Clarysse. 2015. Does the possibility to make equity investments in crowdfunding projects crowd out reward-based investments? *Entrepreneurship Theory and Practice* 39: 145–72. [CrossRef]

Clayton, Jay. 2017. Statement on Cryptocurrencies and Initial Coin Offerings. Available online: https://www.sec.gov/news/public-statement/statement-clayton-2017-12-11 (accessed on 1 August 2018).

Coleman, Susan, and Alicia Robb. 2014. *Access to Capital by High-Growth Women-Owned Businesses*; Washington, DC: National Women's Business Council, pp. 1–32.

Colombo, Massimo G., Chiara Franzoni, and Cristina Rossi-Lamastra. 2015. Internal social capital and the attraction of early contributions in crowdfunding. *Entrepreneurship Theory and Practice* 39: 75–100. [CrossRef]

Conley, John P. 2017. *Blockchain and the Economics of Crypto-Tokens and Initial Coin Offerings (No. 17-00008)*. Nashville: Vanderbilt University Department of Economics.

Cosh, Andy, Douglas Cumming, and Alan Hughes. 2009. Outside Entrepreneurial Capital. *Economic Journal* 119: 1494–533. [CrossRef]

Cumming, Douglas J., Lars Hornuf, Moein Karami, and Denis Schweizer. 2016. Disentangling Crowdfunding from Fraudfunding. Max Planck Institute for Innovation and Competition Research Paper No. 16-09. Available online: https://www.researchgate.net/profile/Denis_Schweizer/publication/317997302_Disentangling_Crowdfunding_from_Fraudfunding/links/59f8ea17a6fdcc075ec99ba9/Disentangling-Crowdfunding-from-Fraudfunding.pdf (accessed on 8 August 2018).

De Filippi, Primavera, and Samer Hassan. 2018. Blockchain technology as a regulatory technology: From code is law to law is code. *arXiv*, arXiv:1801.02507.

Deakins, David, and Mark S. Freel. 2003. *Entrepreneurship and Small Firms*. London: McGraw Hill Higher Education.

Du, Qianzhou, Weiguo Fan, Zhilei Qiao, Gang Wang, Xuan Zhang, and Mi Zhou. 2015. Money talks: A predictive model on crowdfunding success using project description. Paper presented at Americas Conference on Information Systems (AMCIS), Puerto Rico, Territory, August 13–15.

Dubosson-Torbay, Magali, Alexander Osterwalder, and Yves Pigneur. 2002. E-business model design, classification, and measurements. *Thunderbird International Business Review* 44: 5–23. [CrossRef]

Fisch, Christian. 2019. Initial coin offerings (ICOs) to finance new ventures. *Journal of Business Venturing* 34: 1–22. [CrossRef]

Florin, Juan, Michael Lubatkin, and William Schulze. 2003. A social capital model of high-growth ventures. *Academy of Management Journal* 46: 374–84.

Frehen, Rik G. P., William N. Goetzmann, and K. Geert Rouwenhorst. 2013. New evidence on the first financial bubble. *Journal of Financial Economics* 108: 585–607. [CrossRef]

Gimmon, Eli, and Jonathan Levie. 2010. Founder's human capital, external investment, and the survival of new high-technology ventures. *Research Policy* 39: 1214–26. [CrossRef]

Griffin, Zachary J. 2012. Crowdfunding: Fleecing the American masses. *Case Western Reserve Journal of Law, Technology and the Internet* 4: 375. [CrossRef]

Hall, John, and Charles W. Hofer. 1993. Venture capitalists' decision criteria in new venture evaluation. *Journal of Business Venturing* 8: 25–42. [CrossRef]

Harrison, Richard, and Colin Mason. 1996. Developments in the promotion of informal venture capital in the UK. *International Journal of Entrepreneurial Behaviour and Research* 2: 6–33. [CrossRef]

Hellmann, Thomas, and Manju Puri. 2002. Venture capital and the professionalization of start-up firms: Empirical evidence. *Journal of Finance* 57: 169–97. [CrossRef]

Hofstede, Geert. 1984. Cultural dimensions in management and planning. *Asia Pacific Journal of Management* 1: 81–99. [CrossRef]

Hornuf, Lars, and Armin Schwienbacher. 2017. Market mechanisms and funding dynamics in equity crowdfunding. *Journal of Corporate Finance* 50: 556–74. [CrossRef]

Hsu, David H. 2007. Experienced entrepreneurial founders, organizational capital, and venture capital funding. *Research Policy* 36: 722–41. [CrossRef]

Iansiti, Marco, and Karim R. Lakhani. 2017. The truth about blockchain. *Harvard Business Review* 95: 118–27.

Jentzsch, Christoph. 2016. Decentralized Autonomous Organization to Automate Governance. Available online: https://download.slock.it/public/DAO/WhitePaper.pdf (accessed on 8 August 2018).

Jin, Fujie, Andy Wu, and Lorin Hitt. 2017. Social Is the New Financial: How Startup Social Media Activity Influences Funding Outcomes. *Academy of Management Proceedings* 1: 13329. [CrossRef]

Joshi, Archana Prashanth, Meng Han, and Yan Wang. 2018. A survey on security and privacy issues of blockchain technology. *Mathematical Foundations of Computing* 1: 121–47. [CrossRef]

Kim, Jin-Hyuk, and Liad Wagman. 2016. Early-stage entrepreneurial financing: A signaling perspective. *Journal of Banking and Finance* 67: 12–22. [CrossRef]

Lechner, Christian, Michael Dowling, and Isabell Welpe. 2006. Firm networks and firm development: The role of the relational mix. *Journal of Business Venturing* 21: 514–40. [CrossRef]

Lee, Ji Hyung, and Peter C. B. Phillips. 2016. Asset pricing with financial bubble risk. *Journal of Empirical Finance* 38: 590–622. [CrossRef]

Lee, Choonwoo, Kyungmook Lee, and Johannes M. Pennings. 2001. Internal capabilities, external networks, and performance: A study on technology-based ventures. *Strategic Management Journal* 22: 615–40. [CrossRef]

Linn, Laure A., and Martha B. Koo. 2016. Blockchain for health data and its potential use in health it and health care related research. In *ONC/NIST Use of Blockchain for Healthcare and Research Workshop*; Gaithersburg: ONC/NIST.

Macht, Stephanie A., and John Robinson. 2009. Do business angels benefit their investee companies? *International Journal of Entrepreneurial Behavior and Research* 15: 187–208. [CrossRef]

Malmendier, Ulrike, and Devin Shanthikumar. 2007. Are small investors naive about incentives? *Journal of Financial Economics* 85: 457–89. [CrossRef]

Manning, Willard G., and John Mullahy. 2001. Estimating log models: to transform or not to transform? *Journal of Health Economics* 20: 461–94. [CrossRef]

McGrath, Rita Gunther. 2010. Business models: A discovery driven approach. *Long Range Planning* 43: 247–61. [CrossRef]

Mollick, Ethan R. 2013. Swept Away by the Crowd? Crowdfunding, Venture Capital, and the Selection of Entrepreneurs. Available online: https://ssrn.com/abstract=2239204 (accessed on 1 August 2018).

Muzyka, Dan, Sue Birley, and Benoit Leleux. 1996. Trade-offs in the investment decisons of European venture capitalists. *Journal of Business Venturing* 11: 273–87. [CrossRef]

Nakamoto, Satoshi. 2008. Bitcoin: A Peer-to-Peer Electronic Cash System. Available online: https://bitcoin.org/bitcoin.pdf (accessed on 12 June 2018).

Nevin, Sean, Rob Gleasure, Philip O'Reilly, Joseph Feller, Shanping Li, and Jerry Cristoforo. 2017. Social Identity and Social Media Activities in Equity Crowdfunding. Paper presented at 13th International Symposium on Open Collaboration, Galway, Ireland, August 23–25; p. 11.

Osgood, Ryan. 2016. The Future of Democracy: Blockchain Voting. In *COMP116: Information Security, Tufts University Department of Computer Science*. Available online: http://www.cs.tufts.edu/comp/116/archive/fall2016/rosgood.pdf (accessed on 5 August 2018).

Pástor, Ľuboš, and Pietro Veronesi. 2006. Was there a Nasdaq bubble in the late 1990s? *Journal of Financial Economics* 81: 61–100. [CrossRef]

Pastor, Lubos, and Pietro Veronesi. 2009. Learning in financial markets. *Annual Review of Financial Economics* 1: 361–81. [CrossRef]

Powell, Anne, John Galvin, and Gabriele Piccoli. 2006. Antecedents to team member commitment from near and far: A comparison between collocated and virtual teams. *Information Technology and People* 19: 299–322. [CrossRef]

Puthal, Deepak, Nisha Malik, Saraju P. Mohanty, Elias Kougianos, and Gautam Das. 2018. Everything You Wanted to Know About the Blockchain: Its Promise, Components, Processes, and Problems. *IEEE Consumer Electronics Magazine* 7: 6–14. [CrossRef]

Robb, Alicia M., and David T. Robinson. 2014. The capital structure decisions of new firms. *Review of Financial Studies* 27: 153–79. [CrossRef]

Sandner, Philipp G., and Joern Block. 2011. The market value of R and D, patents, and trademarks. *Research Policy* 40: 969–85. [CrossRef]

Schwienbacher, Armin, and Benjamin Larralde. 2010. Crowdfunding of small entrepreneurial ventures. In *Handbook of Entrepreneurial Finance*. Oxford: Oxford University Press.

Scott, Brett. 2016. How Can Cryptocurrency and Blockchain Technology Play a Role in Building Social and Solidarity Finance? No. 2016-1. UNRISD Working Paper. Available online: https://www.econstor.eu/bitstream/10419/148750/1/861287290.pdf (accessed on 22 August 2018).

SEC. 2017a. U.S. Securities and Exchange Commission. Investor Bulletin: Initial Coin Offerings. Available online: https://www.sec.gov/oiea/investor-alerts-and-bulletins/ib_coinofferings (accessed on 17 August 2018).

SEC. 2017b. U.S. Securities and Exchange Commission. Securities and Exchange Commission, Securities Exchange Act of 1934, Release No. 81207/25 July 2017, Report of Investigation Pursuant to Section 21(a) of the Securities Exchange Act of 1934: The DAO. Available online: www.sec.gov/litigation/investreport/34-81207.pdf (accessed on 17 August 2018).

SEC. 2017c. U.S. Securities and Exchange Commission. Securities Act of 1933 Release no. 10445/11 December 2017. Administrative Proceeding File no. 3-18304. Order Instituting Cease-Anddesist Proceedings Pursuant to Section 8a of the Securities Act of 1933, Making Findings, and Imposing a Cease-and-Desist ordeR. Available online: www.sec.gov/litigation/admin/2017/33-10445.pdf (accessed on 17 August 2018).

Shafer, Scott M., H. Jeff Smith, and Jane C. Linder. 2005. The power of business models. *Business Horizons* 48: 199–207. [CrossRef]

Shepherd, Dean A., and Evan J. Douglas. 1999. *Attracting Equity Investors: Positioning, Preparing and Presenting the Business Plan*. Thousand Oaks: Sage.

Solomon, Michael, Rebekah Russell-Bennett, and Josephine Previte. 2012. *Consumer Behaviour*. Melbourne: Pearson Higher Education AU.

Spence, Michael. 1973. Job market signaling. *Quarterly Journal of Economics* 87: 355–74. [CrossRef]

Sprenger, Timm O., Philipp G. Sandner, Andranik Tumasjan, and Isabell M. Welpe. 2014. News or noise? Using Twitter to identify and understand company-specific news flow. *Journal of Business Finance and Accounting* 41: 791–830. [CrossRef]

Stuart, Toby E., Ha Hoang, and Ralph C. Hybels. 1999. Interorganizational endorsements and the performance of entrepreneurial ventures. *Administrative Science Quarterly* 44: 315–49. [CrossRef]

Tankhiwale, Shekhar. 2009. Exploring the interrelationship between Telco business model innovation and the change in business process architecture. *Journal of Telecommunications Management* 2: 126–37.

Thaler, Richard H., and Eric J. Johnson. 1990. Gambling with the house money and trying to break even: The effects of prior outcomes on risky choice. *Management Science* 36: 643–60. [CrossRef]

Timmers, Paul. 1998. Business models for electronic markets. *Electronic Markets* 8: 3–8. [CrossRef]

Vismara, Silvio. 2016. Information cascades among investors in equity crowdfunding. *Entrepreneurship Theory and Practice*. [CrossRef]

Wheale, Peter Robert, and Laura Heredia Amin. 2003. "Bursting the dot. com" bubble': A case study in investor behaviour. *Technology Analysis and Strategic Management* 15: 117–36. [CrossRef]

Witt, Peter. 2004. Entrepreneurs' networks and the success of start-ups. *Entrepreneurship and Regional Development* 16: 391–412. [CrossRef]

Wood, Gavin. 2014. Ethereum: A secure decentralised generalised transaction ledger. *Ethereum Project Yellow Paper* 151: 1–32.

Yang, Song, and Ron Berger. 2017. Relation between start-ups' online social media presence and fundraising. *Journal of Science and Technology Policy Management* 8: 161–80. [CrossRef]

Yermack, David. 2013. *Is Bitcoin a Real Currency? An Economic Appraisal*. No. w19747. Cambridge: National Bureau of Economic Research.

Zacharakis, Andrew, and Dean A. Shepherd. 2005. A non-additive decision-aid for venture capitalists' investment decisions. *European Journal of Operational Research* 162: 673–89. [CrossRef]

Zelizer, Viviana A. Rotman. 1994. *The Social Meaning of Money*. New York: Basic Books.

Zott, Christoph, Raphael Amit, and Lorenzo Massa. 2011. The business model: Recent developments and future research. *Journal of Management* 37: 1019–42. [CrossRef]

Journal of
Risk and Financial Management

MDPI

Article

Inflation Propensity of Collatz Orbits: A New Proof-of-Work for Blockchain Applications

Fabian Bocart

Independent Researcher, Jackson Height, NY 11372, USA; fabian.bocart@gmail.com

Received: 20 September 2018; Accepted: 19 November 2018; Published: 27 November 2018

Abstract: Cryptocurrencies such as Bitcoin rely on a proof-of-work system to validate transactions and prevent attacks or double-spending. A new proof-of-work is introduced which seems to be the first number theoretic proof-of-work unrelated to primes: it is based on a new metric associated to the Collatz algorithm whose natural generalization is algorithmically undecidable: the inflation propensity is defined as the cardinality of new maxima in a developing Collatz orbit. It is numerically verified that the distribution of inflation propensity slowly converges to a geometric distribution of parameter $0.714 \approx \frac{(\pi-1)}{3}$ as the sample size increases. This pseudo-randomness opens the door to a new class of proofs-of-work based on congruential graphs.

Keywords: geometric distribution; collatz conjecture; inflation propensity; systemic risk; cryptocurrency; blockchain; proof-of-work

MSC: 60E05; 62E17

JEL Classification: C46; C65; O39

---

1. Introduction

A decentralized electronic payment system relies on a ledger of transactions shared on a network. The decentralization of a transaction ledger raises the question of security and integrity of the ledger. In the original Bitcoin protocol, the problem of double-spending or alteration of the ledger is solved by the use of blockchain, a system that requires proof-of-work by a network of computers to confirm transactions. In cryptography, intensive computation as proof-of-work allows one party to verify with little computational effort that a counterparty has spent a large amount of computational effort. The concept was originally developed by Dwork and Naor (1992) as a spam prevention technique. Nakamoto (2008) used, for Bitcoin, a proof-of-work based on Back (2002). The protocol consists in finding a nonce value such that the application of the SHA-256 hashing algorithm to a combination of that nonce and a block of information gives a hash starting with series of zeroes by targetting a given threshold. The idea behind the proof-of-work is that participants have an incentive to cooperate rather than to cheat because the computational power required to cheat is too large. However, as cryptocurrencies became more popular and diverse, an over-reliance on mainstream proof-of-work protocols, such as hashcash-SHA256, Ethash (Wood 2014) or hashcash-Scrypt based proof-of-work (Percival 2009) creates a new type of systemic risk in which a cryptographic breakdown would jeopardize cryptocurrencies that rely on these standard proofs-of-work. A weakness of proofs-of-work in cryptocurrency applications is the threat that a single individual (or a coordinated group) would be able to generate blocks faster than 50% of the network. In that case, this entity would completely control the blockchain-based validation system of transactions. In practice, attacks on hash functions could prevent new transactions or alter past ones. In financial markets, exchanges have the possibility to cancel trades in case of infrastructure breakdown or malfunction. By opposition, a systemic failure of the proof-of-work system in decentralized cryptocurrency markets could mean the destruction of the whole history of transactions. Potential risks clouding the proof-of-work system include innovation in technology, mathematics and cryptography that could compromise the existing protocols. Proofs-of-work entirely based on existing hash algorithms such as SHA-256 have been under stress in recent years. Rubin (2017) documented a well-known mining optimization ("ASIC-BOOST") that allowed to mine Bitcoin blocks faster than the network average by taking advantage of a technical flaw in SHA-256. A specific optimization of the mining instruments allowed reducing the problem's complexity by exploiting collision attacks on the SHA-256 hash algorithm. The multiplication of proofs-of-work help mitigate this type of hyper-specialized hardware attack. Bitcoin, Ethereum, Bitcoin Cash and Litecoin overwhelmingly dominate the market capitalization of minable coins. Such concentration of the volumes into a few cryptocurrencies represent equally a significant systemic risk. When looking at the top 25 cryptocurrencies by diluted market capitalization (see Table 1), eight of them use Scrypt as underlying hash algorithm for proof-of-work. Introducing new types of proof-of-work is needed to help networks diversifying the protocols in case of increased concentration of hyper-specialized computational power.

Table 1. The 25 top cryptocurrencies as of 15 October 2018 as can be seen on https://onchainfx.com/v/SMT45r.

Name	~Fully Diluted (Y2050) Marketcap/15 October 2018	Underlying Algorithm
Bitcoin (BTC)	$134,308,812,450	SHA-256
Ethereum (ETH)	$29,787,293,584	SHA-3
Bitcoin Cash (BCH)	$9,225,442,784	SHA-256
Litecoin (LTC)	$4,430,985,913	Scrypt
Dash (DASH)	$2,956,683,098	X11
Monero (XMR)	$2,300,499,210	CryptoNight
ZCash (ZEC)	$2,262,517,311	Equihash
Ethereum Classic (ETC)	$2,161,731,159	SHA-3
Dogecoin (DOGE)	$1,402,169,807	Scrypt
Siacoin (SC)	$564,862,312	Blake-2b
Bitcoin Gold (BTG)	$526,927,423	Equihash
Digibyte (DGB)	$483,402,492	SHA-256 and others
ReddCoin (RDD)	$447,635,857	Scrypt
Bitcoin Diamond (BCD)	$343,664,370	X13
ZenCash (ZEN)	$275,245,426	SHA-3
Verge (XVG)	$229,929,732	Scrypt
Zcoin (XZC)	$194,506,940	Equihash
Monacoin (MONA)	$124,690,762	Scrypt
Syscoin (SYS)	$81,207,881	Scrypt
Zclassic (ZCL)	$67,149,925	Equihash
Vertcoin (VTC)	$53,917,212	Lyra2REv2
Bitcoin Private (BTCP)	$51,124,537	Equihash
LBRY Credits (LBC)	$41,220,511	LBRY
Einsteinium (EMC2)	$25,808,910	Scrypt
GameCredits (GAME)	$13,734,781	Scrypt

So, even though there exist hundreds of different hash functions already, more diversification of proofs-of-work could further mitigate cryptographic risks and improve robustness of the nascent crypto-economy. Several types of proof-of-work have been designed using new hash functions, such as prime numbers verification (King 2013), graph-theoretic proof-of-work (Tromp 2015) or proof-of-work based on the generalized birthday problem (Biryukov and Khovratovich 2017). Post-quantum algorithms are currently being developed in the field of security, see, for example, Bae et al. (2017). In particular, Kiktenko et al. (2018) propose a quantum-safe blockchain that utilizes quantum key distribution. The application presented in the following sections seems to be the first documented attempt to establish a number theoretic proof-of-work unrelated to primes. The hash proposed is based on properties of the Collatz algorithm. In order to describe this algorithm, consider the following function from $\mathbb{N}_0$ to $\mathbb{N}_0$:

$$T(x) = \begin{cases} x/2 & \text{if } x \text{ is even} \\ (3x+1)/2 & \text{if } x \text{ is odd} \end{cases} \tag{1}$$

Now, apply the following iterate of T:

$$\begin{cases} T^0(x) = x \\ T^{(k+1)}(x) = T(T^k(x)) \end{cases} \tag{2}$$

The Collatz conjecture states that $\forall\, x \in \mathbb{N}_0, \exists$ a finite k such that $T^k(x) = 1$. Lagarias (2010) uses the following terminology: the "total stopping time" is defined as $\sigma_\infty(x) = \inf\{k : T^k(x) = 1\}$. The "stopping time" $\sigma(x)$ is $\inf\{k : T^k(x) < x\}$. The "gamma value" is defined as $\gamma(x) = \frac{\sigma_\infty(x)}{\log(x)}$.

For instance, let us consider the case for $x = 3$:

$$\begin{cases} T^0(3) = 3, \\ T^1(3) = (3 \times 3 + 1)/2 = 5, \\ T^2(3) = (5 \times 3 + 1)/2 = 8, \\ T^3(3) = 8/2 = 4, \\ T^4(3) = 4/2 = 2, \\ T^5(3) = 2/2 = 1. \end{cases} \tag{3}$$

In this example, the Collatz sequence[1] is $\left\{ 3, 5, 8, 4, 2, 1 \right\}$ and $\sigma_\infty(3)$ equals to 5 while $\sigma(3) = 4$. By definition, the value of $\sigma_\infty(x)$ depends on the starting point of the algorithm. For example $\forall\, \alpha \in \mathbb{N}_0$, $\sigma_\infty(2^\alpha) = \alpha$ as

$$T^\alpha(2^\alpha) = 1. \tag{4}$$

Analyzing the total stopping time $\forall\, x \in \mathbb{N}_0$ has proven challenging: the lack of clear patterns and the absence of an analytical shortcut to estimate $\sigma_\infty(x)$ have left practitioners with numerical methods to compute it and verify the conjecture. e Silva (2010) proved computationally that the conjecture holds up until $x = 20 \times 2^{58}$. Current computational capabilities have allowed confirming the conjecture for very large numbers. For example, Honda et al. (2017) introduced a GPU-based method to verify the Collatz algorithm. The authors could verify 1.31e12 64-bit numbers per second. A probabilistic approach is also a frequent workaround to justify the validity of the Collatz conjecture: assuming function $T^k(x)$ is "random enough", Crandall (1978) showed that half of the time, the next number in the sequence will be $(3x+1)/2$, then for the next iteration, $1/4$ of the time it will be $(3x+1)/4$, then for the next iteration, $1/8$ of the time it will be $(3x+1)/8$ and so on so that the average growth in the sequence will be $(\frac{3}{2})^{1/2}(\frac{3}{4})^{1/4}(\frac{3}{8})^{1/8}(\frac{3}{16})^{1/16}(\frac{3}{32})^{1/32}... = \frac{3}{4} < 1$. Terras (1976) demonstrated that the set of integers $\{x\!:\!-\, x$ has stopping time $\leq k\}$ has a limiting asymptotic density $F(k)$ with $F(k) \to 1$ as $k \to \infty$. These elements tend to indicate that $T^k(x)$ does not diverge to infinity as k grows. Using Minsky (1961) machines, Conway (1972) showed that a problem generalizing the Collatz conjecture is not algorithmically decidable. Kurtz and Simon (2007) extended the proof to show that this generalization is Π_0^2 complete. If the problem is truly algorithmically undecidable, then no information about the future inflation of the Collatz map is passed from one step k to the next step $k + 1$. To explore that hypothesis and the properties of this "pseudo-randomness", let us define

---

[1]   also called "trajectory" or "forward orbit".

the *inflation propensity of order K* $\xi(x, K)$ as the cardinality of the set of steps that lead to a number strictly larger than all previous numbers in the same sequence:

$$\xi(x, K) = \mathbf{card}\left\{ k : T^k(x) > \max(M_{x,k}) \right\}, k = 1, ..., k, ...K, \tag{5}$$

where $M_{x,k} = \left\{ T^0(x), T^1(x), ..., T^{k-1}(x) \right\}$. $\xi(x, \sigma_\infty(x))$ is a particular case. For the ease of notation: $\xi(x) = \xi(x, \sigma_\infty(x))$. In the above example of $x = 3$, $\xi(3) = 2$. Indeed, the set of numbers strictly larger than the previous maxima in the sequence are $\{5, 8\}$ so that $\xi(3) = \mathbf{card}\{5, 8\} = 2$. In the other example presented supra with $x = 2^\alpha$, $\xi(2^\alpha) = 0 \ \forall \ \alpha \in \mathbb{N}_0$ since no number in their sequences can be strictly larger than the initial one.

This research paper investigates the distribution of $\xi(x)$, the inflation propensity as a deterministic variable that resembles a random behavior. If past maxima anywhere in the sequence are independent from new maxima later computed in that orbit, we should have that $\xi(x) \sim G(\rho)$, a geometric distribution of parameter ρ with density $f(\xi(x) = y) = \rho^y(1 - \rho)$. The interests of fitting a density distribution to $\xi(x)$ are multiple. First, in absence of proof of the Collatz conjecture, numerical analysis of the problem stays relevant towards resolving the question. Second, by properly addressing the behavior of the series for large numbers, one can help anticipate the computational challenges related to exploring the orbits of the Collatz map. Third, identifying pseudo-random behavior of Collatz inflation propensity directly leads to a new class of proofs-of-work for blockchain applications. The remainder of this document is built as follows. The next section discusses the empirical distributions of $\sigma_\infty(x)$, $\sigma(x)$ and $\xi(x) \ \forall \ x \in \mathbb{N}_0$. The third section details the observed density of $\xi(x)$. The density parameter of a geometric distribution is estimated using all natural numbers up to 1×10^{11} as sample. The fourth section presents a new proof-of-work based on inflation propensity, while the last section is a conclusion.

2. Inflation Propensity

Lagarias (1985) describes the $3x + 1$ conjecture as "a deterministic process that simulates random behavior" and goes further to mention that the problem seems "structureless". Urvoy (2001) formally proves the non-regularity of the Collatz's graph. As a visual illustration of this "structurelessness", the total stopping time for the first 1×10^6 natural numbers as a function of their value is presented in Figure 1. The equally "structureless" empirical distribution of the total stopping time for the same numbers is presented in Figure 2. In this context, "structureless" means that it is impossible to anticipate the frequency of the total stopping time. This is unfortunate since it means observing the total stopping times over a region of $\mathbb{N}_0$ gives no information whatsoever on the Collatz problem apart from strictly verifying its convergence. The mean of the total stopping time totally depends on the region over which it is computed, and, even when considering a closed subset of $\mathbb{N}_0$, the distribution of the total stopping time appears to be erratic and does not seem to follow any regular pattern. As such, the total stopping time has no apparent statistical properties that could be useful in applications such as, for instance, generating random numbers.

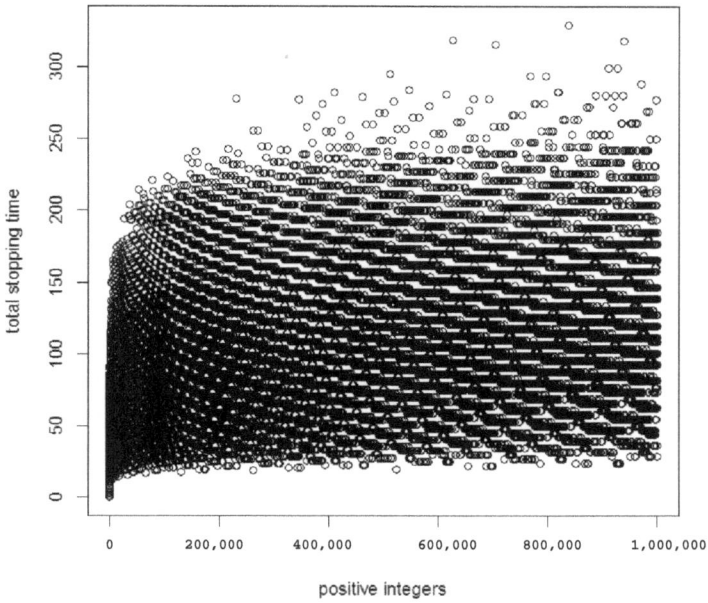

Figure 1. "Structureless" total stopping time for the first 1×10^6 natural numbers.

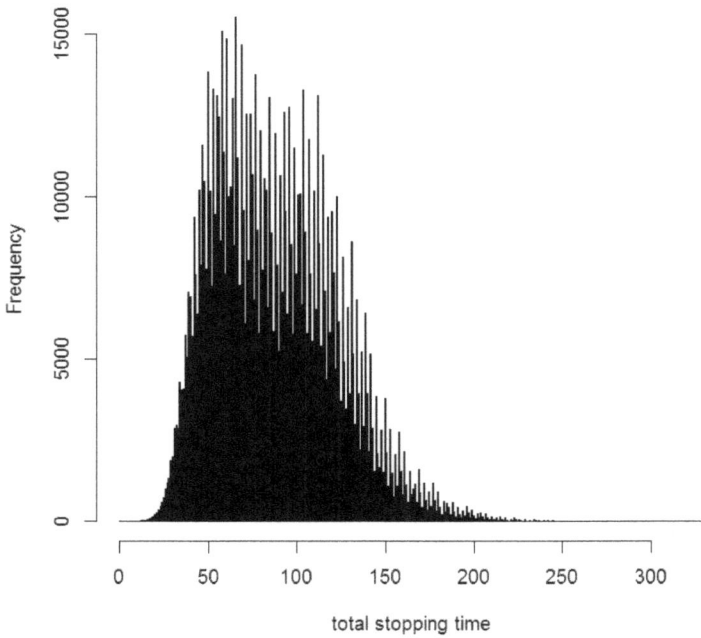

Figure 2. "Structureless" distribution of the total stopping time for the first 1×10^6 natural numbers.

Precisely because the Collatz graph is non-regular, its complexity gives rise to a pseudo-random behavior. Nichols (2018) and Kontorovich and Lagarias (2010) explore similarities between the Collatz model and the following dynamical system:

$$\log_2 T^K(x) \approx \log_2 x - K + b_3 \sum_{k=0}^{K} Y_k, \tag{6}$$

where b_3 is a constant and Y_k are IID (independent and identically distributed) Bernouilli random variables. The stochastic models predict that all orbits converge to a bounded set and that the total stopping time $\sigma_\infty(x)$ for the $3x + 1$ map of random starting point x is about 6.95212 $\log x$ steps, as $x \to \infty$ have a normal distribution centered around that value. The authors point out that a suitable scaling limit for the trajectories is a geometric Brownian motion. This approach is extended in the current research in order to find a discrete metric that could exhibit some type of consistency and is independent from the starting point x. If a geometric Brownian motion can properly describe trajectories of large orbits, it means its Markov property can be exploited: each marginal step in the orbit is independent from the previous step. As a consequence, the probability to find new maxima after any random point $T^k(x)$ of a large orbit does not depend on how many new maxima were discovered before that point. In other words, for any $x >> 4 \in \mathbb{N}$:

$$P\Big(\xi(x) > M \mid \xi(x) \geq \xi(x,k)\Big) = P\Big(\xi(x) > M - \xi(x,k)\Big), \tag{7}$$

where $M > \xi(x,k)$ and $M \in \mathbb{N}$. If the inflation propensity is memoryless as described by Equation (7), it directly implies that the density $f(\xi(x) = y)$ follows a geometric distribution. It would mean that

$$f(\xi(x) = y) = \rho^y(1 - \rho) \tag{8}$$

with $\rho \in \,]0;1[$ and $y \in \mathbb{N}$. The moment generating function is

$$\mu_n = Li_{-n}(\rho) - \rho Li_{-n}(\rho), \tag{9}$$

where $Li_n(\rho)$ is the nth polylogarithm of ρ and

$$\hat{\rho} = \frac{\mu_1}{1 + \mu_1} \tag{10}$$

is the corresponding estimator of ρ based on Equation (9). It is also the maximum likelihood estimator. The empirical distribution of $\xi(x)$ defined in (5) is presented in Figure 3. The next step is to test the hypothesis that $\xi(x) \sim G(\rho)$.

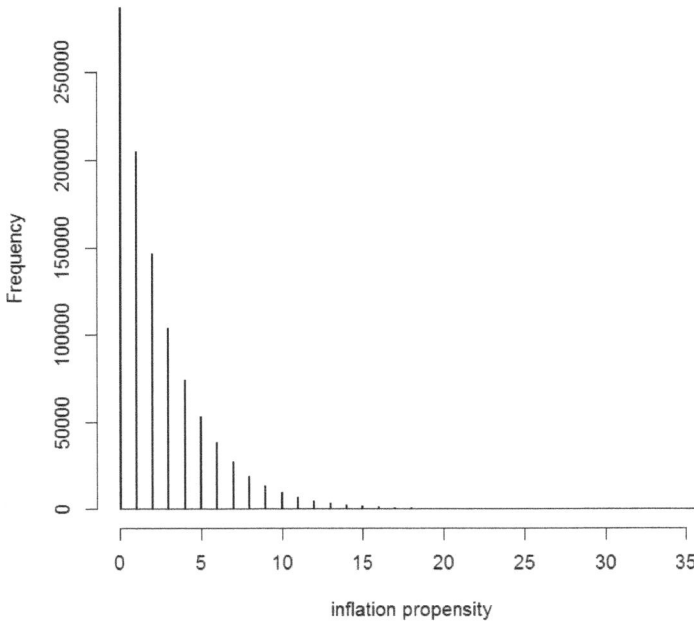

Figure 3. Quasi-geometric distribution of the inflation propensity for the first 1×10^6 natural numbers.

3. Empirical Results

The samples consist in the first 1×10^8, 1×10^9, 1×10^{10} and 1×10^{11} positive integers. For each sample, the maximum likelihood estimator of ρ is computed, then tests are performed to see if elements of the distribution follow a geometric distribution of parameter ρ:

$$H_0 : P(\xi(x) = n) = (1 - \rho)^{n-1}\rho \quad \forall n = 1, ..., q \tag{11}$$

$$H_1 : P(\xi(x) = n) \neq (1 - \rho)^{n-1}\rho \quad \forall n = 1, ..., q \tag{12}$$

where $q \in [0, N]$ and N is the largest observed maximum in the sample. When $q = N$, the entire distribution is tested for goodness of fit with a geometric distribution of parameter $\hat{\rho}$. The tests are performed using Pearson's χ^2 test at a 10% confidence level. Table 2 summarizes the results of the tests. As the sample size increases, the hypothesis is not rejected when it comes to considering the first quantiles of the distribution. For the last sample (1×10^{11}), the hypothesis that the distribution of the inflation propensity follows a geometric distribution cannot be rejected up to the 91th percentile, compared to the 49th percentile for the 1×10^9 sample. Computational limitations prevent at this stage investigating larger sample sizes so that the geometric behavior of the inflation propensity over the entire domain ($\mathbb{N}_0$) needs to be conjectured. Interestingly, the estimator for ρ seems also to converge to a given value as the size of the sample increases and is very close to $\frac{\pi-1}{3}$, which is coincidentally the solution to the equation $3x + 1 = \pi$ (see Figure 4). Table A1 in Appendix A indicates the distribution of inflation propensities for the first 1×10^{11} integers.

Table 2. Pearson's χ^2 tests for goodness of fit with a geometric distribution.

		Sample 1×10^8	Sample 1×10^9	Sample 1×10^{10}	Sample 1×10^{11}
$\hat{\rho}$		0.7133482	0.7135956	0.713667	0.713681
q	Percentile	*p*-Value	*p*-Value	*p*-Value	*p*-Value
0	29	0.01	**0.15**	**0.70**	**0.64**
1	49	0.04	**0.19**	**0.70**	**0.14**
2	64	0.09	0.00	**0.23**	**0.25**
3	74	**0.15**	0.00	**0.36**	**0.39**
4	82	0.08	0.00	**0.11**	**0.35**
5	87	0.05	0.00	0.01	**0.37**
6	91	0.07	0.00	0.00	**0.13**
7	93	**0.11**	0.00	0.00	0.03
8	95	0.00	0.00	0.00	0.04
9	97	0.00	0.00	0.00	0.03
10	98	0.00	0.00	0.00	0.00

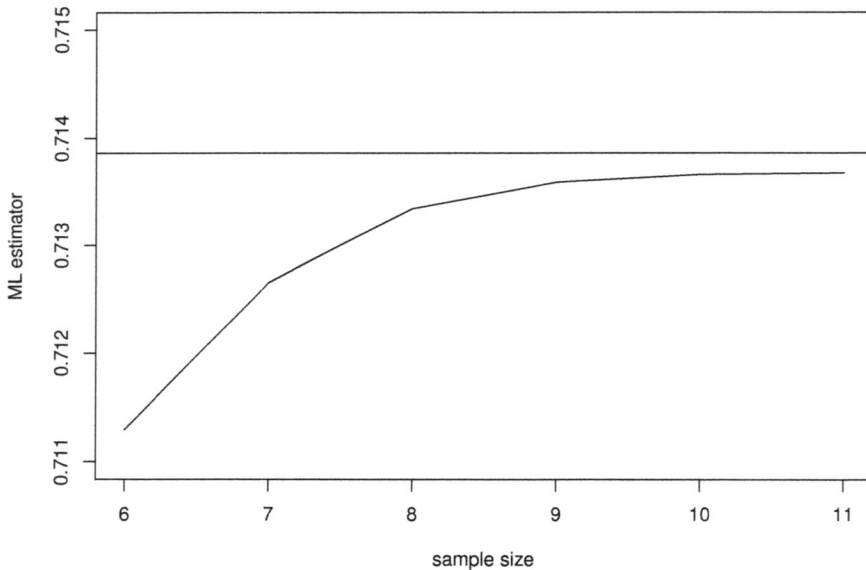

Figure 4. $\hat{\rho}$ as a function of the sample size (log10-scale).

4. Application

4.1. Collatz-Based Proof-of-Work

Because the distribution of the inflation propensity of Collatz orbits can be assumed to be geometric over large samples, and that a natural generalization of the Collatz algorithm has been proven to be undecidable, the inflation propensity can be considered as a new candidate to generate proofs-of-work, conjecturing the Collatz algorithm is also undecidable. Consider the following problem: find any set X made of n natural numbers $\{X_1, ..., X_i, ..., X_n\}$ whose values are between B and $B^* = B + \alpha$, a larger number, and that have inflation propensities of given values $\{Q_1, ..., Q_i, ..., Q_n\}$ with $n \ll \alpha$. In other terms, find a solution to the problem

$$Q_i = \xi(X_i) \quad \forall i \in \{1, ..., n\}, \tag{13}$$

where Q_i is known, $X_i \in [B, B^*]$ and $X_i \neq X_j \quad \forall i \neq j \in \{1, ..., n\}$. $\alpha, B, B^*, Q, X \in \mathbb{N}_0$. B is the unsigned integer value corresponding to a 256 bits block of hashed information. α is set to an arbitrarily large value, for example $\alpha = 2^{64}$. Note that this is still a fraction of the value for B so that pre-computation is virtually impossible in practice.

Since $P(\xi(X_i) = Q_i) \approx (\frac{\pi-1}{3})^{Q_i}(1 - \frac{\pi-1}{3})$ the difficulty to the problem can be designed in a straightforward manner: solutions for higher targets Q_i will be exponentially more difficult to find. Nevertheless, verifying the proof given inputs X and B is immediate, a desirable property for a proof-of-work. Once a valid solution set X has been found, the nounce ν is simply:

$$\nu = X - B, \tag{14}$$

which in practice is an array if X is a set and is an integer if X is a scalar. At the exception of the nonce and the target Q, the remainder of blockchain application based on Collatz is identical to the existing Bitcoin protocol. In practice, the target set Q can be selected by the network so that, similar to Bitcoin, six blocks are mined per hour. Every 2016 blocks, clients can compare the performance of the network and adjust the difficulty accordingly. Thanks to the geometric nature of the inflation propensity, a protocol for this adjustment is straightforward. Let us assume U_0 is the average amount of time required by the network to find any single value $\xi(x)$. Any total computational time $U_T \geq U_0$ can be easily selected by finding a set Q solving the following problem:

$$U_T = \sum_{q \in Q} \frac{1}{\rho^q} U_0 + \epsilon. \tag{15}$$

Two additional constraints must be considered for the protocol to be properly defined: the set Q must be chosen so that $0 \leq \epsilon \leq U_0$ and the cardinality of the set must be as small as possible.

4.2. Example: Bitcoin Genesis Hash

A new Bitcoin genesis hash is created using original inputs by Nakamoto (2008), but exploiting inflation propensity proof-of-work instead of hashcash. The inputs are: a hash merkle root that condenses all information related to the first Bitcoin transaction, a version number, a public key, a date, a time stamp that is used as coinbase parameter, and a target for complexity. A genesis block is the first block of a blockchain. Figure 5 illustrates the proof-of-work system. To create a genesis hash using inflation propensity as proof-of-work, only two adjustments to the Bitcoin protocol are required. First, the target for complexity is expressed with an integer, which is the targeted inflation propensity. This directly relates to a specific probability of occurrence. Second, the hashcash is replaced with the inflation propensity algorithm. In practice, the block header is hashed using SHA-256 then converted into an integer using hexadecimal encoding. This corresponds to B in Equation (14). The target set Q is arbitrarily set to a single value of 40 for the generation of this first hash, which corresponds to a probability of occurence of $\sim 4 \times 10^{-7}$. The value of B given Nakamoto's other initial inputs is of $\sim 2.52 \times 10^{76}$. The X nonce is then incrementally added to the integer B and inflation propensity is computed until the target of 40 is reached. The values obtained from each iteration are hereafter named "Xis". In the Python implementation of the algorithm, 2056 Xis are computed per second on an Intel Core i7-4700MQ CPU with 8×2.40 GHz. After 28 min of computation, the solution is found. Verification of the solution is done in $\approx 5 \times 10^{-4}$ seconds on the same machine. Table 3 describes diagnostics and results of the genesis hash. Using this first instance to calibrate the computational difficulty, the smallest set Q that solves Equation (15) that would yield an expected computational time of 10 min for the next block would be $\{2, 6, 16, 19, 22, 26, 31, 36, 41\}$. The Python code to generate the Genesis Hash is provided in Appendix B.

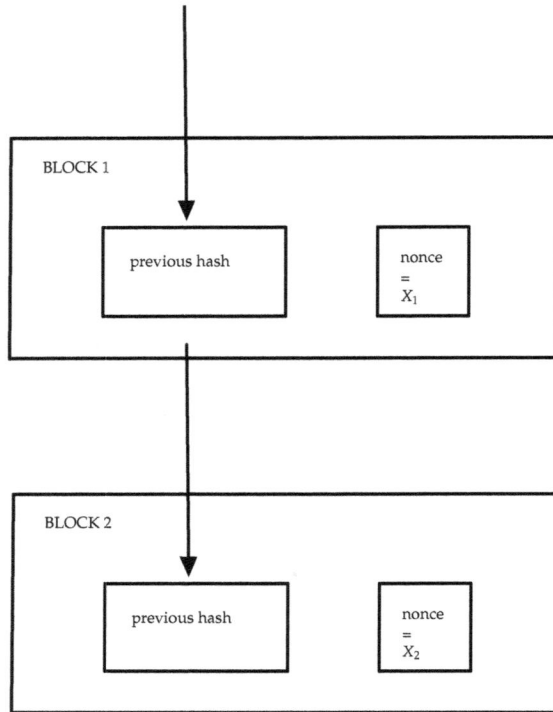

Figure 5. Proof-of-work system in the blockchain.

Table 3. A genesis hash based on original Bitcoin's inputs for genesis but using inflation propensity as proof-of-work.

block header hash	37d25f7f472fde7bb5b84f4bb319097c580383911b45eff10e68afa06073d6c0
corresponding integer	25248903652996148805237565338196318809513309980842754974279018460154571249344
merkle hash	4a5e1e4baab89f3a32518a88c31bc87f618f76673e2cc77ab2127b7afdeda33b
pszTimestamp	The Times 3 January 2009 Chancellor on brink of second bailout for banks
pubkey	04678afdb0fe5548271967f1a67130b7105cd6a828e03909a67962e0ea1f61deb649f6bc3f4cef38c4f 35504e51ec112de5c384df7ba0b8d578a4c702b6bf11d5f
time	1231006505
inflation propensity target	40 (0 × 28)
nounce	3420991
genesis hash	9ed4d59e375c60e568524ac7fdfcce2c36dd8d449a20b0be8c9f6f9dbd2f8709
computational time	28 min

4.3. Advantages of the Collatz-Based Proof-of-Work

The advantages of a Collatz-based proof-of-work are many. From a practitioner perspective, the algorithm is easy to implement in code since the underlying problem is made of simple arithmetic operations, however, bigint arithmetics are needed in case values inflate beyond 2^{256}. Also, the natural generalization of the Collatz algorithm is known to be algorithmically undecidable. If this holds for Collatz algorithm, asymmetry is guaranteed: it is difficult to find the targeted value but easy to verify. From an engineering point of view, difficulty control based on a geometric distribution is significantly more complex than one based on hashcash, however, from a statistical perspective, the geometric distribution allows a very convenient tailoring of the computational complexity. It is very easy to adjust a specific targeted inflation-propensity, or a combination of targets. The same algorithm can also be indefinitely extended to meet new computational improvements since the upper bound of the orbits is infinity. In addition to this scalability, it could be possible to generalize the $3x + 1$ algorithm to other congruential graphs exhibiting the same properties (for example, the $5x + 1$ graph). Provided further research confirms this hypothesis, such a feature could allow more possibilities to generate new proofs-of-work.

5. Conclusions

For the classical $3x + 1$ map, it is conjectured that inflation propensity $\xi(x) = \textbf{card}\left\{ k : T^k(x) > \max(M_{x,k}) \right\}, k = 1, ..., k, ...\sigma_\infty(x)$ has a geometric density distribution whose parameter's value $\rho \approx \frac{\pi - 1}{3}$. This has been verified numerically for the first 1×10^{11} integers. The inflation propensity of Collatz orbits is a new metric that exhibits properties particularly well suited to be the base for new cryptography applications. A new proof-of-work is suggested: finding a set X of n integers greater than a hashed block of information B but smaller than a threshold B^* such that their inflation propensities be of n given values $Q_1, ..., Q_n$. Advantages of this approach are multiple, including an infinite scalability and the possibility to easily tune complexity of the algorithm. This work seems to be the first number theoretic proof-of-work unrelated to primes. Further research is needed to generalize this type of proof-of-work to a larger class of congruential graphs.

Funding: This research received no external funding.

Conflicts of Interest: The author declares no conflicts of interest.

Appendix A. Distribution of Inflation Propensity for the First 1×10^{11} Integers

Table A1. Distribution of inflation propensity $\xi(x)$ for the first 1×10^{11} integers.

$\xi(x)$	Observations
0	28,631,964,381
1	20,434,254,718
2	14,583,348,496
3	10,407,804,534
4	7,427,954,284
5	5,301,161,512
6	3,783,166,989
7	2,699,976,430
8	1,927,052,441
9	1,375,229,862
10	981,424,318
11	700,353,911
12	499,868,474
13	356,795,944
14	254,706,290
15	181,761,315
16	129,757,032
17	92,628,127
18	66,127,176
19	47,199,172
20	33,676,458
21	24,024,158
22	17,138,021
23	12,231,945
24	8,727,118
25	6,225,787

Table A1. *Cont.*

$\zeta(x)$	Observations
26	4,432,544
27	3,162,432
28	2,251,004
29	1,599,248
30	1,139,341
31	814,975
32	583,455
33	416,994
34	298,683
35	212,914
36	150,443
37	106,613
38	76,749
39	55,452
40	39,947
41	28,495
42	20,259
43	14,253
44	10,396
45	7791
46	5431
47	3690
48	2640
49	1984
50	1448
51	1041
52	745
53	595
54	467
55	347
56	234
57	170
58	127
59	72
60	41
61	21
62	20
63	17
64	17
65	9
66	2
67	0
68	1
69	0

Appendix B. Python Code for Genesis Block

Modified from Hartikka (2017).

```python
import hashlib, struct, binascii, time, sys, optparse

from construct import *

def main():
    options = get_args()
    input_script = create_input_script(options.timestamp)
    output_script = create_output_script(options.pubkey)
    tx = create_transaction(input_script, output_script,options)
    hash_merkle_root = hashlib.sha256(hashlib.sha256(tx).digest()).digest()
    print_block_info(options, hash_merkle_root)
    block_header    = create_block_header(hash_merkle_root, options.time, options.bits, options.nonce)
    genesis_hash, nonce = generate_hash(block_header, options.nonce, options.bits)
    announce_found_genesis(genesis_hash, nonce)

def get_args():
    parser = optparse.OptionParser()
    parser.add_option("-t", "--time", dest="time", default=int(1231006505), type="int", help="the (unix) time when the genesisblock is created")
    parser.add_option("-z", "--timestamp", dest="timestamp", default=
    "The Times 03/Jan/2009 Chancellor on brink of second bailout for banks",
    type="string", help="the pszTimestamp found in the coinbase of the genesisblock")
    parser.add_option("-n", "--nonce", dest="nonce", default=0,
    type="int", help="the first value of the nonce that will be incremented when searching the genesis hash")
    parser.add_option("-p", "--pubkey", dest="pubkey", default="04678afdb0fe5548271967f1a67130b7105cd6a828e03909a67962e0ea1f61deb649f6bc3f4cef38c4f35504e51ec112de5c384df7ba0b8d578a4c702b6bf11d5f",
    type="string", help="the pubkey found in the output script")
    parser.add_option("-v", "--value", dest="value", default=5000000000,
    type="int", help="the value in coins for the output, full value (exp. in bitcoin 5000000000)
    - To get other coins value: Block Value * 100000000)")
    parser.add_option("-b", "--bits", dest="bits",
```

```python
        type="int", help="the target in compact representation, associated to a difficulty of 1")
    (options, args) = parser.parse_args()
    if not options.bits:
        options.bits = 40
    return options

def create_input_script(psz_timestamp):
    psz_prefix = ""
    if len(psz_timestamp) > 76: psz_prefix = '4c'
    script_prefix = '04ffff001d0104' + psz_prefix + chr(len(psz_timestamp)).encode('hex')
    print (script_prefix + psz_timestamp.encode('hex'))
    return (script_prefix + psz_timestamp.encode('hex')).decode('hex')

def create_output_script(pubkey):
    script_len = '41'
    OP_CHECKSIG = 'ac'
    return (script_len + pubkey + OP_CHECKSIG).decode('hex')

def create_transaction(input_script, output_script, options):
    transaction = Struct("transaction",
        Bytes("version", 4),
        Byte("num_inputs"),
        StaticField("prev_output", 32),
        UBInt32('prev_out_idx'),
        Byte('input_script_len'),
        Bytes('input_script', len(input_script)),
        UBInt32('sequence'),
        Byte('num_outputs'),
        Bytes('out_value', 8),
        Byte('output_script_len'),
        Bytes('output_script', 0x43),
        UBInt32('locktime'))

tx = transaction.parse('\x00'*(127 + len(input_script)))
tx.version        = struct.pack('<I', 1)
```

```python
tx.num_inputs       = 1
tx.prev_output      = struct.pack('<qqqq', 0,0,0,0)
tx.prev_out_idx     = 0xFFFFFFFF
tx.input_script_len = len(input_script)
tx.input_script     = input_script
tx.sequence         = 0xFFFFFFFF
tx.num_outputs      = 1
tx.out_value        = struct.pack('<q' ,options.value)
tx.output_script_len = 0x43
tx.output_script    = output_script
tx.locktime         = 0
return transaction.build(tx)


def create_block_header(hash_merkle_root, time, bits, nonce):
block_header = Struct("block_header",
Bytes("version",4),
Bytes("hash_prev_block", 32),
Bytes("hash_merkle_root", 32),
Bytes("time", 4),
Bytes("bits", 4),
Bytes("nonce", 4))


genesisblock = block_header.parse('\x00'*80)
genesisblock.version            = struct.pack('<I', 1)
genesisblock.hash_prev_block = struct.pack('<qqqq', 0,0,0,0)
genesisblock.hash_merkle_root = hash_merkle_root
genesisblock.time            = struct.pack('<I', time)
genesisblock.bits            = struct.pack('<I', bits)
genesisblock.nonce           = struct.pack('<I', nonce)
return block_header.build(genesisblock)

#Collatz inflation propensity
def inflation_propensity(x):
xMax=x
stepToMaximum=0
```

```python
    while x > 1:
        if x % 2 == 0:
            x = x / 2
        else:
            x = (3 * x + 1) / 2
        if x > xMax:
            xMax=x
        stepToMaximum+= 1
    return stepToMaximum

def generate_hash(data_block, start_nonce, bits):
    print 'Searching for genesis hash..'
    nonce       = start_nonce
    last_updated    = time.time()
    header_hash = generate_hashes_from_block(data_block)
    print(binascii.hexlify(header_hash))
    orbitTrajectory=int(header_hash.encode('hex_codec'), 16)
    print(orbitTrajectory)
    timeInit=time.time()
    while True:
        xi=inflation_propensity(orbitTrajectory)
        last_updated = calculate_hashrate(nonce, last_updated, orbitTrajectory,timeInit)
        if xi==bits:
            return (generate_hashes_from_block(data_block), nonce)
        else:
            nonce      = nonce + 1
            orbitTrajectory += 1
            data_block = data_block[0:len(data_block) - 4] + struct.pack('<I', nonce)

def generate_hashes_from_block(data_block):
    header_hash = hashlib.sha256(hashlib.sha256(data_block).digest()).digest()[::-1]
    return header_hash

def calculate_hashrate(nonce, last_updated, orbitTrajectory, timeinit):
    if nonce % 10000 == 0:
```

```
now            = time.time()
hashrate       = round(10000/(now - last_updated))
sys.stdout.write("\r%s Xis/s, Orbit: %s, Total time: %s minutes "
%(str(hashrate), str(orbitTrajectory), str((now-timeinit)/60)))
sys.stdout.flush()
return now
else:
return last_updated

def print_block_info(options, hash_merkle_root):
print "merkle hash: " + hash_merkle_root[::-1].encode('hex_codec')
print "pszTimestamp: " + options.timestamp
print "pubkey: "       + options.pubkey
print "time: "         + str(options.time)
print "bits: "         + str(hex(options.bits))

def announce_found_genesis(genesis_hash, nonce):
print "genesis hash found!"
print "nonce: "        + str(nonce)
print "genesis hash: " + genesis_hash.encode('hex_codec')

main()
```

References

Back, Adam. 2002. Hashcash-A Denial of Service Counter-Measure. Available online: http://hashcash.org/papers/hashcash.pdf (accessed on 25 November 2018).

Bae, Minyoung, Ju-Sung Kang, and Yongjin Yeom. 2017. A Study on the One-to-Many Authentication Scheme for Cryptosystem Based on Quantum Key Distribution. Paper presented at IEEE Conference on Platform Technology and Service (PlatCon), Busan, Korea, February 13–15, pp. 1–4.

Biryukov, Alex, and Dmitry Khovratovich. 2017. Equihash: Asymmetric proof-of-work based on the generalized birthday problem. *Ledger* 2: 1–30. [CrossRef]

Conway, John H. 1972. Unpredictable iterations. Paper presented at 1972 Number Theory Conference, Boulder, CO, USA, August 14–18, pp. 49–52.

Crandall, Richard E. 1978. On the 3x + 1 problem. *Mathematics of Computation* 32: 1281–92.

Dwork, Cynthia, and Moni Naor. 1992. Pricing via processing or combatting junk mail. Paper presented at Annual International Cryptology Conference, Santa Barbara, CA, USA, August 16–20. Berlin and Heidelberg: Springer, pp. 139–47.

e Silva, T. Oliveira. 2010. Empirical verification of the 3x+ 1 and related conjectures. In *The Ultimate Challenge: The 3x+ 1 Problem*. Edited by Jeffrey C. Lagarias. Providence: American Mathematical Society, pp. 189–207. ISBN 978-0821849408.

Hartikka, Lauri. 2017. GenesisH0. Available online: https://github.com/lhartikk/GenesisH0 (accessed on 1 September 2018).

Honda, Takumi, Yasuaki Ito, and Koji Nakano. 2017. GPU-accelerated Exhaustive Verification of the Collatz Conjecture. *International Journal of Networking and Computing* 7: 69–85. [CrossRef]

King, Sunny. 2013. Primecoin: Cryptocurrency with Prime Number Proof-of-Work. *Bitcoin Magazine*, July 7.

Kiktenko, Evgeniy O., Nikolay O. Pozhar, Maxim N. Anufriev, Anton S. Trushechkin Ruslan R. Yunusov, Yuri V. Kurochkin, and Aleksey K. Fedorov. 2018. Quantum-secured blockchain. *Quantum Science and Technology* 3: 035004. [CrossRef]

Kontorovich, Alex V., and Jeffrey C. Lagarias. 2010. Stochastic models for the 3x+ 1 and 5x+ 1 problems and related problems. In *The Ultimate Challenge: The 3x+ 1 Problem*. Edited by Jeffrey C. Lagarias. Providence: American Mathematical Society, pp. 131–88. ISBN 978-0821849408.

Kurtz, Stuart A., and Janos Simon. 2007. The undecidability of the generalized Collatz problem. Paper presented at International Conference on Theory and Applications of Models of Computation, Shanghai, China, May 22–25. Berlin and Heidelberg: Springer, pp. 542–53.

Lagarias, Jeffrey C. 1985. The 3x+ 1 problem and its generalizations. *The American Mathematical Monthly* 92: 3–23. [CrossRef]

Lagarias, Jeffrey C., ed. 2010. The 3x+1 problem: An overview. In *The Ultimate Challenge: The 3x+ 1 Problem*. Providence: American Mathematical Society, pp. 3–30. ISBN 978-0821849408.

Minsky, Marvin L. 1961. Recursive unsolvability of Post's problem of "tag" and other topics in the theory of Turing machines. *Annals of Mathematics* 74: 437–55. [CrossRef]

Nakamoto, Satoshi. 2008. *Bitcoin: A Peer-to-Peer Electronic Cash System*. Self-published.

Nichols, Daniel. 2018. Analogues of the 3x + 1 Problem in Polynomial Rings of Characteristic 2. *Experimental Mathematics* 27: 100–10. [CrossRef]

Percival, Colin. 2009. *Stronger Key Derivation via Sequential Memory-Hard Functions*. Self-published.

Rubin, Jeremy. 2017. *The Problem with ASICBOOST*. Self-published.

Terras, Riho. 1976. A stopping time problem on the positive integers. *Acta Arithmetica* 30: 241–52. [CrossRef]

Tromp, John. 2015. Cuckoo cycle: A memory bound graph-theoretic proof-of-work. Paper presented at International Conference on Financial Cryptography and Data Security, San Juan, PR, USA, January 26–30. Berlin and Heidelberg: Springer, pp. 49–62.

J. Risk Financial Manag. **2018**, *11*, 83

Urvoy, Tanguy. 2001. Regularity of congruential graphs. Paper presented at Mathematical Foundations of Computer Science 2000, MFCS 2000, Bratislava, Slovakia, August 28–September 1. Edited by Mogens Nielsen and Branislav Rovan. Lecture Notes in Computer Science. Berlin and Heidelberg: Springer, vol. 1893.

Wood, Gavin. 2014. Ethereum: A secure decentralised generalised transaction ledger. *Ethereum Project Yellow Paper* 151: 1–32.

Journal of
*Risk and Financial
Management*

MDPI

Article

Trend Prediction Classification for High Frequency Bitcoin Time Series with Deep Learning

Takuya Shintate and Lukáš Pichl *

Graduate School of Arts and Sciences, International Christian University, Osawa 3-10-2, Mitaka, Tokyo 181-8585, Japan; g196729a@icu.ac.jp
* Correspondence: lukas@icu.ac.jp; Tel.: +81-422-33-3286

Received: 25 December 2018; Accepted: 17 January 2019; Published: 21 January 2019

Abstract: We provide a trend prediction classification framework named the random sampling method (RSM) for cryptocurrency time series that are non-stationary. This framework is based on deep learning (DL). We compare the performance of our approach to two classical baseline methods in the case of the prediction of unstable Bitcoin prices in the OkCoin market and show that the baseline approaches are easily biased by class imbalance, whereas our model mitigates this problem. We also show that the classification performance of our method expressed as the F-measure substantially exceeds the odds of a uniform random process with three outcomes, proving that extraction of deterministic patterns for trend classification, and hence market prediction, is possible to some degree. The profit rates based on RSM outperformed those based on LSTM, although they did not exceed those of the buy-and-hold strategy within the testing data period, and thus do not provide a basis for algorithmic trading.

Keywords: cryptocurrency; metric learning; classification framework; time series; trend prediction

1. Introduction

Machine learning (ML) methods adapted from among deep learning algorithms have been recently applied to financial time series prediction with a number of publications in computer science journals (Greff et al. 2017; Fe-Fei et al. 2003; Zhang et al. 2018), as well as in economics and finance journals (Koutmos 2018; Kristoufek 2018). There is a gap in the existing literature, however, which is pronounced in the uncovered field of the applications of machine learning methods for time series to cryptocurrency trading data. In this work, we aim to provide a benchmark as to how efficient the modern ML algorithms can be in view of their applicability to the high-frequency trading data on the minute scale. The application of deep learning techniques faces a difficult trade-off: deep learning algorithms require a large number of data samples to learn from, implying in practice high-frequency data, such as minute-sampled trade records, whereas the training patterns over long periods are not always stationary, meaning varying patterns may be extracted from different segments of the training dataset.

The applicability of deep learning to high-frequency market prediction is still an open problem. Recently, some empirical results (Mäkinen et al. 2018; Sirignano and Cont 2018; Zhang et al. 2018) with deep learning algorithms showed that there might be a universal price formulation for the deterministic part of trading behavior to some degree, which implies financial data at high frequency exhibit some stylized facts and could posses learnable patterns that are stationary over long time periods. The aforementioned references used order-driven data (limit order book) and trained recurrent neural networks with the huge number of data. In this paper, we take a different approach: we provide a metric learning-based (Cinbis et al. 2011; Koch 2015; Vinyals et al. 2016; Xing et al. 2003) method, which we call the random sampling method (RSM). We measure the similarity between the input pattern and the training samples with the novel sampling scheme, which we describe below. Then, the label of the most similar data point becomes an output candidate for the prediction of our model.

The present approach is motivated by the highly non-stationary dynamics in digital assets as volatile as cryptocurrencies, in particular Bitcoin. State-of-the-art deep learning algorithms for time series, such as the long short-term memory (LSTM) method (Gers et al. 2000; Hochreiter and Schmidhuber 1997) require large datasets for training, and thus suffer from the fact that the causal patterns in the cryptocurrency time series may change quite substantially in the training and testing datasets, resulting therefore in insufficient prediction performance, noise fitting, and inconsistent results. For Bitcoin, recent data patterns are more relevant for trend prediction than more distant data, which practically limits the number of samples for each class. Here, we therefore adapt the metric learning method in which the algorithm finds the best recent patterns to be labeled for optimal prediction (Fe-Fei et al. 2003; Lake et al. 2014, 2011, 2015; Li et al. 2006). The works in (Graves et al. 2014; Koch 2015; Santoro et al. 2016; Vinyals et al. 2016) showed how to deploy deep learning algorithms for such purposes in various applications.

2. Task Settings

2.1. Classification Problem

First, assume that there are three possible events where the price at time step t can move, i.e., up, down, or static (Equation (2)). Precisely, the meaning is given by taking the histogram of the logarithmic return defined as:

$$R_t = \log \left(\frac{P_t}{P_{t-1}} \right) \tag{1}$$

and partitioning it by 1/3 and 2/3 quantiles. The distribution of R_t is approximately symmetric and stationary. We will denote by $p_t^{(up)}$, $p_t^{(down)}$, and $p_t^{(static)}$ the probabilities with which each event happens, and we estimate them later in our model. Thus, we now have a classification problem,

$$X_t \in \{up, down, static\} \tag{2}$$

2.2. Non-Stationarity

In particular, we consider the situation where $p_t^{(up)}$, $p_t^{(down)}$, and $p_t^{(static)}$ are changing as a function of time. From the viewpoint of machine learning algorithms, it may happen that the models trained on such a dataset are more biased to some class and possibly cannot deal with class imbalance correctly when these are evaluated on a totally different regime. In order to alleviate this problematic situation, we resort to the so-called walk forward optimization method (Dixon et al. 2017) (cf. Figure 1), which trains a model on limited data points in a train window and tests in a test window, then moves both windows to the right and trains the model again. This method enables us to utilize the assumption that the distribution behind the dataset is stationary, and the learning thus becomes more stable. However, data-driven methods such as deep learning could not generalize well with the limited train data, and a model may suffer from non-stationarity even on a limited length dataset.

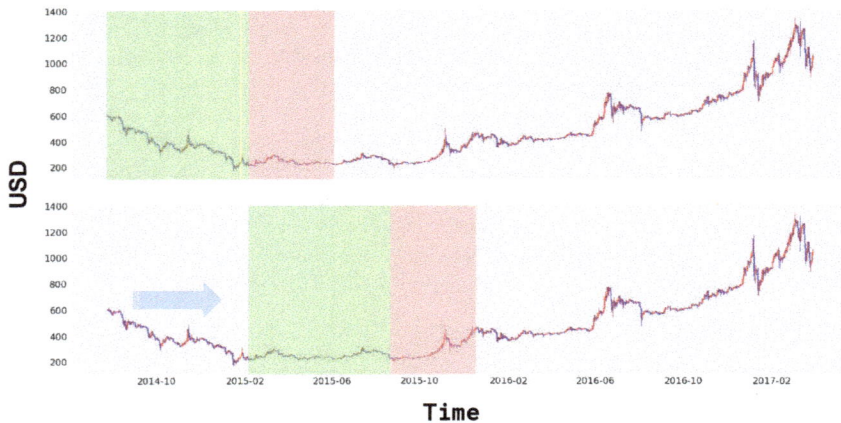

Figure 1. Visualization for walk-forward optimization. It uses the data points in a train window (green box) and a test window (red box), one at a time. After finishing training a model with the dataset, the two windows move to the right, and training begins again until the windows hit the end of the time series.

The principle of the algorithm is as follows. We assume that if a pair of sequences (e.g., $x_{t-1}, x_{t-2} \cdots, x_{t-T-1}$, and $x_{i-1}, x_{i-2}, \cdots, x_{i-T-1}$) is similar to some measure, the distribution $p_t^{(up)}$, $p_t^{(down)}$, and $p_t^{(static)}$ and $p_i^{(up)}$, $p_i^{(down)}$, and $p_i^{(static)}$, which are conditioned on each sequence, are also similar. Therefore, we train our model to learn how to measure a pair of sequences in order to forecast the future trend label.

3. Random Sampling Method

In this section, we detail the sampling scheme and the model developed in this paper. The model is also compared to the reference baseline cases.

3.1. Concept

Our approach was broadly inspired by recent deep learning (DL) developments in the field of image processing. According to (Hilliard et al. 2018), "Learning high quality class representations from few examples is a key problem in metric-learning approaches to few-shot learning". We faced the same problem, i.e., the limitation of the number of data relevant to training and the absence of knowledge about a suitable feature space transform that enters the similarity metric. Similar to (Hilliard et al. 2018), instead of using a static metric comparison, we trained the network to learn how to compare among sequence patterns belonging to different classes. The work in (Hilliard et al. 2018) found that such a flexible architecture provides superior results in the case of image classification task. In our case of cryptocurrency time series, it helped us to address the highly non-stationary character of the time series and to mitigate the class imbalance problem. Our metric learning implementation for the classification task of trend prediction follows (Lake et al. 2011; Li et al. 2006). Our approach is novel in adapting the above outlined classification framework to the field of time series and has yet to be applied to cryptocurrency data and Bitcoin in particular, according to the best of our knowledge.

In particular, we assumed that the similarity of a pair of sequences can be characterized by the classes to which they belong, e.g., a sequence labeled up was more similar to a sequence labeled up than sequences labeled down or static. In this sense, we optimized parametrized models (neural networks in this case) to output the hidden representations, where the hidden representations of inputs labeled by the same class were more similar to the predicted output than those of other classes, using the cosine similarity measure.

In our framework, the input was a pair of a sequence, which we wanted to classify, and sequences (there were three sequences labeled as up, down, and static, respectively) sampled from the recent past (Figure 2). Then, we obtained hidden representations by encoding each sequence independently and output the most similar class by comparing the hidden representation of the input sequence and the hidden representations of the sampled sequences.

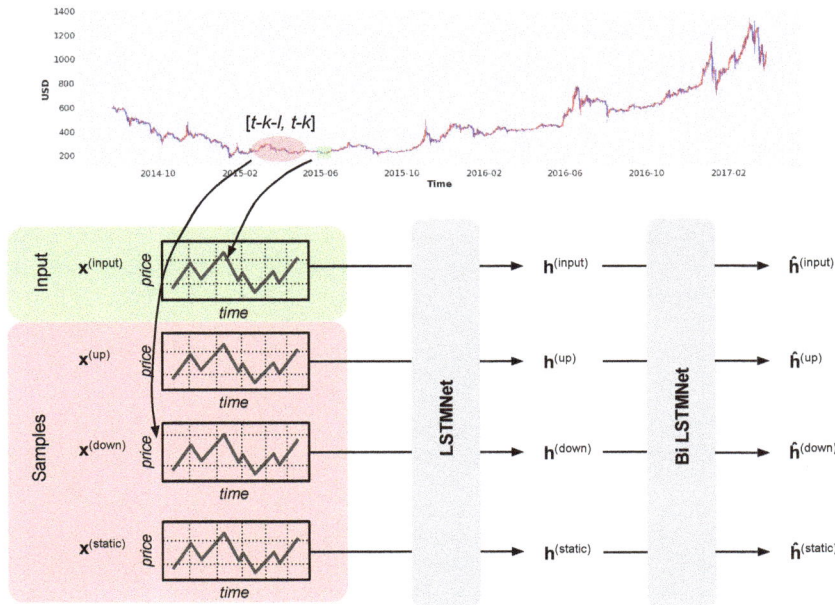

Figure 2. Visualization of the pipeline. Given inputs $x_t^{(input)}$, sequences $x_t^{(up)}$, $x_t^{(down)}$, $x_t^{(static)}$ are randomly sampled in the red window. Then, the input and samples are independently encoded with LSTMNet (Equation (3)) and bi-directional LSTMNet (Equation (4)). Refer to the text for more details.

3.2. Sampling Scheme

We set a sampling scheme based on the assumption that financial data are non-stationary. Therefore, we assumed we needed to sample sequences only observed recently. Formally, given input sequence x_t, our sampling scheme was to sample sequences from the closed interval $[t - k - l, t - k]$ where k is a window size for the simple moving average (see Section 5.2 for details) and l is a hyperparameter to determine the size of this interval (we set it to 10,080). We perform an experiment on how changing the sampling scheme affects the model performance in a later section.

We did rather minimal preprocessing of the dataset, removing the obvious outliers. In particular, we removed a sequence labeled up or down if $|R_t| > \alpha$ was satisfied (R_t is defined in Equation (1)). Here, α is the threshold, and we set it to 0.3 for BTCCNY and 0.1 for BTCUSD.

3.3. Encoder

Encoder (Figure 2) was used to lift a sequence to a corresponding hidden representation. We used cosine similarity to measure the similarity of a pair of hidden representations.

Encoder is composed of two modules. Here, we call a tth input sequence $x_t^{(input)}$ and the tth samples $x_t^{(up)}$, $x_t^{(down)}$, and $x_t^{(static)}$. Then, a tth input sequence and the samples are converted to $h_t^{(input)}$, $h_t^{(up)}$, $h_t^{(down)}$ and $h_t^{(static)}$ independently by LSTMNet defined in Equation (3) (we omit superscripts for simplicity). LSTMNet is an LSTM network (a recurrent neural network composed of LSTM units is called an LSTM network in this paper). In our settings, the LSTMNet had two layers, and each layer had 32 LSTM units.

$$\mathbf{h}_t = \text{LSTMNet}\,(\mathbf{x}_t) \tag{3}$$

Then, $\mathbf{h}_t^{(input)}$, $\mathbf{h}_t^{(up)}$, $\mathbf{h}_t^{(down)}$, and $\mathbf{h}_t^{(static)}$ are related to each other by a bi-directional LSTM network (Schuster and Paliwal 1997; Yao and Huang 2016), which takes as an input the aligned sequence of $\mathbf{h}_t^{(input)}$, $\mathbf{h}_t^{(up)}$, $\mathbf{h}_t^{(down)}$, and $\mathbf{h}_t^{(static)}$. It processes the aligned sequence in the order $\mathbf{h}_t^{(input)}$, $\mathbf{h}_t^{(up)}$, $\mathbf{h}_t^{(down)}$, and $\mathbf{h}_t^{(static)}$ and in the reversed order $\mathbf{h}_t^{(static)}$, $\mathbf{h}_t^{(down)}$, $\mathbf{h}_t^{(up)}$, and $\mathbf{h}_t^{(input)}$. It outputs the result of the addition (Equation (4)) where $\overrightarrow{\mathbf{h}}_{ti}$ is the ith output of the bi-directional LSTM network (on the tth sequence and the samples) in the aligned order, and $\overleftarrow{\mathbf{h}}_{ti}$ is the ith output in the reversed order. We refer to (Vinyals et al. 2016) for this operation. In our settings, the bi-directional LSTM network also had two layers, and each layer had 32 LSTM units. The total hidden feature $\hat{\mathbf{h}}_{ti}$ is given by the encoder equation below.

$$\hat{\mathbf{h}}_{ti} = \overrightarrow{\mathbf{h}}_{ti} + \overleftarrow{\mathbf{h}}_{ti} + \mathbf{h}_{ti} \tag{4}$$

We measured the similarity between hidden representations of an input sequence and samples with cosine similarity and the class to which the sample that was the most similar belongs became the output.

4. Dataset

We used the OkCoin Bitcoin market (CNY and USD) time series data at a minute frequency. The dataset was provided commercially by Kaiko data. Figure 3 shows OHLC (Open, High, Low, Close) price time series in CNY and the transaction volume dynamics in Bitcoin. The horizontal axis is time, and the vertical axis is the price of Bitcoin in CNY. The data ranged from 13 June 2013–18 March 2017. We chose this dataset because as Figure 3 may suggest, the distribution behind each class changes rapidly, which is in accord with our non-stationarity assumption. Figure 4 shows the OHLC price time series in USD and the transaction volume dynamics in Bitcoin. The data ranged from 25 July 2014–29 March 2017. We have computed the high frequency returns on a minute scale and a half-an-hour scale for reference, which are shown in Figure 5. It can be seen that on the minute scale, there was a difference between the exchange markets in the two fiat currencies, with larger volatility in CNY minute prices; the difference almost disappeared, however, on the aggregation scale of 30 min. We have performed the Kolmogorov–Smirnov test, which strictly ruled out the Gaussian shape of all distributions, both for CNY and USD, on the scales of 1 min and 30 min. Heavy tails were observed in all datasets, which cannot be explained by the normal distribution hypothesis. These features are in good accord with the statistical analysis in (Bariviera et al. 2017; Gkillas and Katsiampa 2018; Gkillas et al. 2018), which provided a much more detailed record of the long-range behavior of Bitcoin returns and their stylized facts.

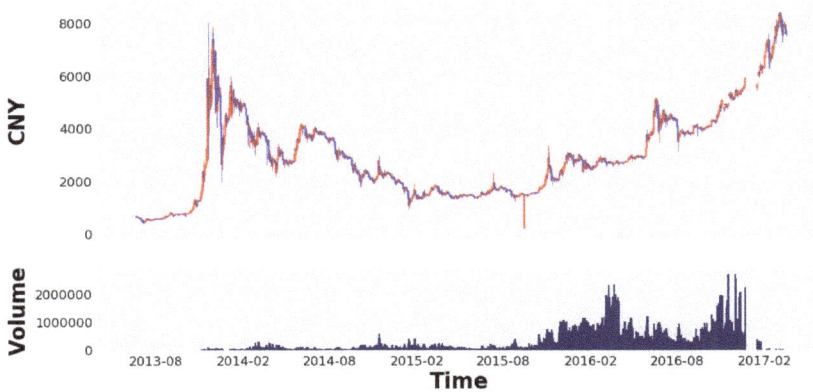

Figure 3. OHLC plot (Bitcoin price in CNY). The price peaks at the end of 2013 and gradually decreases toward the middle of 2015. Then, it recovers and peaks at the beginning of 2017. The price forms a u-shape in the long run. Note that the price highly fluctuates at the beginning of 2017 when Bitcoin markets were regulated in China. This caused class imbalance in the testing dataset (Figure 6).

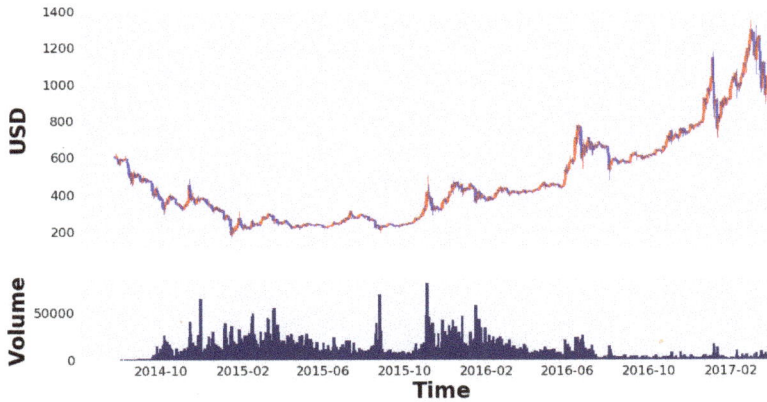

Figure 4. OHLC plot (Bitcoin price in USD). The dataset begins at the latter half of 2014. The price peaks at the beginning of 2017 in the same way as CNY, cf. Figure 3. Transaction volume was relatively constant before June 2016, whereas the volume of BTCCNY transactions in Figure 3 increased dramatically after the beginning of 2016.

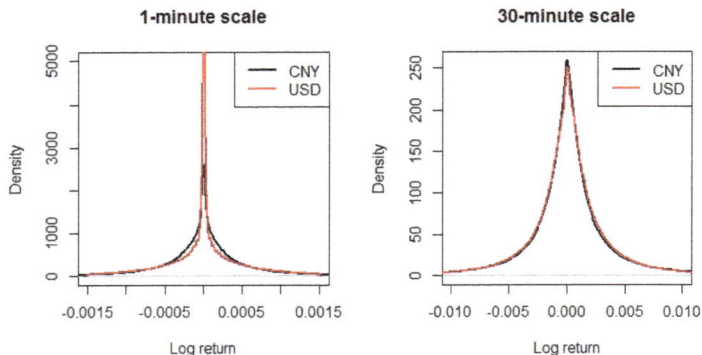

Figure 5. Distribution of high-frequency returns computed from closing prices on a minute scale and a half-an-hour scale for Bitcoin prices in CNY (black) and USD (red). A non-Gaussian shape is observed in all cases.

5. Preprocessing of Data

5.1. Input

We used raw OHLC time series as input. Each input sequence had a length $j = 32$. Since OHLC time series are assumed non-stationary, we first extracted a sequence from the dataset and then applied max-min normalization (Equation (5)) to it. Here, $\mathbf{x}_{ti}$ means the ith OHLC data in the tth time point's input sequence, and the normalization reads

$$\hat{\mathbf{x}}_{ti} = \frac{\mathbf{x}_{ti} - \min(\mathbf{x}_t)}{\max(\mathbf{x}_t) - \min(\mathbf{x}_t)},\tag{5}$$

where the operations of taking the minimum and maximum are applied to the components of $\mathbf{x}_{ti}$ for all $i = 1, \ldots, 4$ in the range of $[t - 31, \ldots, t]$.

5.2. Target

The target is represented as one-hot vectors in which the true class was set to one and the others were set to zero. Our model was trained to minimize the cross-entropy loss function.

Let us denote by m_t the average of prices over a moving window sized $T = 30$ min preceding time t. Then, the target labeling follows Equation (6),

$$y_t = \begin{cases} -1, & \text{if } m_t > m_{t+T} + \epsilon \\ 1, & \text{if } m_t < m_{t+T} - \epsilon \\ 0, & \text{otherwise} \end{cases}\tag{6}$$

Here, ϵ is the threshold parameter to control the class balance (we set it to 1.55 for BTCCNY and 0.24 for BTCUSD to adjust the class balance over the entire dataset). The distribution of the labels in the training and testing datasets is shown in Figure 6.

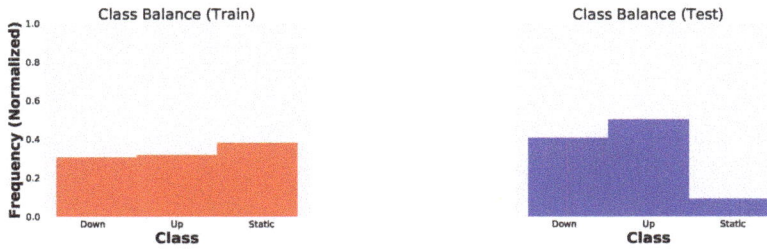

Figure 6. Comparative histogram of training and testing data points (BTCCNY in the OkCoin market). It shows that there was a crucial class imbalance in the testing data, whereas the data points in the training data were relatively balanced. This imbalance is also implied in Figure 3.

6. Experiment

6.1. Settings

The rectified linear unit (ReLU) was used as the activation function in all layers (without the output layer,) which leverages sparsity and improves learning stabilization, even in deep architectures (Glorot et al. 2011). We used as the optimizer the method of Adam (Kingma and Ba 2014). The learning rate was set to 10^{-3}, and we used the same hyperparameter values as the reference paper suggested.

The dataset (BTCCNY) was separated into the training, validation, and testing segments, as follows. For the baseline models, the training set consisted of 920,484 min, validation of 120,000 min, and testing of 120,000 min. For the present method, RSM, the training period was shortened to 910,352 min, whereas the validation and testing sets were both 120,000 min long. Multiple evaluations were performed for each method and evaluated on the validation dataset using early stopping. The coefficient of variation of the validation results between various runs was at the level of 0.1%, meaning the first two significant digits were stable in the validation phase. The selected model was then benchmarked on the testing set using standard metrics for all tables reported in the following subsections.

6.2. Trend Prediction

We have used multi-layer perceptron (MLP) and an LSTM network as baselines (see Appendix A for more details about LSTM). Both MLP and the LSTM network had two layers, and each layer had 32 hidden units. We computed the probability distribution and selected the class with the maximum probability. Metric scores of accuracy, recall, precision, and the F1 measure are given in Table 1 for BTCCNY dataset and in Table 2 for BTCUSD data set.

Table 1. Model evaluation scores on accuracy, recall, precision, and F1 measure. Bitcoin price in Chinese yuan (BTCCNY) from the OkCoin market is used as the dataset. We use the last 120k data points for the evaluation, which were not used in training and validation. RSM, random sampling method. The highest score among the methods is printed in bold in each column.

	Accuracy	Recall	Precision	F1 Score
MLP	0.4766	0.4570	0.4822	0.4511
LSTM	0.4688	0.4877	**0.5581**	0.4657
RSM (*ours*)	**0.5353**	**0.5182**	0.5458	**0.5092**

Table 2. Model evaluation scores on accuracy, recall, precision, and F1 measure. Bitcoin price in U.S. dollar (BTCUSD) from the OkCoin market was used as the dataset. We used the last 120k data points for the evaluation, which were not used in training and validation.

	Accuracy	Recall	Precision	F1 Score
MLP	0.5559	0.4945	0.4978	0.4786
LSTM	0.5759	0.5464	**0.5717**	0.5034
RSM (*ours*)	**0.6264**	**0.5538**	0.5488	**0.5367**

It can be seen that the three-valued classification $F1$ measure increased with noise reduction and was the highest for the present model. Note that the LSTM network obtained the highest precision score because it was biased to output static. It follows that the numbers of the true positives for up and down decreased, and consequently the recall and F1 scores worsened. The reference levels for uniform class distribution in a purely-random process would be $0.33\overline{3}$, which were clearly exceeded by the present results by all methods. Confusion matrices for the LSTM methods and the present RSM method for both currencies, CNY and USD, are given in Figures 7 and 8.

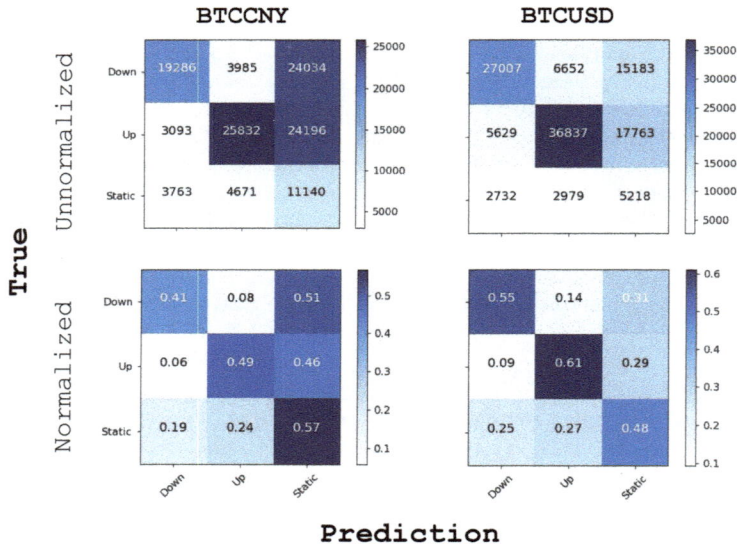

Figure 7. Confusion matrices (LSTM). The x-axis is the prediction, and the y-axis is the true label. Matrices at the top are unnormalized, and the ones at the bottom are normalized. Both unnormalized and normalized matrices are given because there was a crucial class imbalance (Figure 6). As compared to the matrices of Figure 8, the ratio of static prediction became higher.

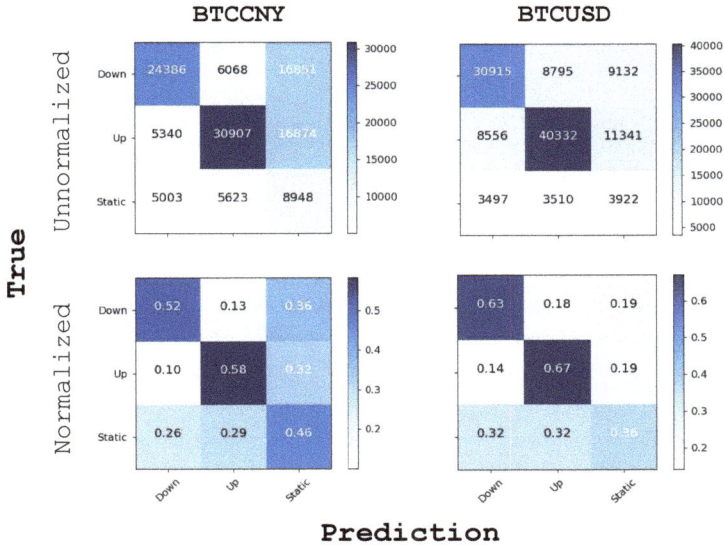

Figure 8. Confusion matrices (RSM). Refer to Figure 7 for the axis labels. As compared to the confusion matrices of an LSTM network, it can be seen that our model was less biased to the static class.

6.3. Profitability

We examine the profitability of baselines and our model, based on the prediction we obtained from the above experiment: up, down, or static for the simple moving average (the result is shown in Table 3). We define a simple trading strategy: buy Bitcoin (all funds) for prediction up; sell Bitcoin (all funds to CNY or USD) for down prediction; and no change in position (either BTC or CNY, based on the current situation) if the prediction is static. Using the present dataset sampled by minutes and the predicted classes for half-an-hour averages, we evaluated the prediction performance using a half-an-hour sampling step. The length of the testing dataset was 120k-min steps. In this setting, we used the log return defined in Equation (7) where P_t is the closing price at time t and $k = 30$.

$$R_t = \log\left(\frac{P_t}{P_{t-k}}\right) \tag{7}$$

Table 3. The profitability factor of BTCCNY and BTCUSD in the OkCoin market. BTCCNY and BTCUSD prices showed two bubble bursts (Figures 3 and 4). The values are exponentials of the log return accumulated from trades. Market reference values were 1.5643 for BTCCNY and 1.4122 for BTCUSD (a value of 1 represents 100% of the initial investment). Refer to the text for details.

	CNY	USD
MLP	**1.5787**	1.1055
LSTM	1.2124	1.3157
RSM (*ours*)	1.4761	**1.3346**

Dynamic trading results measured on a half-an-hour trading scale are given in Figure 9. The green curve (our method) should be compared with the red curve (buy-and-hold strategy). While all strategies remained profitable in the long run, none of them outperformed the market, except for very rare intermittent periods.

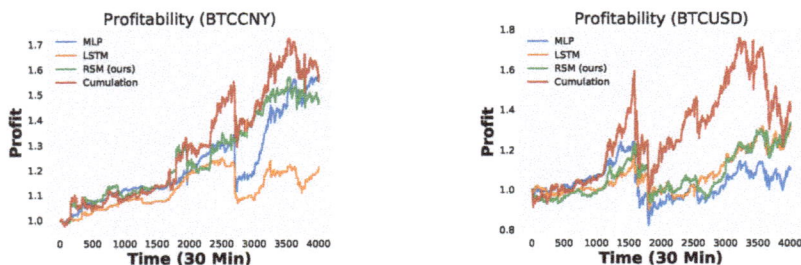

Figure 9. Visualization for profitability of BTCCNY (**left**) and BTCUSD (**right**) at each time step. Cumulation on each graph denotes the exponential of the cumulative log return value at that time step. Refer to Figures 3 and 4 for price.

It remains to be established whether a more elaborate trading scheme based on the present classification method would be able to outperform the market. An example could be using n-grams of past prediction labels, evaluating their correctness, and conditioning the next trading move based on the results. We remark here that the present success in predicting the market trend already rules out the applicability of the strong form of the efficient market hypothesis; in addition, a profitable trading strategy would rule out also its weaker form, which forbids the existence of such algorithms. Practical differences may arise for instance from the transaction fees or because of the time required to record the transactions in the blockchain (about 10 min for Bitcoin).

6.4. Alternative Sampling Schemes

We studied how changing the sampling scheme affects the performance (Table 4). We evaluated our model using the original and the alternative sampling methods. If the sampling scheme does not affect the performance, this may imply that the market dynamics does not change between the two sampling selections. To test this hypothesis, we compared sample sequences from the very first part of the dataset to classify the input sequences around the very end of the dataset, which is the essence of the alternative sampling method.

Table 4. Model evaluation scores on BTCCNY. We deployed 2 different sampling schemes. Refer to the text for details.

	Accuracy	Recall	Precision	F1 Score
first week	0.4031	0.4860	0.6076	0.4152
global	0.5364	0.5238	0.5503	0.5124

The alternative sampling thus took all samples from the first week. Interestingly, the performance of BTCUSD did not change much, whereas the performance of BTCCNY degraded dramatically. BTCCNY price at the end of 2013 went up sharply and heavily fluctuated during a few months. This degradation might be caused by this strong fluctuation, which is not observed in BTCUSD time series. The global sampling scheme used the option that all samples are taken from the whole past.

6.5. Universal Patterns

For the sake of completeness, we studied the degree of the existence of universal patterns (see (Sirignano and Cont 2018) for the formulation) empirically. We deployed the pre-trained model with fixed settings and evaluated it on the different dataset. If there were any relation among distributions of an asset on which a model was trained and another asset on which the model was tested, we could deploy the same model among different assets. The work in (Sirignano and Cont 2018) studied this type of universality extensively. Here, we used Lite Coin (LTC) in the same market as a test dataset. We used RSM, which was trained on BTCUSD (we used the same number of train data points as the experiment above) to test it on the last 120k data points of LTCCNY and LCTUSD, which were not observed in the training data. The results are shown in Tables 5 and 6. Both the LSTM network and our model worked reasonably, and our model performed better for most information metric scores, except the precision score, for which the reason is the same as in the above section.

Table 5. Universal patterns (LTCCNY). Model evaluation scores use the same metric as in Table 1. We evaluated the same baselines and our model on a different dataset from the dataset on which they were trained. Lite Coin Chinese yuan (LTCCNY) in the OkCoin market was used as the evaluation dataset. We used the parameters optimized on BTCUSD.

	Accuracy	Recall	Precision	F1 Score
MLP	0.4992	0.5004	0.5176	0.5005
LSTM	0.5475	0.5452	0.5668	0.5492
RSM (*ours*)	**0.5746**	**0.5695**	**0.5762**	**0.5713**

Table 6. Universal patterns (LTCUSD). Model evaluation scores use the same metric as in Table 1. We evaluated the same baselines and our model on a different dataset from the dataset on which they were trained. Lite Coin US dollar (LTCUSD) in the OkCoin market was used as the evaluation dataset. We used the parameters optimized on BTCUSD.

	Accuracy	Recall	Precision	F1 Score
MLP	0.4917	0.4927	0.5052	0.4905
LSTM	0.5242	0.5332	**0.5752**	0.5291
RSM (*ours*)	**0.5526**	**0.5504**	0.5637	**0.5499**

7. Conclusions

We proposed a new trend prediction classification learning method and showed that it performed well in the domain where taking the non-stationarity assumption was quite fair. We conducted experiments with very small scaled models to distinguish the effect of our method and confirmed its superiority in comparison with the MLP and LSTM baselines. The present method can be applied to other financial time series and is not confined to cryptocurrency markets.

Author Contributions: Conceptualization, L.P., T.S.; methodology, T.S., L.P.; software, T.S.; validation, T.S., L.P.; formal analysis, T.S., L.P.; investigation, T.S., L.P.; resources, L.P.; data curation, T.S., L.P.; writing—original draft preparation, T.S., L.P.; writing—review and editing, L.P., T.S.; visualization, T.S., L.P.; supervision, L.P.; project administration, L.P.; funding acquisition, L.P.

Funding: This research received no external funding.

Conflicts of Interest: The authors declare no conflict of interest.

Appendix A. Long Short-Term Memory

Long short-term memory (LSTM) (Gers et al. 2000; Hochreiter and Schmidhuber 1997) is a unit for recurrent neural networks (Figure A1). LSTM deploys the gating mechanism, which is designed to solve input (output) weight conflict. It enables LSTM to capture long time dependencies and encode relatively long sequences ((Greff et al. 2017) conducted experiments on the performance of the varieties of LSTM models extensively). Because of this advantageous property, LSTM has been used in many research works (Andrychowicz et al. 2016; Bahdanau et al. 2014; Luong et al. 2015; Sutskever et al. 2014;

Ravi and Larochelle 2017; Wu et al. 2016) as a core technique. Equations (A1)–(A6) are the formulation (we refer to (Greff et al. 2017)),

$$\mathbf{z}^t = g\left(\mathbf{W}_z\mathbf{x}^t + \mathbf{R}_z\mathbf{y}^{t-1} + \mathbf{b}_z\right) \tag{A1}$$

$$\mathbf{i}^t = \sigma\left(\mathbf{W}_i\mathbf{x}^t + \mathbf{R}_i\mathbf{y}^{t-1} + \mathbf{b}_i\right) \tag{A2}$$

$$\mathbf{f}^t = \sigma\left(\mathbf{W}_f\mathbf{x}^t + \mathbf{R}_f\mathbf{y}^{t-1} + \mathbf{b}_f\right) \tag{A3}$$

$$\mathbf{c}^t = \mathbf{z}^t \odot \mathbf{i}^t + \mathbf{c}^{t-1} \odot \mathbf{f}^t \tag{A4}$$

$$\mathbf{o}^t = \sigma\left(\mathbf{W}_o\mathbf{x}^t + \mathbf{R}_o\mathbf{y}^{t-1} + \mathbf{b}_o\right) \tag{A5}$$

$$\mathbf{y}^t = h\left(\mathbf{c}^t\right) \odot \mathbf{o}^t \tag{A6}$$

where $\mathbf{W}_z, \mathbf{W}_i, \mathbf{W}_f$, and $\mathbf{W}_o$ are weight parameters for input, $\mathbf{R}_z, \mathbf{R}_i, \mathbf{R}_f$, and $\mathbf{R}_o$ are weight parameters for recurrent input, and $\mathbf{b}_z, \mathbf{b}_i, \mathbf{b}_f$, and $\mathbf{b}_o$ are biases, respectively. x_t and y_{t-1} are input and recurrent input (note that y_{t-1} has a gap in time because it is a recurrent input). g, σ, and h are non-linear functions (usually, the hyperbolic tangent function is selected as g and h and the logistic sigmoid function as σ). Capital letters in bold denote matrices, whereas lower case in bold is used for vectors. $\odot$ stands for element-wise multiplication.

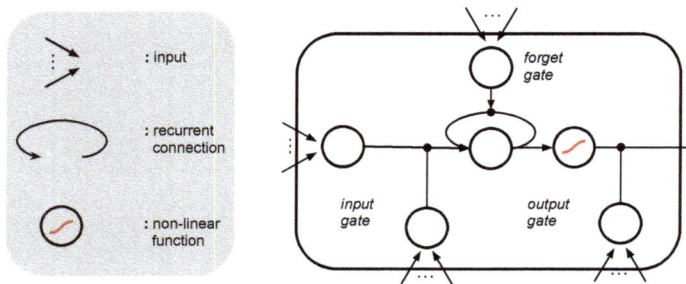

Figure A1. Abstract visualization of LSTM. A set of components on the left describes their roles in a unit on the right.

In Equation (A1), LSTM selectively extracts information necessary to output desired values, and the information extracted passes the input gate where LSTM determines how much information should be loaded into its memory (memory at time step t is represented as $\mathbf{c}^t$) in Equation (A2). If the gate outputs one, then all the extracted information flows into its memory, and if it outputs zero, none of the extracted information is read in its memory. The forget and output gates work in the same way to adjust information flow in memory-to-memory and memory-to-output propagation segments.

References

Andrychowicz, Marcin, Misha Denil, Sergio Gomez, Matthew W. Hoffman, David Pfau, Tom Schaul, Brendan Shillingford, and Nando De Freitas. 2016. Learning to learn by gradient descent by gradient descent. In *Advances in Neural Information Processing Systems*. Cambridge: The MIT Press, pp. 3981–89.

Bahdanau, Dzmitry, Kyunghyun Cho, and Yoshua Bengio. 2014. Neural machine translation by jointly learning to align and translate. *arXiv*, arXiv:1409.0473.

Bariviera, Aurelio F., Maria Jose Basgall, Waldo Hasperue, and Marcelo Naiouf. 2017. Some stylized facts of the bitcoin market. *Physica A: Statistical Mechanics and its Applications* 484: 82–90. [CrossRef]

Cinbis, Ramazan Gokberk, Jakob Verbeek, and Cordelia Schmid. 2011. Unsupervised metric learning for face identification in tv video. Paper presented at the 2011 IEEE International Conference on Computer Vision (ICCV), Barcelona, Spain, November 6–13, pp. 1559–66.

Dixon, Matthew, Diego Klabjan, and Jin Hoon Bang. 2017. Classification-based financial markets prediction using deep neural networks. *Algorithmic Finance* 6: 67–77. [CrossRef]

Gers, Felix A., Jürgen Schmidhuber, and Fred A. Cummins. 2000. Learning to forget: Continual prediction with lstm. *Neural Computation* 12: 2451–71. [CrossRef] [PubMed]

Gkillas, Konstantinos, and Paraskevi Katsiampa. 2018. An application of extreme value theory to cryptocurrencies. *Economics Letters* 164: 109–11. [CrossRef]

Gkillas, Konstantinos, Stelios Bekiros, and Costas Siriopoulos. 2018. Extreme Correlation in Cryptocurrency Markets. Available online: https://ssrn.com/abstract=3180934 (accessed on 14 January 2019) .

Glorot, Xavier, Antoine Bordes, and Yoshua Bengio. 2011. Deep sparse rectifier neural networks. Paper presented at the Proceedings of the Fourteenth International Conference on Artificial Intelligence and Statistics, Ft. Lauderdale, FL, USA, April 11–13, pp. 315–23.

Graves, Alex, Greg Wayne, and Ivo Danihelka. 2014. Neural turing machines. *arXiv*, arXiv:1410.5401.

Greff, Klaus, Rupesh K. Srivastava, Jan Koutník, Bas R. Steunebrink, and Jürgen Schmidhuber. 2017. Lstm: A search space odyssey. *IEEE Transactions on Neural Networks and Learning Systems* 28: 2222–32. [CrossRef] [PubMed]

Hilliard, Nathan, Lawrence Phillips, Scott Howland, Artem Yankov, Courtney D. Corley, and Nathan O. Hodas. 2018. Few-shot learning with metric-agnostic conditional embeddings. *arXiv*, arXiv:1802.04376.

Hochreiter, Sepp, and Jürgen Schmidhuber. 1997. Long short-term memory. *Neural Computation* 9: 1735–80. [CrossRef] [PubMed]

Kingma, Diederik P., and Jimmy Ba. 2014. Adam: A method for stochastic optimization. *arXiv*, arXiv:1412.6980.

Koch, Gregory. 2015. Siamese neural networks for one-shot image recognition. Paper presented at the 32 nd International Conference on Machine Learning, Lille, France, July 6–11.

Koutmos, Dimitrios. 2018. Bitcoin returns and transaction activity. *Economics Letters* 167: 81–85. [CrossRef]

Kristoufek, Ladislav. 2018. On bitcoin markets (in)efficiency and its evolution. *Physica A: Statistical Mechanics and its Applications* 503: 257–62. [CrossRef]

Lake, Brenden, Chia-ying Lee, James Glass, and Josh Tenenbaum. 2014. One-shot learning of generative speech concepts. Paper presented at Annual Meeting of the Cognitive Science Society, Quebec City, QC, Canada, July 23–26, vol. 36.

Lake, Brenden, Ruslan Salakhutdinov, Jason Gross, and Joshua Tenenbaum. 2011. One shot learning of simple visual concepts. Paper presented at Annual Meeting of the Cognitive Science Society, Boston, MA, USA, July 20–23, vol. 33.

Lake, Brenden M., Ruslan Salakhutdinov, and Joshua B. Tenenbaum. 2015. Human-level concept learning through probabilistic program induction. *Science* 350: 1332–38. [CrossRef] [PubMed]

Li, Fe-Fei, Rob Fergus, and Pietro Perona. 2003. A bayesian approach to unsupervised one-shot learning of object categories. Paper presented at the 2003 Ninth IEEE International Conference on Computer Vision, Nice, France, October 13–16, pp. 1134–41.

Li, Fei-Fei, Rob Fergus, and Pietro Perona. 2006. One-shot learning of object categories. *IEEE Transactions on Pattern Analysis and Machine Intelligence* 28: 594–611.

Luong, Minh-Thang, Hieu Pham, and Christopher D. Manning. 2015. Effective approaches to attention-based neural machine translation. *arXiv*, arXiv:1508.04025.

Mäkinen, Milla, Juho Kanniainen, Moncef Gabbouj, and Alexandros Iosifidis. 2018. Forecasting of jump arrivals in stock prices: New attention-based network architecture using limit order book data. *arXiv*, arXiv:1810.10845.

Ravi, Sachin, and Hugo Larochelle. 2017. Optimization as a model for few-shot learning. Paper presented at International Conference on Learning Representations (ICLR), Toulon, France, April 24–26.

Santoro, Adam, Sergey Bartunov, Matthew Botvinick, Daan Wierstra, and Timothy Lillicrap. 2016. One-shot learning with memory-augmented neural networks. *arXiv*, arXiv:1605.06065.

Schuster, Mike, and Kuldip K Paliwal. 1997. Bidirectional recurrent neural networks. *IEEE Transactions on Signal Processing* 45: 2673–81. [CrossRef]

Sirignano, Justin, and Rama Cont. 2018. Universal Features of Price Formation in Financial Markets: Perspectives From Deep Learning. Available online: https://ssrn.com/abstract=3141294 (accessed on 1 December 2018).

Sutskever, Ilya, Oriol Vinyals, and Quoc V. Le. 2014. Sequence to sequence learning with neural networks. In *Advances in Neural Information Processing Systems*. Cambridge: The MIT Press, pp. 3104–12.

J. Risk Financial Manag. **2019**, *12*, 17

Vinyals, Oriol, Charles Blundell, Timothy Lillicrap, Koray Kavukcuoglu, and Daan Wierstra. 2016. Matching networks for one shot learning. In *Advances in Neural Information Processing Systems*. Cambridge: The MIT Press, pp. 3630–38.

Wu, Yonghui, Mike Schuster, Zhifeng Chen, Quoc V. Le, Mohammad Norouzi, Wolfgang Macherey, Maxim Krikun, Yuan Cao, Qin Gao, Klaus Macherey, and et al. 2016. Google's neural machine translation system: Bridging the gap between human and machine translation. *arXiv*, arXiv:1609.08144.

Xing, Eric P., Michael I. Jordan, Stuart J. Russell, and Andrew Y. Ng. 2003. Distance metric learning with application to clustering with side-information. In *Advances in Neural Information Processing Systems*, Cambridge: The MIT Press, pp. 521–28.

Yao, Yushi, and Zheng Huang. 2016. Bi-directional LSTM recurrent neural network for chinese word segmentation. *arXiv*, arXiv:1602.04874.

Zhang, Zihao, Stefan Zohren, and Stephen Roberts. 2018. Deeplob: Deep convolutional neural networks for limit order books. *arXiv*, arXiv:1808.03668.

Journal of
Risk and Financial Management

MDPI

Article

Testing Stylized Facts of Bitcoin Limit Order Books

Matthias Schnaubelt *, Jonas Rende and Christopher Krauss

Department of Statistics and Econometrics, University of Erlangen-Nürnberg, Lange Gasse 20,
90403 Nürnberg, Germany; jonas.rende@fau.de (J.R.); christopher.krauss@fau.de (C.K.)
* Correspondence: matthias.schnaubelt@fau.de

Received: 21 December 2018; Accepted: 30 January 2019; Published: 5 February 2019

Abstract: The majority of electronic markets worldwide employ limit order books, and the recently emerging exchanges for cryptocurrencies pose no exception. With this work, we empirically analyze whether commonly observed empirical properties from established limit order exchanges transfer to the cryptocurrency domain. Based on the literature, we establish a structured methodological framework to conduct analyses in a systematic and comprehensive way. We then present results from a unique and extensive limit order data set acquired from major cryptocurrency exchanges for the currency pair Bitcoin to US Dollar. We recover many observations from mature markets, such as a symmetry between the average ask and the average bid side of the order book, autocorrelation in returns on the smallest time scales only, volatility clustering and the timing of large trades. We also observe some idiosyncrasies: The distributions of trade size and limit order prices deviate from commonly observed patterns. Also, we find limit order books to be relatively shallow and liquidity costs to be relatively high when compared to established markets.

Keywords: limit order book; cryptocurrency; stylized fact; high-frequency finance; liquidity costs; transaction costs

---

1. Introduction

With this paper, we aim to empirically characterize limit order books (LOBs) from several Bitcoin exchanges, and to examinine stylized facts typically observed at a large range of traditional markets. Cryptocurrency markets are of academic interest for several reasons: Leaving technological advances aside, cryptocurrency markets represent a unique opportunity to study properties of an emerging market for a largely unregulated asset, which does not (yet) "fulfill the main properties of a standard currency" (Bariviera et al. 2017). It is, therefore, of interest to contrast the extensive body of results on traditional limit order exchanges with analyses on cryptocurrency exchanges.

Despite the unprecedented ease of access to high-frequency and rich market data from cryptocurrency exchanges using their open interfaces, we found only a single study employing LOB data: Donier and Bouchaud (2015) focus on the role of liquidity in market crashes. Donier and Bonart (2015) use trade data to reconstruct "metaorders" and investigate the price impact of these orders. Other works focus on stylized facts of price time series (Bariviera et al. 2017; Brandvold et al. 2015; Chan et al. 2017; Chu et al. 2017; Easwaran et al. 2015; Zargar and Kumar 2019; Zhang et al. 2018) or the liquidity at the best bid and best ask—see Dimpfl (2017) and Dyhrberg et al. (2018).

Clearly, there is a vast body of literature on LOBs in traditional markets. For a comprehensive survey of literature on LOBs for traditional assets we refer to Gould et al. (2013). We review further works when we present our methodology and results. In one of the first empirical works on LOBs, Biais et al. (1995)

report a symmetry in the average shape of the LOB from the Paris Bourse, and find that incoming orders are most likely placed close to the current price. In contrast, depth is largest further away from the current price. When analyzing conditional probabilities of certain events, they find that market participants place orders within the bid-ask spread when volume at the quotes is high or the bid-ask spread wide. Both Bouchaud et al. (2002) and Zovko and Farmer (2002) study the arrival rates of limit orders at the Paris Bourse and the London Stock exchange as a function of the price difference to the current price, and find that it follows a power law. Focusing on levels deeper in the LOB, Gomber et al. (2015) study liquidity costs for large volumes and their reaction after liquidity shocks in the form of large trades. Gopikrishnan et al. (2000) focus on statistics of trades from LOBs for many major US stocks, and report power laws in the distribution of trade size. Other works assess the price impact of limit orders, i.e., the change in price following a limit order. Bouchaud (2009) provides an overview of the concept. Cont et al. (2014) empirically demonstrate that short-term returns are mainly driven by order flow imbalances.

With this paper, we contribute to close the research gap in the cryptocurrency domain and make the following contributions:

1. *Structured framework for analyzing limit order book data:* First, following the literature, we establish a structured framework for the extraction of empirical properties from LOB data and trade flows. The substantial body of literature addressing LOB data from established exchanges serves as a baseline for our work as well as other studies addressing cryptocurrencies.

2. *Recovery of common qualitative facts:* Second, using a large-scale limit order data set, we can confirm that many empirical observations from more mature markets also transfer to major exchanges for the BTC/USD currency pair, most notably:

   - **Symmetric average limit order book:** We recover the commonly observed symmetry between the bid and the ask side of the time-averaged LOB.
   - **Dispersion of liquidity:** Liquidity is dispersed over many levels of the order book, and small values of depth at the best bid and ask occur with highest probability.
   - **No autocorrelation in lower-frequency returns:** We do not observe significant autocorrelation in the series of returns on time scales from minutes to days.
   - **Negative autocorrelation in tick-level returns (bid-ask bounce):** The series of trade-to-trade price changes exhibits negative autocorrelation in the first lags.
   - **Volatility clustering:** The autocorrelation of volatility measures exhibits significant positive values even after multiple days.
   - **Non-normality of returns:** The distribution of returns on different time scales shows heavy tails and deviates strongly from the normal distribution.
   - **Timing of large trades:** Trades of large size seem to be executed when liquidity costs are relatively low.
   - **Power tails in trade size distribution:** For trades larger than the minimum order size, we recover a power tail in the distribution of trade size.

3. *Idiosyncratic observations:* Third, we can identify the following key idiosyncrasies:

   - **Relatively shallow limit order book:** Despite narrow bid-ask spreads, liquidity costs increase rapidly once higher volumes are traded. This finding is consistent with Bitcoin traders being retail traders rather than institutional investors.
   - **Weak intraday patterns:** Depending on the exchange, we observe either absent or weak intraday patterns in liquidity costs and weak patterns in trade frequency and size. Contrary to traditional

markets, there is continuous trading at cryptocurrency exchanges, and our results might indicate a superposition of automated trading and worldwide market participation.

- **Frequent minor trades:** Many trades are of very small size, i.e., close to the minimum size increment. Unlike most traditional assets, Bitcoin can be traded in increments of 10^{-8} BTC with typical minimum order sizes in the order of 10^{-3} BTC. These two limits and the predominance of retail trading seems to explain the very broad empirical distribution of trade size with a minimum at the minimum size increment.

- **Broad distribution of limit order prices:** A large part of limit order volume and changes thereof is located very far away from the current price. Possible reasons are the unlimited lifetime of orders at cryptocurrency exchanges, the speculative placement of orders far away from the current price and the absence of regulatory limits such as price caps for submitted orders.

The remainder of this paper is structured as follows: In Section 2, we provide a brief overview of cryptocurrency exchange market structure. Our data set is described in Section 3. We cover our methodology in Section 4 and embed analyses from the literature in a comprehensive framework, which then also guides the presentation of our results in Section 5. We conclude in Section 6.

2. Cryptocurrency Exchange Market Structure

There are several ways to acquire cryptocurrencies: First, units of a cryptocurrency can be earned through the process of mining, e.g., by contributing computing power to append blocks to the block chain (compare Böhme et al. (2015) for an introductory review). Second, cryptocurrencies can be used as form of payment, and be obtained by offering goods or services. Third, cryptocurrencies can be exchanged for traditional currencies and other cryptocurrencies at several exchange platforms, which are operated by private companies. Although the Bitcoin network itself is largely decentralized and the technical setup for an exchange is relatively straightforward, there are drivers that force exchanges to a small number of countries. Regulatory requirements and the need for a secure infrastructure limit the number of exchanges (Böhme et al. 2015). In addition, the origin of an investor determines a preference for certain base currencies, which in turn constitutes a preference for the exchange's place of business.

Cryptocurrency exchanges come in several varieties: brokers offering exchange at fixed prices, direct peer-to-peer exchange venues and trading platforms similar to conventional currency or stock exchanges. In this paper, we focus on currency exchanges operating LOBs, which are also used by most traditional markets worldwide (Gould et al. 2013). In this respect, cryptocurrency limit order exchanges replicate common features from their traditional counterparts: Traders express their intention by submitting orders with a price limit and a fixed amount, which are then matched with other orders to yield transactions or are transferred to the LOB. One prominent difference to conventional exchanges is that cryptocurrency exchanges operate continuously and thus do not hold opening or closing auctions often found at (hybrid) stock exchanges.

In Table 1, we exemplarily compare several cryptocurrency exchanges along several dimensions for the currency pair Bitcoin (BTC) against US Dollar (USD). We list the availability of several special order types: *Stop orders* (also called *stop-loss* or *take-profit* orders) are executed once previously set conditions on the current price are met. *Fill-or-kill* orders are to be executed either immediately to the full requested quantity or canceled. *Immediate-or-cancel* orders are executed immediately and to the largest extent possible, and not transferred to the LOB. *Hidden* orders (also called *iceberg* orders) are not shown with their full quantity in the publicly visible order book and serve to hide liquidity. The table also lists the range of fees to be paid at the exchanges. Most exchanges charge fees following a fee schedule depending on traded volume, and differ between taker and maker fees, which we list separately: *Maker fees* are paid for trades following the provision of liquidity (e.g., after posting a new limit order), and *taker fees* are charged on trades taking liquidity out of the market by submitting some immediately executed order. We also list fees payable when withdrawing or depositing traditional fiat currency. The listed resolution parameters specify the smallest price increment (*tick size*) and the smallest order size (*minimum order size*).

Table 1. **Comparison of cryptocurrency limit order exchanges along the dimensions order type, fee structure and resolution parameters.** *FOK*: fill-or-kill orders, *IOC*: immediate-or-cancel orders, *hidden*: publicly invisible limit orders, *taker fees*: range of fees payable for taking liquidity from the market, *maker fees*: range of fees payable when submitting orders subsequently taken by other traders. All information is retrieved on 1 November 2018.

Exchange	Order Type					Fees				Resolution	
	Market	Stop	FOK	IOC	Hidden	Taker [bp]	Maker [bp]	Deposit	Withdrawal	Tick Size (USD)	Min. Order Size (BTC)
BitFinex [1]	✓	✓	✓	✓	✓	20–5.5	10–0	10 bp/20 USD	10 bp/20 USD	10^{-1}	2×10^{-3}
BitStamp [2]	✓	✓				25–10	25–10	5 bp/7.5 USD	9 bp/15 USD	10^{-2}	$\approx 10^{-3}$
Bittrex [3]				✓		25	25	NA	NA	10^{-3}	10^{-4}
Coinbase/GDAX [4]	✓	✓	✓	✓		30–10	0	10 USD	25 USD	10^{-2}	10^{-3}
Gemini [5]	✓		✓	✓		100–10	100–0	none	none	10^{-2}	10^{-5}
Kraken [6]	✓	✓				26–10	16–0	5 USD	5 USD	10^{-1}	2×10^{-3}
Poloniex [7]		✓				20–10	10–0	none	10 bp/50 USD	10^{-8}	10^{-4}

[1] http://www.bitfinex.com/features; http://www.bitfinex.com/fees; http://api.bitfinex.com/v1/symbols_de tails; [2] http://www.bitstamp.net/api/v2/trading-pairs-info/; http://www.bitstamp.net/faq/; http://www.bits tamp.net/fee_schedule/; [3] http://support.bittrex.com/hc/en-us/articles/115000199651-What-fees-does-Bittrex-charge-; http://support.bittrex.com/hc/en-us/articles/202227464-What-is-Time-in-Force-; http://support.bitt rex.com/hc/en-us/articles/115003004171-What-are-my-trade-limits-; [4] http://support.pro.coinbase.com/cus tomer/en/portal/articles/2945310-fees; http://support.pro.coinbase.com/customer/en/portal/articles/29453 13-overview-of-order-types-and-settings-stop-limit-market-; http://www.coinbase.com/legal/trading_rules; [5] http://gemini.com/trading-fee-schedule/; http://gemini.com/transfer-fee-schedule/; http://gemini.com/m arketplace/#order-types; http://docs.gemini.com/rest-api/#symbols-and-minimums; [6] http://www.kraken.com /en-us/help/fees; http://support.kraken.com/hc/en-us/articles/360001389366-Price-and-volume-decimal-p recision; http://support.kraken.com/hc/en-us/articles/360000423043-Fiat-currency-withdrawal-fees; http:// support.kraken.com/hc/en-us/articles/360000279946-Fiat-currency-deposit-fees; [7] http://poloniex.com/fees/; http://thecryptobot.com/2017/11/27/markets-minimum-trade-sizes-poloniex-bittrex-kraken/; http://supp ort.usdc.circle.com/hc/en-us/articles/360015471331.

3. Data

We select data from several different exchanges, and focus on the BTC/USD market, which is the leading cryptocurrency pair by traded volume and order book depth. For this currency pairs, we determine the largest exchanges by volume and collect data from BitFinex, Bitstamp and Coinbase[1].

We retrieve data from selected exchanges and for selected currency pairs by directly connecting to the exchange's application programming interface (API). We collect both transactions (trades) and limit order data. For trades, we record the timestamp of the transaction, its volume, price and a buy/sell flag. The collected limit order data contains the limit order book depth at all price steps. Our data set comprises data from 2 December 2017 to 12 October 2018, i.e., close to one calendar year and covers the time of peak interest in cryptocurrencies with the highest ever achieved prices and high volatility, as well as a time of relatively stable prices. In total, we have obtained over 140 GB of raw data.

To prepare limit order data for further analyses, we first reconstruct the state of the LOB at a minutely sampling frequency. We restore LOBs to the largest depth available during the time of retrieval via the

---

[1]   Formerly called GDAX.

exchange's API. For example, we reconstruct roughly 450 thousand states of the LOB for our evaluation period and the BitFinex BTC/USD market. Finally, we aggregate order books to extract relevant measures.

4. Methodology

We continue by describing the methodology for our study. Section 4.1 introduces the basic notation used throughout the remainder of this paper. Then, Sections 4.2 and 4.3 detail our approach for extracting the empirical properties of cryptocurrency data.

4.1. Basic Notation

Our notation builds upon the mathematical description of LOBs introduced by Gould et al. (2013). The atomic building block of a limit order exchange is the limit order denoted by the vector $x = (p_x, \omega_x, t_x)$. In case of a positive volume $\omega_x > 0$ (negative volume $\omega_x < 0$), the order is a sell-order (buy-order), expressing the intention to sell (buy) no more than $|\omega_x|$ of the traded asset at a price of at least p_x (no more than p_x). t_x denotes the time of submission of the order. Limit orders usually need to adhere to some discretization of price (tick size) and quantity (lot size) imposed by the exchange. A special case of the limit order is the market order. It constitutes the commitment to sell at any price (therefore, $p_x = -\infty$) or buy at any price (hence, $p_x = \infty$). Upon order submission, the trade matching algorithm of the exchange checks whether the newly submitted order can be matched with active limit orders, i.e., if the limit price p_x to sell (buy) is below the limit price of any buy-order (above the limit price of any sell-order). A matched order leads to a transaction (trade) denoted by $M = (p_M, \omega_M, t_M)$. Herein, $|\omega_M|$ is the amount traded, and p_M is the price of the transaction. The sign of ω_M is determined by the order initiating the trade. A partial execution of orders may lead to a trade covering only a fraction of the initial order, leaving the remainder in the LOB. An order enters the order book if it has not been fully executed and its execution flags do not specify a differing behavior. Orders in the LOB are called active and remain active until they are canceled, matched or expire. We denote the set of orders in the LOB at time t as $\mathcal{L}(t)$. The bid side $\mathcal{B}(t)$ at time t contains all buy-orders, i.e., $\mathcal{B}(t) = \{x \in \mathcal{L}(t) \mid \omega_x < 0\}$. Similarly, the set of sell orders (ask side) is defined as $\mathcal{A}(t) = \{x \in \mathcal{L}(t) \mid \omega_x > 0\}$. The evolution of an order book state $\mathcal{L}(t_1)$ to another order book state $\mathcal{L}(t_2)$, $t_2 > t_1$ is driven by the flow of incoming orders $\{x_t \mid t_1 < t \le t_2\}$.

Hence, we can have two different approaches to analyze the evolution of LOBs: First, we can either look at the series of snapshots of the (static) state of the LOB, sampled at a Δt-second timescale. Second, alternatively, analyses can cover the (dynamic) flow of limit orders $\{x_i\}$ leading to changes of the order book or the resulting flow of trades $\{M_i\}$. Both perspectives are used in the literature, and for the sake of a clear structure of the remainder of this paper, we use this differentiation and practical considerations to guide our methodology and the presentation of results. Consequently, we first describe the statistics of static LOB states $\mathcal{L}(t)$ in Section 4.2. In the subsequent Section 4.3, we turn to the analysis of order flows $\{x_i\}$ and the resulting flow of transactions $\{M_i\}$.

4.2. Measures of the Static Limit Order Book

We first focus on derived measures of the static LOB at some time t, i.e., $\mathcal{L}(t)$. In other words, we consider some function f which we apply to the static state of the LOB, i.e., $f(\mathcal{L}(t))$. Most of the quantities introduced in this section are visualized in Figure 1. One of the most important properties of $\mathcal{L}(t)$ is its *depth profile*, which is the total available limit order volume at a given price p and is given by

$$n^b(p, t) = \sum_{\{x \in \mathcal{B}(t) \mid p_x = p\}} \omega_x, \tag{1}$$

for the bid side, and similarly for the ask side. We write the i-th best price of the ask side (bid side) as $a_i(t), i \in \{1, \ldots, |\mathcal{A}(t)|\}$ $(b_i(t), i \in \{1, \ldots, |\mathcal{B}(t)|\})$. The total order volume at level i is given by $q_i^a(t) = n^a(a_i(t), t)$ and $q_i^b(t) = n^b(b_i(t), t)$, respectively. The first ask-side level $a_1(t) = \min_{x \in \mathcal{A}(t)} p_x$ is the *best ask price* of the order book, and $b_1(t) = \max_{x \in \mathcal{B}(t)} p_x$ is the *best bid price*. The average of best ask and best bid price is the *mid price* given by $m(t) = (a_1(t) + b_1(t))/2$. The difference between the best ask and the best bid price is the *bid-ask spread*, i.e., $s(t) = a_1(t) - b_1(t)$. Similarly, we can define the *volume-weighted average price (VWAP)* function for the imaginary immediate execution of a market order of size ω, assuming no other orders interfere at the same instant:

$$v_a(\omega, t) = \frac{1}{\omega} \sum_i a_i(t) \cdot \min \left(\max \left(\omega - \sum_{k=1}^{i} q_k^a(t), 0 \right), q_i^a(t) \right). \tag{2}$$

Herein, the index i iterates over price levels in a price-ordered fashion, and we assume that the order book is deep enough to provide the requested volume ω. The definition for the bid-side VWAP function $v_b(\omega, t)$ is analogous.

To increase the comparability of different order books at different times, it is common practice to consider prices relative to the current mid price. We define the transformation of a price $p(t)$ to the relative price scale as $\tilde{p}(t) = (p(t) - m(t))/m(t)$. In this scale, the *relative bid-ask spread* is given by $\tilde{s}(t) = \tilde{a}(t) - \tilde{b}(t)$. The bid-ask spread often serves as a measure of market liquidity, as it quantifies the liquidity premium one needs to pay for immediately executing a trade by submitting a market order. However, it is only an accurate estimate for the liquidity premium for order volumes smaller than the order book depth at the best bid/best ask price. To correctly valuate the liquidity cost for a given volume ω, we can similarly define the two-sided VWAP spread as $\tilde{vs}(\omega, t) = \tilde{v}_a(\omega, t) - \tilde{v}_b(\omega, t)$.[2]

---

[2] Two-sided in this case refers to both the bid and the ask side of the order book, and is used for comparability to the (two-sided) bid-ask spread. Please note that this is equal to the exchange liquidity measure (XLM) of Gomber et al. (2015).

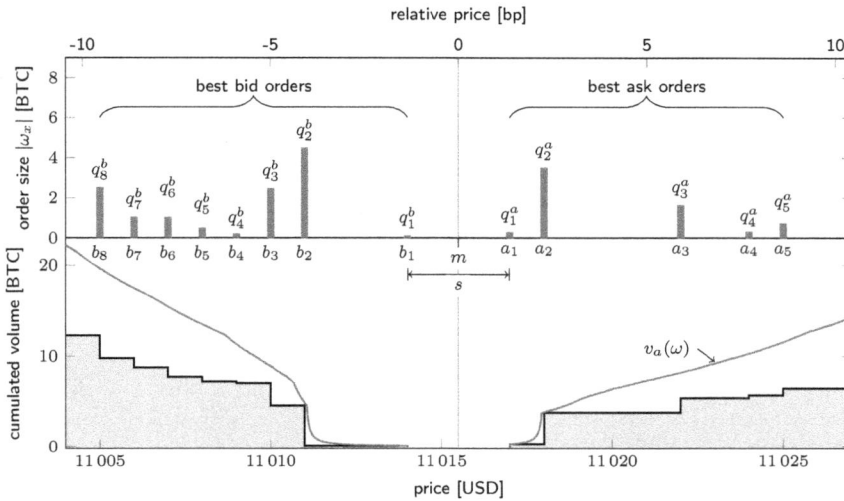

Figure 1. Schematic visualization of a limit order book. The figure visualizes the order book state $\mathcal{L}(t)$ for the BitFinex BTC/USD market as of 2 December 2017 22:01:26 (UTC).

We split further analyses on measures of the static LOB into three canonical subgroups: First, we can perform cross-sectional descriptive statistics in the sense that we ignore the time series nature of the data. Second, we can take the time series nature of the derived measures into account and study their evolution over time. Third, we can evaluate descriptive statistics of derived measures subject to some condition.[3] Table 2 provides an overview of the analyses which we describe in the following, and includes the commonly observed fact under investigation as well as relevant references from works focusing on traditional limit order markets.

---

[3] To keep the three groups canonical, the third group is limited to conditions other than the own past of the data, i.e., the time series, which was already addressed in the second group.

Table 2. Overview of commonly found facts and supporting analyses on static limit order books. Type refers to the class of analysis and is one of U (unconditional statistic), TS (time series statistic) and C (conditional statistic).

Common Fact	Measure Considered for Analysis	Key References	Type
Symmetric mean cumulative depth profiles	Time-averaged depth profile $(\bar{\tilde{a}}, \bar{\tilde{b}}, \overline{q^a}, \overline{q^b})_i$ (Equations (3) and (4)) and time-averaged relative price differences between adjacent steps of the LOB $(\overline{\Delta \tilde{a}}, \overline{\Delta \tilde{b}})_i$ (Equation (5))	Biais et al. (1995), Cao et al. (2009) and Potters and Bouchaud (2003)	U
Gamma-distributed depth at best bid and best ask	Unconditional empirical distribution of the total volume (depth) at the best bid (or ask), i.e., $\{q_0^a(t)\}_t$ and $\{(q_0^b(t)\}_t$	Bouchaud et al. (2002)	U
Hump-shaped mean depth profile	Empirical distribution of the time-averaged volume from the depth profile ($q_i^a(t)$ and $q_i^b(t)$) as a function of the (relative) price difference to the ask or bid price	Bouchaud et al. (2002), Potters and Bouchaud (2003) and Gu et al. (2008)	U
Increase in liquidity costs beyond the best bid/ask	Unconditional distribution of the relative bid-ask spread $\{\tilde{s}(t)\}_t$ and the relative VWAP spread $\{\tilde{vs}(\omega, t)\}_t$	Gomber et al. (2015)	U
Heavy tails of mid-price returns	Unconditional distribution of mid-price returns $\{r(t, \Delta t)\}_t$ analyzed with kurtosis estimates and Hill estimator (Equations (10) and (11))	Hill (1975), Balanda and MacGillivray (1990) and Lux and Marchesi (2000)	TS
No autocorrelation of returns	Autocorrelation of logarithmic mid-price returns $C(n)$ (Equation (8))	Lux and Marchesi (2000) and Cont (2001)	TS
Volatility clustering	Autocorrelation of absolute or squared logarithmic mid-price returns, i.e., the functions $C_1(n)$ and $C_2(n)$, respectively (Equation (9))	Lux and Marchesi (2000) and Cont (2001)	TS
Non-constant liquidity costs	Average daily liquidity costs (i.e., the bid-ask spread $\tilde{s}(t)$ and the VWAP spread $\tilde{vs}(\omega, t)$)	Dyhrberg et al. (2018)	TS
U-shaped intraday patterns of liquidity costs	Average liquidity costs (i.e., the bid-ask spread $\tilde{s}(t)$ and the VWAP spread $\tilde{vs}(\omega, t)$) conditional on the hour of the day	McInish and Wood (1992) and Gomber et al. (2015)	C
Liquidity resiliency and timed large trades	Distribution of average liquidity costs (i.e., the bid-ask spread $\tilde{s}(t)$ and the VWAP spread $\tilde{vs}(\omega, t)$) for large trades conditional on the event time τ of the trade (Equation (12))	Cummings and Frino (2010) and Gomber et al. (2015)	C

4.2.1. Descriptive Statistics of Unconditional Limit Order Book Measures

We can now introduce cross-sectional statistics of measures based on the static LOB $\mathcal{L}(t)$. We start from a set of T LOB states $\{\mathcal{L}(t)\}_{t=1}^{T}$ and derive the corresponding set of values of some measure f, i.e., $\{f(\mathcal{L}(t))\}_{t=1}^{T}$. In a first set of analyses, we consider distributional characteristics of the values of f. Thereby, we focus on two important measures for liquidity costs, namely on the relative bid-ask spread ($f = \tilde{s}$) and on the two-sided VWAP spread for different order volumes ω ($f = \tilde{vs}$). The second set of analyses considers the average depth profile, where we average over all states $\mathcal{L}(t)$ of the LOB at different points in time t. We first define the time-averaged relative ask (bid) price of LOB step i, i.e.,

$$\bar{\tilde{a}}_i = \frac{1}{T} \sum_{t=1}^{T} \tilde{a}_i(t) \qquad \text{and} \qquad \bar{\tilde{b}}_i = \frac{1}{T} \sum_{t=1}^{T} \tilde{b}_i(t). \tag{3}$$

Following Biais et al. (1995), we consider the time-averaged cumulated depth up to a step i, i.e.,

$$\overline{q_i^a} = \frac{1}{T} \sum_{t=1}^{T} \sum_{j=1}^{i} q_j^a(t) \qquad \text{and} \qquad \overline{q_i^b} = \frac{1}{T} \sum_{t=1}^{T} \sum_{j=1}^{i} q_j^b(t). \tag{4}$$

The vectors $\left(\bar{\tilde{a}}, \bar{\tilde{b}}, \overline{q^a}, \overline{q^b} \right)_i$ represent the time-averaged shape of the cumulated LOB. A different definition is used by Bouchaud et al. (2002) to discuss the average shape of the LOB: They consider the time-averaged distribution of non-cumulated volume q_i^a (or q_i^b) as a function of the difference in price to the current bid or ask. Complementing the analyses of the average shape of the order book, we also consider time-averaged differences between the relative price at level i and level $i + 1$, i.e.,

$$\overline{\Delta \tilde{a}_i} = \frac{1}{T} \sum_{t=1}^{T} \tilde{a}_{i+1}(t) - \tilde{a}_i(t) \qquad \text{and} \qquad \overline{\Delta \tilde{b}_i} = \frac{1}{T} \sum_{t=1}^{T} \tilde{b}_{i+1}(t) - \tilde{b}_i(t). \tag{5}$$

4.2.2. Time Series Properties of Limit Order Book Measures

Instead of considering cross-sectional properties of the LOB state $\mathcal{L}(t)$, we can consider the time series of values of some measure f, i.e., $(f(\mathcal{L}(t)))_{t=1}^{T}$. Our analyses will focus on measures of liquidity costs (relative bid-ask spread $\tilde{s}$ and the two-sided VWAP spread $f = \tilde{v}s$) and the mid price m. Also, we consider logarithmic mid-price returns on the time scale Δt given by

$$r^{mid}(t, \Delta t) = \ln\left(m(t + \Delta t)\right) - \ln\left(m(t)\right). \tag{6}$$

We calculate the log-realized volatility $rv(t_1, t_2, \Delta t)$ between times t_1 and t_2 as

$$rv(t_1, t_2, \Delta t) = \sqrt{\sum_{t=t_1}^{t_2} \left(r^{mid}(t, \Delta t)\right)^2}. \tag{7}$$

Following Cont (2001), we also compute the autocorrelation function of logarithmic mid-price returns and the k-th power of absolute logarithmic mid-price returns, i.e.,

$$C^{mid}(n) = \text{corr}\left(r^{mid}(t, \Delta t), r^{mid}(t + n\Delta t, \Delta t)\right), \text{ and} \tag{8}$$

$$C_k^{mid}(n) = \text{corr}\left(|r^{mid}(t, \Delta t)|^k, |r^{mid}(t + n\Delta t, \Delta t)|^k\right). \tag{9}$$

Herein, n denotes the lag, and corr is the sample correlation function.

Tails of the distribution of mid-price returns are analyzed in terms of two kurtosis measures and a tail index estimator. As kurtosis metrics we consider the empirical fourth standardized moment (henceforth: m_4, compare Bacon (2008)) and a second metric based on Balanda and MacGillivray (1990), using quantiles (henceforth: $\gamma_{p,q}$). The computation of $\gamma_{p,q}$ is as follows:

$$\gamma_{p,q} = \frac{F^{-1}(1-p) - F^{-1}(p)}{F^{-1}(1-q) - F^{-1}(q)}, \quad \text{with} \quad 0 < p < q < 0.5. \tag{10}$$

Please note that F^{-1} denotes the quantile function and p and q are p-quantiles. If the underlying distribution F is symmetric, then we can use $\gamma_{p=0.025,q=0.125}$ to measure heavy tails (Büning 1991). To measure deviation from normality we compute the excess version of both metrics, i.e., $\gamma_{p=0.025,q=0.125}^{e} = \gamma_{p=0.025,q=0.125} - 1.706$ and $m_4^{e} = m_4 - 3$. A time series is classified as platykurtic if the excess metric of interest is smaller than zero, mesokurtic if the excess metric is equal to zero and leptokurtic if the excess metric is larger than zero. Thereby, for both metrics larger positive values are associated with heavier tails, while smaller negative values indicate lighter tails. Financial time series are typically leptokurtic (Cont 2001).

The tail index is a measure of the frequency of extreme returns (Lux and Marchesi 2000) and is estimated with a Hill estimator (Hill 1975). As a prerequisite to compute the Hill estimator the time series must be descendingly ordered, i.e., $r_n^{mid} \geq \cdots \geq r_{n-a}^{mid} \geq \cdots \geq r_1^{mid}$. Thereby, r_n^{mid} denotes the largest mid-price return in the time series and r_1^{mid} the smallest. The number of observations included in the tail

J. Risk Financial Manag. **2019**, *12*, 25

analysis solely depends on the value for a. In recent decades a large body of literature has focused on how to determine a.[4] Following Lux and Marchesi (2000) and Kelly and Jiang (2014), we set a to a fixed percentage p of data points, namely 10, 5 and 2.5 percent. Given the ordered time series, we can compute the Hill estimator with the following equation (Lux and Marchesi 2000):

$$H_p = \frac{1}{\frac{1}{a}\sum\limits_{l=1}^{a}\left[\ln\left(r_{n-l+1}^{mid}\right) - \ln\left(r_{n-a}^{mid}\right)\right]}. \tag{11}$$

4.2.3. Statistics of Conditional Limit Order Book Measures

In the third category, we subsume many analyses from the literature which evaluate measures of the static LOB conditional on some condition $\mathcal{C}$. Following our notation, we evaluate order book measures f for the subset given by $\mathcal{C}$, i.e., consider the set $\{f(\mathcal{L}(t)) \mid \mathcal{L}(t) \in \mathcal{C}\}$. We investigate the intraday dynamics of liquidity measures to test for commonly observed patterns—see, among others, McInish and Wood (1992), Biais et al. (1995), Danielsson and Payne (2001), Ranaldo (2004) and Gomber et al. (2015). In this case, $\mathcal{C}$ selects only those order book states from a given hour of the day, and we evaluate mean bid-ask spreads ($f = \bar{s}$) and VWAP spreads ($f = \bar{vs}$). Another class of studies covers the concept of *market resiliency*, which we define in the sense of Foucault et al. (2005) and Gomber et al. (2015) as the recovery of market liquidity following liquidity shocks, and which is considered to be one of the main characteristics of liquid markets (Black 1971; Kyle 1985). We follow several previous studies (compare, for example, Degryse et al. (2005), Large (2007), Cummings and Frino (2010) and Gomber et al. (2015)) and analyze the evolution of market liquidity around large trades in a conditional event study: We condition the analysis onto a set of selected events $\mathcal{E}_C$, which is given by the set of trades with exceptionally large volume, and transform the timestamp t of a LOB state $\mathcal{L}(t)$ to the event time scale τ of event e, i.e., calculate $\tau = t - t_e$. We then consider the average avg of a measure f over all LOB states that are a time difference τ away from a selected trade $e \in \mathcal{E}_C$:

$$\bar{f}(\tau) = \text{avg}\left(\{f(\mathcal{L}(t)) \mid t - t_e = \tau, \ e \in \mathcal{E}_C\}\right). \tag{12}$$

In the analyses presented in this paper, $\bar{f}$ evaluates averages of the bid-ask spread and the VWAP spread around large trades.

4.3. Dynamics of the Limit Order Book: Order and Trade Flows

We now turn to the analysis of the two event streams translating one static state of the LOB $\mathcal{L}(t_1)$ to a subsequent state $\mathcal{L}(t_2)$: the flow of limit orders $\{x_i\}$ leading to changes of the order book and the resulting flow of trades $\{M_i\}$. We use the index i to count limit order or trade events, while index t refers to the wall-clock time. We directly observe trades with information $M_i = (p_M, \omega_M, t_M)_i$, with the traded amount $|\omega_M|$, the execution price p_M and its time t_M. The sign of ω_M is determined by the order initiating the trade. In contrast, we are unable to observe every single limit order between LOB states at different times. Nevertheless, we can compute the change in depth profile between order book states sampled at times t and $t + \Delta t$ as the absolute change in limit order depth at a given price p, i.e.,

$$\Delta n^b(p, t) = |n^b(p, t + \Delta t) - n^b(p, t)| \tag{13}$$

---

4   There are theoretical-based methods and heuristics. For an overview about the different methods see Danielsson et al. (2016).

for the bid side, and similarly for the ask side. For newly submitted or canceled limit orders that are not executed, $\Delta n^b(p,t)$ corresponds to the net limit order volume flow between t and $t + \Delta t$. The limit order volume flow close to the current price is underestimated as some orders are executed in between.

As for static LOB measures, we use three canonical subgroups (unconditional, time series and conditional properties) to structure our analyses. Table 3 provides an analogous overview of analyses with commonly found facts from other works.

Table 3. Overview of commonly found facts and supporting analyses on trades and limit orders. Type refers to the class of analysis and is one of U (unconditional statistic), TS (time series statistic) and C (conditional statistic).

Common Fact	Measure Considered for Analysis	Key References	Type
Number preference for trade sizes	Empirical distribution of trade size ω_M	Mu et al. (2009)	U
Power tail in the distribution of trade size	Empirical distribution of trade size ω_M	Gopikrishnan et al. (2000), Maslov and Mills (2001) and Mu et al. (2009)	U
Power-law decay of order frequency with relative price	Time-average of changed limit order volume, i.e., $\overline{\Delta n^b(p)}$ and $\overline{\Delta n^a(p)}$ (Equation (14))	similar to Bouchaud et al. (2002) and Zovko and Farmer (2002)	U
Negative autocorrelation of trade prices (bid-ask bounce)	Autocorrelation of the series of trade price changes $C^{tp}(n)$ (Equation (15))	Cont (2001) and Russell and Engle (2010)	TS
Autocorrelation of trade sizes	Autocorrelation in the series of trade sizes $C^{size}(n)$ (Equation (16))		TS
Intraday patterns in trade frequency and volume	Average trade frequency and average trade size conditional on the hour of the day	Biais et al. (1995) and Danielsson and Payne (2001)	C

4.3.1. Descriptive Statistics of Unconditional Measures

Several authors study the frequency of limit orders and their size as a function of the price difference to the current bid or ask (among others, Bouchaud et al. (2002), Potters and Bouchaud (2003) and Gu et al. (2008)). To analyze the limit order flow as a function of price using available data, we consider the time-averaged absolute change in limit order depth as a function of price, which is for the bid side given by

$$\overline{\Delta n^b(p)} = \frac{1}{T}\sum_{t=1}^{T}\Delta n^b(p,t), \tag{14}$$

and analogously for the ask side $(\overline{\Delta n^a(p)})$. Another class of works studies the empirical frequency distribution of transaction sizes, for example Gopikrishnan et al. (2000), Maslov and Mills (2001) and Mu et al. (2009). We repeat these analyses with the available cryptocurrency data and consider distributional properties of the series of trade size, i.e., $\{\omega_{M_i}\}$.

4.3.2. Time Series Properties

To evaluate the evolution of trade properties, we sample trade data onto lower timescales by considering some trade statistics f_T of all transactions between time t_1 and t_2, i.e., the set $\{M_i|\, t_1 \leq t_{M_i} < t_2\}$. We consider the average trade size, the total trade volume as well as trade counts (i.e., the trade frequency).

Time series of changes in trade price are known to exhibit autocorrelation for the first few lags (compare, for example, Cont (2001) and Russell and Engle (2010)). We therefore define the series of changes between trade prices, i.e., $\Delta p_i = p_{M_{i+1}} - p_{M_i}$, and compute its autocorrelation as

$$C^{tp}(n) = \text{corr}\left(\Delta p_i, \Delta p_{i+n}\right). \tag{15}$$

Similarly, we analyze the autocorrelation in the series of trade sizes by considering

$$C^{size}(n) = \text{corr}\left(\omega_{M_i}, \omega_{M_{i+n}}\right). \tag{16}$$

4.3.3. Statistics of Conditional Trade Measures

Similar to the analysis of intraday patterns of liquidity costs, we consider average properties of cryptocurrency transactions conditional on the hour of the day (trade frequency, total traded volume, average trade size). Biais et al. (1995) and Danielsson and Payne (2001) perform similar analyses.

5. Results

Following the methodology outlined in the previous section, we now present results for the cryptocurrency exchange BitFinex and the currency pair BTC/USD. We focus our analyses on this exchange as it has the highest trading volume in the time period of our study. We also evaluate data for the currency pair BTC/USD for the second and third largest exchange (Coinbase and Bitstamp), and compare the results to check robustness. Parts of those results are included in the appendix, and we discuss major differences in the following. Most LOB measures are unlikely to be stationary, and might therefore differ with market phases. To check robustness in this regard, we divide our data into a subperiod of high volatility (*SP1* from 2 December 2017 to 7 May 2018) and a subperiod with relatively stable prices (*SP2* from 7 May 2018 to 12 October 2018).[5] We first analyze statistics of measures of the static LOB in Section 5.1, which we divide into three parts to separately discuss unconditional, time series and conditional statistics. In Section 5.2, we analyze the dynamics of LOBs.

5.1. Analysis of the Static Limit Order Book

5.1.1. Descriptive Statistics of Unconditional Limit Order Book Measures

We first present unconditional descriptive statistics of measures of the static LOB, and begin by discussing the average shape of the LOB.

Time-averaged depth profile: Figure 2a displays the time-averaged cumulated depth profile of the LOB, i.e., plots the quantities $(\bar{\bar{a}}, \bar{\bar{b}}, \overline{q^a}, \overline{q^b})_i$ (Equations (3) and (4)) for the first 25 limit orders of each side, on a relative price scale. Table 4 presents further descriptive statistics of the prices and volumes of the first ten steps of the depth profile. We make the following observations:

1. *Symmetry between bid and ask side:* There is a high degree of symmetry in the average depth profile of the bid and the ask side: Average prices exhibit very similar absolute values, and depths agree surprisingly well at corresponding steps *i*. This symmetry is well-known for limit order stock markets (see, for example, Biais et al. (1995), Potters and Bouchaud (2003) and Cao et al. (2009)).
2. *Dispersion of liquidity:* The liquidity provided at the best bid or the best ask price is only a very small part of overall liquidity, and the incremental liquidity provided by each level deeper in the LOB is

---

5   Whenever possible, results for subperiods are shown alongside main results. Omitted results are available on request.

comparably small. Biais et al. (1995) observe this pattern for equity data from the Paris Bourse, and we find that it is very pronounced in the Bitcoin market: The average level contributes an additional volume of 2 BTC (corresponding to roughly 20000 USD). These small depths may be driven by the fact that the cryptocurrency markets are still dominated by retail trading activity, and that there is still potential for further institutional market making activities—see Chaparro (2017) and Arnold (2018). Furthermore, we find that the average volume at the best ask/bid is triple the volume contributed by levels deeper in the book, which contrasts with Biais et al. (1995) who point out that it is slightly lower.

3. *Approximately linear price schedule:* In agreement with Biais et al. (1995), we observe that the price schedule, i.e., the dependence of the price on demanded or offered quantity, can be approximated very well by linearity and is weakly concave. The concavity seems to be a consequence of an unequal spacing of average price levels rather than a consequence of increasing average volume at each price level. To analyze this in detail, Figure 2b displays the average relative spread between adjacent price levels $\left(\overline{\Delta a}, \overline{\Delta b} \right)_i$ (Equation (5)) as function of the level number i. The bid and the ask side of the LOB behave very similarly. The largest average difference in price is found directly after the best bid/best ask and amounts to roughly 1.2 bp, which is larger than the average bid-ask spread (0.97 bp). This value then declines to lower values and remains constant at roughly 0.7 bp for higher price levels $(i \geq 15)$.[6] The first 25 price levels in the static LOB are therefore denser further away from the bid-ask spread. We might interpret this observation as a consequence of the execution of market orders reducing the limit order volume at the center of the LOB. Orders deeper in the book are less likely to be executed, leading to more densely spaced price levels on average.

Robustness checks: The observed symmetry between bid and ask side of the LOB and the roughly linear price schedule holds also for subperiods SP1 and SP2 (compare the light gray lines in Figure 2a) as well as for the Coinbase and Bitstamp exchanges (compare Figure A1 in the Appendix A). Surprisingly, for Coinbase, the price schedule is convex, and consequently, the average price spread between LOB levels increases with i.

---

[6] The question arises whether these results are a consequence of the limited price increment of the exchange. With average mid prices in the order of 10,000 USD and a price increment of 0.1 USD, we obtain a technical limit for relative price differences of 0.1 bp, which is still one order of magnitude larger than the observed average price differences.

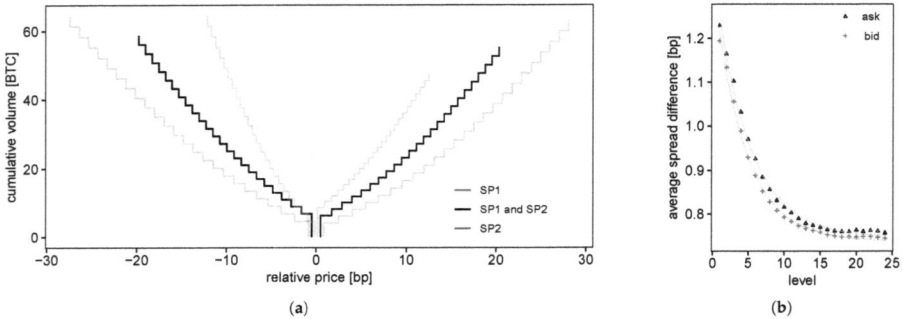

Figure 2. Average limit order book and relative spread between adjacent order book depths. (**a**) Average limit order depth. We plot the time-averaged spread (relative to the respective mid-price) and time-averaged cumulated volume for each level of the order book and for the different subperiods (SP1, SP2) of the data. (**b**) Time-averaged relative spread difference between adjacent depth steps. The gray lines are fits of exponential functions to guide the eye.

Distribution of volume at the (best) bid and ask: Figure 3 shows the joint distribution of volume at the best bid and the best ask (q_1^b and q_1^a, respectively). We calculate the common logarithm of the volume in units of the minimum order size (0.002 BTC, compare Table 1) and calculate the histogram. The empirical distribution shares the main characteristic properties with the results by Bouchaud et al. (2002) for the Paris Bourse: First, the empirical distributions agree very well and fit to a Gamma distribution $p(q_1) \propto q_1^{\gamma-1} \exp(-q_1/\theta)$ with a shape parameter $\gamma \approx 0.28 \leq 1$ and a scale parameter $\theta \approx 10.94$ BTC. From the fit to the Gamma distribution follows that the most probable volume at the best bid or best ask is zero, but the expected value is rather large. Second, the distribution deviates from the Gamma distribution for specific, equally spaced values: Apparently, there is a number preference for the order size, which gets apparent for smaller depth values, where it is more likely that only a single limit order provides the complete depth. Preferred values seem to be 0.1 BTC, 0.5 BTC, and especially 1.0 BTC. Third, the distributions of the bid and the ask side are very similar (not shown).

Robustness checks: Despite differences in estimated parameters γ and θ, we find the empirical distribution for subperiods SP1 and SP2 to be very similar. When comparing results to those of the Coinbase and Bitstamp exchanges, we find that the volume at the best bid and best ask is considerably lower (compare Tables A1 and A2 in the Appendix A) for both exchanges. The distribution seems to be largely affected by a trader's preference for certain order sizes and is not well described by the Gamma distribution, which might be a consequence of a much smaller trading volume at these exchanges.

Table 4. Descriptive statistics of the average order book. The table reports descriptive statistics for the relative prices ($\bar{a}_i$ and $\bar{b}_i$) and depths (q_i^a and q_i^b) at the first ten steps of the LOB.

	$\bar{a}_1$ [bp]	$\bar{a}_2$ [bp]	$\bar{a}_3$ [bp]	$\bar{a}_4$ [bp]	$\bar{a}_5$ [bp]	$\bar{a}_6$ [bp]	$\bar{a}_7$ [bp]	$\bar{a}_8$ [bp]	$\bar{a}_9$ [bp]	$\bar{a}_{10}$ [bp]
mean	0.4831	1.7123	2.8763	3.9788	5.0104	5.9803	6.9070	7.7917	8.6484	9.4799
sd	1.2024	2.3147	2.9969	3.6133	4.1442	4.6576	5.1445	5.6122	6.0846	6.5424
q25	0.0675	0.3759	1.0092	1.6425	2.3193	2.9572	3.5081	4.0941	4.6438	5.1234
median	0.0777	1.0470	2.0961	3.0733	3.9880	4.8294	5.5362	6.2500	6.9267	7.5638
q75	0.4392	2.1786	3.7341	5.1103	6.4375	7.6628	8.8376	9.9623	11.0422	12.1047

	$\bar{b}_1$ [bp]	$\bar{b}_2$ [bp]	$\bar{b}_3$ [bp]	$\bar{b}_4$ [bp]	$\bar{b}_5$ [bp]	$\bar{b}_6$ [bp]	$\bar{b}_7$ [bp]	$\bar{b}_8$ [bp]	$\bar{b}_9$ [bp]	$\bar{b}_{10}$ [bp]
mean	−0.4831	−1.6766	−2.8087	−3.8629	−4.8509	−5.7797	−6.6675	−7.5188	−8.3457	−9.1531
sd	1.2024	2.2548	2.9204	3.4579	3.9502	4.4140	4.8690	5.3263	5.7785	6.2391
q25	−0.4392	−2.1422	−3.6505	−5.0113	−6.2035	−7.3812	−8.4742	−9.5624	−10.6170	−11.6707
median	−0.0777	−1.0301	−2.0679	−3.0492	−3.9324	−4.7487	−5.3844	−6.0720	−6.7132	−7.3242
q75	−0.0675	−0.3608	−0.9902	−1.6176	−2.2711	−2.9088	−3.4496	−4.0167	−4.5456	−5.0245

	q_1^a [BTC]	q_2^a [BTC]	q_3^a [BTC]	q_4^a [BTC]	q_5^a [BTC]	q_6^a [BTC]	q_7^a [BTC]	q_8^a [BTC]	q_9^a [BTC]	q_{10}^a [BTC]
mean	6.2519	1.9335	1.8313	1.8295	1.8376	1.8579	1.8727	1.8916	1.8991	1.9668
sd	20.2119	14.0038	9.5268	9.3860	10.6332	9.5688	9.6347	10.2464	9.9094	17.8200
q25	0.5049	0.1000	0.1000	0.1049	0.1093	0.1226	0.1270	0.1322	0.1300	0.1338
median	2.1400	0.5225	0.5008	0.5000	0.5000	0.5000	0.5000	0.5000	0.5000	0.5000
q75	6.6157	1.6600	1.5000	1.4802	1.4634	1.4722	1.4860	1.4990	1.5000	1.5000

	q_1^b [BTC]	q_2^b [BTC]	q_3^b [BTC]	q_4^b [BTC]	q_5^b [BTC]	q_6^b [BTC]	q_7^b [BTC]	q_8^b [BTC]	q_9^b [BTC]	q_{10}^b [BTC]
mean	6.7553	2.1255	2.0309	2.0423	2.0494	2.0255	1.9986	2.0195	2.0211	2.0247
sd	21.0636	10.3102	11.5825	12.0838	11.7907	12.6380	12.7130	12.8436	12.1750	10.6579
q25	0.5972	0.1000	0.1000	0.1000	0.1000	0.1063	0.1121	0.1194	0.1270	0.1251
median	2.2928	0.5394	0.5000	0.5000	0.5000	0.5000	0.5000	0.5000	0.5000	0.5000
q75	6.8141	1.7280	1.5360	1.5000	1.4770	1.4512	1.4300	1.4440	1.4743	1.5000

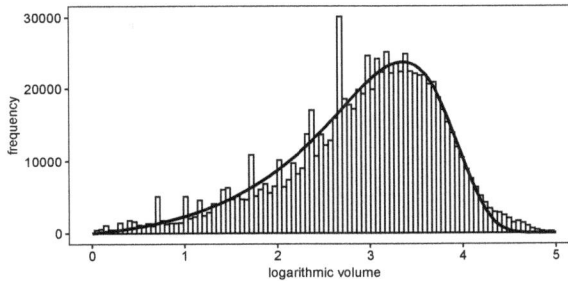

Figure 3. Distribution of volume at the best bid and best ask. We plot the empirical distribution of the common logarithm of the volume at the best bid and ask in units of the minimum order size (0.002 BTC). The solid line corresponds to a fit of a Gamma distribution with $\gamma \approx 0.28$ and $\theta \approx 10.94$ BTC.

Broad distribution of limit order prices and hump-shaped average order book: Several authors have reported empirical time-averaged limit order volumes as a function of the price difference to the current bid or ask (see Bouchaud et al. (2002), Potters and Bouchaud (2003) and Gu et al. (2008)). Figure 4 presents the density of limit order depth $\overline{q_i^a}$ (or $\overline{q_i^b}$) as a function of relative price $\tilde{p}$ (Figure 4), which we estimate using a kernel density estimator with bandwidth 0.25 bp. We identify the following main characteristics:

1. *Global maximum at (best) bid and ask:* Consistent with the findings from the time-averaged cumulated depth profile, we find the global maximum of volume at the current bid or ask of the LOB. This structure resembles the finding by Potters and Bouchaud (2003) for the SPY exchange-traded fund at Island ECN, where maximum limit order volume is found at the best bid and ask.

2. *Maximum away from current price:* There is a second, local maximum further away from the current bid (or ask), which we locate at relative prices in the order of $\bar{p} \approx 1\%$. We find the location of this maximum to be roughly symmetric between the ask and bid side of the order book. Both Bouchaud et al. (2002) and Gu et al. (2008) report a maximum in the average shape of the LOB located several ticks deep in the order book, yielding a *hump-shaped average order book*. In contrast to data from the Bitcoin exchange, this maximum is in relation closer to the current price.

3. *Broad distribution of time-averaged volume:* Bouchaud et al. (2002) find that orders are placed as far as 50 percent away from the current mid price; however most limit order volume is located within the first 100 ticks surrounding the current price, consistent with the analyses of Potters and Bouchaud (2003) and Gu et al. (2008). In contrast, we find a very broad distribution of volume around the current mid price, which extends with significant shares of the total limit order volume to up to 100 percent of the current mid price, and for the case of ask orders even further.

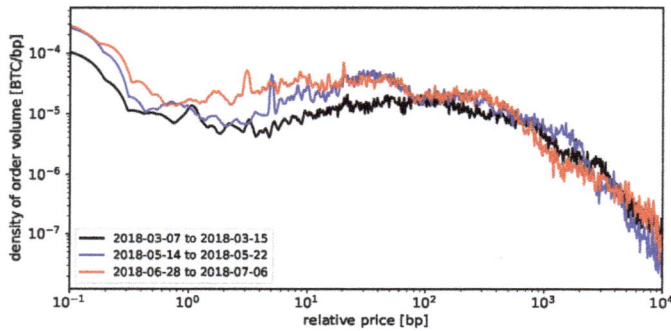

Figure 4. Time-averaged limit order depth in dependence of price. The plots show the time-averaged total limit order volume $q_i^a(t)$ (or $q_i^b(t)$) as a function of relative price for different subperiods of the sample.

To gain a better understanding of our results, we refer to the work by Roşu (2009), who models the hump-shaped volume distribution as an equilibrium: On the one hand, traders are optimistic that limit orders placed away from the current price will eventually execute at a favorable price. On the other hand, they fear that limit orders too far away from the current price will never be executed. Following this picture, there seems to be a pronounced optimism in Bitcoin markets that limit orders far away from the current price will eventually match, which may seem likely for market participants in the light of highly volatile prices. In addition, Bitcoin markets do not close during night, and limit orders can have unlimited lifetime, leading to significant limit order volume at highly speculative prices far away from the current mid price. Bitcoin markets are unregulated, with exchanges, to our knowledge, not imposing any restrictions that limit orders need to be placed within a fixed bandwidth around the current mid price. This stands in contrast to more mature markets, where such conditions may be imposed—see Interactive Brokers (2019). The observed second local maximum might therefore correspond to the hump observed in other markets, but much further away from the current price.

Robustness checks: The general shape of the average limit order depth is similar for different subperiods of data (compare Figure 4). Results from other exchanges are generally consistent with these results.

Liquidity costs: Knowledge of the full depth profile of the LOB at any time t allows to determine the liquidity premium for the virtual immediate execution of a market order of size $|\omega|$. This is particularly interesting since liquidity costs make up an important part of transaction costs, which are critical, e.g., for the profitability of high-turnover statistical arbitrage strategies. Table 5 reports descriptive statistics of the VWAP spread[7] $\bar{v}s(\omega, t)$ for different volumes ω and the bid-ask spread $\bar{s}$.

Table 5. Descriptive statistics of liquidity cost measures. We list descriptive statistics of the bid-ask spread $\bar{s}$ and volume-weighted average price spreads $\bar{v}s$ for different order volumes ω.

| | | ω [BTC] | | | | | | ω [USD] | |
	$\bar{s}$	0.1	0.5	1.0	2.0	5.0	10.0	10^5	10^6
min	0.1000	0.1000	0.1000	0.1000	0.1000	0.1000	0.1000	0.1000	0.1291
max	327.2825	327.2825	327.2825	327.2825	327.2825	327.7916	330.2782	327.9760	381.7934
mean	0.9663	1.1993	1.6364	2.0350	2.7790	4.8564	7.8754	8.3667	39.6270
sd	2.4048	2.6776	3.1408	3.5267	4.1727	5.7297	7.6235	6.7230	14.9090
q25	0.1350	0.1405	0.1488	0.1520	0.1604	1.0064	2.9504	4.0599	31.2217
q50	0.1554	0.1591	0.4497	0.7421	1.2843	3.2525	5.8831	7.0778	37.0837
q75	0.8783	0.9870	1.8381	2.5691	3.7175	6.5002	10.2739	10.8947	45.1485
skew	17.0203	13.9014	10.0866	8.2406	6.4527	4.2931	3.2508	3.4022	2.6558
kurt	1201.9088	831.4204	465.3095	309.4683	183.0332	74.8028	37.9242	49.7824	17.6048

We find an average bid-ask spread of 0.97 bp with a distribution skewed towards lower bid-ask spreads (median spread of 0.16 bp, skewness $\approx$ 17). For a similar time period but different exchanges, Dyhrberg et al. (2018) find comparable average quoted bid-ask spreads ranging from 0.54 bp to 7.8 bp and point out that these are "significantly lower than the average quoted (effective) spread [...] of stocks on the NYSE" (Dyhrberg et al. 2018, p. 141). However, taking into account liquidity deeper into the order book, we find that liquidity costs rise fast for larger volumes ω: Two-sided VWAP spreads for 1 BTC are on average twice as high as the bid-ask spread, and rise by roughly one order of magnitude (8.37 bp) for a volume of 10^5 USD, which still is a relatively small amount for traditional institutional investors. When compared to a similar analysis by Gomber et al. (2015), the depth of the LOB beyond the best bid or ask is limited: For DAX stocks, the ratio between liquidity costs for 10^6 EUR and the bid-ask spread is between 5 and 12, whereas we find a value of roughly 41.

Robustness checks: When considering subperiods of data, we find that average liquidity costs for small volumes depend on the current market phase (also compare Section 5.1.2). In SP1, liquidity is on a generally higher level, but the scaling of liquidity costs with volume is similar. The scaling of liquidity costs with volume is even more extreme for the second largest exchange (Coinbase): With 0.20 bp, the bid-ask spread is narrower on average (compare Table A3), which might be a consequence of the smaller price increment of 0.01 USD. However, liquidity costs rise fast, and assume values similar to the BitFinex exchange for larger volumes. The ratio between liquidity costs for 10^6 USD and the bid-ask spread is at 282.

5.1.2. Time Series Characteristics of Statistics

We now turn to the study of time series properties of selected measures of the static LOB.

Non-normal return distribution: Figure 5 displays the evolution of the last mid-price $m(t)$ of the day, as well as the daily realized volatility (Equation (7)). Besides the expected non-stationarity of this time series, we observe high volatility with double-digit percentage price changes during the first months of our data. This picture is reinforced by the descriptive statistics of mid-price returns $r^{mid}(t, \Delta t)$ in Table 6, for different time scales Δt. Both positive and negative daily logarithmic returns have extremal values

---

[7] The reported VWAP spreads are upper bounds as BitFinex allows hidden limit orders which might provide further liquidity.

close to 20 percent. Median and mean returns are close to zero. Daily returns are slightly skewed to the left, minutely returns are slightly skewed to the right.

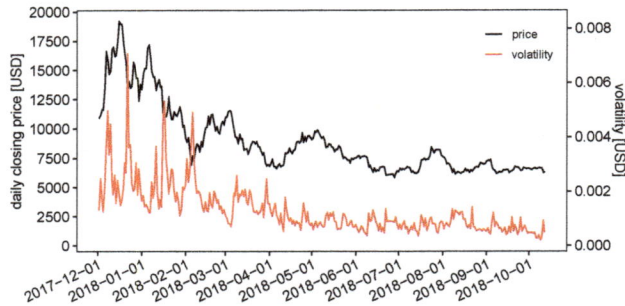

Figure 5. Daily closing prices and volatility. We plot the last available mid-price $m(t)$ of each day in universal coordinated time and the realized volatility $rv(t-1\,\text{day}, t, 1\,\text{min})$ for the respective day.

Table 6. Descriptive return statistics. This table lists statistical properties of logarithmic mid-price returns $r^{mid}(t, \Delta t)$ on different time scales Δt, in units of 1 bp (where applicable).

	$\Delta t = 1\,\text{min}$	$\Delta t = 1\,\text{h}$	$\Delta t = 1\,\text{day}$
min	-363.0070	-1273.4918	-2039.0606
max	454.4009	1127.3911	2063.1761
mean	-0.0219	-0.6505	-15.1541
sd	15.3572	115.6858	497.8412
q25	-3.4865	-35.9549	-232.2230
q50	0.0000	1.2460	5.8898
q75	3.5754	35.1836	187.2999
skew	0.1583	0.0309	-0.0797

Next, we will evaluate the tail index estimates. Table 7 summarizes the results of the tail analysis for minutely and daily data. For the Hill estimator H_p (Equation (11)) to be meaningful, approximately 2000 observations are needed (Lux and Marchesi 2000), and we therefore do not show Hill estimates for daily data (313 observations). Our tail index estimates range between 1.94 and 3.67, which is in line with the literature. Smaller estimates indicate heavier tails. Estimates for the tail index smaller than four are associated with infinite fourth moments making m_4 unreliable. Thus, we show excess kurtosis values m_4^e but do not interpret them. A typical pattern for stocks can also be found in our context, namely that the tail index estimator increases with the number of observations considered as being in the tails (Lux and Marchesi 2000). Our results provide evidence that mid returns exhibit heavy tails, i.e., the probability of extreme events is higher compared to a normal distribution. For the case where we do not distinguish between the two tails of the distribution (columns "both"), this can be seen from the quantile-based excess kurtosis metric $\gamma^e_{p=0.025, q=0.125}$ close to 0.6.[8] The Hill estimates between 2.05 and 2.90 ($\Delta t = 1\,\text{min}$) as well as 2.27 and 3.30 ($\Delta t = 1\,\text{h}$) point into the same direction. According to both metrics, we can draw the following further conclusions: First, minute data have heavier tails than hourly data, i.e., excess kurtosis values are larger, and Hill estimates smaller. Second, the left tail is heavier than the right tail for minute data

---

[8] There is only weak skewness (Table 6) giving no indication that the symmetry assumption underlying the metric is violated.

and vice versa for hourly data. The latter holds true independent of the number of observations declared as tail. In a recent contribution, Zhang et al. (2018) use the m_4 kurtosis metric and the Hill estimator to analyze the tails of eight cryptocurrencies, among them Bitcoin. For two years of daily returns, computed from closing prices, the authors point out that all examined cryptocurrencies exhibit heavy tails. Overall, we can reproduce the stylized facts on the empirical distribution of returns as summarized by Cont (2001): The distribution of mid-price returns has a sharp peak centered around zero and exhibits fat tails, and is therefore insufficiently described by the normal distribution.

Robustness checks: We recalculate tail measures for subperiods of the data (columns "SP1" and "SP2" in Table 7). The patterns for SP1 are in line with those observed for the SP1 and SP2. Also, we find similar tail patterns when comparing results to those obtained for the Coinbase and Bitstamp exchange.

Table 7. Analysis of tails of the return distribution. This table shows measures for the tails of the distribution of logarithmic mid-price returns on different time scales Δt. We use kurtosis metrics based on the fourth standardized moment (m_4^e) and based on quantiles ($\gamma_{p=0.025,q=0.125}^e$), as well as tail indices from a Hill estimator (H_p). The measures are applied to the full distribution as well as to the left and right side of the distribution only. SP1 and SP2 refer to subperiods of data.

		SP1 and SP2						SP1		SP2	
Δt		1 min			1 h			1 min	1 h	1 min	1 h
	Side	Both	Left	Right	Both	Left	Right	Both	Both	Both	Both
m_4^e		44.3497	41.5939	47.3472	17.6771	18.0461	17.3392	32.219	11.6763	77.9707	30.7078
$\gamma_{p=0.025,q=0.125}^e$		0.6481	0.7975	0.6004	0.5784	0.4773	0.6922	0.3992	0.2830	0.5555	0.9727
$H_{p=10\%}$		2.0521	1.9382	2.1681	2.2681	2.4375	2.1438	2.4160	2.6743	2.0854	1.8972
$H_{p=5\%}$		2.4823	2.3919	2.5650	2.8674	2.8448	2.8233	2.8642	3.2549	2.3750	2.1826
$H_{p=2.5\%}$		2.8954	2.8852	2.9079	3.2968	3.6668	2.9610	3.2203	3.7743	2.4933	2.7144

Autocorrelation of returns and volatility clustering: We check the common fact that "price movements in liquid markets do not exhibit any significant autocorrelation" (Cont 2001, p. 229), and compute the autocorrelation function of mid-price returns $C^{mid}(n)$ on different time scales (Table 8): We find a small positive autocorrelation of 0.0343 on the minute time scale for a lag of one minute. Turning to daily data, we do not find significant structure in the autocorrelation, which is confirmed by the Ljung-Box test (Ljung and Box 1978) with the null hypothesis of no autocorrelation.[9]

---

[9] We obtain a *p*-value of 0.6340. Given the large sample sizes for minutely and hourly data, applying the Ljung-Box test is not meaningful, because even the smallest estimated autocorrelation is significant (Lux and Marchesi 2000).

Table 8. **Autocorrelation of logarithmic, absolute and squared returns.** We compute the autocorrelation functions $C^{mid}(n)$, $C_1^{mid}(n)$ and $C_2^{mid}(n)$ for different lags n, different time scales Δt and different subperiods.

	lag n	$\Delta t = 1\,\text{min}$			$\Delta t = 1\,\text{h}$			$\Delta t = 1\,\text{day}$		
		$C^{mid}(n)$	$C_2^{mid}(n)$	$C_1^{mid}(n)$	$C^{mid}(n)$	$C_2^{mid}(n)$	$C_1^{mid}(n)$	$C^{mid}(n)$	$C_2^{mid}(n)$	$C_1^{mid}(n)$
SP1 and SP2	1	0.0342	0.2847	0.4667	−0.0722	0.1625	0.2962	0.0004	0.1443	0.1209
	2	−0.0172	0.2357	0.4295	0.0134	0.2028	0.3259	0.0179	0.0436	0.1205
	3	−0.0055	0.2198	0.4121	−0.0208	0.1690	0.3071	0.0107	0.0766	0.1681
	4	−0.0015	0.2324	0.4041	−0.0364	0.1366	0.2833	−0.0862	0.2132	0.1960
	5	−0.0074	0.2069	0.4005	−0.0083	0.2034	0.3264	0.0441	0.0796	0.1203
	6	−0.0093	0.2112	0.3961	0.0212	0.1386	0.2850	0.0174	0.0887	0.1428
	7	−0.0169	0.1976	0.3885	−0.0120	0.1785	0.3083	−0.0201	0.0733	0.1395
	8	−0.0097	0.1858	0.3835	0.0071	0.2399	0.3399	0.0531	0.1511	0.2352
	9	−0.0068	0.1873	0.3784	−0.0427	0.2007	0.3056	−0.0229	0.0528	0.0892
	10	−0.0055	0.1944	0.3801	0.0535	0.2099	0.2927	−0.0307	0.1126	0.1503
SP1	1	0.0306	0.2706	0.4019	−0.0900	0.1324	0.2084	−0.0044	0.0678	−0.0331
	2	−0.0186	0.2267	0.3683	0.0170	0.1793	0.2588	0.0071	−0.0532	−0.0188
	3	−0.0066	0.2119	0.3523	−0.0256	0.1432	0.2421	0.0116	−0.0107	0.0539
	4	−0.0001	0.2265	0.3452	−0.0403	0.1067	0.2109	−0.1007	0.1495	0.0927
	5	−0.0080	0.1995	0.3432	−0.0098	0.1822	0.2663	0.0533	0.0075	0.0164
SP2	1	0.0592	0.2883	0.3813	0.0157	0.0757	0.1497	0.0189	−0.0040	0.0720
	2	−0.0076	0.1446	0.2933	−0.0162	0.0029	0.0512	0.0613	0.0169	0.0044
	3	0.0019	0.1071	0.2538	−0.0005	0.0342	0.0651	−0.0042	−0.0530	−0.0213
	4	−0.0112	0.0914	0.2339	0.0019	−0.0044	0.0359	−0.0424	−0.0098	−0.0080
	5	−0.0033	0.0810	0.2190	−0.0035	−0.0073	0.0292	0.0132	−0.0785	−0.0848

On the other hand, nonlinear functions of returns are known to show significant autocorrelation, which is referred to as volatility clustering (Cont 2001). As for a wide range of other markets, we find that the autocorrelation of squared returns is positive and decays slowly with the lag n. Following several other authors, we fit a power law $C_2^{mid}(n) \sim n^{-\beta}$ and obtain coefficients of $\beta \approx 0.16$ and $\beta \approx 0.24$ for the decay of autocorrelation on the minutely and hourly time scale, respectively, which is at the lower end of the range given by Cont (2001) ($\beta \in [0.2, 0.4]$). The effect size of autocorrelation in squared and absolute returns decreases with the frequency. For absolute and squared daily returns, we test the null hypothesis of no autocorrelation using the Ljung-Box test (Ljung and Box 1978), which we can reject (p-value of 0.0000). Our findings for daily data are in line with Zhang et al. (2018). The authors report for all eight analyzed cryptocurrencies that autocorrelation decays at a fast rate for returns and slowly for absolute returns. In addition, they found significant volatility clustering.

Robustness checks: The subperiod analysis for SP1 and SP2 (panels "SP1" and "SP2" in Table 8) reveals that the general results for the full time period carry over to the subperiods. When comparing results with other exchanges, we obtain a similar picture.

Evolution of liquidity costs: Figure 6 displays the evolution of the daily averages of the relative bid-ask spread $\tilde{s}(t)$ and the VWAP spread $\tilde{v}s(\omega, t)$ for virtual market orders of different sizes ω. We make the following observations: First, the bid-ask spread $\tilde{s}(t)$ varies over approximately one order of magnitude from 3 bp in late 2017/early 2018 to roughly 0.3 bp after May 2018. This stark change is in line with the evolution of the average weekly bid-ask spread for several Bitcoin exchanges found by Dyhrberg et al. (2018). Second, we find that the variation in the level of liquidity costs for higher volumes is less pronounced: For example, the VWAP spread $\tilde{v}s(\omega, t)$ for a value of 10^6 USD remains—in relation to the bid-ask spread—closer to the long-term average value of 39.62 bp. Third, the analysis shows that the costs of liquidity provision are higher in times of high Bitcoin price and high volatility: The linear correlation coefficients between the daily closing price are $\rho \approx 0.73$ for the bid-ask spread and $\rho \approx 0.21$ for the VWAP spread for 10^6 USD.

Robustness checks: We find that results from the exchanges Coinbase and Bitstamp exhibit a similar evolution of liquidity cost measures (compare Figure A2 in the Appendix A).

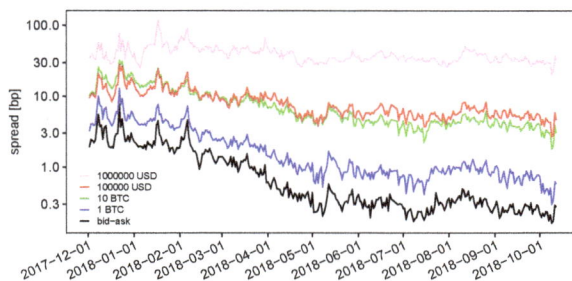

Figure 6. Evolution of daily average liquidity costs. The figure displays the evolution of the daily averages of the bid-ask spread $\tilde{s}(t)$ and the volume-weighted average price spread $\tilde{v}s(\omega, t)$ for different volumes ω.

5.1.3. Conditional Statistics of the Limit Order Book

Finally, we present two selected analyses based on conditional statistics of measures of the static LOB, namely intraday patterns of liquidity costs and liquidity resiliency.

Intraday patterns of liquidity costs: A common result for limit order markets is that the bid-ask spread has a U-shaped intraday pattern: McInish and Wood (1992) find for NYSE data that averaged bid-ask spreads are highest at the beginning and the end of the trading day. Similar results have been obtained for a foreign exchange market (Danielsson and Payne 2001), the Swiss Stock Exchange (Ranaldo 2004) and the Paris Bourse (Biais et al. 1995). Gomber et al. (2015) demonstrate that VWAP spreads are approximately doubled near the start and end of the continuous trading session for Xetra-traded DAX stocks. Figure 7 displays the change of the average hourly distribution of the bid-ask spread $\tilde{s}(t)$ and liquidity costs $\tilde{v}s(\omega, t)$ for 10 BTC and 10^6 USD relative to the mean value at the BitFinex BTC/USD market. We observe that average liquidity cost measures vary only slightly across the day (with relative changes of a few percent) with no clearly visible pattern.[10] Dyhrberg et al. (2018) make the same observation for averaged bid-ask spreads from three Bitcoin markets and attribute this to the continuous trading at every hour of the day at cryptocurrency markets. In addition, we conjecture that these results could be explained by a worldwide market participation leading to a superposition of intraday patterns from different time zones and the presence of automated trading, such that no clear picture can emerge.

---

[10] Following McInish and Wood (1992), we additionally perform a regression of the bid-ask spread $\tilde{s}(t)$ on dummy variables for each hour of the day. In line with previous results, regression results do not yield a significant pattern.

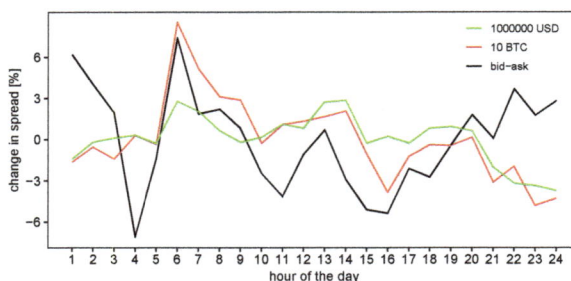

Figure 7. Intraday dynamics of liquidity costs. We display the relative deviation from the mean value of the average hourly distribution of the bid-ask spread $\bar{s}(t)$ and liquidity costs $\bar{v}s(\omega, t)$ for 10 BTC and 10^6 USD, with the hour of the day given in the local exchange time zone (Hong Kong time).

Robustness checks: As expected, the observed average hourly changes in liquidity are not robust when considering subperiods of data, which supports the conclusion of absent intraday patterns. We find a clear but weak U-shaped intraday pattern in liquidity costs for the Bitstamp exchange (compare Figure A3 in the Appendix A), which could be due to a focus of trading activity on the European market.[11] In contrast, we observe larger variations at the Coinbase exchange, but no universal pattern emerges when comparing bid-ask spread and liquidity costs for higher volumes. Overall, we observe a mixed picture: Hourly average liquidity costs differ largely between cryptocurrency exchanges, and pronounced patterns known from established markets are largely absent.

Liquidity resiliency and timing of large trades: We now characterize the recovery of limit order liquidity after liquidity shocks, and analyze whether large trades are timed in the sense that they occur when liquidity is high. We examine average liquidity costs (precisely, the relative bid-ask spread $f = \bar{s}$ and VWAP spread $f = \bar{v}s$) as a function of the event time τ in temporal vicinity of large trades (Equation (12)). We consider the one percent largest trades ($N = 510{,}584$) to obtain sufficient statistics. Figure 8 displays results for the bid-ask spread and the VWAP spreads for 10^5 USD and 10^6 USD. Compared to relevant literature, we make the following observations:

---

[11] As for BitFinex, we run a dummy variable regression which supports the existence of the U-shaped pattern.

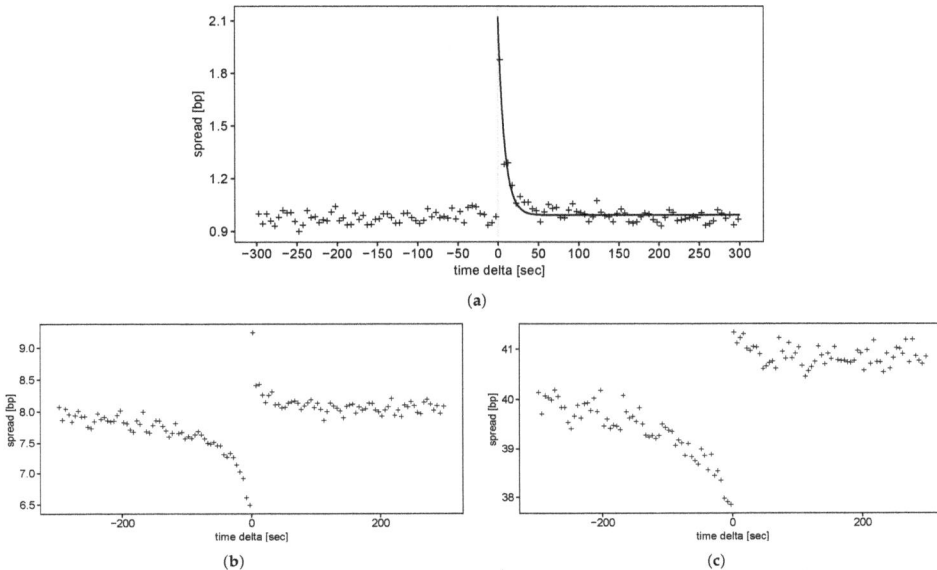

Figure 8. Resiliency of liquidity costs. The figures display three different average measures of liquidity cost in the event time τ of the 1 percent largest trades. (**a**) Evolution of the average bid-ask spread $\bar{s}(\tau)$. We fit an exponential function with time constant 8.3 s to guide the eye.; (**b**) Evolution of the average volume-weighted average price spread $\bar{v}s(\omega, \tau)$ for a volume of $\omega = 10^5$ USD; (**c**) Evolution of the average volume-weighted average price spread $\bar{v}s(\omega, \tau)$ for a volume of $\omega = 10^6$ USD.

1. *Recovery of the bid-ask spread:* We first consider the typical speed at which liquidity recovers after a large trade. We find that the average bid-ask spread increases to roughly 2 bp directly following the trade and subsequently recovers to its pre-event value of about 1 bp (Figure 8a). We fit an exponential decay function $\bar{s}(\tau) \sim \exp(-\tau/T)$ to estimate the decay time constant as $T \approx 8.3$ s (corresponding to a half-life of $T_{1/2} \approx 5.8$ s). Surprisingly, this is well in line with the finding of Cummings and Frino (2010) for large block trades of interest rate futures at the Sydney Futures Exchange: Considering only the largest block trades, they find that excess bid-ask spreads after the largest block purchases recover to a normal level on a time scale of approximately 7 s. They find that recovery is faster for the largest trades. Similarly, Large (2007) estimates a half-life time of about 20 s for a stock at the London Stock Exchange.

2. *Recovery of liquidity beyond the (best) bid and ask:* For liquidity provided from deeper levels of the LOB, we find that liquidity does not quite recover to pre-event levels in the considered time window of 300 s (compare Figure 8b,c). Gomber et al. (2015) find that "it takes longer to restore large depth than to restore a small spread" (Gomber et al. 2015, p. 67). They estimate that it takes about four minutes to restore liquidity costs for 10^5 EUR. For similar volumes (Figure 8b) we observe that average liquidity after the trade still differs slightly from pre-trade values.

3. *Pre-trade liquidity increase and timing of large transactions:* For average liquidity costs for 10^5 USD and 10^6 USD, we find—at first quite surprisingly—that liquidity increases prior to a large trade. This effect is observed in time windows of 2–3 min preceding the trade. Gomber et al. (2015) report a very similar finding for the evolution of the average exchange liquidity measure: Liquidity costs for 10^5 EUR and

DAX stocks decrease over an interval of about three minutes before large trades. Noticing that the increase in liquidity takes place on the side of the market where the trade occurs, they interpret this effect in terms of timed large transactions: Market participants prefer to execute large trades when liquidity is exceptionally high, and the execution of large trades relatively cheap. Our results indicate that the timing of large transactions is also present in Bitcoin markets.

Robustness checks: We obtain similar results for subperiods SP1 and SP2 of our data. To check that results are not driven by clusters of trades, we follow Gomber et al. (2015) and redo calculations for all large trades that are not followed by other large trades within 15 min. We observe very similar results and conjecture that our results are not dominated by the clustering of trades. When comparing results to the exchange Coinbase (compare Figure A4 in the Appendix A), we observe similar patterns in the recovery of liquidity. However, results are different for the smallest exchange in our sample (Bitstamp), where we observe an increase of liquidity costs after the trade. These results could be due to a market maker or some other idiosyncrasy of the exchange, for example the generally lower liquidity or differences in trade and order sizes.

5.2. Analysis of the Dynamics of the Limit Order Book: Order and Trade Flows

5.2.1. Unconditional Descriptive Statistics of Trades and Order Book Changes

We next present unconditional descriptive statistics of measures of the dynamic LOB, i.e., properties of trades and the limit order flow, and begin by discussing the distribution of trade size.

Distribution of trade size: Table 9 lists descriptive statistics of the price p_M and size ω_M of all trades in our sample ($N = 51{,}058{,}356$). There seems to be a large amount of retail trading: With a median trade value of roughly 634 USD (0.0752 BTC), most trades are comparably small. Figure 9 displays the rich structure in the distribution of trade size ω_M, for which we observe the following:

1. *Two regimes separated by the minimum order size:* The distribution of trade size exhibits a large jump at the minimum order size of 0.002 BTC, and separates two regimes: For smaller trades, trade frequency increases with trade size, but exhibits discontinuities. For larger trade sizes, the distribution exhibits a convex plateau and a power tail for trades larger 1 BTC.

2. *Power-law dependence of volume for large trades:* For trade sizes exceeding the minimum order size, the empirical distribution of trade size agrees well with results from the literature: Similar to the results of Mu et al. (2009), the empirical distribution of trade sizes larger than the minimum order size fits well to a q-Gamma distribution $p(\omega_M) \propto (\omega_M)^\beta \left[1 - (1-q)\frac{\omega_M}{\theta}\right]^{(1-q)^{-1}}$ with parameters $\beta \approx 10^{-4}$, $\theta \approx 5.28 \cdot 10^{-2}$ and $q \approx 1.41$. The asymptotic tail exponent of this distribution is given by $\alpha = \frac{1}{q-1} - \beta - 1 \approx 1.44$. Gopikrishnan et al. (2000) and Maslov and Mills (2001) find power tails with comparable values for US stock markets ($\alpha = 1.53 \pm 0.07$) and the NASDAQ ($\alpha = 1.4 \pm 0.1$).

3. *Significant share of trades smaller than the minimum order size:* A large share of trades has a size smaller than the minimum order size. We interpret these results in the light of a minimum order size increment (10^{-8} BTC) much smaller than the minimum order size (0.002 BTC), leading to trade sizes much smaller than the minimum order size. For example, an ask order with initial volume 0.0021 BTC could be partially matched with a bid order of 0.002 BTC, leaving a small ask order active that could subsequently lead to a trade of size 0.0001 BTC.

4. *Number preference:* Mu et al. (2009) reported that traders seem to prefer certain numbers for order sizes, which also manifests in the distribution of trade size. Similarly, we observe peaks in trade frequency for certain sizes, for example at 0.01 BTC, 0.02 BTC, 0.1 BTC, 0.5 BTC and 1 BTC.

Contrary to traditional equity markets investigated in the literature, minimum order size and the order size increment differ largely for cryptocurrency markets due to the divisibility of Bitcoin, leading to the observation a different trade size distribution.

Robustness checks: The shape of the empirical distribution of trade size is robust with respect to considering subperiods SP1 and SP2 of our data. We obtain very similar empirical distributions for the other two exchanges, albeit slightly different minimum order sizes (compare Table 1).

Table 9. Descriptive statistics of trades. This table lists descriptive statistics of the price p_M, the value $\omega_M \cdot p_M$ and the size ω_M for all trades.

	p_M [USD]	$\omega_M \cdot p_M$[USD]			ω_M [BTC]		
	All	All	Ask-Initiated	Bid-Initiated	All	Ask-Initiated	Bid-Initiated
count	51,058,356	51,058,356	26,112,746	24,945,610	51,058,356	26,112,746	24,945,610
mean	8665.11	3053.87	3059.75	3047.72	0.3643	0.3658	0.3627
sd	2493.81	13,658.82	14,155.62	13,118.64	1.6686	1.7441	1.5857
q25	6710.00	138.14	134.45	143.19	0.0170	0.0160	0.0180
q50	8011.30	634.33	626.23	641.15	0.0752	0.0748	0.0760
q75	9602.40	2431.44	2419.27	2440.93	0.2938	0.2906	0.2970
skew	1.52	89.51	97.32	78.79	94.84	92.21	97.75

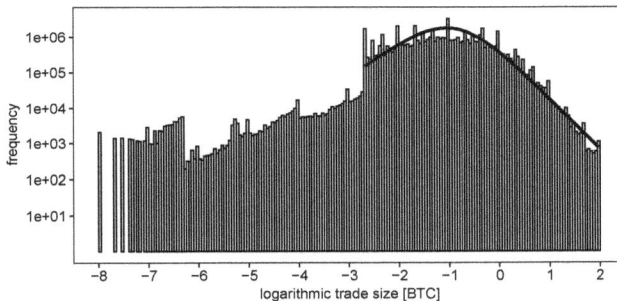

Figure 9. Distribution of trade size. We plot the empirical distribution of trade size ω_M in log-log scale. The line corresponds to a fit to the q-Gamma distribution.

Distribution of changes in limit order depth: Next, we consider the flow of limit order volume to and from the LOB. In Figure 10, we plot the time-averaged empirical density of changed limit order volume in the LOB, i.e., $\overline{\Delta n^b(p)}$ and $\overline{\Delta n^a(p)}$ (Equation (14)) on a price scale relative to the current mid price. We make the following observations:

1. *Power tail away from the current price:* Further away from the current mid price, the changed limit order volume declines rapidly. Figure 10 includes dashed straight lines with a slope of roughly −2.8, and the empirical density in log-log axes declines at a roughly similar rate. Power tails in the distribution of order frequency as a function of the difference to the price have been found before (compare, for example, Bouchaud et al. (2002), Zovko and Farmer (2002) and Potters and Bouchaud (2003). These analyses consider all incoming orders, whereas we consider the total change in depth in the LOB. Therefore, a different distribution close to the mid price would be expected.
2. *Constant changed order volume near the current price:* We find a roughly constant density in changed limit order volume up to a relative price of 1 percent. We may cautiously conclude that this finding is

still consistent with the literature: Several authors (for example, Bouchaud et al. (2002), Zovko and Farmer (2002) and Potters and Bouchaud (2003)) found that most orders arrive at the current bid or ask price. These orders are, however, executed immediately or with high profitability, and thus cannot be observed in our analysis, leading to the observed plateau in the distribution of changed limit order volume. Orders arriving further away from the current price are less likely executed and lead to persistent changes in limit order depth, which we observe in our analysis.

3. *Peaked activity away from the current price:* Quite surprisingly, we see distinct peaks in changed order volume at relative prices of 4 and 6 percent. These could be the consequence of speculative order placement or the traders' preference for certain round order prices.

These results are well in line with the previously found broad distribution of limit order volume (compare Section 5.1.1). Specifically, we conjecture that speculative order placement plays an important role in these markets, which is—in contrast to established markets—not restricted by exchanges or regulators by imposing caps on order prices.

Robustness checks: The distributions of LOB changes for all subperiods in Figure 10 are similar, and we find generally consistent results for the other exchanges.

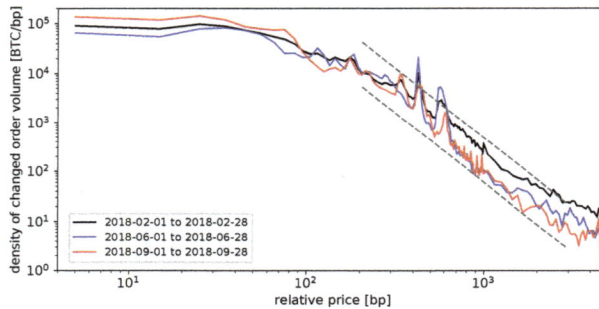

Figure 10. Distribution of changed limit order volume. We plot the time-averaged empirical density of changed limit order volume in the limit order book (Equation (14)) on a relative price scale. The three plots correspond to different four-week periods of our data. The dashed lines have a slope of -2.8.

5.2.2. Time Series Characteristics of Trade Properties

Evolution of trading volume and trade size: Figure 11 displays the evolution of daily averages of the trade size, the number of trades and the cumulated volume (compare Section 4.3.2). We make the following observations: First, both the number of trades and cumulated volume are higher during the phase of comparably high prices. Second, peaks in cumulated volume and trade frequency coincide with peaks in volatility of the mid price (compare Figure 5). Third, the average trade size is relatively stable, and decreases in the high-price phase, which might be a consequence of increased retail trading due to higher interest in cryptocurrencies.

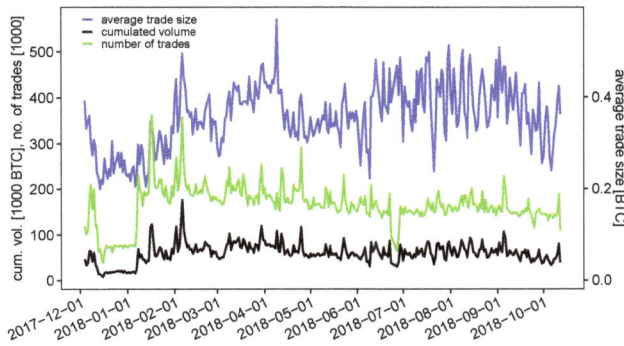

Figure 11. Daily trading volume, number of trades and daily average trade size. We aggregate the daily volume and the daily number of trades in universal coordinated time.

Autocorrelation of trade price changes and sizes: While return time series on time scales of minutes to days do typically not possess any significant autocorrelation, high-frequency return time series are found to have negative autocorrelation at the first lags. This is attributed to the bid-ask bounce, i.e., the oscillation of trade prices between prices of the bid side of the LOB and prices at the ask side (Cont 2001; Russell and Engle 2010). Table 10 lists values of the autocorrelation function of trade price changes $C^{tp}(n)$ (Equation (15)). We observe negative autocorrelations $C^{tp}(n)$ in the first lags, and $C^{tp}(1) \approx -0.18$ is comparable in size with results by Russell and Engle (2010). When looking at sell and buy trades separately, we find that $C^{tp}(1)$ drops to roughly -0.08, which is consistent with autocorrelations being driven mainly by the bid-ask bounce. Results for the autocorrelation function of trade sizes $C^{size}(n)$ (Equation (16)) exhibit positive values in the order of 0.12, which does not depend on whether we include all trades or only sell or buy trades.

Robustness checks: We obtain similar results when repeating the analyses for subperiods of data (panels SP1 and SP2 of Table 10). Autocorrelation functions for trade price changes and trade sizes behave similarly for the other Bitcoin exchanges.

Table 10. Autocorrelation of trade properties. We compute the autocorrelation functions of trade price changes $C^{tp}(n)$ and trade sizes $C^{size}(n)$ for lags $n = 1, \ldots, 10$. We show results for all trades, for ask-initiated trades ($\omega_M > 0$) and bid-initiated trades ($\omega_M < 0$) separately.

	lag n	$C^{size}(n)$ All	$\omega_M > 0$	$\omega_M < 0$	$C^{tp}(n)$ All	$\omega_M > 0$	$\omega_M < 0$
SP1 and SP2	1	0.1225	0.1398	0.1176	−0.1759	−0.0790	−0.0833
	2	0.1045	0.1106	0.1128	−0.0529	−0.0204	−0.0234
	3	0.0926	0.0995	0.0946	−0.0302	−0.0110	−0.0147
	4	0.1092	0.1219	0.1061	−0.0107	−0.0001	−0.0033
	5	0.0743	0.0775	0.0796	−0.0128	−0.0059	−0.0066
	6	0.0893	0.0947	0.0931	−0.0032	0.0059	0.0045
	7	0.0672	0.0728	0.0694	−0.0091	−0.0018	−0.0018
	8	0.0890	0.1013	0.0832	−0.0020	0.0048	0.0036
SP1	1	0.1024	0.1314	0.0854	−0.1775	−0.0787	−0.0831
	2	0.0675	0.0718	0.0773	−0.0532	−0.0204	−0.0236
	3	0.0611	0.0644	0.0665	−0.0294	−0.0101	−0.0140
	4	0.0596	0.0609	0.0671	−0.0111	−0.0006	−0.0042
	5	0.0496	0.0505	0.0580	−0.0114	−0.0044	−0.0054
SP2	1	0.1406	0.1464	0.1513	−0.1378	−0.0834	−0.0871
	2	0.1380	0.1419	0.1501	−0.0468	−0.0207	−0.0205
	3	0.1211	0.1278	0.1239	−0.0483	−0.0276	−0.0276
	4	0.1541	0.1713	0.1469	−0.0024	0.0099	0.0121
	5	0.0965	0.0993	0.1021	−0.0458	−0.0320	−0.0288

5.2.3. Conditional Statistics Across All Trades

Intraday patterns of trading activity: We now analyze intraday patterns in trading activity. Contrary to commonly found patterns in the bid-ask spread, results from the literature differ depending on the market, and range from U-shaped patterns for stocks at the Paris Bourse (Biais et al. 1995) to M-shaped patterns in data from an FX market (Danielsson and Payne 2001). Figure 12 displays the average trade size and trade frequency conditional on the hour of the day. We make the following observations: First, we find some weakly visible patterns and a similarity between the average trade size ω_M and the number of trades. Second, we find the trade frequency to vary in the order of 10 percent during the day. Third, we observe a slightly lower average trade size during night time.

Robustness checks: Similar patterns can be observed for the other exchanges (compare Figure A6). Here, we find that the trade frequency is highest in the afternoon and lowest during night (or morning hours) in the local time zone of the exchange. Nevertheless, there is a strong trading activity baseline for all exchanges, which might indicate that large cryptocurrency exchanges for the US Dollar attract market participants from all over the world, or that trading is to a large degree automated.

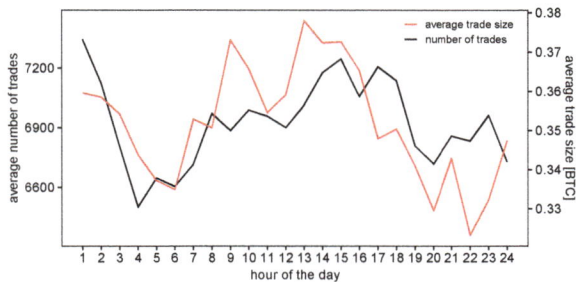

Figure 12. Intraday dynamics of trading activity. We plot the average hourly trade size and the average hourly number of trades as a function of the hour of the day in Hong Kong time.

6. Conclusions

In this work, we have empirically characterized limit order books and resulting trades from major cryptocurrency exchanges, thereby using a structured and comprehensive framework of analyses and commonly observed facts derived from the literature. We have focused on the presentation of descriptive statistical facts, which we have compared to commonly found facts from established exchanges. Also, we have provided possible qualitative interpretations for our findings. Limit order data from cryptocurrency exchanges exhibit many of the properties found for other limit order exchanges, for example a symmetric average limit order book, autocorrelation of returns only at the tick level and the timing of large trades. In contrast, we have found that cryptocurrency exchanges exhibit a relatively shallow limit order book with quickly rising liquidity costs for larger volumes, many small trades and an extended distribution of limit order volume far beyond the current mid price. Further research could focus on the origin of order placements further away from the current mid price and on the source of the differences in curvature of the average limit order book, as well as on comparisons to limit order exchanges allowing to trade between two cryptocurrencies.

Author Contributions: Conceptualization, M.S. and C.K.; methodology, M.S. and C.K.; software, J.R. and M.S.; validation, M.S., J.R. and C.K.; investigation, J.R. and M.S.; data curation, M.S.; writing—original draft preparation, M.S. and J.R.; writing—review and editing, C.K.; visualization, J.R.

Funding: This research received no external funding.

Acknowledgments: We thank the editor and two anonymous referees for their valuable comments. The authors have benefited from helpful discussions with Ingo Klein and Thomas Fischer.

Conflicts of Interest: The authors declare no conflict of interest.

Appendix. Results for Further Exchanges

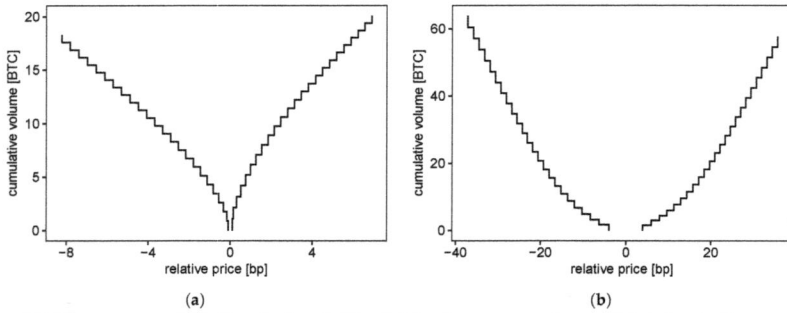

(a)   (b)

Figure A1. Time–averaged limit order book. We plot the time-averaged spread (relative to the respective mid price) and time-averaged volume for each level of the order book. (**a**) Coinbase BTC/USD market; (**b**) Bitstamp BTC/USD market.

Table A1. Descriptive statistics of the average order book for the Coinbase BTC/USD market. The table reports descriptive statistics for the relative prices ($\tilde{a}_i$ and $\tilde{b}_i$) and depths (q_i^a and q_i^b) at the first five limit order steps.

	$\tilde{a}_1$ [bp]	$\tilde{a}_2$ [bp]	$\tilde{a}_3$ [bp]	$\tilde{a}_4$ [bp]	$\tilde{a}_5$ [bp]	$\tilde{b}_1$ [bp]	$\tilde{b}_2$ [bp]	$\tilde{b}_3$ [bp]	$\tilde{b}_4$ [bp]	$\tilde{b}_5$ [bp]
mean	0.0992	0.1532	0.3097	0.5102	0.7390	−0.0992	−0.1638	−0.3407	−0.5685	−0.8364
sd	9.4231	0.9120	1.3032	1.6700	2.0189	9.4231	0.9466	1.3670	1.7763	2.2484
q25	0.0056	0.0057	0.0058	0.0060	0.0061	−0.0076	−0.0077	−0.0078	−0.0085	−0.4824
median	0.0067	0.0068	0.0071	0.0074	0.0075	−0.0067	−0.0068	−0.0070	−0.0073	−0.0075
q75	0.0076	0.0077	0.0078	0.0085	0.3317	−0.0056	−0.0057	−0.0058	−0.0059	−0.0060

	q_1^a [BTC]	q_2^a [BTC]	q_3^a [BTC]	q_4^a [BTC]	q_5^a [BTC]	q_1^b [BTC]	q_2^b [BTC]	q_3^b [BTC]	q_4^b [BTC]	q_5^b [BTC]
mean	1.0937	1.0352	1.0407	1.0242	1.0012	0.8994	0.8716	0.8330	0.8478	0.8355
sd	3.5183	3.4218	3.5283	3.5174	3.5246	2.7554	2.7223	2.6287	2.7821	2.7304
q25	0.0047	0.0029	0.0030	0.0025	0.0023	0.0077	0.0064	0.0060	0.0063	0.0063
median	0.1130	0.1000	0.0932	0.0800	0.0662	0.1200	0.1002	0.1000	0.1000	0.0958
q75	1.0000	1.0000	1.0000	1.0000	1.0000	1.0000	1.0000	0.9725	0.9683	0.9460

Table A2. Descriptive statistics of the average order book for the Bitstamp BTC/USD market. The table reports descriptive statistics for the relative prices ($\tilde{a}_i$ and $\tilde{b}_i$) and depths (q_i^a and q_i^b) at the first five limit order steps.

	$\tilde{a}_1$ [bp]	$\tilde{a}_2$ [bp]	$\tilde{a}_3$ [bp]	$\tilde{a}_4$ [bp]	$\tilde{a}_5$ [bp]	$\tilde{b}_1$ [bp]	$\tilde{b}_2$ [bp]	$\tilde{b}_3$ [bp]	$\tilde{b}_4$ [bp]	$\tilde{b}_5$ [bp]
mean	3.9306	5.9740	7.8983	9.6986	11.3785	−3.9306	−6.2516	−8.3233	−10.2498	−12.0205
sd	3.6971	5.0798	5.9524	6.6103	7.1657	3.6971	5.2242	6.1008	6.7221	7.2437
q25	1.3370	2.6456	3.9142	5.1897	6.5248	−5.3879	−7.9980	−10.6020	−12.8396	−14.7508
median	3.1511	4.7447	6.4603	8.2124	9.8818	−3.1511	−4.9946	−6.9114	−8.8283	−10.5893
q75	5.3879	7.6499	10.1350	12.3066	14.2027	−1.3370	−2.8920	−4.3039	−5.7707	−7.2550

	q_1^a [BTC]	q_2^a [BTC]	q_3^a [BTC]	q_4^a [BTC]	q_5^a [BTC]	q_1^b [BTC]	q_2^b [BTC]	q_3^b [BTC]	q_4^b [BTC]	q_5^b [BTC]
mean	1.5771	1.4164	1.4532	1.5579	1.7032	1.6735	1.5641	1.6563	1.8360	1.9904
sd	6.7095	5.3325	4.6641	4.6641	4.7830	9.1645	6.3446	4.9995	5.1847	5.3419
q25	0.0697	0.0380	0.0341	0.0350	0.0396	0.0855	0.0941	0.1000	0.1000	0.1000
median	0.5244	0.4200	0.4200	0.4440	0.5000	0.6273	0.6000	0.6691	0.8000	0.9397
q75	1.4285	1.3380	1.4226	1.5000	1.5114	1.5000	1.5000	1.5146	1.6483	1.8762

Table A3. Descriptive statistics of liquidity cost measures for the Coinbase (panel A) and the Bitstamp BTC/USD market (panel B). We list descriptive statistics of the bid-ask spread $\tilde{s}$ and volume-weighted average price spreads $\tilde{v}s$ for different order volumes ω.

			ω [BTC]							ω [USD]	
		$\tilde{s}$	0.1	0.5	1.0	2.0	5.0	10.0	10^5	10^6
A	mean	0.1984	0.4565	0.8852	1.2585	1.9590	3.9038	6.9085	8.2644	55.9732
	sd	18.8463	1.6903	3.0141	2.7074	3.3185	4.6643	6.2279	6.4667	72.2166
	q25	0.0112	0.0116	0.0121	0.0124	0.0137	0.2657	2.5405	3.7401	42.1128
	q50	0.0133	0.0142	0.0150	0.0155	0.3297	2.6565	5.7849	7.4037	51.9763
	q75	0.0152	0.0157	0.4227	1.3888	2.8715	5.7636	9.5908	11.4203	63.9471
	skew	208.2537	9.5766	173.4533	5.0151	3.9150	2.8447	2.3831	2.0350	129.3065
	kurt	43464.80	228.58	69382.36	63.09	37.55	19.99	14.23	12.14	21011.61
B	mean	7.8612	9.0643	10.5030	11.6672	13.7398	18.2892	23.5749	24.9565	73.5508
	sd	7.3941	7.9357	8.7012	9.3081	10.0856	11.6074	13.0441	11.7406	21.6807
	q25	2.6739	3.6618	4.7017	5.4402	6.9664	10.7988	15.4833	17.8222	58.9856
	q50	6.3022	7.4225	8.6849	9.6938	11.7622	16.0878	20.7755	22.8481	69.9553
	q75	10.7758	12.2041	13.8400	15.1248	17.3629	22.0618	27.1251	28.6737	83.7376
	skew	2.2649	2.1057	2.0129	1.9788	1.9183	1.8158	1.7826	1.7740	1.7231
	kurt	17.3872	14.8690	11.7922	10.3188	8.9804	6.9622	5.8785	7.1700	7.5178

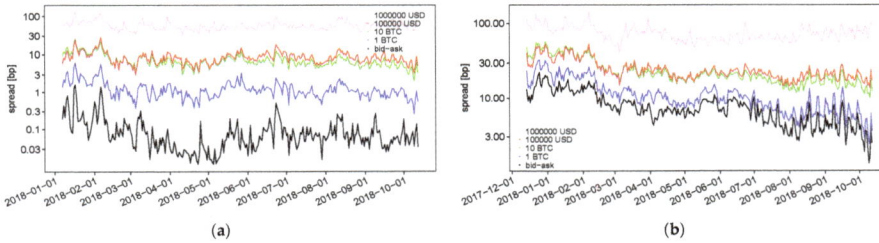

Figure A2. Evolution of daily average liquidity costs. The figure displays the daily averages of the bid-ask spread $\tilde{s}(t)$ and the volume-weighted average price spread $\tilde{v}s(\omega,t)$ for different volumes ω. (a) Coinbase BTC/USD market; (b) Bitstamp BTC/USD market.

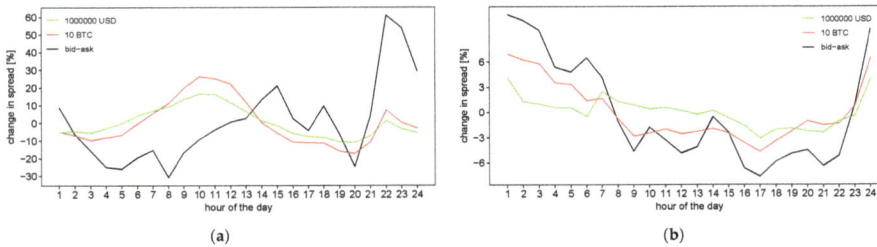

Figure A3. Intraday dynamics of liquidity costs. We display the relative deviation of the average hourly distribution of the bid-ask spread $\tilde{s}(t)$ and liquidity costs $\tilde{v}s(\omega,t)$ for 10 BTC and 10^6 USD from the mean value. (a) Coinbase BTC/USD market. The hour of the day is given in San Francisco time; (b) Bitstamp BTC/USD market. The hour of the day is given in Berlin time.

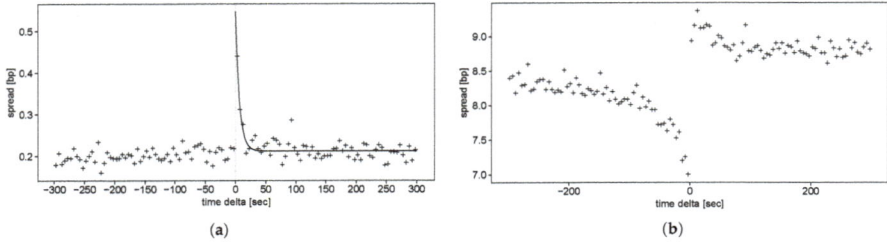

Figure A4. Resiliency of liquidity costs for the Coinbase BTC/USD market. The figures display three different average measures of liquidity cost in the event time τ of the 1 percent largest trades. (**a**) Evolution of the average bid-ask spread $\bar{s}(\tau)$. We include the fit of an exponential function with exponential time constant $T \approx 6.3$ s to guide the eye; (**b**) Evolution of the average volume-weighted average price spread $\bar{v}s(\omega, \tau)$ for a volume of $\omega = 10^5$ USD.

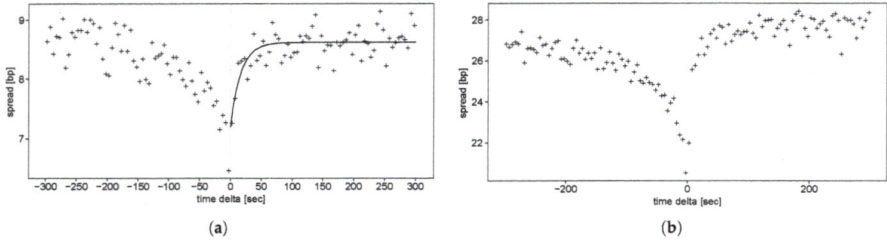

Figure A5. Resiliency of liquidity costs for the Bitstamp BTC/USD market. The figures display three different average measures of liquidity cost in the event time τ of the 1 percent largest trades. (**a**) Evolution of the average bid-ask spread $\bar{s}(\tau)$. We include the fit of an exponential function with exponential time constant $T \approx 16.6$ s to guide the eye; (**b**) Evolution of the average volume-weighted average price spread $\bar{v}s(\omega, \tau)$ for a volume of $\omega = 10^5$ USD.

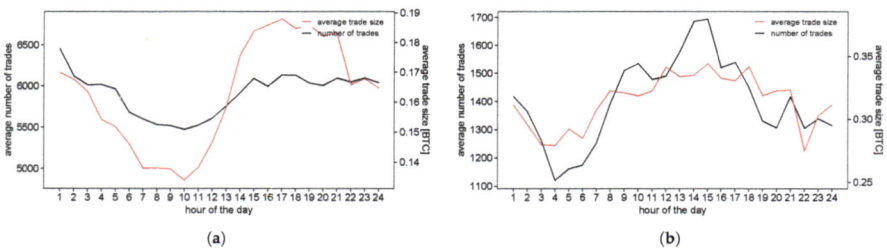

Figure A6. Intraday dynamics of trading activity. We plot the average hourly trade size and the average hourly number of trades as a function of the hour of the day. (**a**) Coinbase BTC/USD market. The hour of the day is given in San Francisco time; (**b**) Bitstamp BTC/USD market. The hour of the day is given in Berlin time.

J. Risk Financial Manag. **2019**, *12*, 25

References

Arnold, Andrew. 2018. How Institutional Investors Are Changing The Cryptocurrency Market. *Forbes*. Available online: https://www.forbes.com/sites/andrewarnold/2018/10/19/how-institutional-investors-are-changing-the-cryptocurrency-market/ (accessed on 17 January 2019).

Bacon, Carl R. 2008. *Practical Portfolio Performance Measurement and Attribution*. The Wiley Finance Series. Hoboken: Wiley & Sons.

Balanda, Kevin P., and Helen L. MacGillivray. 1990. Kurtosis and spread. *Canadian Journal of Statistics* 18: 17–30. [CrossRef]

Bariviera, Aurelio F., María José Basgall, Waldo Hasperué, and Marcelo Naiouf. 2017. Some stylized facts of the Bitcoin market. *Physica A: Statistical Mechanics and Its Applications* 484: 82–90. [CrossRef]

Biais, Bruno, Pierre Hillion, and Chester Spatt. 1995. An empirical analysis of the limit order book and the order flow in the Paris Bourse. *The Journal of Finance* 50: 1655–89. [CrossRef]

Black, Fischer. 1971. Toward a fully automated stock exchange, part I. *Financial Analysts Journal* 27: 28–35. [CrossRef]

Bouchaud, Jean-Philippe. 2009. Price Impact. *arXiv*, arXiv:0903.2428.

Bouchaud, Jean-Philippe, Marc Mézard, and Marc Potters. 2002. Statistical properties of stock order books: Empirical results and models. *Quantitative Finance* 2: 251–56. [CrossRef]

Brandvold, Morten, Peter Molnár, Kristian Vagstad, and Ole C. A. Valstad. 2015. Price discovery on Bitcoin exchanges. *Journal of International Financial Markets, Institutions and Money* 36: 18–35. [CrossRef]

Böhme, Rainer, Nicolas Christin, Benjamin Edelman, and Tyler Moore. 2015. Bitcoin: Economics, technology, and governance. *Journal of Economic Perspectives* 29: 213–38. [CrossRef]

Büning, Herbert. 1991. *Robuste und Adaptive Tests*. Berlin: De Gruyter.

Cao, Charles, Oliver Hansch, and Xiaoxin Wang. 2009. The information content of an open limit-order book. *Journal of Futures Markets* 29: 16–41. [CrossRef]

Chan, Stephen, Jeffrey Chu, Saralees Nadarajah, and Joerg Osterrieder. 2017. A statistical analysis of cryptocurrencies. *Journal of Risk and Financial Management* 10: 12. [CrossRef]

Chaparro, Frank. 2017. A small band of trading specialists are taking calls about $50 million bitcoin deals. *Business Insider Deutschland*. Available online: https://www.businessinsider.de/bitcoin-trading-matures-as-institutions-pour-in-2017-11 (accessed on 17 January 2019).

Chu, Jeffrey, Stephen Chan, Saralees Nadarajah, and Joerg Osterrieder. 2017. GARCH modelling of cryptocurrencies. *Journal of Risk and Financial Management* 10: 17. [CrossRef]

Cont, Rama. 2001. Empirical properties of asset returns: Stylized facts and statistical issues. *Quantitative Finance* 1: 223–36. [CrossRef]

Cont, Rama, Arseniy Kukanov, and Sasha Stoikov. 2014. The Price Impact of Order Book Events. *Journal of Financial Econometrics* 12: 47–88. [CrossRef]

Cummings, James Richard, and Alex Frino. 2010. Further analysis of the speed of response to large trades in interest rate futures. *Journal of Futures Markets* 30: 705–24. [CrossRef]

Danielsson, Jon, Lerby M. Ergun, Laurens de Haan, and Casper G. de Vries. 2016. *Tail Index Estimation: Quantile Driven Threshold Selection*. SSRN Scholarly Paper ID 2717478. Rochester: Social Science Research Network.

Danielsson, Jon, and Richard Payne. 2001. *Measuring and Explaining Liquidity on an Electronic Limit Order Book: Evidence from Reuters D2000-2*. SSRN Scholarly Paper ID 276541. Sochester: Social Science Research Network.

Degryse, Hans, Frank De Jong, Maarten Van Ravenswaaij, and Gunther Wuyts. 2005. Aggressive orders and the resiliency of a limit order market. *Review of Finance* 9: 201–42. [CrossRef]

Dimpfl, Thomas. 2017. *Bitcoin Market Microstructure*. SSRN Scholarly Paper ID 2949807. SSochester: Social Science Research Network.

Donier, Jonathan, and Julius Bonart. 2015. A million metaorder analysis of market impact on the Bitcoin. *Market Microstructure and Liquidity* 1: 1550008. [CrossRef]

Donier, Jonathan, and Jean-Philippe Bouchaud. 2015. Why do markets crash? Bitcoin data offers unprecedented insights. *PLoS ONE* 10: e0139356. [CrossRef] [PubMed]

Dyhrberg, Anne H., Sean Foley, and Jiri Svec. 2018. How investible is Bitcoin? Analyzing the liquidity and transaction costs of Bitcoin markets. *Economics Letters* 171: 140–43. [CrossRef]

Easwaran, Soumya, Manu Dixit, and Sitabhra Sinha. 2015. itcoin dynamics: The inverse square law of price fluctuations and other stylized facts. In *Econophysics and Data Driven Modelling of Market Dynamics*. Edited by Frédéric Abergel, Hideaki Aoyama, Bikas K. Chakrabarti, Anirban Chakraborti and Asim Ghosh. New Economic Windows. Cham: Springer International Publishing, pp. 121–28..

Foucault, Thierry, Ohad Kadan, and Eugene Kandel. 2005. Limit order book as a market for liquidity. *The Review of Financial Studies* 18: 1171–217. [CrossRef]

Gomber, Peter, Uwe Schweickert, and Erik Theissen. 2015. Liquidity dynamics in an electronic open limit order book: An event study approach. *European Financial Management* 21: 52–78. [CrossRef]

Gopikrishnan, Parameswaran, Vasiliki Plerou, Xavier Gabaix, and Harry E. Stanley. 2000. Statistical properties of share volume traded in financial markets. *Physical Review E* 62: R4493. [CrossRef]

Gould, Martin D., Mason A. Porter, Stacy Williams, Mark McDonald, Daniel J. Fenn, and Sam D. Howison. 2013. Limit order books. *Quantitative Finance* 13: 1709–42. [CrossRef]

Gu, Gao-Feng, Wei Chen, and Wei-Xing Zhou. 2008. Empirical shape function of limit-order books in the Chinese stock market. *Physica A: Statistical Mechanics and its Applications* 387: 5182–88. [CrossRef]

Hill, Bruce M. 1975. A simple general approach to inference about the tail of a distribution. *The Annals of Statistics* 3: 1163–74. [CrossRef]

Interactive Brokers. 2019. Order Handling Using Price Capping. Available online: https://www.interactivebrokers.com/en/index.php?f=14186 (accessed on 17 January 2019).

Kelly, Bryan, and Hao Jiang. 2014. Tail risk and asset prices. *The Review of Financial Studies* 27: 2841–71. [CrossRef]

Kyle, Albert S. 1985. Continuous auctions and insider trading. *Econometrica* 53: 1315–35. [CrossRef]

Large, Jeremy. 2007. Measuring the resiliency of an electronic limit order book. *Journal of Financial Markets* 10: 1–25. [CrossRef]

Ljung, Greta M., and George E. P. Box. 1978. On a measure of lack of fit in time series models. *Biometrika* 65: 297–303. [CrossRef]

Lux, Thomas, and Michele Marchesi. 2000. Volatility clustering in financial markets: A microsimulation of interacting agents. *International Journal of Theoretical and Applied Finance* 3: 675–702. [CrossRef]

Maslov, Sergei, and Mark Mills. 2001. Price fluctuations from the order book perspective—Empirical facts and a simple model. *Physica A: Statistical Mechanics and its Applications* 299: 234–46. [CrossRef]

McInish, Thomas H., and Robert A. Wood. 1992. An analysis of intraday patterns in bid/ask spreads for NYSE stocks. *The Journal of Finance* 47: 753–64. [CrossRef]

Mu, Guo-Hua, Wei Chen, János Kertész, and Wei-Xing Zhou. 2009. Preferred numbers and the distributions of trade sizes and trading volumes in the Chinese stock market. *The European Physical Journal B* 68: 145–52. [CrossRef]

Potters, Marc, and Jean-Philippe Bouchaud. 2003. More statistical properties of order books and price impact. *Physica A: Statistical Mechanics and its Applications* 324: 133–40. [CrossRef]

Ranaldo, Angelo. 2004. Order aggressiveness in limit order book markets. *Journal of Financial Markets* 7: 53–74. [CrossRef]

Roşu, Ioanid. 2009. A dynamic model of the limit order book. *The Review of Financial Studies* 22: 4601–41. [CrossRef]

Russell, Jeffrey R., and Robert F. Engle. 2010. Analysis of high-frequency data. In *Handbook of Financial Econometrics: Tools and Techniques*. Edited by Yacine Ait-Sahalia and Lars Peter Hansen. San Diego: North-Holland, vol. 1, pp. 383–426.

Zargar, Faisal N., and Dilip Kumar. 2019. Long range dependence in the Bitcoin market: A study based on high-frequency data. *Physica A: Statistical Mechanics and its Applications* 515: 625–40. [CrossRef]

J. Risk Financial Manag. **2019**, *12*, 25

Zhang, Wei, Pengfei Wang, Xiao Li, and Dehua Shen. 2018. Some stylized facts of the cryptocurrency market. *Applied Economics* 50: 5950–65. [CrossRef]

Zovko, Ilija, and J. Doyne Farmer. 2002. The power of patience: A behavioural regularity in limit-order placement. *Quantitative Finance* 2: 387–92. [CrossRef]

Journal of
Risk and Financial
Management

MDPI

Article

Statistical Arbitrage in Cryptocurrency Markets

Thomas Günter Fischer *,†, Christopher Krauss and Alexander Deinert

Department of Statistics and Econometrics, University of Erlangen-Nürnberg, 90403 Nürnberg, Germany;
christopher.krauss@fau.de (C.K.); alexander.deinert@fau.de (A.D.)
* Correspondence: thomas.g.fischer@fau.de
† Current address: University of Erlangen-Nurnberg, Department of Statistics and Econometrics, Lange Gasse 20, 90403 Nurnberg, Germany.

Received: 30 December 2018; Accepted: 7 February 2019; Published: 13 February 2019

Abstract: Machine learning research has gained momentum—also in finance. Consequently, initial machine-learning-based statistical arbitrage strategies have emerged in the U.S. equities markets in the academic literature, see e.g., Takeuchi and Lee (2013); Moritz and Zimmermann (2014); Krauss et al. (2017). With our paper, we pose the question how such a statistical arbitrage approach would fare in the cryptocurrency space on minute-binned data. Specifically, we train a random forest on lagged returns of 40 cryptocurrency coins, with the objective to predict whether a coin outperforms the cross-sectional median of all 40 coins over the subsequent 120 min. We buy the coins with the top-3 predictions and short-sell the coins with the flop-3 predictions, only to reverse the positions after 120 min. During the out-of-sample period of our backtest, ranging from 18 June 2018 to 17 September 2018, and after more than 100,000 trades, we find statistically and economically significant returns of 7.1 bps per day, after transaction costs of 15 bps per half-turn. While this finding poses a challenge to the semi-strong from of market efficiency, we critically discuss it in light of limits to arbitrage, focusing on total volume constraints of the presented intraday-strategy.

Keywords: statistical arbitrage; cryptocurrencies; machine learning

---

1. Introduction

The cryptocurrency markets are a phenomenon. During the year of 2017, Bitcoin has reached a total market capitalization of more than USD 300 bn—next to more than one thousand smaller cryptoassets with less significant capitalization (coinmarketcap.com 2018). Despite these heights, the market has remained fairly unregulated by governmental institutions (Dyhrberg 2016). We hypothesize that this unique, early-stage environment may exhibit pricing inefficiencies that can potentially be detected and exploited by statistical arbitrage strategies. So far, only few academic studies have touched upon this question, and most of them only focus on a few selected cryptocurrencies.

One of the first works addressing this question is Shah and Zhang (2014). Specifically, the authors aim for predicting price changes of Bitcoin during a six month period in 2014 with a Bayesian regression model. The results are astonishing, with a return of 89 percent and a Sharpe ratio of 4.10 during a period of merely 50 trading days. However, no transaction costs are taken into account, perfect liquidity is assumed, and only one cryptocurrency is considered. Utilizing some of the ideas proposed by Shah and Zhang (2014), Madan et al. (2015) deploy several classification models to predict the sign of Bitcoin price changes, leveraging information on prices, transaction volume, and data about the underlying blockchain. A binomial generalized linear model and a random forest perform exceptionally well with 98.7 percent and

95.0 percent accuracy for the daily sign, respectively. However, the authors note that these results may very well be due to, in general, rising long-term prices in the market—a naive buy-and-hold strategy would have achieved similar results in ever-rising crypto markets at that time. Lintilhac and Tourin (2017) develop a pairs trading strategy for Bitcoin, following ideas of Tourin and Yan (2013), and other representatives of the stochastic control approach—for an overview see Krauss (2017). Balcilar et al. (2017) find that volume can help in predicting returns, based on a Granger-causal relationship between these two variables. Another innovative idea for constructing explanatory variables is to include social signals. Garcia and Schweitzer (2015) build a vector autoregressive (VAR) model to predict the sign of future returns of Bitcoin on a daily basis. The model is provided with market information, such as returns, transaction volumes, as well as social signals. These signals include relative search popularity based on Google trends data, the volume of tweets containing the term "bitcoin", and the emotional valence and sentiment expressed in these tweets[1]. Daily returns above 0.3 percent and a Sharpe ratio of over 1.75, prior to transaction costs, are generated. Up to transaction costs of 25 bps, the results remain profitable. Also related to social signals and the "fear of missing out" (FOMO) of uniformed investors is the recent work by Baur and Dimpfl (2018). The authors analyze asymmetric volatility effects for 20 cryptocurrencies and find, as opposed to equities markets, that positive shocks lead to a stronger increase of volatility compared to negative shocks. In a similar spirit, Koutmos (2018) observes an increase in the frequency of return and volatility spillovers in recent times, especially during major news events and oftentimes driven by Bitcoin. Beneki et al. (2019) dive deeper into this topic and test for volatility spillovers and hedging abilities between Bitcoin and Ethereum using impulse response analysis and a multivariate BEKK-GARCH model. In their study, the authors find a significant reduction of the diversification potential due to a delayed positive response and large changes in time-varying correlation among the two cryptocurrencies. Colianni et al. (2015) explore the predictive information potentially comprised in Twitter data. With the use of text-processing, the authors analyze the negativity, positivity, and neutrality of words contained in tweets relating to Bitcoin. Based on these data, features are generated. These features are processed with several classification models that manage to accomplish astonishingly high accuracy values when predicting the hour-to-hour and day-to-day sign change of Bitcoin. Instead of utilizing Twitter data, Kim et al. (2016) base their model on sentiment expressed in user forums relating to cryptocurrencies. The authors' framework consists of three steps. First, they crawl text data from the relevant forums where participants express opinions about the coin. Second, a sentiment for each comment is derived with the VADER algorithm[2]. Third, an averaged one-dependence-estimator is applied as a predictive model for future price fluctuations. With a simple trading strategy, profits of over 35 percent are accumulated. As of the day of writing, very few studies have introduced deep learning to predictive tasks in the cryptocurrency market. McNally et al. (2018) investigate the performance of state-of-the-art deep learning models, such as a long short-term memory (LSTM) network, in predicting future price changes of Bitcoin. Using a rolling window of 100 days of input data, this model achieves a predictive accuracy of 52.78 percent in forecasting the price change of the next day. Jiang and Liang (2017) follow a different approach based on deep reinforcement learning. Recently, Ha and Moon (2018) use genetic programming to detect profitable technical trading patterns for cryptocurrencies, and find that their system performs better than a buy-and-hold strategy.

However, to our knowledge, none of these studies have systematically transferred a well-established statistical arbitrage approach from more mature markets to the cryptocurrency space. With the present paper, we aim to fill this void and make the following contributions to the literature:

---

[1] The emotional valence and opinion polarization are computed on a daily basis as proposed by Warriner et al. (2013).

[2] Vader = Valence Aware Dictionary for sEntiment Reasoning. This algorithm allows to interpret slang, neologisms, and emoticons, which are oftentimes found on social media platforms. Further information on this algorithm can be found in Gilbert (2014).

- Development of an advanced, machine-learning-based statistical arbitrage approach for the cryptocurrency space: we build our approach on the ideas of Fischer and Krauss (2018); Huck (2009, 2010); Krauss et al. (2017); Moritz and Zimmermann (2014); Takeuchi and Lee (2013), who have developed similar methods for U.S. cash equities, but on much lower frequencies (days to months). With the present manuscript, we successfully show that relative-value arbitrage opportunities exist in this young and aspiring market, given that a random forest is able to produce daily returns of 7.1 bps after transaction costs.
- Consideration of microstructural effects: advancing to higher frequencies, e.g., minute-binned data, brings along substantial challenges. First, trading volume needs to be taken into account. In cash equities, many strategies are backtested on the closing price, which captures 7 percent of daily liquidity for NYSE listed stocks—see Intercontinental Exchange (2018). In stark contrast, liquidity needs to be carefully assessed for every minute bar in the cryptocurrency space, especially in case of smaller coins. We incorporate this effect in our study and only execute trades in case liquidity is present. Second, micro-structural effects, and especially the bid-ask bounce, need to be considered. We therefore introduce a lag between the price on which the prediction is generated, and the subsequent price on which execution is taking place. Hence, we eliminate the bid-ask bounce see, e.g., (Gatev et al. 2006) and we render the strategy realistic in the digital age, given that there is sufficient time for signal generation, order routing, and order execution.
- Shining light into the black box: machine learning models often have the downside of being intransparent and opaque. Hence, we analyze feature importances, and we compare the random forest to the transparent logistic regression. We find that both methods capture short-term characteristics in the data, with past returns over the past 60 min contributing most when explaining future returns over the subsequent 120 min.

The remainder of this paper is organized as follows. Section 2 covers the data sample as well as software and Section 3 the methodology. Sections 4 and 5 present the results and discuss the key findings. Finally, Section 6 concludes.

2. Data and Software

2.1. Data

In this paper, we use minute-binned price and volume data from 5 January 2018 to 7 September 2018, collected from www.cryptocompare.com via their official application programming interface (cryptocompare.com 2018). For each minute, we collect *Open*, *High*, *Low*, *Close*, *Volume$_{from}$*, *Volume$_{to}$*, and *Timestamp* data. *Open*, *High*, *Low*, and *Close* denote the first, highest, lowest, and last price paid for a coin c in minute t, respectively. *Volume$_{from}$* and *Volume$_{to}$* quantify the volume of coins being traded during that period of time and the equivalent value in USD. *Timestamp* is the UNIX-timestamp, i.e., is the number of seconds that have passed since 1 January 1970 (IEEE and The Open Group 2018).

The initial collection of coins and possible exchanges consist of the 100 coins with the highest market capitalization according to coinmarketcap.com (2018) and all 78 exchanges available with respect to the *API*, both as of 27 December 2017. To this large database, we apply several filters, ensuring minimum liquidity requirements and data quality, and rigorously drop many of the coin-exchange combinations. Going forward, we work with 40 coins and the data from their most liquid exchange—the combinations are listed in Appendix A.

2.2. Software

The code for this study is written in Python 3.5 (Python Software Foundation 2016). It involves the preprocessing and formatting of the data, the training of the models and the backtesting engine, as well as the evaluation of the performance, i.e., the calculation of risk and return metrics. Data preparation mostly relies on the packages *numpy* (van der Walt et al. 2011) and *pandas* (McKinney 2010), which are powerful tools for handling large amounts of data. Furthermore, the package *sci-kit learn* (Pedregosa et al. 2011) is used for the random forest and logistic regression model and the packages *SciPy* (Jones et al. 2014) and *Empyrical* (Quantopian Inc. 2016) are deployed for the calculation of the statistical properties and performance analysis of the results.

3. Methodology

Following Krauss et al. (2017), the methodology of this paper consists of four steps. First, the entire data set is split into a training set and a trading set. Second, the features (explanatory variables) and targets (dependent variables) are created. Third, a random forest, and a simpler logistic regression model are trained in the training period (in-sample data). Fourth, with each trained model, out-of-sample predictions are made on the respective trading set to test the effectiveness of the model and its trading performance. The rest of this section follows the outlined structure.

3.1. Generation of Training and Trading Set

Of the data available for each coin, the first two thirds of the time-series are used as training data (in-sample) while the remaining third makes up the trading period (out-of-sample). The training and trading sets are strictly non-overlapping to ensure that no look-ahead bias is introduced. As minute-binned data since the beginning of January 2018 up to the beginning of September 2018 are used, one complete time-series consists of close to 360,000 data points.[3] Taking into account the $n = 40$ coins, this results in approximately $40 \cdot 360,000 \cdot \frac{2}{3} \approx 9.6$ million training examples and 4.8 million trading examples for the models.

3.2. Feature and Target Generation

3.2.1. Features—Multiperiod Returns

Loosely following the logic of Takeuchi and Lee (2013), each feature sequence (input) is generated in the following way: Let $P^c = (P_t^c)_{t \in T}$ denote the price process of coin c, with $c \in \{1, \dots, 40\}$, and $R_{t,t-m}^c$ the simple return for a coin c over the last m periods, i.e.,

$$R_{t,t-m}^c = \frac{P_t^c}{P_{t-m}^c} - 1, \tag{1}$$

where the periods are in minutes. Each feature sequence then consists of the set $\{R_{t,t-m}^c\}$ with $m \in \{\{20, 40, 60, 80, 100, 120\} \cup \{240, \dots, 1320, 1440\}\}$. Hence, the model first puts emphasis on the returns of the last 120 min and then switches to a less granular resolution to focus on the returns of the last $k \cdot 120$, with $k \in \{2, \dots, 12\}$, points in time. With this approach, we follow the logic of Takeuchi and Lee (2013)

---

[3] Not all time-series examined are complete in the sense that they cover the whole period from January to September 2018. This could be due to several reasons such as the delisting of a coin. It is noteworthy that such time-series are not eliminated but traded according to the available data.

and transfer it to minute-binned data with the aim of forecasting the return of the next two hours or 120 min, while using information of the returns of the last 24 h.

3.2.2. Targets

As in Krauss et al. (2017), a binary response variable $\mathcal{Y}^c_{t+121,t+1} \in \{0,1\}$ is introduced. All target values of the cross-section are classified as class "1" if the return over the 120 min after the predict time t (including a one minute gap), i.e., $R_{t+121,t+1}$, is at or above the cross-sectional median of all coins, and "0" otherwise. Therefore, instead of predicting the actual value of the future 120 min returns, the probability $\mathcal{P}_{t+121,t+1}$ of the coin outperforming the cross-sectional median is predicted. This approach is promising, as classification problems have found to work better than regression problems in the context of financial market predictions (Enke and Thawornwong 2005; Leung et al. 2000).

3.3. Models

3.3.1. Logistic regression

As a baseline model, we include a transparent (we can interpret the regression coefficients to better understand what leads to a prediction) logistic regression (LR). The model's name "logistic regression" stems from the logistic function which is used to model the binary response variable. As our classification problem comprises two classes (hence, binary), i.e., "the coin outperforms the cross-sectional median of all coins over the following 120 min" (class 1) and "the coin does not outperform" (class 0), our model is a linear function of the form

$$f(x) = y = \frac{1}{1 + e^{-(\alpha + \beta x)}}, \tag{2}$$

with α, β denoting the intercept and coefficients, y the dependent and x the independent variable/feature vector (Berkson 1953; Kleinbaum and Klein 2010). The coefficients can be estimated by maximum likelihood using the observations from the training set—further details are available in Hastie et al. (2008).

For this paper, we rely on the implementation of Pedregosa et al. (2011) for the logistic regression and follow the parameters outlined in Fischer and Krauss (2018), i.e., the optimal L2-regularization is determined among 100 values on a logarithmic scale from 0.0001 to 10,000 via 5-fold cross-validation on the respective training set and L-BFGS is deployed to find an optimum. Further, we restrict the maximum number of iterations to 100.

3.3.2. Random forest

Following Krauss et al. (2017), who find the random forest (RF) to yield the best trading performance in their empirical study for the S&P 500 constitutents, we opt for this model as our machine learning benchmark. Random forests Breiman (1996, 2001); Ho (1995, 1998) are ensemble learners consisting of many decorrelated decision trees which can be understood as their building blocks. During the learning phase, the decision trees are trained individually on random subsets of the training samples. Hereby, each tree is "grown" with the objective of separating the training samples as pure as possible with respect to their class (the target value "0" or "1"). At each split (node of the tree), the samples are divided into two buckets depending on whether or not the respective sample fulfills the learned split criterion, e.g., whether or not the value of the feature "return over the past 60 min" exceeds 3 percent. This process is repeated recursively until all buckets are pure or another stop criterion, e.g., max depth J of the tree, is reached. Once all trees are trained, the random forest model can be applied to make predictions for the unseen data. Hereby, each tree of the forest predicts the class of the new sample based on its learned split criterions—simply speaking, if the new sample is sorted into a "0" bucket, the tree predicts "0", otherwise "1". In the last step, the predictions of all *B* trees of the forest are averaged to compute the final prediction—a value between 0 and 1 which can be interpreted as the probability that the sample belongs to class "1". Further details and a comprehensive description of the algorithm are available in Raschka (2015).

As random forest implementation, we use Pedregosa et al. (2011) and largely follow Fischer and Krauss (2018) and Krauss et al. (2017) with respect to the parameters of random forest model. Specifically, we set the number of trees *B* to 1000 and the maximum tree depth *J* to 15. For the random feature selection, we follow the default value $m = \sqrt{p}$ for classification, whereby *p* denotes the number of features—see (Pedregosa et al. 2011).

3.4. Forecasting, Ranking and Trading

Once the two models are trained using the features and targets of the training set (Note: we train universal models, i.e., each of the two models is trained using the samples of all coins), the learned parameters are fixed and the two models are transferred to the trading phase. In this phase, only the features are used (which are limited to the information an investor would have known at the respective point in time) and out of sample predictions are made. Specifically, at the end of each minute *t* of the trading period, each model forecasts the price development of all individual coins over the next two hours, i.e., the probability to outperform the cross-sectional median. We hence obtain two lists (one list per model) with 40 probabilities (one for each coin) which we sort in descending order. At the top of the lists, we find the coins that are most likely to outperform the cross-section of coins, whereas at the bottom, we find those coins most likely to underperform. Based on that ranking, we enter a long position for the top-3 coins, and a short position for the flop-3 coins. Finally, we reverse all positions at the end of the two hours holding period. To simulate the whole trading period from 18 June 2018 to 7 September 2018, the above procedure is repeated for each minute of the trading set resulting in 120 parallel portfolios active at each point in time (each portfolio is funded with 1/120th of the overall capital and comprises three long and three short positions at leverage 1). To render the backtest more realistic, we incorporate several execution constraints and transaction cost assumptions:

- *Execution gap*: We create the trading signal at the end of minute *t* and place the order for execution at the closing price of the following minute *t* + 1. In other words, we introduce a one period gap between signal generation and execution to account for the time frame required for data processing, prediction making, and order management.
- *Volume constraint (opening of position)*: A position is only opened when at least one unit of the currency pair is traded at the respective point in time—otherwise, the order is canceled and the amount of capital foreseen for the position is kept in cash for the two hours period.
- *Volume constraint (closing of position)*: Once the position has reached its two hours lifetime, a closing order is triggered and executed at the first bar with sufficient volume.
- *Elimination of starting point bias*: To avoid any bias related to the starting point (point in time at which the first portfolio is opened), we open a new portfolio at every minute $t \in \{1, 2, ..., 120\}$ and average the results across the 120 portfolios that are opened at each time *t*.
- *Transaction costs*: We assume 15 bps per half turn, based on analyses on transaction costs and liquidity costs provided in Schnaubelt et al. (2019) on cryptocurrency limit order book data.

Finally, at the end of the backtesting period, we analyze the financial performance for each of the two models based on the logged trades.

4. Results

In this section, we evaluate the financial performance of the RF and the LR model (when investing in the top-3 and flop-3 coins), and contrast them to a simple buy-and-hold strategy in Bitcoin (BTC) as well as the general market (MKT). The latter shall be defined as an equally-weighted investment in all coins at the beginning of the trading period. We proceed in three steps. First, we analyze the performance on trade level. Next, we aggregate the individual trades to daily returns and explore the development of the financial performance over time. Finally, we move beyond financial results and shed light on the patterns the employed predictive models exploit to select coins for trading.

4.1. Trade-Level Results

First, we evaluate the predictive performance of the logistic regression (LR) and the random forest (RF) model on the level of individual round trip trades.

Table 1 depicts the results of the more than 100,000 round trip trades over the full out-of-sample period from 18 June 2018 until 7 September 2018 after transaction costs of 30 bps. We make the following observations:

- *Positive mean returns:* Both models yield positive and statistically significant mean returns with the RF (3.8 bps) clearly outperforming the LR (2.0 bps) by a factor of almost two. Looking at the contribution from long trades and short trades, we find that the latter are more profitable (−2.1 bps. vs. 5.6 bps (LR) and 0.2 bps. vs. 6.4 bps. (RF))—a finding that is likely driven by the overall decline of the cryptocurrency market during this period.
- *Extreme price movements:* Looking at the minimum (−42.8 percent) and maximum returns (34.4 percent), we find astonishingly high values given the two hour holding period. However, these observations can be attributed to the extreme price movements in cryptocurrency markets—see Osterrieder and Lorenz (2017). The 25 percent and 75 percent quartiles are less extreme with values between −1.2 and 1.3 percent for both models.
- *Negative median:* We further notice that both, the RF and the LR model, have negative median returns. In other words, more trades lead to a loss than to a profit. However, taking into account the magnitude of the profits and losses, we find that the profits surpass the losses by approximately 5 bps (LR) and 10 bps (RF) on average (simply speaking, more money is made when the model is right than lost when it is wrong). In result, the mean trade of the RF is positive, i.e., $0.49587 \times 0.01774 + 0.50413 \times (-0.01669) = 0.00038 > 0$.
- *Skewness and Kurtosis:* Both, LR and RF exhibit positive skewness, which is a favorable property for investors, given that the right tail tends to be more pronounced than the left tail. By contrast, kurtosis values above 9 indicate leptokurtic behavior, and that significant risk lies in the extremes—see Osterrieder and Lorenz (2017).
- *Differing number of trades:* Finally, we observe that the number of executed trades differs between the two models as well as the long and short leg. As described in the previous section, our backtesting engine cancels orders in case no volume is available to execute the respective trade. We may therefore cautiously conclude that the RF model selects a larger share of less liquid coins (119,829 executed trades) compared to the LR model (158,408 trades). Note: the overall high number of trades results from the backtesting logic in which we open a new portfolio with three long orders and three short orders by the end of each minute to avoid starting point bias.

Table 1. Key return characteristics on the level of individual round trip trades for the logistic regression (LR) and the random forest model (RF) when investing in the top-3 and flop-3 coins, after transaction costs of 30 bps for the round trip trade.

	LR			RF		
	Long	Short	Total	Long	Short	Total
No. trades	73319	85089	158408	49689	70140	119829
Mean return	−0.00021	0.00056	0.00020	0.00002	0.00064	0.00038
Standard error	0.00009	0.00009	0.00006	0.00011	0.00010	0.00008
t-Statistic	−2.35284	6.19182	3.17475	0.19865	6.39796	5.14330
Minimum	−0.17736	−0.42764	−0.42764	−0.17649	−0.42764	−0.42764
25% Quantile	−0.01169	−0.01086	−0.01127	−0.01140	−0.01064	−0.01094
Median	−0.00141	0.00109	−0.00004	−0.00192	0.00095	−0.00015
75% Quantile	0.00993	0.01313	0.01172	0.00990	0.01299	0.01183
Maximum	0.29043	0.34424	0.34424	0.26296	0.34424	0.34424
Share > 0	0.46677	0.52671	0.49897	0.45622	0.52395	0.49587
Standard dev.	0.02449	0.02656	0.02563	0.02490	0.02653	0.02587
Skewness	1.00453	−0.44146	0.14509	1.03417	−0.38629	0.14070
Kurtosis	9.26031	9.46260	9.41992	8.98506	9.55134	9.36387
Mean return positive trade	0.01726	0.01750	0.01739	0.01802	0.01757	0.01774
Mean return negative trade	−0.01551	−0.01828	−0.01691	−0.01508	−0.01799	−0.01669

4.2. Return Development over Time

Next, we aggregate the individual trades to daily returns and further explore the financial performance. Table 2 depicts daily and annualized risk-return metrics for the logistic regression (LR) and the random forest (RF) compared to Bitcoin (BTC) as well as the general market (MKT), i.e., an equal investment in all coins at the beginning of the trading period.

Table 2. Daily and annualized risk-return metrics for the logistic regression (LR) and the random forest model (RF) model when investing in the top-3 and flop-3 coins, versus Bitcoin (BTC) and the general market (MKT), i.e., an equal investment in all coins at the beginning of the trading period. Panel A depicts daily return characteristics, panel B depicts risk and panel C annualized risk-return metrics.

		LR	RF	BTC	MKT
A	Mean return	0.00049	0.00071	−0.00005	−0.00281
	Standard dev.	0.00661	0.00534	0.03260	0.03680
	Minimum	−0.02583	−0.01027	−0.10016	−0.10805
	25% Quantile	−0.00323	−0.00212	−0.01598	−0.02270
	Median	0.00025	0.00020	0.00111	0.00069
	75% Quantile	0.00388	0.00324	0.01458	0.01829
	Maximum	0.01920	0.02115	0.08777	0.11555
	Share > 0	0.51807	0.53012	0.50602	0.50602
B	Historic VaR 1%	−0.01523	−0.01025	−0.09112	−0.10461
	Historic VaR 5%	−0.00809	−0.00756	−0.05482	−0.05978
	Maximum drawdown	−0.05892	−0.02432	−0.26738	−0.32908
C	Annual return	0.18762	0.29012	−0.18754	−0.71640
	Annual volatility	0.12632	0.10203	0.62284	0.70310
	Sharpe ratio	1.42394	2.54785	−0.02755	−1.46060
	Sortino ratio	2.16255	4.51777	−0.03787	−1.90273

We make the following findings:

- *Panel A—daily return characteristics:* With regard to mean return, the random forest surpasses the logistic regression by 2.2 bps per day (7.1 bps vs. 4.9 bps). We further observe that both, the maximum and minimum daily returns, are within reasonable levels of −2.6 percent (LR) and +2.1 percent (RF), respectively. The underlying reason is the large number of active positions at each point in time (see Section 3.4) which also explains the low standard deviation of 66 bps (LR) and 53 bps (RF). Looking at Bitcoin (BTC) and the general market (MKT), we find mean returns of −0.5 bps per day and −28.1 bps, respectively.
- *Panel B—risk metrics:* Panel B reveals favorable risk metrics for the random forest with a 1-percent value at risk of −1.0 percent compared to −1.5 percent for the logistic regression. Moreover, we find a significantly lower maximum drawdown of −2.4 percent for the RF and -5.9 percent for the LR compared to −26.7 percent for Bitcoin and −32.9 percent for the general market. The difference is caused by the short leg of the portfolio, i.e., the investment in the flop-3 coins which helps in eliminating market risk.
- *Panel C—annualized risk-return metrics:* Finally, panel C depicts annualized risk-return metrics. We observe annualized returns of 29.0 percent for the random forest and 18.8 percent for the logistic regression, compared to vastly negative results for the buy-and-hold benchmarks. Given the low volatility, these results translate into a Sharpe ratio of 1.4 (LR) and 2.5 (RF) respectively—hereby outperforming both Bitcoin and the general market by a clear margin.

Finally, Figure 1 depicts the cumulative profits for the random forest model (RF), and compares it to the development of Bitcoin (BTC) and the general market (MKT) over the duration of the out-of-sample trading period from 18 June 2018 to 7 September 2018:

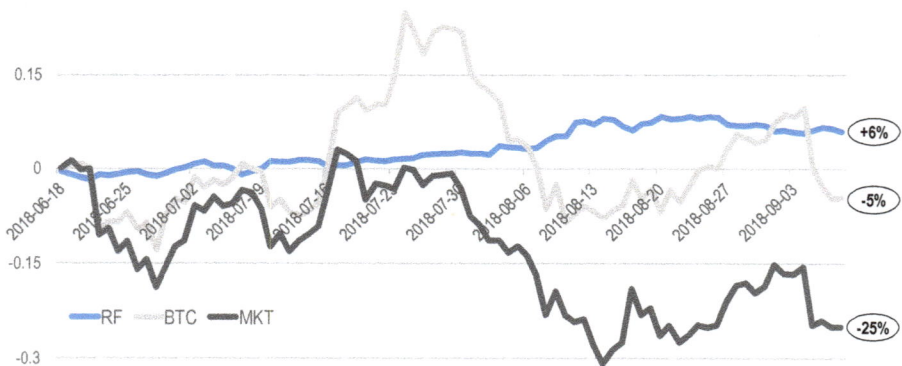

Figure 1. Development of financial performance of random forest model (RF) when investing in the top-3 and flop-3 coins vs. Bitcoin (BTC) and general market (MKT), i.e., an equal investment in all coins at the beginning of the trading period.

We observe that the RF model shows fairly steady growth at low volatility levels—which is in stark contrast to the rugged nature and wild swings of Bitcoin and the general market. By the end of the trading period, the random forest has accumulated profits of +6 percent, whereas Bitcoin (BTC) and the general market (MKT) yield negative profits of −5 percent and −25 percent respectively.

4.3. Beyond Returns—Shedding Light Into the Patterns Exploited for Trading

In the following paragraphs, we move beyond the financial results and shed light into specific aspects of our predictive models. Specifically, we extract the feature importance of the random forest and contrast it with the regression coefficients of the logistic regression. We hereby aim to gain insights into the patterns our models exploit in order to select coins for trading. Figure 2 depicts the feature importance (RF) and regression coefficients (LR) respectively:

We make the following observations:

- *Feature importance analysis:* The upper half of the figure shows the features (explanatory variables) used by the random forest, sorted by feature importance in descending order. The most important features are the returns over the past 20, 40 and 60 min. In other words, the random forest pays most attention to the price development over the past hour. By contrast, the longer term price development (past 12–24 h) does not seem to have a substantial contribution to predicting the price change over the next two hours.

- *Coefficient analysis:* Looking at the lower part of the figure, we take advantage of the high transparency and explanatory value of the logistic regression model. The highest regression coefficient of approximately −6.5 belongs to the return over the past 20 min, followed by the coefficients for the 40 and 60 min returns. Moreover, we find that almost all regression coefficients exhibit a negative sign—in other words, the model likely produces a positive forecast (long), in case the respective coin has experienced a decline in the recent past (negative feature values which are multiplied with negative regression coefficients) and vice versa. We may therefore cautiously conclude that the model capitalizes on short-term mean-reversion—see Jegadeesh (1990); Lehmann (1990).

Feature importance random forest

High importance: price development
over the past 60 minutes

Lower importance: price development over the past 12-24
hours (i.e., price development over a longer time period
compared to the forecast horizon of two hours)

Coefficients logistic regression

Negative coefficients: indication
for capitalization of reversal effect

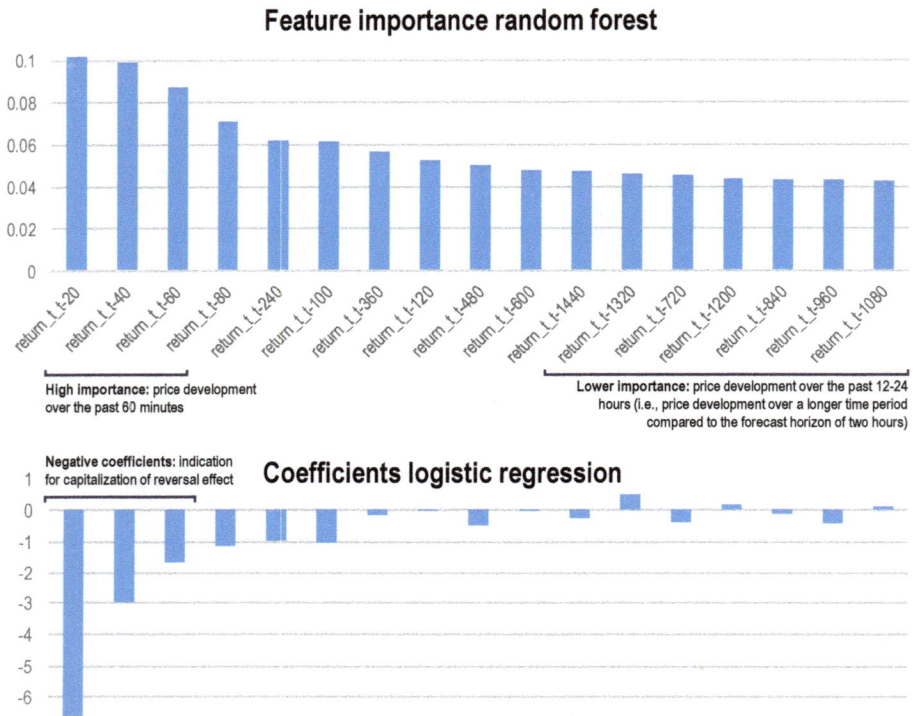

Figure 2. Feature importance extracted from the random forest and regression coefficients for the logistic regression model. The features (explanatory variables) are sorted in descending order based on their importance extracted from the random forest model. The coefficients of the logistic regression model are plotted following the same order.

5. Discussion—Limits to Arbitrage

We would like to discuss our findings in light of limits to arbitrage. The most prominent effect that may adversely affect returns, is market microstructure. Inadvertently trading the bid-ask bounce in a backtest leads to high and statistically significant returns that may yet not be captured in reality. Hence, we have followed Gatev et al. (2006) and representatives of the high-frequency pairs trading literature—see Bowen and Hutchinson (2016); Liu et al. (2017), and only trade (i) when volume is present for a coin and (ii) with a one period gap after signal generation. In other words, when the signal is generated at the end of minute t, we only enter the market at the closing price of minute $t + 1$, as long as volume is present. To corroborate our findings, and to take into account potential liquidity issues, we further delay execution by additional periods—see Table 3 for our findings. We see that executing without gap—as is often the baseline in the literature—would lead to returns of 20.5 bps per round trip[4]. This value drops

---

[4]   More precisely, by executing at the opening price of minute $t + 1$, we still leave a small gap compared to an execution at the closing price of minute t (which is used to make the prediction).

drastically to 3.8 bps when delaying execution to minute $t + 1$—our base case used throughout this study. A delay to minute $t + 2$ leads to returns of 2.4 bps and a delay to minute $t + 3$ to 1.6 bps—both of them still statistically significant. When delaying execution to minute $t + 4$, returns are still positive at 0.9 bps, albeit not statistically significant. As of minute $t + 5$, the alpha has vanished. Hence, we may conclude that fast execution after signal generation is paramount to the success of such a strategy. The latter is technically possible, but still a challenge. A second limit to arbitrage are short-selling constraints—which are commonly known in equity markets, see Gregoriou (2012). For cryptocurrencies, at the time of writing, several exchanges offer short selling (e.g., Poloniex, Bitfinex, etc.), but it is questionable whether the desired coin is always available at reasonable costs and in reasonable quantities. Given that the majority of the RF profits stem from the short leg in a downward market environment, this limit poses a challenge to any investor implementing such a strategy. The third major limit to arbitrage is capacity. An intraday strategy for cryptocurrencies may offer high Sharpe ratios. By contrast, costs for productionizing and operating such a strategy would be significant, when taking into account human capital and technical infrastructure. The reward may be fairly thin. The average trading volume per coin and minute is 7000 USD for the considered coin-exchange combinations (see Appendix A). Assuming a participation rate of 5 percent and a six-positions portfolio (top-3 long, flop-3 short) would lead to an estimated capacity of $0.05 \times 7000 \times 6 = 2100$ [USD] per minute—a fairly low value, compared to more mature markets.

Table 3. Key return characteristics on the level of individual round trip trades for the random forest (RF) model when investing in the top-3 and flop-3 coins, after transaction costs of 30 bps. Each column represents the gap between signal generation and signal execution, i.e., gap 0 refers to signal generation at the closing price of bar t and execution at the opening price of bar $t + 1$. Gap 1 refers to a delayed execution at the closing price of bar $t + 1$, gap 2 to a delayed execution at the closing price of bar $t + 2$, and so forth.

	Gap 0	Gap 1	Gap 2	Gap 3	Gap 4	Gap 5
No. trades	119829	119829	118948	118424	118055	117630
Mean return	0.00205	0.00038	0.00024	0.00016	0.00009	−0.00001
Standard error	0.00008	0.00008	0.00008	0.00008	0.00008	0.00007
t−Statistic	26.97626	5.14330	3.24117	2.15184	1.15309	−0.09429
Minimum	−0.42764	−0.42764	−0.40397	−0.43317	−0.40940	−0.37498
25% Quantile	−0.00974	−0.01094	−0.01104	−0.01113	−0.01120	−0.01126
Median	0.00097	−0.00015	−0.00031	−0.00043	−0.00053	−0.00061
75% Quantile	0.01330	0.01183	0.01163	0.01146	0.01135	0.01124
Maximum	0.34424	0.34424	0.34424	0.34424	0.34424	0.34424
Share > 0	0.52342	0.49587	0.49294	0.49070	0.48810	0.48605
Standard dev.	0.02626	0.02587	0.02574	0.02566	0.02566	0.02552
Skewness	0.32786	0.14070	0.11708	0.09076	0.04651	0.09360
Kurtosis	9.19105	9.36387	9.14659	9.35075	9.76571	9.47677
Mean return positive trade	0.01869	0.01774	0.01763	0.01756	0.01755	0.01745
Mean return negative trade	−0.01623	−0.01669	−0.01666	−0.01660	−0.01656	−0.01651

6. Conclusions

With our paper, we have successfully transferred an advanced machine-learning-based statistical arbitrage approach from the U.S. equities markets to a large universe of 40 cryptocurrency coins on minute-binned data. Using returns over the past 1440 min (24 hours) and a random forest classifier, we aim to forecast the development of each coin for the subsequent 120 min. When going long the top-3 and short the flop-3 predictions, we find statistically and economically significant excess returns of 3.8 bps per round-trip trade—even after delaying order execution by one period, incorporating volume constraints for the opening and closing of the position, and transaction costs of 15 bps per half-turn. These results outperform a naive buy-and-hold strategy of Bitcoin, and of all 40 participating coins, equally-weighted by far—thereby indicating that this young and aspiring market may not (yet) follow the semi-strong form of market efficiency (Fama 1970). By analyzing the feature importances of the random forest and by comparing it to the coefficients of a logistic regression model, we observe that both methods capture short-term characteristics in the data, with returns over the past 60 min contributing most when explaining future returns over the subsequent 120 min. Moreover, the regression coefficients of the logistic regression model suggest the capitalization on short-term mean reversion—a well-documented phenomena in the finance literature (see Jegadeesh 1990; Lehmann 1990). Finally, we critically discuss these findings in light of potential limits to arbitrage. Hereby, we find the returns to remain positive and statistically significant when waiting up to three minutes after signal generation—so timely execution is paramount. Furthermore, potential short-selling constraints and overall market liquidity, which limits the capacity of the strategy, pose additional challenges on the implementation of statistical arbitrage strategies in the yet developing cryptocurrency markets.

Author Contributions: Conceptualization, T.G.F. and C.K.; Data curation, A.D.; Investigation, T.G.F., C.K. and A.D.; Methodology, T.G.F. and C.K.; Software, T.G.F. and A.D.; Validation, T.G.F., C.K. and A.D.; Visualization, T.G.F. and C.K.; Writing—original draft, T.G.F., C.K. and A.D.; Writing—review & editing, T.G.F. and C.K.

Funding: This research received no external funding.

Acknowledgments: The authors have benefited from many helpful discussions with Ingo Klein. We are further grateful to the "Open Access Publikationsfonds", which has covered 75 percent of the publication fees.

Conflicts of Interest: The authors declare no conflict of interest.

Abbreviations

The following abbreviations are used in this manuscript:

BTC   Bitcoin
LR   logistic regression
MKT   market, i.e., an equal investment in all coins at the beginning of the trading period
RF   random forest
VaR   value at risk

Appendix

Table A1. Overview of coins and corresponding exchanges used throughout this study. Note: All coins are denominated in USD prices as provided by www.cryptocompare.com.

No	Coin	Exchange	No	Coin	Exchange
1	ADA	BitTrex	21	QTUM	Bitfinex
2	BCH	Bitfinex	22	RDD	Yobit
3	BCN	HitBTC	23	SAN	Bitfinex
4	BTC	Bitfinex	24	SNT	Bitfinex
5	BTG	Bitfinex	25	STRAT	HitBTC
6	CND	HitBTC	26	TNB	Bitfinex
7	CVC	HitBTC	27	TNT	HitBTC
8	DASH	Bitfinex	28	TRX	Bitfinex
9	DATA	Bitfinex	29	USDT	Kraken
10	EOS	Bitfinex	30	VIB	HitBTC
11	ETC	Bitfinex	31	WAVES	Yobit
12	ETH	Bitfinex	32	XDN	HitBTC
13	ETP	Bitfinex	33	XEM	Yobit
14	GNT	Bitfinex	34	XLM	Poloniex
15	LTC	Bitfinex	35	XMR	Bitfinex
16	MANA	Bitfinex	36	XRP	Bitfinex
17	NEO	Bitfinex	37	XVG	BitTrex
18	NXT	Poloniex	38	YOYOW	Bitfinex
19	OMG	Bitfinex	39	ZEC	Bitfinex
20	QASH	Bitfinex	40	ZRX	Bitfinex

References

Balcilar, Mehmet, Elie Bouri, Rangan Gupta, and David Roubaud. 2017. Can volume predict Bitcoin returns and volatility? A quantiles-based approach. *Economic Modelling* 64: 74–81.

Baur, Dirk G., and Thomas Dimpfl. 2018. Asymmetric volatility in cryptocurrencies. *Economics Letters* 173: 148–51. [CrossRef]

Beneki, Christina, Alexandros Koulis, Nikolaos A. Kyriazis, and Stephanos Papadamou. 2019. Investigating volatility transmission and hedging properties between Bitcoin and Ethereum. *Research in International Business and Finance* 48: 219–27. [CrossRef]

Berkson, Joseph. 1953. A statistically precise and relatively simple method of estimating the bio-assay with quantal response, based on the logistic function. *Journal of the American Statistical Association* 48: 565–99. [CrossRef]

Bowen, David A., and Mark C. Hutchinson. 2016. Pairs trading in the UK equity market: Risk and return. *The European Journal of Finance* 22: 1363–87. [CrossRef]

Breiman, Leo. 1996. Bagging predictors. *Machine Learning* 24: 123–40. [CrossRef]

Breiman, Leo. 2001. Random forests. *Machine Learning* 45: 5–32. [CrossRef]

coinmarketcap.com. 2018. Overview of available cryptocurrencies. Available online: coinmarketcap.com (accessed on 27 July 2018).

Colianni, Stuart, Stephanie Rosales, and Michael Signorotti. 2015. Algorithmic Trading of Cryptocurrency Based on Twitter Sentiment Analysis. Working Paper, Stanford University, Stanford, CA, USA.

cryptocompare.com. 2018. Overview of CryptoCompare API. Available online: cryptocompare.com (accessed on 6 September 2018).

Dyhrberg, Anne Haubo. 2016. Bitcoin, gold and the dollar—A GARCH volatility analysis. *Finance Research Letters* 16: 85–92. [CrossRef]

Enke, David, and Suraphan Thawornwong. 2005. The use of data mining and neural networks for forecasting stock market returns. *Expert Systems with Applications* 29: 927–40. [CrossRef]

Fama, Eugene F. 1970. Efficient capital markets: A review of theory and empirical work. *The Journal of Finance* 25: 383–417. [CrossRef]

Fischer, Thomas, and Christopher Krauss. 2018. Deep learning with long short-term memory networks for financial market predictions. *European Journal of Operational Research* 270: 654–69. [CrossRef]

Garcia, David, and Frank Schweitzer. 2015. Social signals and algorithmic trading of Bitcoin. *Royal Society Open Science* 2: 150288. [CrossRef] [PubMed]

Gatev, Evan, William N. Goetzmann, and K. Geert Rouwenhorst. 2006. Pairs trading: Performance of a relative-value arbitrage rule. *Review of Financial Studies* 19: 797–827. [CrossRef]

Gilbert, Clayton J. Hutto Eric. 2014. Vader: A parsimonious rule-based model for sentiment analysis of social media text. Paper presented at Eights International Conference on Weblogs and Social Media, Ann Arbor, MI, USA, June 1–4.

Gregoriou, Greg N. 2012. *Handbook of Short Selling*. Amsterdam and Boston: Academic Press.

Ha, Sungjoo, and Byung-Ro Moon. 2018. Finding attractive technical patterns in cryptocurrency markets. *Memetic Computing* 10: 301–6. [CrossRef]

Hastie, Trevor, Robert Tibshirani, and Jerome Friedman. 2008. *The Elements of Statistical Learning: Data Mining, Inference, and Prediction*, 2nd ed. Series in Statistics. New York: Springer.

Ho, Tin Kam. 1995. Random decision forests. Paper presented at the third International Conference on Document Analysis and Recognition, Montreal, QC, Canada, August 14–16. vol. 1, pp. 278–82.

Ho, Tin Kam. 1998. The random subspace method for constructing decision forests. *IEEE Transactions on Pattern Analysis and Machine Intelligence* 20: 832–44.

Huck, Nicolas. 2009. Pairs selection and outranking: An application to the S&P 100 index. *European Journal of Operational Research* 196: 819–25.

Huck, Nicolas. 2010. Pairs trading and outranking: The multi-step-ahead forecasting case. *European Journal of Operational Research* 207: 1702–16. [CrossRef]

IEEE, and The Open Group. 2018. The open group base specifications. 7. Available online: http://pubs.opengroup.org/onlinepubs/9699919799/basedefs/V1_chap04.html#tag_04_16 (accessed on 6 September 2018).

Intercontinental Exchange. 2018. Behind the Scenes—An insider's guide to the NYSE closing auction. Available online: https://www.nyse.com/article/nyse-closing-auction-insiders-guide (accessed on 30 December 2018).

Jegadeesh, Narasimhan. 1990. Evidence of predictable behavior of security returns. *The Journal of Finance* 45: 881. [CrossRef]

Jiang, Zhengyao, and Jinjun Liang. 2017. Cryptocurrency portfolio management with deep reinforcement learning. *arXiv* arXiv:1612.01277v5.

Jones, Eric, Travis Oliphant, and Pearu Peterson. 2014. SciPy: open source scientific tools for Python. Available online: http://www.scipy.org/ (accessed on 30 December 2018).

Kim, Y. Bin, Jun G. Kim, Wook Kim, Jae H. Im, Tae H. Kim, Shin J. Kang, and Chang H. Kim. 2016. Predicting fluctuations in cryptocurrency transactions based on user comments and replies. *PLoS ONE* 11: e0161197. [CrossRef] [PubMed]

Kleinbaum, David G., and Mitchel Klein. 2010. *Logistic Regression: A Self-Learning Text*. New York: Springer.

Koutmos, Dimitrios. 2018. Return and volatility spillovers among cryptocurrencies. *Economics Letters* 173: 122–27. [CrossRef]

Krauss, Christopher. 2017. Statistical arbitrage pairs trading strategies: Review and outlook. *Journal of Economic Surveys* 31: 513–45. [CrossRef]

Krauss, Christopher, Xuan Anh Do, and Nicolas Huck. 2017. Deep neural networks, gradient-boosted trees, random forests: Statistical arbitrage on the S&P 500. *European Journal of Operational Research* 259: 689–702.

Lehmann, Bruce N. 1990. Fads, martingales, and market efficiency. *The Quarterly Journal of Economics* 105: 1. [CrossRef]

Leung, Mark T., Hazem Daouk, and An-Sing Chen. 2000. Forecasting stock indices: A comparison of classification and level estimation models. *International Journal of Forecasting* 16: 173–90. [CrossRef]

Lintilhac, Paul S., and Agnes Tourin. 2017. Model-based pairs trading in the Bitcoin markets. *Quantitative Finance* 17: 703–16. [CrossRef]

Liu, Bo, Lo-Bin Chang, and Hélyette Geman. 2017. Intraday pairs trading strategies on high frequency data: The case of oil companies. *Quantitative Finance* 17: 87–100. [CrossRef]

Madan, Isaac, Shaurya Saluja, and Aojia Zhao. 2015. Automated Bitcoin Trading via Machine Learning Algorithms. Working Paper, Stanford University, Stanford, CA, USA.

McKinney, Wes. 2010. Data structures for statistical computing in python. Paper presented at the 9th Python in Science Conference, Austin, TX, USA, June 28–July 3. vol. 445, pp. 51–56.

McNally, Sean, Jason Roche, and Simon Caton. 2018. Predicting the price of Bitcoin using machine learning. Paper presented at the 26th International Conference on Parallel, Distributed and Network-Based Processing, Cambridge, UK, March 21–23. pp. 339–43.

Moritz, Benjamin, and Tom Zimmermann. 2014. Deep Conditional Portfolio Sorts: The Relation between Past and Future Stock Returns. Working Paper, LMU Munich, Munich, Germany; Harvard University, Cambridge, MA, USA.

Osterrieder, Joerg, and Julian Lorenz. 2017. A statistical risk assessment of Bitcoin and its extreme tail behavior. *Annals of Financial Economics* 12: 1750003. [CrossRef]

Pedregosa, F., G. Varoquaux, A. Gramfort, V. Michel, B. Thirion, O. Grisel, M. Blondel, P. Prettenhofer, R. Weiss, V. Dubourg, and et al. 2011. Scikit-learn: Machine learning in Python. *Journal of Machine Learning Research* 12: 2825–30.

Python Software Foundation. 2016. Python 3.5.2 Documentation. Available online: https://docs.python.org/3.5/ (accessed on 15 December 2018).

Quantopian Inc. 2016. Empyrical: Common Financial Risk Metrics. Available online: https://github.com/quantopian/empyrical (accessed on 15 December 2018).

Raschka, Sebastian. 2015. *Python Machine Learning*. Birmingham: Packt Publishing.

Schnaubelt, Matthias, Jonas Rende, and Christopher Krauss. 2019. Testing Stylized Facts of Bitcoin Limit Order Books. *Journal of Risk and Financial Management* 12: 25. [CrossRef]

Shah, Devavrat, and Kang Zhang. 2014. Bayesian regression and Bitcoin. Paper presented at the 52nd Conference on Communication, Control, and Computing, Monticello, IL, USA, October 1–3. pp. 409–14.

Takeuchi, Lawrence, and Yu-Ying Lee. 2013. Applying Deep Learning to Enhance Momentum Trading Strategies in Stocks. Working Paper, Stanford University, Stanford, CA, USA.

Tourin, Agnès, and Raphael Yan. 2013. Dynamic pairs trading using the stochastic control approach. *Journal of Economic Dynamics and Control* 37: 1972–81. [CrossRef]

Van der Walt, S., S. C. Colbert, and G. Varoquaux. 2011. The NumPy array: A structure for efficient numerical computation. *Computing in Science & Engineering* 13: 22–30. [CrossRef]

Warriner, Amy Beth, Victor Kuperman, and Marc Brysbaert. 2013. Norms of valence, arousal, and dominance for 13,915 English lemmas. *Behavior Research Methods* 45: 1191–207. [CrossRef] [PubMed]

Journal of
Risk and Financial Management

MDPI

Article

Bitcoin at High Frequency

Leopoldo Catania [1],* and Mads Sandholdt [2]

[1]   Department of Economics and Business Economics, Aarhus University and CREATES, Aarhus BSS,
      Fuglesangs Allé 4, DK-8210 Aarhus V, Denmark
[2]   Tvilum A/S, Egon Kristiansens Allé 2, DK-8882 Faarvang, Denmark; mads.sandholdt@me.com
*   Correspondence: leopoldo.catania@econ.au.dk; Tel.: +44-8716-5536

Received: 12 December 2018; Accepted: 30 January 2019; Published: 15 February 2019

Abstract: This paper studies the behaviour of Bitcoin returns at different sample frequencies. We consider high frequency returns starting from tick-by-tick price changes traded at the Bitstamp and Coinbase exchanges. We find evidence of a smooth intra-daily seasonality pattern, and an abnormal trade- and volatility intensity at Thursdays and Fridays. We find no predictability for Bitcoin returns at or above one day, though, we find predictability for sample frequencies up to 6 h. Predictability of Bitcoin returns is also found to be time–varying. We also study the behaviour of the realized volatility of Bitcoin. We document a remarkable high percentage of jumps above 80%. We also find that realized volatility exhibits: (i) long memory; (ii) leverage effect; and (iii) no impact from lagged jumps. A forecast study shows that: (i) Bitcoin volatility has become more easy to predict after 2017; (ii) including a leverage component helps in volatility prediction; and (iii) prediction accuracy depends on the length of the forecast horizon.

Keywords: bitcoin; realized volatility; HAR; high frequency

1. Introduction

One of the reasons why cryptocurrencies—and in particular Bitcoin introduced by Nakamoto (2009)—became so popular in 2017 has been their huge price increase which caught the attention from both the media and regular people. Indeed, we find that approximately 65% of all Bitcoin transactions happened in 2017 or later.[1] As a consequence of this huge interest, Bitcoin experienced a price increase of 1324% from the begin to the end of 2017. The financial industry and the academics have also been very interested in Bitcoin over the last years. For example, the Chicago Mercantile Exchange (CME) as well as Nasdaq and the Tokyo Financial Exchange started to negotiate Bitcoin futures during 2017 and 2018, see CME (2017), Bloomberg (2017), and Cryptocoinsnews (2017). Academics working in the field of financial econometrics have studied Bitcoin using well known methodologies, such as ARMA–GARCH models. For example, Dyhrberg (2016) compared Bitcoin with gold and the American dollar and classified the behavior of Bitcoin in between these two assets. Bariviera (2017) found long memory in the Bitcoin volatility measured as the logarithmic difference between intraday highest and lowest prices. Phillip et al. (2018) document long memory in cryptocurrencies as well. Additional results about the time–dependence properties of cryptocurrencies are reported in Zhang et al. (2019). Ardia et al. (2018) and Stavroyiannis (2018) model and forecast the value at risk for Bitcoin. Recently, Catania and Grassi (2017) show that standard volatility models, like GARCH, are generally not suitable for cryptocurrency time–series and suggest to use a more sophisticated modelling technique based on the score driven approach, see Creal et al. (2013) and Harvey (2013). The predictability of cryptocurrencies returns and volatility has been studied in Catania et al. (2019) and Catania et al. (2018),

---

[1]   Specifically, 54.42% for the Bitstamp exchange and 68.78% for the Coinbase exchange.

respectively. Understanding the behavior of Bitcoin volatility has important implications for individual investors and public institutions. Individual investors – people not in the finance industry but interested in trading cryptocurrencies – should be informed about how the Bitcoin volatility evolves and whether these investment opportunities match with their risk profile. Public institutions, like the central banks of Ecuador, Tunisia, and Sweden who are considering issuing their own cryptocurrency, should be interested in the behavior of Bitcoin due to the possible systemic risk they would face by entering in this new market.

In this paper, we study the Bitcoin returns at high frequency and its realized volatility measure. We start by describing the construction of our dataset from the raw transactions downloaded from the Bitstamp and Coinbase exchanges.[2] The first part of our analysis focuses on the in sample properties of Bitcoin returns sampled at different frequencies. We study the autocorrelation structure of Bitcoin returns as well as the intraday and intraweek seasonalities of Bitcoin volatility and traded volumes. Results indicate strong presence of both intraday and intraweek seasonality in the volatility. We also document that seasonality is different across exchanges. Specifically, Coinbase follows the US trading activity, while Bitstamp the European one. The second part the paper focuses on predicting realized volatility for Bitcoin using several forecasting models. Realized volatility is a consistent estimator of the quadratic variation of the price process and is presently widely used in financial and risk management applications, see Bauwens et al. (2012) for a recent overview. We consider the baseline HAR-RV model of Corsi (2008) as well as its generalization with the inclusion of jumps (Andersen et al. 2007; Barndorff-Nielsen 2004; Barndorff-Nielsen and Shephard 2003; Barndorff-Nielsen et al. 2006) and the leverage component (Corsi et al. 2012). Our results suggest that: (i) the predictability of Bitcoin realized volatility has increased over time; (ii) including the leverage component helps in predicting future volatility levels; and (iii) predictability varies with the forecast horizon. Both in sample and out of sample results are reported for the two exchanges as well as for the subperiod 2017–2018 which coincides with the explosion in the interest of Bitcoin. Overall, our results indicate several peculiarities of Bitcoin volatility compared to the volatility of alternative investment opportunities. First, we find that the frequency of jumps is much higher compared to common findings. Second, in contrast to Catania and Grassi (2017) and Ardia et al. (2018) who find an "inverted" leverage effect, our results show that Bitcoin exhibits a leverage effect similar to that of equity assets when this is measured using the Realized Volatility estimator. This last point also supports the arguments of Dyhrberg (2016) who classify Bitcoin as an asset and not as an exchange rate. Indeed, the leverage effect is of little importance for exchange rates as documented for example by Hansen and Lunde (2005) and Ardia et al. (2018).

The structure of the paper is organized as follows. Section 2 details the dataset we build starting from tick–by–tick price changes to equally spaced logarithmic returns. Section 3 studies the behaviour of Bitcoin returns sampled at different frequencies. Section 4 analyses the realized volatility of Bitcoin. Conclusions are drawn in Section 5.

2. Data

Our dataset is composed by tick-by-tick traded prices recorded at the two exchanges Bitstamp and Coinbase over which the majority of the transactions takes place. From both exchanges we collect the tick-by-tick transaction data using the freely available API at www.api.bitcoincharts.com. The raw data include the transaction price for every trade, along with the amount of Bitcoins traded. Observations start the 13 September 2011 on Bitstamp and the 1 December 2014 on Coinbase and are reported in UTC

---

[2] Among several exchanges where Bitcoin is traded we have selected two of the most active ones. Another possibility would have been to consider GDAX instead of Coinbase since this exchange might give a better representation of Bitcoin. However, we have decided to use Coinbase since, differently from GDAX and Bitstamp which are traditional exchanges, it is a click and buy exchange which allows investor to immediately invest in Bitcoin. We thank an anonymous referee for pointing out this to us.

time. We record data up to 18 March 2018 for a total of 22,457,894 trades for Bitstamp and 39,439,004 for Coinbase. Unfortunately, trades are reported with a precision of one second. However, even though it is not reported in the exchanges documentations, we conjecture that trades within a second are reported in a chronological order. Overall, we find that 47.35% and 70.40% of the recorded transactions happen simultaneously with at least one other trade for Bitstamp and Coinbase, respectively.

Data Cleaning

Similar to standard high-frequency financial time-series, raw tick-by-tick Bitcoin prices are contaminated by wrongly reported observations. As suggested by Barndorff-Nielsen et al. (2009), we start by removing all those transactions associated with zero or negative volume. As a second step of data cleaning, we apply the methodology of Brownlees and Gallo (2006) to filter each transaction price. Specifically, let p_i be the price of Bitcoin associated with trade i in our dataset, we apply the following rule:

$$(|p_i - \bar{p}_i(k)| < 3s_i(k) + \gamma) = \begin{cases} \text{True,} & p_i \text{ is kept} \\ \text{False,} & p_i \text{ is removed} \end{cases}, \qquad (1)$$

where $\bar{p}_i(k)$ and $s_i(k)$ denote δ-trimmed mean and sample standard deviation of a neighborhood of k observations around i, respectively. According to Brownlees and Gallo (2006), the positive integer k should be chosen as a function of the trading intensity, which for Bitcoin is relative high since there is no minimum buy-level. The additional tuning parameter $\gamma \in (0, 1)$ is a granularity parameter and should prevent a zero standard deviation caused by sequences of k equal prices. Finally, $\delta \in (0, 1)$ helps to reduce the effect of extreme observations during the filtering procedure. We run the filter reported in Equation (1) using different choices of γ, and k. Table 1 reports results from the cleaning procedure in terms of percentage of outliers eliminated over the full sample and on a daily basis, for different choices of the tuning parameters $\gamma \in \{0.02, 0.04, 0.06\}$ and $k \in \{40, 60, 80\}$. We set $\delta = 5\%$ and found that results are robust to this choice.

Table 1. Number of outliers and average number of outliers per day in percentage points as a function of the rolling trimmed mean parameter k and the granularity parameter γ. Results are reported for Coinbase and Bitstamp using Equation (1) with $\delta = 5\%$.

(k, γ)	$(40, 0.02)$	$(40, 0.04)$	$(40, 0.06)$	$(60, 0.02)$	$(60, 0.04)$	$(60, 0.06)$	$(80, 0.02)$	$(80, 0.04)$	$(80, 0.06)$
				Bitstamp					
Number of outliers	141,029	134,584	128,934	104,018	99,007	85,593	82,623	78,603	75,438
Average outliers per day	0.51%	0.46%	0.42%	0.38%	0.34%	0.30%	0.31%	0.27%	0.25%
				Coinbase					
Number of outliers	118,162	107,936	100,570	98,037	89,922	84,009	85,499	78,482	73,521
Average outliers per day	0.24%	0.20%	0.17%	0.19%	0.16%	0.14%	0.17%	0.14%	0.12%

The percentage of outliers we find are consistent with the findings of Brownlees and Gallo (2006) and Barndorff-Nielsen et al. (2009). For $k = 80$ and $\gamma = 0.06$ we find almost half the amount of outliers than for the case $k = 40$ and $\gamma = 0.02$. In general, we see a clear decreasing pattern in the amount of outliers when increasing the surrounding neighborhood as well as the granularity parameter. Consistently with Brownlees and Gallo (2006), we also find that the amount of outliers increases along with the increase in the number transactions. Indeed, for the case $k = 60$ and $\gamma = 0.02$, we find that 58.66% and 81.95% of the outliers are from 2017 or later for Bitstamp and Coinbase, respectively. Generally, we find that the outcome of the cleaning procedure is similar to that of Brownlees and Gallo (2006) suggesting that no particular attention should be made when dealing with high-frequency Bitcoin prices compared to the standard procedure employed for other financial series. Therefore, we stick to Brownlees and Gallo (2006) and use price series filtered using $(k, \gamma) = (60, 0.02)$ for our analysis. Starting from the filtered series of prices, we compute an equally spaced sequence of one–second prices and volumes. When multiple transactions are available within the same second, we set the final price to the median price computed over that second. Days with less then 40 observations have been removed for the dataset. We removed 167 days for Bitstamp and 16 days for Coinbase from the begin of the sample. Beside this, in order to remain with a time series without missing days, we let our data set to start from 17 March 2013 for Bitstamp and from 2 February 2015 for Coinbase. In order to isolate the effect of 2017, for the rest of the paper results are reported for the full sample as well as for the sub-sample after 1 January 2017 at midnight labelled as "Hype". Table 2 summarizes the results from the cleaning procedure.

Table 2. This table summarizes the results from the cleaning procedure. Starting from the raw dataset, transactions associated with non positive volume are removed. Outliers are identified following the procedure of Brownlees and Gallo (2006). The "Simultaneous ticks" reports the number of transactions that occurs within the same second. The row "Final sample size in seconds" and " Trading days" report the number of equally spaced observations in second and the number of trading days, respectively. Results are reported for the two exchanges Bitstamp and Coinbase as well as for the full sample and the sub–sample "Hype".

	Bitstamp		Coinbase	
	Full Sample	**Hype**	**Full Sample**	**Hype**
Raw observations	22,346,195	12,217,195	39,285,138	27,126,897
Volume ≤ 0	1112	98	0	0
Outliers	104,295	61,350	103,071	85,418
Simultaneous ticks	9,976,748	5,338,296	28,400,400	18,861,682
Final sample size in seconds	12,263,584	6,817,445	10,781,667	8,179,797
Trading days	1825	442	1132	442

3. High Frequency Bitcoin Returns and Realized Volatiltiy

We start our analysis by computing the series of percentage Bitcoin logarithm returns at second $s = 1, \ldots, 86,400$ in day t as:

$$r_{s,t} = 100 \times [\log(p_{s,t}) - \log(p_{s-1,t})],$$

where $p_{s,t}$ and $p_{s-1,t}$ are two subsequent Bitcoin prices for day t. One second logarithmic returns are subsequently aggregated at different frequencies as reported below. We also compute the realized volatility for day t as in Andersen et al. (2001b). As suggested by Liu et al. (2015) realized volatility is computed using 5-min returns, as:

$$RV_t = \sum_{j=1}^{288} \tilde{r}^2_{j(300),t},$$

where $\tilde{r}_{j(N),t} = \sum_{s=\underline{m}_j}^{\overline{m}_j} r_{s,t}$ and $\underline{m}_j = (j-1) \times N + 1$ and $\overline{m}_j = j \times N$ and we set $N = 300$ to achieve 5-min. aggregation. Table 3 reports a comparison between the realized variance of Bitcoin and the variance of S&P 500 measured with the VIX. We note that the volatility of Bitcoin and that of S&P 500 are comparable during the years 2015 and 2016. On the contrary, in the period 2017–2018 the volatility of Bitcoin is considerably higher compared to that of S&P 500. We also note that volatility of Bitcoin is higher during the bear market period of 2018 than during the bubble period of 2017. Overall, results indicate that the volatility of volatility is much higher for Bitcoin than for the S&P 500.

Descriptive statistics for Bitcoin percentage log returns aggregated at the 5-min. frequency are reported in Table 4. We observe that both series are characterized by extreme observations. We find that returns traded at the Bitstamp exchange exhibit higher volatility. However, we also note that returns traded at Coinbase are characterized by more pronounced negative skewness and higher excess of kurtosis. Overall, departure from Gaussianity is evident from the data. To conclude the analysis of Bitcoin returns at 5-min, in Figure 1 we report Gaussian kernel densities estimated on the mean, standard deviation, skewness, and kurtosis coefficients computed over each trading day available in our dataset. Interestingly, while the skewness and the excess of kurtosis coefficients are similar across exchanges and sub–samples, we note that the distribution of the standard deviation is considerably shifted to the right during the Hype period. Furthermore, it is also evident that during the Hype period we observe more dispersed average returns.

Table 3. Comparison over the period 2015–2018 between daily average realized variance of Bitcoin, measured using Coinbase and Bitstamp 5-min returns and S&P 500 measured using the volatility index VIX. The first four columns report the sample while the last four columns the standard deviation (i.e., the volatility of volatility).

	Mean				Standard Deviation			
	2015	2016	2017	2018	2015	2016	2017	2018
S&P 500	16.67	15.83	11.09	16.64	4.34	3.97	1.36	5.09
Coinbase	11.25	6.89	37.24	59.02	29.76	17.26	78.46	67.15
Bitstamp	23.10	10.08	37.46	64.88	72.48	14.69	57.19	62.44

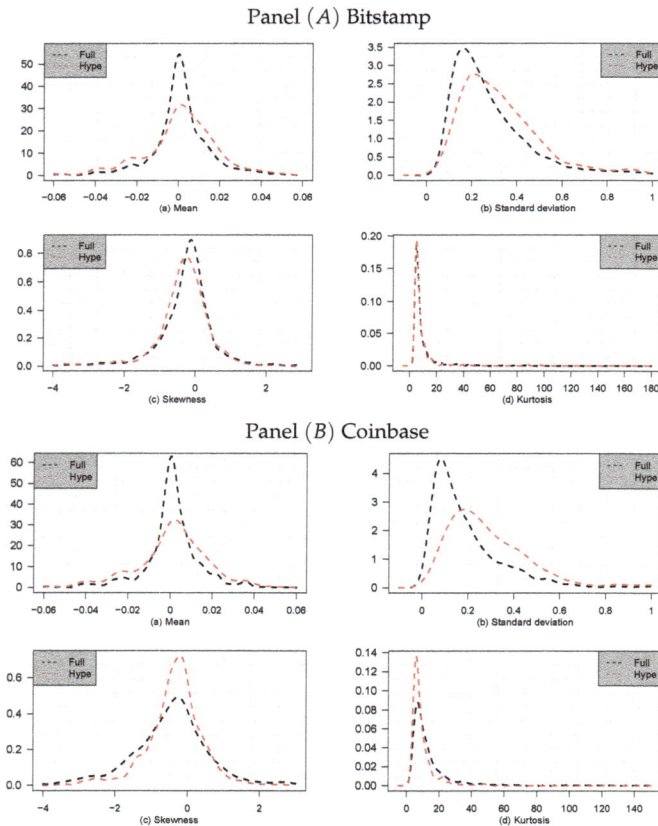

Figure 1. Gaussian kernel densities estimated using 5 min returns over the daily mean (a); standard deviation (b); skewness (c) and excess of kurtosis (d) coefficients for Bitstamp (panel **A**) and Coinbase (panel **B**). Results are reported for the full sample (black) and for the Hype period (red).

Table 4. Summary statistics of the 5 min Bitcoin log returns. Results are reported for the two exchanges Bitstamp and Coinbase over the full period "Full" and conditional on the Hype period.

	Bitstamp		Coinbase	
	Full	Hype	Full	Hype
Maximum	61.09	7.41	10.62	10.62
Minimum	−36.89	−15.54	−21.02	−21.02
Mean	0.00	0.00	0.00	0.00
Median	0.00	0.00	0.00	0.00
Std. Dev.	0.31	0.33	0.20	0.31
Skewness	−0.28	−0.38	−0.58	−0.40
Excess of kurtosis	8.84	8.28	14.36	10.22

3.1. Are Bitcoin Returns Predictable?

Catania et al. (2019) investigate the predictability of Cryptocurrencies returns—and in particular Bitcoin—at one–day horizon.[3] They find evidence of predictability for Bitcoin returns at the one–day frequency when averaging over a large number of Dynamic Linear Models resorting to the Dynamic Model Averaging technique. In this section, we only focus on the plain autoregressive model of order one defined as:

$$\tilde{r}_{j(N),t} = \mu_N + \phi_N \tilde{r}_{j(N)-1,t} + \sigma \varepsilon_{j(N),t}, \quad \varepsilon_{j(N),t} \overset{iid}{\sim} (0,1),$$

where ϕ_N is the first order autoregressive coefficients for frequency N. Figure 2 plots the estimated coefficient ϕ_N for Bitstamp and Coinbase according to different values of N starting from $N = 300$ (five minutes) to $N = 2,592,000$ (30 days). Results for the Hype period are also reported. We find that ϕ_N is negative and statistical different from zero when returns are aggregated up to 6 h. The autoregressive coefficient follows an upward trend and a peculiar curve around the 12 h aggregation frequency. After this point, the estimated coefficient decreases again and start being quite noisy around 0. We find that this behaviour is consistent across exchanges and also holds during the Hype sub-sample.

We conclude that there is no strict evidence indicating that Bitcoin returns can be predicted using a first order autoregressive model when looking at horizons longer than a day. However, by looking at intraday horizons, and especially within the first 6 hours, it seems like there is some predictability, even though the statistical significance is limited.[4]

Gencay et al. (2001) note that the first order autocorrelation of high frequency financial assets is time–varying resulting in different patterns of predictability over time. We follow their approach and investigate the stability of the estimated ϕ_N over time for different N. We expect that due to the increase in the number of transactions the Bitcoin market has become more efficient over time, resulting in insignificant predictability based on prior observations. Thus, we estimate ϕ_N for $N = 900$ (15 min), $N = 1800$ (30 min), and $N = 3600$ (one hour) using only observations available in the previous month of data and update its value according to a rolling window of fixed length. Figure 3 displays the estimated ϕ_N coefficients for Bitstamp and Coinbase. We find that during the begin of the sample Bitstamp shows a significant predictability pattern for both the 30 min and one hour intervals. Though, from the beginning of 2015, this predictability seems to have shrinkage down and lead into the 95% confidence range indicating insignificant predictability. This pattern indicates that Bitcoin traded at Bitstamp has become more efficient especially during the Hype period. Differently, in the Coinbase exchange we do not find the same predictability pattern. A possible explanation could be the more

---

[3] See also Balcilar et al. (2017) who examine the causal relation between Bitcoin return/volatility and traded volumes.

[4] However, we acknowledge that at the time of writing there is a lag of 10.83 min between the placement and execution of a trade on Bitstamp. Differently, on Coinbase trade execution is immediate.

substantial amount of trades for the Coinbase exchange compared to Bitstamp, which implies that
Coinbase is a more liquid and efficient market.

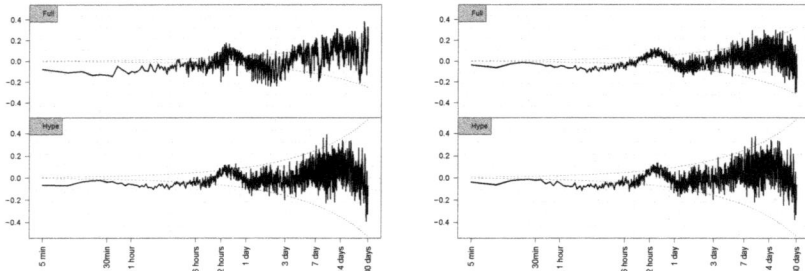

Figure 2. Linear correlation coefficient calculated as a function of the size of the time interval of returns
for Bitstamp left and Coinbase right. The horizontal axis is the logarithmic of the time interval.

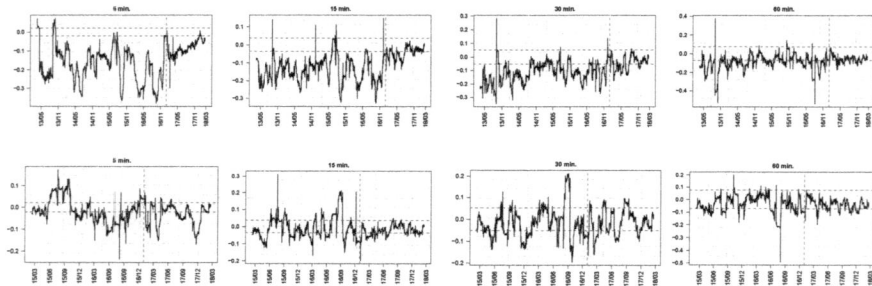

Figure 3. First order serial autocorrelation coefficient estimated using a fixed rolling windows of one
month for Bitstamp (top figures) and Coinbase (bottom figures). Horizontal dashed lines indicate the
95% confidence interval. The dashed vertical line indicates the start of the Hype period at the begin of
January 2017. Results are reported for Bitcoin logarithmic returns sampled at 5, 15, 30, and 60 min.

3.2. Seasonality in Bitcoin's Volatility

Similar to foreign exchange rates, also Bitcoin exhibits a large amount of seasonality in its volatility,
see for example Dacorogna et al. (1993), Taylor and Xu (1997), and Breedon and Ranaldo (2013).
We investigate the daily seasonality pattern by looking at the intraday realized volatility computed
at 30 min over the full sample and over the Hype period, as well as the average traded volumes
computed at the same frequency.

Figure 4 reports a graphical illustration of the intraday realized volatility and average volumes
every 30 min. The figure shows a clear seasonality pattern for the average traded volume (vertical lines)
and intraday realized volatility (red line). It is interesting to see the differences in the two exchanges
peak hours, referring to the fact that Bitstamp is a European-based exchange, and Coinbase is a
US-based exchange. Hence, they have spikes in different timezones associated with their working
hours. Asia should be represented in both exchanges but does not seem to influence the two figures.
We also note that the seasonal pattern has not changed during the Hype period.

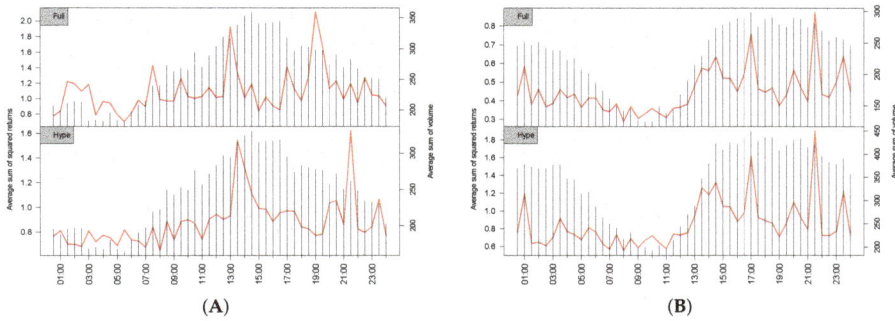

Figure 4. Intraday realized volatility (red lines, left axis) and average volumes (vertical bars, right axis) computed every 30 min for Bitcoin traded at the Bitstamp (panel **A**) and Coinbase (panel **B**) exchanges.

Besides the analysis of the intra-daily seasonality, we also investigate whether there is presence of intra-weekly seasonality. Following Dacorogna et al. (1993), we divide the week into a sequence of 2 h equally spaced observations. Figure 5 reports the weekly sequence based on average realized volatility (red line) and the average sum of volume (vertical lines). The effect of the weekends is clear from the figure. However, we note that this effect is more pronounced during the Hype period reported in the top panel of the figure. Interestingly, we also find evidence of intra–weekly seasonality for other days. Indeed, for both the exchanges we observe increasing activity from Monday to Thursday–Friday and then a decreasing curve over Saturday and Sunday. Remarkably, this effect during working days is not present for regular financial trading assets.

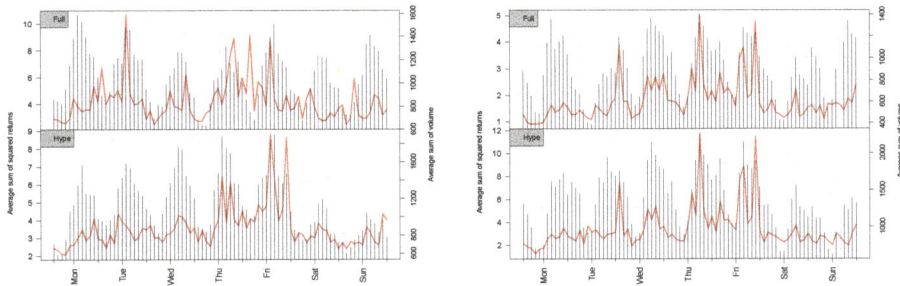

Figure 5. Weekly seasonality computed for the Bitstamp (left figures) and Coinbase (right figures) exchanges over the full sample and Hype period. Red lines report the average realized volatility (**left axis**) while the vertical bars report the average sum of volume (**right axis**).

4. Modelling and Predicting Bitcoin Realized Volatility

In this section, we report on an in sample and out of sample forecast analysis of the Bitcoin's realized volatility using several Heterogeneous Autoregressive (HAR) specifications. HAR has been originally introduced by Corsi (2008) in order to approximate the slow decay of the autocorrelation function of realized volatility. The model builds on the assumption of three different types of investors creating three different types of volatility. The investors are: (i) short-term traders with daily activity; (ii) medium investors who typically regulate their portfolio once a week; and (iii) long-term investors with horizon around a month or longer. Corsi (2008) and Corsi et al. (2012) argue that while the level of short-term volatility does not affect the long-term traders, the level of long-term volatility does affect the short-term traders, as it determines the expectation to the future size of trends and risks. Hence, the short-term volatility is dependent on the longer horizon volatility, while the long-term volatility only consist of an $AR\,(1)$ structure, then the model can be written in a hierarchical system defined by

$$
\begin{aligned}
\tilde{\sigma}_{t+1m}^{m} &= c^{m} + \phi RV_{t}^{m} + \tilde{\omega}_{t+1m}^{m} \\
\tilde{\sigma}_{t+1w}^{w} &= c^{w} + \phi^{w} RV_{t}^{w} + \gamma^{w} E_{t}\left[\tilde{\sigma}_{t+m}^{m}\right] + \tilde{\omega}_{t+1m}^{w} \\
\hat{\sigma}_{t+1d}^{d} &= c^{d} + \phi^{d} RV_{t}^{d} + \gamma^{d} E_{t}\left[\tilde{\sigma}_{t+w}^{w}\right] + \tilde{\omega}_{t+1d}^{d}
\end{aligned}
\tag{2}
$$

where RV_{t}^{d}, RV_{t}^{w} and RV_{t}^{m} are the daily, weekly and monthly realized volatility and $\tilde{\omega}_{t+1d}^{d}$, $\tilde{\omega}_{t+1w}^{w}$, and $\tilde{\omega}_{t+1m}^{m}$ are the volatility innovations for the daily, weekly and monthly horizons, respectively. The economic interpretation of this hierarchical system is that each horizon volatility component consists of two parameters: (i) the expectation to the next period volatility; and (ii) an expectation for the longer horizon volatility, which is shown to have an impact on the future volatility. The HAR model can be written in a cascade of previous values for one day, one week and one month. By straightforward recursive substitutions we obtain a forecasting model for the realized volatility as:

$$
RV_{t,t+h}^{d} = c + \beta^{d} RV_{t}^{d} + \beta^{w} RV_{t}^{w} + \beta^{m} RV_{t}^{m} + \epsilon_{t,t+h}
\tag{3}
$$

where $h \geq 0$ is the forecast horizon and $\epsilon_{t,t+h}$ is a zero mean serially uncorrelated shocks and $RV_{t}^{w} = \frac{1}{7}\sum_{s=1}^{7} RV_{t-s+1}^{d}$, and $RV_{t}^{m} = \frac{1}{28}\sum_{s=1}^{28} RV_{t-s+1}^{d}$ are the weekly and monthly volatility, respectively.[5] This model is labelled as "HAR-RV". Andersen et al. (2007) extended the HAR-RV model to include a jump component in the cascade of lagged volatility measures. Jumps are defined as:

$$
J_{t+1} \equiv \max\left(RV_{t+1} - BV_{t+1}, 0\right)
\tag{4}
$$

where:

$$
BV_{t+1} = \mu_{1}^{-2} \sum_{i=2}^{n} |r_{t+i}|\,\left|r_{t+(i-1)}\right|,
\tag{5}
$$

with $\mu_{1} = \sqrt{2/\pi}$ is the bipower variation introduced by Barndorff-Nielsen and Shephard (2003) and Barndorff-Nielsen (2004). By including the jump component into the HAR model we obtain the "HAR-RV-J" defined as:

$$
RV_{t,t+h}^{d} = c + \beta^{d} RV_{t}^{d} + \beta^{w} RV_{t}^{w} + \beta^{m} RV_{t}^{m} + \alpha^{d} J_{t}^{d} + \epsilon_{t,t+h}.
\tag{6}
$$

A related specification has been further introduced by Barndorff-Nielsen et al. (2006) by including the so called "significant jumps" component. Specifically, let:

$$
TQ_{t+1} = n\mu_{\frac{4}{3}}^{-3} \sum_{i=3}^{n} |r_{t,i}|^{\frac{4}{3}}\, |r_{t,i-1}|^{\frac{4}{3}}\, |r_{t,i-2}|^{\frac{4}{3}}
\tag{7}
$$

be the realized tripower quarticity where $\mu_{\frac{4}{3}} = 2^{\frac{2}{3}} \cdot \Gamma\,(7/6) \cdot \Gamma\,(1/2)^{-1}$. The significant jump component at level $\tau \in (0,1)$ is defined as:

$$
J_{t+1,\tau} = I\left[Z_{t+1} > \Phi_{1-\tau}\right] \cdot \left[RV_{t+1} - BV_{t+1}\right]
\tag{8}
$$

where $I\,[A]$ is the indicator function equal to 1 if A is true and 0 otherwise, and:

$$
Z_{t+1} = \Delta^{-1/2} \times \frac{\left[RV_{t+1} - BV_{t+1}\right] RV_{t+1}^{-1}}{\left[\left(\mu_{1}^{-4} + 2\mu_{1}^{-2} - 5\right) \max\left\{1, TQ_{t+1} BV_{t+1}^{-2}\right\}\right]^{-\frac{1}{2}}}
\tag{9}
$$

---

[5]   Please note that Bitcoin is traded 7 days a week.

is the feasible test statistics arising from the asymptotic distribution of the difference between the realized volatility and the bipower variation, see Barndorff-Nielsen et al. (2006) for more details. Finally, the new HAR model with continuous jumps, HAR-RV-CJ, is defined as:

$$RV_{t,t+h}^d = c + \beta^{cd} C_t^d + \beta^{cw} C_t^w + \beta^{cm} C_t^m + \alpha^{cd} J_{t,\tau}^d + \alpha^{cw} J_{t,\tau}^w + \alpha^{cm} J_{t,\tau}^m + \epsilon_{t,t+h} \tag{10}$$

where:

$$C_{t+1} = I\left[Z_{t+1} \leq \Phi_{1-\tau}\right] RV_{t+1} + I\left[Z_{t+1} > \Phi_{1-\tau}\right] BV_{t+1} \tag{11}$$

selects RV_{t+1} if $Z_{t+1} \leq \Phi_{1-\tau}$ and BV_{t+1} if $Z_{t+1} > \Phi_{1-\tau}$. We perform a sensitivity analysis similar to that reported in Andersen et al. (2007) and set $\tau = 0.01$.

4.1. Including a Leverage Component

A well known stylized fact of equity financial returns is the so called leverage effect, see Black (1976), Nelson (1991) and Zakoian (1994), among others. The leverage effect relates to the different reaction of the volatility of a firm to past positive and negative news. Its original formulation relates to the reaction of the volatility to changes in the debt to equity ratio of a traded company. Specifically, when a bad news arrives, the value of the firm decreases while its debt remains unchanged. This leads to an increase of the debt to equity ratio corresponding to an increase of the riskiness of the firm which translates in more volatility. Of course, the original interpretation of the leverage effect cannot be applied to Bitcoin since it does not have any capital structure. However, previous empirical works have found evidence of leverage effect for Bitcoin, see Catania and Grassi (2017), Katsiampa (2017), Bariviera (2017), and Ardia et al. (2018). We follow Corsi et al. (2012) and introduce a leverage component in the HAR specification by defining:

$$r_t^{-d} = \min\left[\sum_{i=1}^{288} r_{t,i}, 0\right] \tag{12}$$

which indicates the minimum return over the trading day. The variable r_t^{-d} along with its weekly r_t^{-w} and monthly r_t^{-m} averages are included linearly in the HAR-RV, HAR-RV-J, and HAR-RV-CJ specifications. For example, the HAR-RV specification with leverage, HAR-RV-L, is defined as:

$$RV_{t,t+h}^d = c + \beta^d RV_t^d + \beta^w RV_t^w + \beta^m RV_t^m + \gamma^d r_t^{-d} + \gamma^w r_t^{-w} + \gamma^m r_t^{-m} + \epsilon_{t,t+h} \tag{13}$$

4.2. In Sample Results

We consider the realized variance of Bitcoin from 17 March 2013 for Bitstamp and from 2 February 2015 for Coinbase up to 18 March 2018. Similar to previous results, we also consider the Hype period from 1 January 2017 to 18 March 2018. Results are also reported for the realized standard deviation, $RSD = \sqrt{RV}$ and the logarithmic realized variance, $LRV = \log(RV)$. Figure 6 displays: (i) the time series of the log realized variance; (ii) the feasible test statistics; and (iii) the significant logarithmic jump series, $\log(J_{t,\tau} + 1)$ over the full sample for Bitstamp and Coinbase. We find that the logarithmic realized variance for the Coinbase exchange displays an increasing pattern, with the highest values in the end, and especially around December 2017 where the underline value increased significantly. Interestingly, we find that realized volatility is lower during the bubble period of 2017 compared to the bear market period of 2018.

Panel (b) reports the test statistics from Equation (9) for $\tau = 0.01$. The red horizontal line indicates $\Phi_{1-0.01} = 2.32$, i.e., the threshold after which jumps are classified as significant. Interestingly, we find a very large proportion of jumps for Bitcoin compared to the proportion usually found in other asset classes, see e.g., Andersen et al. (2007). Indeed, the proportion of jumps ranges from 27% to 92% depending on different choices of τ. When $\tau = 0.01$, the proportion of jumps over the full period is around 79% for Bitstamp and 85% for Coinbase. If we focus on the Hype period the proportion of jumps is halved for both exchanges. This results further indicates the growing trade intensity and the increased stability of the market over time.

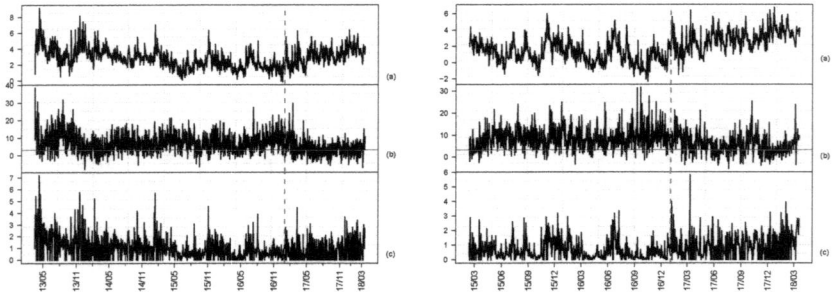

Figure 6. Plot of logarithmic realized variance $log(RV_t)$ (**a**), Z_t (**b**) and logarithmic significant jumps $log(J_t + 1)$ (**c**) over time. Purple vertical dashed lines indicate the start of the Hype period. The horizontal red line indicates the $1 - \tau$ quantile of a standard Gaussian distribution for $\tau = 0.01$. Figures on the left panel are for Bitstamp, figures on the right panel for Coinbase.

Table 5 reports the summary statistics for the realized variance and its transformations. We find that both the median and the standard deviation of the realized variance and jump component are higher during the Hype period. We also find that similar to Andersen et al. (2001a) and Andersen et al. (2001b), we are not able to reject the null hypothesis of normality for the logarithmic realized variance according to the Jarque-Bera test statistics.

Table 5. Summary statistic for the realized variance, realized standard deviation and logarithmic realized variance. Panel (A) reports results for the full sample while panel (B) for the Hype period. The rwo J.test reports the Jarque-Bera test statistics for the null hypothesis of Gaussianity.

Panel (A)—Full sample

	Bitstamp						Coinbase					
	RV_t	$RV_t^{\frac{1}{2}}$	$log(RV_t)$	J_t	$J_t^{\frac{1}{2}}$	$log(J_t+1)$	RV_t	$RV_t^{\frac{1}{2}}$	$log(RV_t)$	J_t	$J_t^{\frac{1}{2}}$	$log(J_t+1)$
Maximum	9374.99	96.82	9.15	1320.43	36.34	7.19	835.73	28.91	6.73	326.73	18.08	5.79
Minimum	0.87	0.93	−0.14	0.12	0.35	0.12	0.01	0.31	−2.31	0.02	0.15	0.02
Mean	54.94	5.23	2.86	7.35	1.85	1.29	21.47	3.41	1.82	1.25	1.25	0.88
Median	15.63	3.95	2.75	2.01	1.42	1.10	5.81	2.41	1.76	1.02	1.00	0.70
Std. Dev.	311.15	5.26	1.23	45.42	1.98	0.87	53.93	3.14	1.57	11.48	1.06	0.73
Skewness	21.19	7.39	0.69	21.16	7.96	1.82	7.51	2.72	0.19	24.81	5.51	1.34
Kurtosis	541.82	94.59	4.11	552.17	102.12	8.60	81.77	14.48	2.55	694.19	74.09	5.77
J.test	$22e^{+6}$	$65e^{+4}$	239				$30e^{+4}$	7612	16.01			

Panel (B)—Hype period

	Bitstamp						Coinbase					
	RV_t	$RV_t^{\frac{1}{2}}$	$log(RV_t)$	J_t	$J_t^{\frac{1}{2}}$	$log(J_t+1)$	RV_t	$RV_t^{\frac{1}{2}}$	$log(RV_t)$	J_t	$J_t^{\frac{1}{2}}$	$log(J_t+1)$
Maximum	588.38	24.26	6.38	37.84	6.15	3.66	835.73	28.91	6.73	326.73	18.08	5.79
Minimum	1.40	1.19	0.34	0.26	0.51	0.23	0.23	0.48	−1.48	0.07	0.26	0.06
Mean	42.23	5.64	3.18	4.62	1.91	1.44	41.04	5.21	2.89	5.16	1.78	1.30
Median	24.56	4.96	3.20	2.90	1.70	1.36	18.70	4.32	2.93	2.19	1.48	1.16
Std. Dev.	58.99	3.23	1.06	5.37	0.99	0.72	76.98	3.73	1.29	21.39	1.42	0.76
Skewness	4.44	1.80	0.06	3.10	1.32	0.53	5.49	2.30	−0.06	14.05	6.77	1.41
Kurtosis	31.60	8.08	2.86	16.08	5.49	2.90	43.11	10.97	3.16	210.54	73.42	7.91
J. test	16,521	714	0.62				31,853	1562	0.67			

Model Estimation

We now estimate by OLS the HAR-RV, HAR-RV-J, and HAR-RV-CJ models to the realized variance, realize standard deviation and logarithmic realized variance over the full sample for the two exchanges.

Specifications that include the leverage component are also estimated and indicated with the additional label "-L". Estimation results are reported in Table 6. Estimated coefficients are in line with those usually found in the literature for other asset classes. Interestingly, we find that specifications that include the leverage component outperform their counterpart without leverage. Regarding the estimated leverage coefficients, we see that these are negative and statistically significant at standard confidence levels. This finding is somehow in contrast with previous results by results by Catania and Grassi (2017) and Ardia et al. (2018) who document an "inverted" leverage effect for Bitcoin. To further investigate this aspect, in Figure 7 we report the empirical autocorrelation at different lags between realized variance and the leverage component, i.e., $cor(RV_t, r_{t-h}^{-d})$ for $h = 1, \ldots, 50$. The plot is reported for the two exchanges for the full sample as well as for the Hype period. Results indicate that correlations are negative and statistically different from zero up to $h = 10$ when computed over the full sample. However, when we focus on the Hype period, evidence of correlation between RV_t and r_{t-h}^{-d} is less strong. This result suggests that the leverage effect has changed over time for Bitcoin and somehow confirms the findings of Ardia et al. (2018).

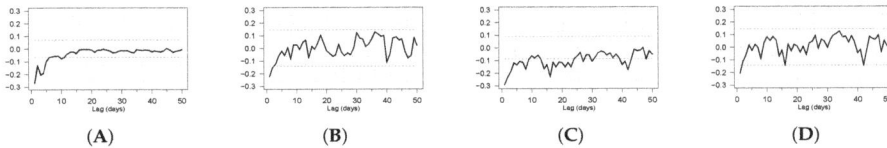

(A)   (B)   (C)   (D)

Figure 7. Empirical cross correlation at different lags between realized variance and the leverage component, $cor(RV_t, r_{t-h}^{-d})$ for $h = 1, \ldots, 50$. Panels (**A**) and (**B**) report results for Bitstamp over the full sample and the Hype period, respectively. Panels (**C**) and (**D**) report results for Coinbase over the full sample and the Hype period, respectively. Horizontal red dashed lines indicate 95% confidence bounds.

4.3. Out of Sample Results

We now conduct an out of sample analysis studying the predictability of Bitcoin realized variance at different horizons. Predictions are made by the models previously introduced at horizons $h = 1$ (one day), $h = 7$ (one week), and $h = 28$ (one month) using the direct method of forecast, see Marcellino et al. (2006). We start making prediction from 21 April 2014 for Bitstamp and 17 March 2016 for Coinbase and than update model parameters each time a new observation becomes available during the whole forecast periods using a fixed rolling window. The length of the out of sample is $F = 1424$ and $F = 731$ for Bitstamp and Coinbase, respectively. Results are compared with the Random Walk (RW) specification defined by:

$$RV_{t+h} = RV_t + \epsilon_{t+h}. \tag{14}$$

Let $\widehat{RV}_{t+h}$ be the prediction made at time t for time $t + h$. Comparison among different specification is performed according to the mean absolute forecast error (MAFE) and root mean square forecast error (RMSFE). MAFE at horizon h is defined as:

$$MAFE_h = \frac{1}{F} \sum_{f=1}^{F} \left| RV_{T+f} - \widehat{RV}_{T+f+h} \right|, \tag{15}$$

while RMSFE as:

$$RMSFE_h = \sqrt{\frac{1}{F} \sum_{f=1}^{F} \left(RV_{T+f} - \widehat{RV}_{T+f+h} \right)^2} \tag{16}$$

where T is the length of the in sample period. Models with lower MAFE and RMSFE are preferred. Table 7 reports the results computed over the full sample. Results for the Hype period are similar and are available upon request to the second author.

Table 6. OLS in sample estimated coefficients for the five different HAR models for Bitstamp (panel A) and Coinbase (panel B). HAC standard errors are reported in parentheses based on the Newey-West correction. The apexes a–d report the significance level, $a = 0.1\%$, $b = 1\%$, $c = 5\%$ and $d = 10\%$.

Panel (A)—Bitstamp

	HAR-RV			HAR-RV-J			HAR-RV-L			HAR-RV-CJ			HAR-RV-CJ-L		
	RV_t	$RV_t^{1/2}$	$Log(RV_t)$	RV_t	$RV_t^{1/2}$	$Log(RV_t)$	RV_t	$RV_t^{1/2}$	$Log(RV_t)$	RV_t	$RV_t^{1/2}$	$Log(RV_t)$	RV_t	$RV_t^{1/2}$	$Log(RV_t)$
c	17.15[a] (2.20)	1.07[a] (0.14)	0.24[a] (0.05)	17.16[a] (2.22)	1.09[a] (0.15)	0.23[a] (0.05)	13.96[c] (6.12)	1.24[a] (0.13)	0.18[b] (0.06)	16.92[a] (1.92)	1.13[a] (0.15)	0.40[a] (0.05)	15.01[c] (6.93)	1.30[a] (0.14)	0.34[a] (0.06)
β^d	0.24[a] (0.07)	0.47[a] (0.05)	0.57[a] (0.03)	0.24[a] (0.06)	0.48[a] (0.05)	0.59[a] (0.03)	0.15 (0.11)	0.37[a] (0.09)	0.51[a] (0.03)	0.28[a] (0.05)	0.49[a] (0.05)	0.53[a] (0.03)	0.17[c] (0.08)	0.38[a] (0.08)	0.47[a] (0.03)
β^w	0.16[c] (0.07)	0.12[d] (0.07)	0.18[c] (0.04)	0.13[b] (0.07)	0.12[d] (0.07)	0.18[c] (0.04)	0.14 (0.09)	0.08 (0.09)	0.20[b] (0.05)	0.09 (0.11)	0.09 (0.08)	0.20[a] (0.05)	0.07 (0.08)	0.04 (0.11)	0.23[a] (0.05)
β^m	0.13[b] (0.04)	0.16[c] (0.04)	0.14[b] (0.04)	0.16[b] (0.04)	0.16[b] (0.04)	0.14[b] (0.03)	0.16[b] (0.06)	0.28[a] (0.08)	0.21[a] (0.05)	0.24 (0.15)	0.19[b] (0.07)	0.14[b] (0.04)	0.31 (0.19)	0.37[b] (0.11)	0.21[a] (0.05)
α^d			−0.02 (0.56)	−0.07 (0.12)	−0.04 (0.03)		−0.15 (0.36)	0.13 (0.21)	−0.01 (0.14)	0.04 (0.03)	0.01 (0.69)	0.01 (0.12)	0.04 (0.02)	0.37[b] (0.11)	
α^w							0.75 (1.17)	−0.10 (0.18)	−0.04 (0.05)	0.75 (1.02)	0.13 (0.20)	−0.06 (0.05)			
α^m							−0.80 (1.11)		0.00 (0.06)	−0.95 (1.25)	−0.19 (0.19)	0.03 (0.06)			
γ^d				−7.41[d] (3.91)	−3.50 (4.70)	−0.19[c] (0.08)	−0.03[d] (0.01)			−7.28[d] (3.75)	−0.18[c] (0.08)	−0.03[d] (0.01)			
γ^w				6.54 (4.58)		0.49 (0.22)	0.01 (0.02)			−4.18 (4.55)	−0.18 (0.14)	0.0 (0.02)			
γ^m					−0.16 (0.14)		0.08[c] (0.03)			8.57 (5.61)	0.55[c] (0.24)	0.10[b] (0.03)			
R^2	23%	50%	67%	23%	50%	67%	25%	51%	68%	23%	50%	67%	25%	51%	68%
adj. R^2	23%	49%	67%	23%	49%	67%	25%	51%	68%	23%	49%	67%	25%	51%	67%

Panel (B)—Coinbase

	HAR-RV			HAR-RV-J			HAR-RV-L			HAR-RV-CJ			HAR-RV-CJ-L		
	RV_t	$RV_t^{1/2}$	$Log(RV_t)$	RV_t	$RV_t^{1/2}$	$Log(RV_t)$	RV_t	$RV_t^{1/2}$	$Log(RV_t)$	RV_t	$RV_t^{1/2}$	$Log(RV_t)$	RV_t	$RV_t^{1/2}$	$Log(RV_t)$
c	4.44[b] (1.70)	0.40[a] (0.12)	0.02 (0.06)	5.01[b] (1.92)	0.44[c] (0.17)	0.05 (0.06)	8.06[c] (3.67)	0.44[a] (0.12)	0.01 (0.06)	6.67[a] (1.81)	0.65[a] (0.17)	0.30[a] (0.06)	8.69[c] (3.69)	0.68[a] (0.18)	0.29[a] (0.07)
β^d	0.33[b] (0.10)	0.51[a] (0.06)	0.56[a] (0.03)	0.33[b] (0.12)	0.52[a] (0.06)	0.59[a] (0.04)	0.12 (0.12)	0.42[a] (0.07)	0.52[a] (0.04)	0.37[a] (0.12)	0.51[a] (0.06)	0.50[a] (0.06)	0.31[c] (0.14)	0.43[a] (0.08)	0.45[a] (0.04)
β^w	0.08 (0.07)	0.13[b] (0.06)	0.24[a] (0.04)	0.08 (0.07)	0.15[b] (0.05)	0.25[a] (0.04)	−0.05 (0.12)	0.11[d] (0.07)	0.27[a] (0.04)	0.04 (0.09)	0.14[d] (0.07)	0.31[a] (0.06)	−0.07 (0.12)	0.11 (0.07)	0.33[a] (0.06)
β^m	0.40[c] (0.18)	0.19[b] (0.06)	0.11[b] (0.04)	0.38[c] (0.19)	0.19[b] (0.06)	0.10[c] (0.04)	0.69[d] (0.36)	0.37[b] (0.13)	0.15[b] (0.06)	0.47[c] (0.23)	0.25[b] (0.08)	0.12[c] (0.05)	0.68[d] (0.37)	0.39[b] (0.13)	0.16[c] (0.06)
α^d			−0.46 (0.32)	−0.10 (0.18)	−0.08 (0.05)		−0.09 (0.23)	−0.12 (0.13)	−0.16[d] (0.09)	0.09[b] (0.05)	−0.18 (0.19)	−0.08 (0.15)	0.08[b] (0.04)		
α^w							0.42 (0.33)	0.02 (0.1)	−0.16[d] (0.09)	0.17 (0.34)	0.00 (0.16)	−0.16[c] (0.09)			
α^m							−1.20 (0.84)	−0.27[d] (0.16)	−0.05 (0.08)	−0.51 (0.53)	−0.18 (0.14)	−0.04 (0.08)			
γ^d				−3.70[b] (1.18)	−3.72 (4.14)	−0.18[b] (0.05)	−0.05[a] (0.01)			−3.70[b] (1.18)	−0.18[b] (0.05)	−0.05[a] (0.01)			
γ^w				12.82 (8.20)	0.56[c] (0.28)	−0.07 (0.16)	0.04 (0.04)			−3.94 (4.01)	−0.07 (0.16)	0.04 (0.04)			
γ^m							0.08 (0.06)			11.01 (7.80)	0.51[d] (0.27)	0.08 (0.06)			
R^2	23%	51%	68%	23%	51%	68%	26%	52%	68%	24%	51%	68%	27%	53%	68%
adj. R^2	23%	50%	68%	23%	51%	68%	26%	52%	68%	24%	51%	68%	26%	53%	68%

Table 7. This table reports the out of sample forecast results for different HAR models. Results for Bitstamp are reported in panel (A) for Coinbase in panel (B) for the three forecast horizons $h = 1$, $h = 7$, and $h = 28$. Diebold Mariano test statistics with respect to the RW model (DM1) and HAR-RV model (DM2) are reported. p-values based on the asymptotic Gaussian distribution with HAC standard errors are reported in parenthesis.

Panel (A)—Bitstamp

Daily $h = 1$

Model	RW			HAR-RV			HAR-RV-J			HAR-RV-L			HAR-RV-CJ			HAR-RV-CJ-L		
	RV_t	$RV_t^{1/2}$	$Log(RV_t)$	RV_t	$RV_t^{1/2}$	$Log(RV_t)$	RV_t	$RV_t^{1/2}$	$Log(RV_t)$	RV_t	$RV_t^{1/2}$	$Log(RV_t)$	RV_t	$RV_t^{1/2}$	$Log(RV_t)$	RV_t	$RV_t^{1/2}$	$Log(RV_t)$
R^2	24.57%	50.18%	63.51	21.21%	51.00%	65.53%	20.79%	50.84%	65.59%	20.70%	50.48%	65.91%	20.40%	50.97%	65.53%	20.30%	50.33%	65.94%
MAFE	16.36	1.20	0.51	24.16	1.24	0.47	24.12	1.24	0.47	25.03	1.27	0.47	23.93	1.25	0.48	25.34	1.27	0.47
RMSFE	52.19	2.12	0.68	47.54	1.97	0.63	47.57	1.97	0.63	48.15	1.98	0.62	47.44	1.97	0.63	48.82	1.98	0.63
DM_1				0.93 (35.13)	1.79 (7.44)	5.59 (0.00)	0.92 (35.63)	1.79 (7.41)	5.65 (0.00)	0.87 (38.37)	1.78 (7.46)	5.87 (0.00)	0.96 (33.67)	1.85 (6.38)	5.28 (0.00)	0.82 (40.98)	1.88 (6.08)	5.65 (0.00)
DM_2							−1.27 (20.27)	−0.36 (71.53)	1.19 (23.38)	−0.31 (76.00)	−0.13 (74.51)	1.76 (7.91)	0.36 (72.11)	0.59 (55.27)	−1.00 (31.90)	−0.59 (55.67)	−0.19 (84.87)	1.11 (26.60)

Weekly $h = 7$

Model	RW			HAR-RV			HAR-RV-J			HAR-RV-L			HAR-RV-CJ			HAR-RV-CJ-L		
	RV_t	$RV_t^{1/2}$	$Log(RV_t)$	RV_t	$RV_t^{1/2}$	$Log(RV_t)$	RV_t	$RV_t^{1/2}$	$Log(RV_t)$	RV_t	$RV_t^{1/2}$	$Log(RV_t)$	RV_t	$RV_t^{1/2}$	$Log(RV_t)$	RV_t	$RV_t^{1/2}$	$Log(RV_t)$
R^2	15.48%	33.56%	47.95%	4.70%	29.47%	46.14%	4.30%	29.71%	46.32%	0.89%	23.37%	46.90%	5.12%	30.05%	46.42%	0.26%	21.74%	46.56%
MAFE	17.86	1.45	0.59	27.04	1.62	0.59	27.14	1.62	0.59	29.52	1.62	0.56	26.65	1.62	0.59	30.36	1.64	0.57
RMSFE	36.05	2.21	0.76	35.15	2.08	0.72	35.33	2.08	0.72	38.34	2.15	0.71	34.91	2.08	0.72	39.66	2.17	0.72
DM_1				0.69 (48.99)	2.66 (0.78)	3.97 (0.01)	0.56 (57.57)	2.65 (0.82)	4.03 (0.01)	−1.71 (8.67)	1.13 (25.68)	4.76 (0.00)	0.88 (37.81)	2.73 (0.64)	3.87 (0.01)	−2.76 (11.50)	0.62 (53.72)	4.37 (0.00)
DM_2							−1.38 (16.71)	0.03 (97.80)	1.33 (18.52)	−8.25 (0.00)	−2.58 (1.01)	2.40 (1.66)	1.69 (9.07)	1.00 (31.84)	−0.24 (81.33)	−8.62 (0.00)	−2.95 (0.32)	1.63 (10.27)

Monthly $h = 28$

Model	RW			HAR-RV			HAR-RV-J			HAR-RV-L			HAR-RV-CJ			HAR-RV-CJ-L		
	RV_t	$RV_t^{1/2}$	$Log(RV_t)$	RV_t	$RV_t^{1/2}$	$Log(RV_t)$	RV_t	$RV_t^{1/2}$	$Log(RV_t)$	RV_t	$RV_t^{1/2}$	$Log(RV_t)$	RV_t	$RV_t^{1/2}$	$Log(RV_t)$	RV_t	$RV_t^{1/2}$	$Log(RV_t)$
R^2	19.46%	24.87%	30.15%	0.37%	14.29%	27.57%	0.37%	14.18%	27.62%	1.41%	8.20%	31.14%	1.41%	20.04%	32.86%	0.54%	9.99%	33.79%
MAFE	16.22	1.52	0.65	28.00	1.88	0.66	28.01	1.88	0.66	31.07	1.83	0.61	27.32	1.83	0.64	31.55	1.83	0.60
RMSFE	24.82	2.05	0.82	31.79	2.13	0.77	31.80	2.13	0.77	36.82	2.17	0.74	31.04	2.08	0.76	38.52	2.23	0.73
DM_1				−10.06 (0.00)	−1.84 (6.54)	3.83 (0.01)	−10.08 (0.00)	−1.87 (6.12)	3.82 (0.01)	−13.54 (0.00)	−2.38 (1.75)	7.49 (0.00)	−8.88 (0.00)	−0.70 (48.18)	5.21 (0.00)	−13.85 (0.00)	−3.48 (0.05)	8.22 (0.00)
DM_2							−2.27 (2.35)	−2.34 (1.93)	−0.71 (47.56)	−12.98 (0.00)	−1.58 (11.33)	5.13 (0.00)	8.79 (0.00)	6.53 (0.00)	5.15 (0.00)	−11.76 (0.00)	−2.94 (0.33)	6.00 (0.00)

Table 7. Cont.

Panel (B)—Coinbase

Daily h = 1

Model	RW			HAR-RV			HAR-RVJ			HAR-RV-L			HAR-RV-CJ			HAR-RV-CJ-L		
	RV_t	RV_t^2	$Log(RV_t)$	RV_t	RV_t^2	$Log(RV_t)$	RV_t	RV_t^2	$Log(RV_t)$	RV_t	RV_t^2	$Log(RV_t)$	RV_t	RV_t^2	$Log(RV_t)$	RV_t	RV_t^2	$Log(RV_t)$
R^2	15.90%	44.46%	67.50%	17.33%	47.51%	69.58%	17.23%	47.10%	69.52%	19.28%	48.70%	69.82%	17.52%	47.92%	69.69%	19.43%	48.83%	69.85%
MAFE	23.24	1.61	0.77	20.15	1.42	0.72	20.79	1.45	0.72	19.97	1.40	0.72	21.11	1.45	0.72	20.74	1.42	0.72
RMSFE	69.21	2.87	1.02	58.25	2.57	0.95	59.34	2.58	0.95	57.48	2.54	0.95	59.37	2.56	0.95	58.36	2.53	0.95
DM_1				2.01 (4.51)	2.99 (0.29)	3.92 (0.01)	2.04 (4.16)	2.98 (0.30)	3.90 (0.01)	2.15 (3.22)	3.34 (0.09)	3.93 (0.01)	2.04 (4.20)	2.97 (0.31)	4.20 (0.00)	2.18 (2.98)	3.26 (0.12)	4.18 (0.00)
DM_2							-1.57 (11.70)	-1.22 (22.26)	0.23 (81.61)	1.34 (18.19)	1.58 (11.57)	0.13 (89.53)	-1.57 (11.68)	0.29 (77.49)	1.32 (18.68)	-0.11 (91.59)	1.07 (28.36)	0.91 (36.36)

Weekly h = 7

Model	RW			HAR-RV			HAR-RVJ			HAR-RV-L			HAR-RV-CJ			HAR-RV-CJ-L		
	RV_t	RV_t^2	$Log(RV_t)$	RV_t	RV_t^2	$Log(RV_t)$	RV_t	RV_t^2	$Log(RV_t)$	RV_t	RV_t^2	$Log(RV_t)$	RV_t	RV_t^2	$Log(RV_t)$	RV_t	RV_t^2	$Log(RV_t)$
R^2	15.88%	38.10%	56.62%	19.01%	37.90%	57.01%	17.87%	37.90%	57.43%	20.18%	41.79%	59.80%	18.79%	38.88%	56.77%	18.09%	41.08%	58.73%
MAFE	23.85	1.72	0.90	20.02	1.73	0.84	20.29	1.73	0.83	20.33	1.67	0.82	20.82	1.72	0.84	21.67	1.69	0.82
RMSFE	42.79	2.47	1.10	36.28	2.48	1.04	36.94	2.48	1.04	36.28	2.39	1.02	37.22	2.46	1.04	38.06	2.40	1.02
DM_1				3.87 (0.01)	3.82 (0.01)	2.83 (0.48)	3.42 (0.07)	3.85 (0.01)	3.25 (0.12)	3.97 (0.01)	4.90 (0.00)	3.50 (1.61)	3.39 (0.07)	4.27 (0.00)	3.25 (0.12)	2.84 (0.47)	4.93 (0.00)	3.66 (0.03)
DM_2							-1.52 (12.90)	-0.33 (74.46)	1.93 (5.38)	0.00 (99.78)	1.97 (4.88)	1.61 (10.76)	-1.91 (5.69)	0.79 (42.80)	1.02 (31.04)	-1.96 (5.02)	1.57 (11.67)	1.67 (9.49)

Monthly h = 28

Model	RW			HAR-RV			HAR-RVJ			HAR-RV-L			HAR-RV-CJ			HAR-RV-CJ-L		
	RV_t	RV_t^2	$Log(RV_t)$	RV_t	RV_t^2	$Log(RV_t)$	RV_t	RV_t^2	$Log(RV_t)$	RV_t	RV_t^2	$Log(RV_t)$	RV_t	RV_t^2	$Log(RV_t)$	RV_t	RV_t^2	$Log(RV_t)$
R^2	32.15%	38.57%	42.45%	31.06%	41.34%	45.15%	30.22%	41.10%	45.86%	36.82%	46.32%	45.13%	33.57%	40.18%	37.76%	33.18%	42.74%	35.17%
MAFE	18.40	1.81	0.93	16.95	1.74	0.93	16.98	1.73	0.92	16.85	1.69	0.95	17.09	1.71	0.95	17.38	1.72	0.98
RMSFE	27.10	2.30	1.14	26.69	2.26	1.10	26.68	2.24	1.09	25.22	2.15	1.12	25.65	2.18	1.12	25.51	2.13	1.16
DM_1				0.51 (61.08)	0.71 (47.67)	1.64 (10.23)	0.52 (60.24)	1.00 (31.76)	2.04 (4.22)	2.59 (0.97)	2.48 (1.32)	0.86 (39.03)	2.07 (3.85)	2.66 (0.81)	0.95 (34.28)	2.41 (1.62)	2.97 (0.31)	-0.55 (58.02)
DM_2							0.06 (95.32)	2.40 (1.68)	3.67 (0.01)	3.91 (0.01)	2.61 (0.91)	-0.73 (46.87)	3.98 (0.01)	4.69 (0.00)	-2.13 (3.39)	2.07 (3.92)	2.84 (0.46)	-2.55 (1.09)

Along with the MAFE and RMSFE measures, the table also reports the R^2 of the Mincer–Zarnowitz regression defined by:

$$RV_{t+h} = c + \beta \widehat{RV}_{t+h} + \epsilon_{t+h}, \qquad (17)$$

as well as the Diebold and Mariano (1994) test statistics of each model with respect to the benchmark RW (DM1) and with respect to the plain HAR-RV model (DM2). Results indicate that predictability is higher for lower forecast horizons. Indeed, looking at the R^2 we find that when $h = 1$, up to 65% of the log realized variance variability can be predicted with the HAR-RV-CJ model. However, when $h = 28$ the R^2 decreases to only 33%. Overall, the inclusion of jumps does not always translate in better predictions. In this respect, results are a bit mixed. Differently, models that include the leverage component seem to generally perform better than the standard HAR-RV model. Looking at the Diebold Mariano test statistic with respect to the benchmark model (DM1), we find strong evidence of predictability of all specifications. Differently, when we focus on predictability with respect to the plain HAR-RV model, results are mixed and do not show a clear pattern. Comparing results between the two exchanges indicates that realized variance is easier to predict in the Coinbase exchange.

To conclude our analysis we study the stability of prediction gains with respect to the RW benchmark over time. To do so, we compute the cumulative absolute error of a forecast model over the cumulative absolute error of the benchmark model. Specifically, the ratio of cumulative absolute errors RCAE at time f is defined as:

$$RCAE_f = \frac{\sum_{s=1}^{f} |e_{j,s}|}{\sum_{s=1}^{f} |e_{i,s}|}, \qquad (18)$$

where $e_{j,s}$ is the forecast error of generic model j at time s and $e_{i,s}$ is the forecast error of the benchmark specification. Results are reported for $i = $ RW and $i = $ HAR-RV. Values of $RCAE_f$ below one indicate outperformance with respect to the benchmark and viceversa. Figure 8 displays the $RCAE_f$ for the log realized variance for different forecast horizons and the two exchanges. In the top graph of each sub-figure the comparison is performed with respect to RW, while in the bottom graphs we use HAR-RV as the benchmark. Results are very clear and show that predictability of the realized variance is increased over time. Indeed, at the start of the sample we observe large losses of all models with respect to RW and HAR-RV probably due to uncertainty in estimated parameters. However, at the end of the forecasting period those losses seem to vanish suggesting that volatility becomes more easy to predict. Across the different specifications we observe that HAR-L and HAR-CJ-L are the top performer. This result confirms the in sample findings and indicates that the leverage component is important for volatility prediction of Bitcoin. A comparison across the two exchanges also suggests that volatility in the Coinbase exchange is easier to predict.

Panel (*A*) Bitstamp

Panel (*B*) Coinbase

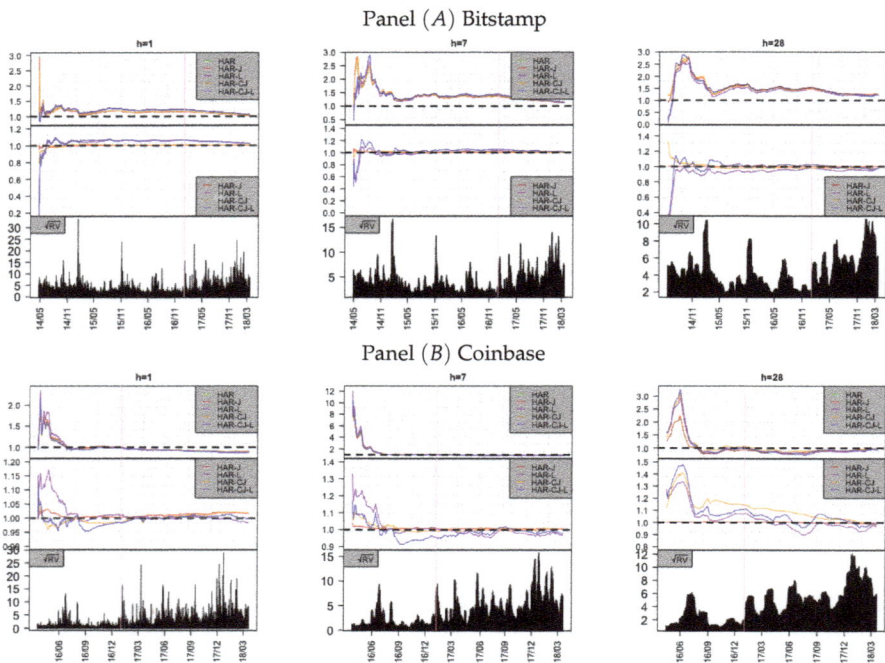

Figure 8. Relative cumulative absolute errors of several forecasting models with respect to RW (first sub-figure) and HAR-RV (second sub-figure). The third sub-figure reports the evolution of the realized standard deviation over time. The red vertical lines correspond to the start of the Hype period. Results are reported for Bitstamp in panel (**A**) and for Coinbase in panel (**B**) for the three forecast horizons $h = 1$, $h = 7$, and $h = 28$.

5. Conclusions

In this paper, we analysed Bitcoin returns sampled at high frequency and its realized variance. Raw Bitcoin transactions have been downloaded from the two exchanges Bitstamp and Coinbase. After detailing how raw data are cleaned, we started our analysis focusing on the in sample properties of Bitcoin logarithmic returns sampled at different frequencies. Results about the autocorrelation structure of Bitcoin returns as well as the intraday and intraweek seasonality of Bitcoin volatility and volumes are reported. The second part the paper focuses on predicting realized variance for Bitcoin using several forecasting models. Our results indicate that the predictability of Bitcoin realized variance is increased over time, and that predictability varies with the forecast horizon. Results extend those reported by Catania et al. (2019) and Catania et al. (2018) to the high frequency case and are consistent with previous findings reported for lower frequencies. We have also documented the presence of leverage effect for Bitcoin when realized variance is used. However, this finding is in contrast with previous results reported by Catania and Grassi (2017) and Ardia et al. (2018) where an "inverted" leverage effect is found. However, we note that differently from Catania and Grassi (2017) and Ardia et al. (2018) who use financial econometrics models to filter the conditional volatility of Bitcoin, in this study we estimate volatility using the realized variance estimator of Andersen et al. (2001a). Furthermore, our results also indicate that the leverage effect is less evident during the Hype period. Through the paper, all results have been detailed with respect to the two exchange rates as well as with a focus on the recent 2017–2018 period.

We believe that our results can be used by private investors as well as by hedge funds to improve their forecasting models for Bitcoin as well as for pricing of derivative securities. Furthermore, central banks who are considering issuing their own digital currency like Ecuador, Tunisia, and Sweden can exploits our results to improve the efficiency and reduce the volatility of the resulting market.

We have not investigated the presence of possible arbitrage opportunities across the two exchanges. Possible extensions can be made in this direction. Additionally, our results can be extended to a multivariate analysis aiming at investigating the lead/lag structure of different cryptocurrencies observed at high frequency.

Author Contributions: L.C. conceived of the presented idea. M.S. implemented the analysis under the supervision of L.C. Both authors discussed the results and contributed to the final manuscript.

Funding: This research received no external funding.

Conflicts of Interest: The authors declare no conflict of interest.

References

Andersen, Torben G., Tim Bollerslev, Francis X. Diebold, and Heiko Ebens. 2001a. The distribution of realized stock return volatility. *Journal of Financial Economics* 61: 43–76. [CrossRef]

Andersen, Torben G., Tim Bollerslev, Francis X. Diebold, and Paul Labys. 2001b. The distribution of realized exchange rate volatility. *SSRN Electronic Journal* 27: 42–55.

Andersen, Torben G., Tim Bollerslev, and Francis X. Diebold. 2007. Roughing it up: Including jump components in the measurement, modeling, and forecasting of return volatility. *Review of Economics and Statistics* 89: 701–20. [CrossRef]

Ardia, David, Keven Bluteau, Kris Boudt, and Leopoldo Catania. 2018. Forecasting risk with markov-switching garch models: A large-scale performance study. *International Journal of Forecasting* 34: 733–47. [CrossRef]

Ardia, David, Keven Bluteau, and Maxime Rüede. 2018. Regime changes in Bitcoin GARCH volatility dynamics. *Finance Research Letters*. [CrossRef]

Balcilar, Mehmet, Elie Bouri, Rangan Gupta, and David Roubaud. 2017. Can volume predict bitcoin returns and volatility? A quantiles-based approach. *Economic Modelling* 64: 74–81. [CrossRef]

Bariviera, Aurelio F. 2017. The inefficiency of bitcoin revisited: A dynamic approach. *Economics Letters* 161: 1–4. [CrossRef]

Barndorff-Nielsen, Ole, Peter R. Hansen, Asger Lunde, and Neil Shephard. 2009. Realized kernels in practice: trades and quotes. *Econometrics Journal* 12: C1–C32. [CrossRef]

Barndorff-Nielsen, Ole E. 2004. Power and bipower variation with stochastic volatility and jumps. *Journal of Financial Econometrics* 2: 1–37. [CrossRef]

Barndorff-Nielsen, Ole E., and Neil Shephard. 2003. Realized power variation and stochastic volatility models. *Bernoulli* 9: 243–65. [CrossRef]

Barndorff-Nielsen, Ole E., Svend Erik Graversen, Jean Jacod, Mark Podolskij, and Neil Shephard. 2006. A central limit theorem for realised power and bipower variations of continuous semimartingales. In *From Stochastic Calculus to Mathematical Finance*. Berlin/Heidelberg: Springer, pp. 33–68.

Bauwens, Luc, Christian M. Hafner, and Sébastien Laurent. 2012. *Handbook of Volatility Models and Their Applications*. New York: John Wiley & Sons, vol. 3.

Black, Fischer. 1976. Studies of Stock Price Volatility Changes. In *Proceedings of the 1976 Meeting of the Business and Economic Statistics Section*. Washington: American Statistical Association, pp. 177–181.

Bloomberg. 2017. Nasdaq Plans to Introduce Bitcoin Futures. Available online: https://www.bloomberg.com/news/articles/2017-11-29/nasdaq-is-said-to-plan-bitcoin-futures-joining-biggest-rivals (accessed on 10 February 2019).

Breedon, Francis, and Angelo Ranaldo. 2013. Intraday patterns in FX returns and order flow. *Journal of Money, Credit and Banking* 45: 953–65. [CrossRef]

Brownlees, Christian T., and Giampiero M. Gallo. 2006. Financial econometric analysis at ultra-high frequency: Data handling concerns. *Computational Statistics & Data Analysis* 51: 2232–245.

Catania, Leopoldo, and Stefano Grassi. 2017. Modelling crypto-currencies financial time-series. *SSRN Electronic Journal*. [CrossRef]

Catania, Leopoldo, Stefano Grassi, and Francesco Ravazzolo. 2019. Forecasting cryptocurrencies under model and parameter instability. *International Journal of Forecasting* 35: 485–501. [CrossRef]

Catania, Leopoldo, Stefano Grassi, and Francesco Ravazzolo. 2018. Predicting the volatility of cryptocurrency time–series. In *Mathematical and Statistical Methods for Actuarial Sciences and Finance: MAF 2018*. Edited by Marco Corazza, María Durbán, Aurea Grané, Cira Perna and Marilena Sibillo. New York: Springer.

CME. 2017. CME Group Announces Launch of Bitcoin Futures. Available online: http://www.cmegroup.com/media-room/press-releases/2017/10/31/cme_group_announceslaunchofbitcoinfutures.html (accessed on 10 February 2019).

Corsi, Fulvio. 2008. A simple approximate long-memory model of realized volatility. *Journal of Financial Econometrics* 7: 174–96. [CrossRef]

Corsi, Fulvio, Francesco Audrino, and Roberto Renò. 2012. HAR modeling for realized volatility forecasting. In *Handbook of Volatility Models and Their Applications*. Hoboken: John Wiley & Sons, Inc., pp. 363–82.

Creal, Drew, Siem Jan Koopman, and André Lucas. 2013. Generalized Autoregressive Score Models with Applications. *Journal of Applied Econometrics* 28: 777–95. [CrossRef]

Cryptocoinsnews. 2017. Tokyo Financial Exchange Plans for Bitcoin Futures Launch. Available online: https://www.cryptocoinsnews.com/breaking-tokyo-financial-exchange-plans-bitcoin-futures-launch/ (accessed on 10 February 2019).

Dacorogna, Michael M., Ulrich A. Müller, Robert J. Nagler, Richard B. Olsen, and Olivier V. Pictet. 1993. A geographical model for the daily and weekly seasonal volatility in the foreign exchange market. *Journal of International Money and Finance* 12: 413–38. [CrossRef]

Diebold, Francis, and Robert Mariano. 1994. Comparing Predictive Accuracy. *Journal of Business and Economic Statistics* 13: 253–65.

Dyhrberg, Anne H. 2016. Bitcoin, gold and the dollar—A GARCH volatility analysis. *Finance Research Letters* 16: 85–92. [CrossRef]

Gencay, Ramazan, Michel Dacorogna, Ulrich A. Muller, Richard Olsen, and Olivier Pictet. 2001. *An Introduction to High-Frequency Finance*. Amsterdam: Elsevier Science Publishing Co. Inc.

Hansen, Peter R., and Asger Lunde. 2005. A forecast comparison of volatility models: Does anything beat a garch (1, 1)? *Journal of Applied Econometrics* 20: 873–89. [CrossRef]

Harvey, Andrew C. 2013. *Dynamic Models for Volatility and Heavy Tails: With Applications to Financial and Economic Time Series*. Cambridge: Cambridge University Press, Vol. 52.

Katsiampa, Paraskevi. 2017. Volatility estimation for bitcoin: A comparison of GARCH models. *Economics Letters* 158: 3–6. [CrossRef]

Liu, Lily, Andrew Patton, and Kevin Sheppard. 2015. Does anything beat 5-minute rv? A comparison of realized measures across multiple asset classes. *Journal of Econometrics* 187: 293–311. [CrossRef]

Marcellino, Massimiliano, James H. Stock, and Mark W. Watson. 2006. A comparison of direct and iterated multistep ar methods for forecasting macroeconomic time series. *Journal of econometrics* 135: 499–526. [CrossRef]

Nakamoto, Satoshi. 2009. Bitcoin: A Peer-to-Peer Electronic Cash System. Available online: https://bitcoin.org/bitcoin.pdf (accessed on 10 February 2019).

Nelson, Daniel B. 1991. Conditional heteroskedasticity in asset returns: A new approach. *Econometrica: Journal of the Econometric Society* 59: 347–70. [CrossRef]

Phillip, Andrew, Jennifer S. K. Chan, and Shelton Peiris. 2018. A new look at cryptocurrencies. *Economics Letters* 163: 6–9. [CrossRef]

Stavroyiannis, Stavros. 2018. Value-at-risk and related measures for the bitcoin. *The Journal of Risk Finance* 19: 127–136. [CrossRef]

Taylor, Stephen J., and Xinzhong Xu. 1997. The incremental volatility information in one million foreign exchange quotations. *Journal of Empirical Finance* 4: 317–40. [CrossRef]

J. Risk Financial Manag. **2019**, *12*, 36

Zakoian, Jean-Michel. 1994. Threshold Heteroskedastic Models. *Journal of Economic Dynamics and Control* 18: 931–55. [CrossRef]

Zhang, Yuanyuan, Stephen Chan, Jeffrey Chu, and Saralees Nadarajah. 2019. Stylised facts for high frequency cryptocurrency data. *Physica A: Statistical Mechanics and Its Applications* 513: 598–612. [CrossRef]

Journal of
Risk and Financial
Management

MDPI

Article

Sentiment-Induced Bubbles in the Cryptocurrency Market

Cathy Yi-Hsuan Chen [1,*] **and Christian M. Hafner** [2]

[1]   Adam Smith Business School, University of Glasgow, Glasgow G12 8QQ, UK
[2]   Louvain Institute of Data Analysis and Modeling, Université catholique de Louvain, 1348 Louvain-la-Neuve, Belgium; christian.hafner@uclouvain.be
*   Correspondence: CathyYi-Hsuan.Chen@glasgow.ac.uk

Received: 18 January 2019; Accepted: 28 March 2019; Published: 1 April 2019

Abstract: Cryptocurrencies lack clear measures of fundamental values and are often associated with speculative bubbles. This paper introduces a new way of testing for speculative bubbles based on StockTwits sentiment, which is used as the transition variable in a smooth transition autoregression. The model allows for conditional heteroskedasticity and fat tails of the conditional distribution of the error term, and volatility may depend on the constructed sentiment index. We apply the model to the CRIX index, for which several bubble periods are identified. The detected locally explosive price dynamics, given the specified bubble regime controlled by a smooth transition function, are more akin to the notion of speculative bubble that is driven by exuberant sentiment. Furthermore, we find that volatility increases as the sentiment index decreases, which is analogous to the commonly called leverage effect.

Keywords: cryptocurrencies; speculative bubbles; sentiment; smooth transition

JEL Classification: C14; C43; Z11

1. Introduction

The current literature on bubble tests is confronted with the difficulty to conclude that a price bubble is not caused by time-varying or regime switching fundamentals (Gürkaynak 2008). Recent tests proposed by (Phillips et al. 2011, 2015) provide powerful tests, essentially based on the supremum of sequential unit root test statistics, and have been applied to the cryptocurrency markets by (Cheung et al. 2015; Corbet et al. 2018; Hafner 2018), where the latter accounts for time-varying volatility. These tests, however, are purely statistical in nature and do not allow us to infer if structural breaks detected in the time series processes of asset prices are evidence of bubbles or are due to breaks in the underlying (unobserved) fundamentals (Pesaran and Johnsson 2018). An inclusion of extracted sentiment information, representing the sentiment in the crypto community with their specific linguistic features, contributes to solving this inconclusive puzzle and adds economic and behavioral information into the statistical settings.

Alternative bubble tests have been proposed e.g., by Pavlidis et al. (2017) based on the gap between spot and futures prices and applied to equities and exchange rates, and Pavlidis et al. (2018) using market expectations of futures prices applied to the oil market—see also Kruse and Wegener (2019). With the lack of liquidity in futures prices of cryptocurrencies, it seems difficult to apply these tests to crypto markets today. Further bubble tests include Cheah and Fry (2015), who use a continuous time model to identify bubbles via anomalous behaviors of the drift and volatility components, and Fry and Cheah (2016), who develop models for financial bubbles and crashes based on statistical physics, with applications to Bitcoin and Ripple.

Bubbles are more prone to emerge in the crypto market than in the stock markets. Theoretical grounds for market efficiency rely crucially on the stabilizing powers of rational speculation—see e.g., (De Long et al. 1990; Glosten and Milgrom 1985; Yang and Brown 2016). Given the presence of limits to arbitrage (e.g., no short-sale venue) and the limited fundamental information in the cryptocurrency market, rational speculation that pulls prices close to its fundamental value is not possible. These constraints result in a hurdle of price discovery.

In this paper, we postulate that a bubble-like behavior of prices is characterized by a smooth transition function that dynamically assigns the probability (loading) to the explosive regime and the random walk regime, given the exogenous sentiment information. By this construction, the speculative bubble can only be pumped up with anomalous sentiment. We therefore develop an econometric framework and a test for a sentiment-induced price bubble.

We target the cryptocurrency-related messages in Stocktwits which attracts the crypto community to share their information, opinions and sentimental moods. We use the sentiment measures constructed by Nasekin and Chen (2018) from this social media as their newly constructed sentiment index is viewed as a representative sentiment from the crypto community, with a consideration of their specific linguistic features. The information content of it is relevant for future market performance and can be used to predict the price and volatility evolution (Chen et al. 2018). As mentioned before, due to the limited knowledge of a fundamental value in this new digital asset class, the mispricing caused by sentiments cannot be promptly corrected or revert to its fundamental value. This is the reason why sentiment entails a short-run predictability because of an inefficient crypto market that defers a price correction process. This slow correction makes sentiment accumulated and amplified; as a consequence, the bubble is able to grow and probably collapse once sentimental bias is finally being corrected.

The econometric framework is that of a smooth transition autoregressive model (STAR), where the transition variable is the sentiment index. The idea is that, in times of a very high sentiment index, corresponding to excessively bullish evaluations, the price dynamics will be driven by an explosive autoregression, while otherwise they follow a random walk. We allow for conditional heteroskedasticity and fat tails by specifying recently proposed score-driven models that are shown to fit the data well. Volatility is allowed to depend explicitly on the sentiment index. This complements previous studies on cryptocurrency volatility as in (Conrad et al. 2018; Kjaerland et al. 2018).

We apply the model to the CRIX index, which is a value weighted index of the cryptocurrency market with endogenously determined number of constituents using statistical criteria. The reallocation of the CRIX happens on a monthly and quarterly basis—see (Trimborn and Härdle 2018) and `thecrix.de` for details. We identify several bubble periods, primarily in 2017. Volatility is negatively depending on the sentiment index, meaning that bad sentiments or news increase volatility, a feature commonly called leverage effect in classical financial markets. Here, the leverage effect is explicitly driven by the sentiment index.

The paper is organized as follows. We first present the sentiment index for cryptocurrencies in Section 2. Then, we introduce the econometric model in Section 3 and discuss its application to the CRIX. Section 4 provides the conclusions.

2. Cryptocurrencies and a Sentiment Index

For the task of sentiment quantification and construction, this section outlines the dataset being analyzed and the methodologies employed for quantification.

2.1. StockTwits Data

StockTwits[1] is a social microblogging platform where investors and traders dedicate to financial and economic discussion. Each message, by StockTwits policy, should start with "cashtag" that explicitly refers to the specific financial asset. Through it, one can easily link the message content with the asset symbol starting with cashtag; subsequently, associate the symbol with the sentiment of message content, after textual analysis. Sentiment analysis is very possible in StockTwits due to its add-in sentiment disclosure applied to each users. Users can also express their sentiment by labeling their messages as "Bearish" (negative) or "Bullish" (positive) via a toggle button. The available labeled data benefits an advance on textual analysis that typically relies on the available training dataset.

Since 2014, StockTwits adds streams and symbology for cryptocurrencies and tokens, expanding from 100 cryptos in the beginning to more than 400 cryptos recently. This brand new and vibrant new asset class have successfully attracted a huge attention from its big community and also from new comers. New cryptocurrencies are regularly added to the list of cashtags supported by StockTwits.[2] A cashtag refers to a cryptocurrency if and only if it ends with ".X" (e.g., $BTC.X for Bitcoin, $LTC.X for Litecoin). We use this convention and StockTwits Application Programming Interface (API) to download all messages containing a cashtag referring to a cryptocurrency. StockTwits API also provides for each message its user's unique identifier, the time it was posted at with a one-second precision, and the sentiment associated by the user ("Bullish", "Bearish" or unclassified). Our final dataset contains 1,220,728 messages from 33,613 distinct users, posted between March 2013 and May 2018, and related to 425 cryptocurrencies. Overall, 472,255 messages are classified as bullish (38.6%) and 92,033 as bearish (7.5%), and the remaining are unclassified. An imbalance between the numbers of positive and negative messages shows that online investors are optimistic on average, as previously found by (Avery et al. 2016; Kim and Kim 2014).

StockTwits, with a focus on financial discussion, offers an advantage to extract the speculative sentiment, which may ultimately trigger a speculative bubble. Another advantage is that the availability of labeled sentiment by users themselves, rendering an application of supervised learning schemes. The detail of statistical learning model applied to Stocktwits dataset will be documented in the following subsection.

2.2. Sentiment Prediction

Nasekin and Chen (2018) propose a state-of-art methodology for semantic sentiment prediction in the cryptocurrency domain. The long short-term memory (LSTM) type of recurrent neural network (RNN), together with word embedding technique provide a superior performance in predicting domain-specific sentiment. The key advantageous feature in the LSTM is to keep the context-specific dependence encoded, so that the important information about semantic structure of sentence won't be lost.

A general architecture of a sentiment prediction LSTM/RNN network is presented in Figure 1 of Nasekin and Chen (2018). This architecture consists of the input sequence, an embedding lookup matrix, several layers of LSTM cells/units, an output sequence, mean pooling and softmax layers. The core of this structure are the LSTM cells. The structure of these cells is presented in Figure 1. The specifications of this structure include several steps: (1) introducing the cell state C_t to keep information about the previous states of LSTM cells. The amount of information stored in the cell state is controlled by the "gates": an input gate i_t, a forget gate f_t and an output gate g_t. The first to act is the forget gate f_t: it determines how much of the previous state C_{t-1} will be kept based on the values of the previous hidden state h_{t-1} and the current input x_t. The sigmoid function $\sigma(x) = 1/(1 + \exp(-x))$ outputs a value between 0 and 1

---

[1] https://stocktwits.com/.
[2] This list can be found at https://api.stocktwits.com/symbol-sync/symbols.csv.

for each number in the cell state C_{t-1}; (2) generating an update to C_{t-1} through a new candidate value of the cell state, $\tilde{C}_t$, and deciding how much of the new candidate state $\tilde{C}_t$ will be inputted into C_t; and (3) updating the value of the cell state C_t as a weighted sum of the previous cell state value C_{t-1} and the new candidate value $\tilde{C}_t$; (4) updating the the hidden state h_t as a filtered value of the cell state C_t, which is put through the tanh nonlinearity and multiplied element-wise by the values of the output gate g_t.

The detail of RNN algorithm can be found in Nasekin and Chen (2018). Its performance in terms of labeling sentiment as bullish or bearish is also documented, with 84% accuracy.

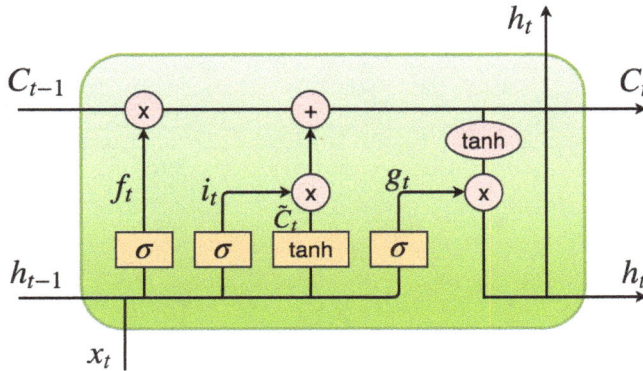

Figure 1. Structure of an LSTM unit.

2.3. Sentiment Index and Cryptocurrency Index

A trained RNN model is used to predict sentiment labels of unlabeled messages which constitute about 60% of the StockTwits' messages' dataset. More specifically, the LSTM setup with pre-trained Word2Vec embeddings are employed for this purpose. Aggregated sentiment in Nasekin and Chen (2018) is constructed in the following way:

$$s_t = \log \left(\frac{M_t^{Bu} - M_t^{Be}}{M_{t-1}^{Bu} - M_{t-1}^{Be}} \right),$$ (1)

where M_t^{Bu} and M_t^{Be} is the number of bullish and bearish messages on day t, respectively. Equation (1) is defined as a logarithmic rate of change of the number of bullish and bearish messages on a day t. This aggregate sentiment is viewed as a representative sentiment from the crypto community in Stocktwits with their specific linguistic features. The information content of it is relevant for future market performance and can be used to predict the price and volatility evolution, given the limited knowledge of fundamental value (Chen et al. 2018). More importantly, due to the limited knowledge of fundamental value in this new digital asset class, the mispricing due to sentiment cannot be promptly corrected or revert to its fundamental value. This is the reason in sentiment carries a short-run predictability. This slow correction makes sentiment accumulated and amplified; as a consequence, the bubble is able to grow and probably collapses as sentimental bias is finally being corrected.

The CRIX (CRyptocurrency IndeX) is created by Trimborn and Härdle (2018) and used to track the entire cryptocurrency market performance as close as possible. It is constructed robustly in the sense it considers a frequently changing market structure, hence the representativity and the tracking performance can be assured. In such a way, the number of constituents is changing over time, depending on market conditions and the relative dominance among cryptos. The data series starting from July 2014 can be downloaded through thecrix.de.

Figure 2 displays an interplay between the time series of crypto-sentiment index and the CRIX index over time, from July 2014 until May 2018. We observe a concurrence between sentiment exuberance and price soar. The next section, based on this observation, is to model a role of sentiment in testing the price bubble.

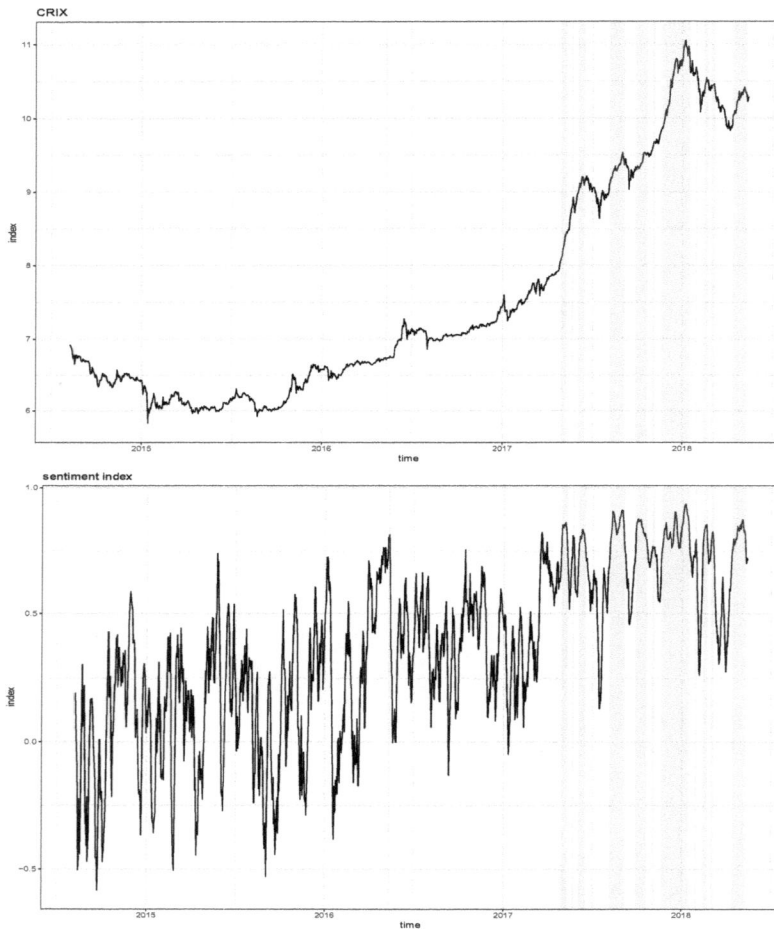

Figure 2. Log CRIX (**upper panel**) and sentiment index **(lower panel)**. The shaded areas correspond to the estimated bubble periods.

3. A Sentiment-Based Model for Locally Explosive Crypto Prices

Suppose we have a series of log prices for the CRIX, denoted y_t, and a series of sentiment indices for the crypto market, called s_t. The idea is to allow for bubble-like behavior of prices, given by a locally explosive autoregressive process, where the explosive regime is determined by a sentiment index of the crypto market. The transition between the random walk and the explosive regime is driven by a smooth transition function as in classical smooth transition AR models (STAR). Furthermore, we take into account conditional heteroskedasticity of the error term and fat tails of the conditional distribution. The model can be written as

$$\Delta y_t = \mu_1 + \{\alpha y_{t-1} + \mu_2\}g(s_{t-1}) + \exp(h_t)\varepsilon_t,$$

where $\alpha > 0$, ε_t is an i.i.d. error term with mean zero and unit variance, h_t is volatility, and $g(s)$ is the logistic function, i.e.,

$$g(\cdot) = \frac{1}{1 + \exp(-\gamma(\cdot - \tau))},$$

with "steepness" parameter γ and "threshold" parameter τ. Essentially, the dynamics of y_t are a mixture of two regimes. When the index s_t is large, then $g(\cdot)$ will be close to unity and more weight is given to the explosive regime, while if it is small, then $g(\cdot)$ is close to zero and more weight is given to the random walk regime. In the limiting case, $\gamma \to \infty$ one obtains as a special case the threshold autoregressive model, as $g(s_t)$ degenerates to the indicator function $I(s_t - \tau > 0)$. It is for this reason that we interpret the situation $s_t - \tau > 0$ as the bubble regime and $s_t - \tau < 0$ as the non-bubble regime, although in the smooth transition model there is strictly speaking a continuum of regimes. See also van Dijk et al. (2002), who adopt the same interpretation.

Estimation of the model can be done by nonlinear least squares—see, e.g., Teräsvirta (1994). However, it will be more efficient to take into account conditional heteroskedasticity and fat tails of the distribution of ε_t by using maximum likelihood estimation (MLE).

The volatility part of the model is taken to be the Beta-t-EGARCH model of (Creal et al. 2011; Harvey 2013). That is, we assume that ε_t follows a student-t distributed random variable with mean zero, scale one, and η degrees of freedom and the volatility dynamics are driven by the score of the likelihood function, i.e.,

$$
\begin{aligned}
h_{t+1} &= \omega + \phi h_t + \kappa u_t, \quad |\phi| < 1, \\
u_t &= \frac{(\eta + 1)\varepsilon_t^2}{\eta + \varepsilon_t^2} - 1.
\end{aligned}
$$

By Proposition 12 of Harvey (2013), we can write alternatively $u_t = (\eta + 1)b_t - 1$, where $b_t = \varepsilon_t^2/(\varepsilon_t^2 + \eta)$ is an IID beta distributed r.v. The reason for using a score driven EGARCH rather than the classical EGARCH model of Nelson (1991) is that many recent empirical studies have found that the news impact function of classical EGARCH tends to overweigh the impact of large shocks on volatility, while the impact functions of score driven models tend to give a more accurate account of the impact of large shocks—see, e.g., Harvey (2013) for a detailed discussion and motivation for score driven models.

The exponential form of volatility is convenient to augment the volatility equation with explanatory variables without having to worry about the positivity of the variance. We consider an additional term based on the first difference of the sentiment index, Δs_t, i.e., the volatility equation becomes

$$h_{t+1} = \omega + \phi h_t + \kappa u_t + \delta \Delta s_t. \tag{2}$$

The motivation for using the first differences of the sentiment index rather than the index level is that changes in the index might be more informative to explain price uncertainty, and hence volatility, than the index itself. The sign of the parameter δ is not a priori clear, as it may be that volatility increases when either the sentiment index increases or decreases. We have tried other functional forms for the impact of the sentiment index, such as $\delta(\Delta s_{t-1} - c)^2$, where c is a constant—for example, the sample mean of the sentiment index. However, and perhaps surprisingly, the best form turned out to be the linear one.

Estimation of the transition parameter γ is often problematic when this parameter is large, as then the transition function is steep and a large number of observations in a neighborhood of $s_t = \tau$ is required to obtain a reliable estimate of γ—see, e.g., Granger and Teräsvirta (1993) for a detailed discussion. In that case, they suggest to first reparameterize g as $1/(1 + \exp(-\gamma(s_{t-1} - \tau)/\hat{\sigma}))$, where $\hat{\sigma}$ is the sample standard deviation of the sentiment index, then set γ to a fixed value, e.g., unity, and estimate the remaining parameters by MLE. The procedure can be reiterated by using a set of fixed values for γ on a grid. We follow their advice here using the grid of integers from 1 to 10 and found that, after rescaling of the transition function, $\gamma = 3$ maximizes the likelihood and gives the best results.

We compare our model with one that ignores the sensitivity index in the conditional mean and variance, i.e.,

$$\Delta y_t = \mu + \exp(h_t)\varepsilon_t,$$
$$h_{t+1} = \omega + \phi h_t + \kappa u_t.$$

We call this model M0, as opposed to the above complete model M1, and we would like to test model M1 versus model M0 to see whether the sensitivity index has a significant contribution to explain locally explosive behavior and volatility. Testing is however non-standard as under the null hypothesis, $H_0 : \alpha = \mu_2 = 0$, there are unidentified parameters, τ and γ. Thus, likelihood ratio test statistics do not have a chi-square distribution under the null. This is a well known problem in STAR models—see, e.g., (Granger and Teräsvirta 1993; van Dijk et al. 2002) for an overview. The simplest solution is to use an LM-type test by estimating the auxiliary regression

$$\Delta y_t = \mu + b y_{t-1} s_{t-1} + e_t, \tag{3}$$

where e_t is an error term, and then test the hypothesis $H_0' : b = 0$. As shown by Luukkonen et al. (1988), testing H_0 is equivalent to testing H_0', as the mean term in the auxiliary regression is the first order Taylor expansion of the logistic regression. See van Dijk et al. (2002) for details.

For the CRIX and sentiment index, daily observations from 8 August 2014 to 15 May 2018, the estimation results are reported in Table 1. In the sentiment-free model M0, the constant μ_1 is positive and significant, while in model M1 the combined term of μ_1 and μ_2 is closer to zero. The estimate of α is small but significant, indicating that the explosive regime is important. In addition, the difference in the log likelihood values suggests that the goodness-of-fit of M1 is substantially higher than that of M0. A classical likelihood ratio test clearly would reject M0 in favor of M1. However, as outlined above, this test is non-standard in our context due to unidentified parameters under the null hypothesis. Instead, we perform the auxiliary regression approach in Equation (3) and obtain the least squares estimator of $\hat{b} = 0.0011$ with a standard error of 0.0002, so that the p-value of the t-test for $H_0' : b = 0$ is very close to zero. Hence, we reject the hypothesis of a random walk in favor of STAR nonlinearity. Rather than estimating the degrees-of-freedom parameter η directly, we estimate its inverse, $1/\eta$, as this often yields more stable results numerically—see, e.g., Harvey (2013). To summarize, our testing approach suggests a significant contribution of the sentiment index to explain locally explosive behavior of the CRIX.

The estimated transition function is given by $g(\cdot) = 1/(1 + \exp(-3(\cdot - \hat{\tau})/\hat{\sigma}))$, where $\hat{\sigma} = 0.3358$ is the standard deviation of the sentiment index. This function is shown in Figure 3, indicating the "bubble regime" for $s_t > \hat{\tau}$. Empirically, this regime occurs in about 16% of the sample period, as, for 219 of 1340 observations, the sentiment index is larger than the estimated value of τ.

Table 1. Estimation results for the model without (M0) and with (M1) sentiment index. Standard errors are in parentheses. $\log L$ is the value of the log likelihood function.

Parameter	Model M0		Model M1	
ω	−0.0929	(0.0323)	−0.0972	(0.0085)
κ	0.1193	(0.0155)	0.1183	(0.0153)
ϕ	0.9759	(0.0081)	0.9709	(0.0000)
$1/\eta$	0.3716	(0.0325)	0.3872	(0.0330)
μ_1	0.0025	(0.0005)	0.0015	(0.0006)
μ_2			−0.0222	(0.0392)
τ			0.7461	(0.1461)
α			0.0061	(0.0012)
δ			−0.2740	(0.1289)
$\log L$	2820.45		2838.78	

Transition function

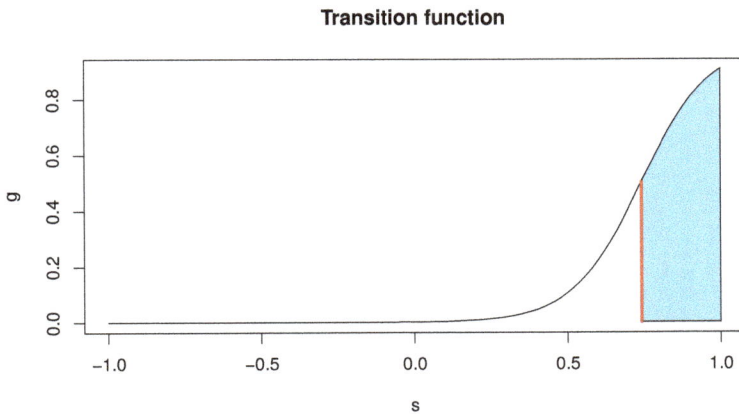

Figure 3. Estimated transition function. The vertical red line indicates the line $s = \hat{\tau} = 0.746$, for which $g(s_t) = 1/2$. Values above this line, i.e., the shaded area, are interpreted as the bubble regime.

Note that the estimated volatility parameters, except for the sentiment term, are rather similar for the two models and characterized by high persistence, i.e., ϕ is close to one, and fat tails of the conditional student-t distribution given by a degrees of freedom parameter η of about 2.6 for both models. However, the parameter related to the sentiment index, δ is significant and negative, indicating that volatility increases whenever there is a drop in the sentiment index. This is similar to financial markets, where negative news tend to have stronger impact on volatility than positive news, often referred to as the "leverage effect" and first noted by (Black 1976; Christie 1982), see Bauwens et al. (2012) for a recent overview. In our case, the asymmetry in the impact of positive and negative innovations on volatility is explicitly modeled by the change of the sentiment index.

Figure 4 shows the estimated log volatility process together with the estimated conditional mean of returns, i.e., $\mu_1 + \{\alpha y_{t-1} + \mu_2\} g(s_{t-1})$. The shaded areas highlight the estimated bubble periods, which mainly occurred in 2017 and parts of 2018. Not surprisingly, the shaded bubble periods correspond to substantially higher conditional mean returns, while it is close to zero for the non-shaded areas. Unlike Hafner (2018) who finds a single bubble regime starting in May 2017 and whose sample ends in December 2017, we find multiple bubble periods, mainly during the period May 2017 to April 2018. Hence, the starting date of these periods coincides with the single regime of Hafner (2018), but, due to the volatility of the sentiment index, this regime is decomposed into several sub-regimes. While the procedure advocated by (Hafner 2018; Phillips et al. 2011) identifies bubble periods that are of long duration and quite inert to price decreases, our approach produces regimes of shorter duration because, as the sentiment index drops, one quickly leaves a bubble regime.

Furthermore, we find that volatility is generally higher in the bubble regimes, with an average log volatility of -3.58 compared with -4.04 outside of a bubble. However, short term movements of volatility tend to react negatively to changes of the sentiment index, as reflected by the negative estimate of δ in model (2). Hence, our approach of using a sentiment index for modelling cryptocurrencies not only identifies locally explosive bubble periods, but also measures its impact on volatility. Moreover, it can be used as a predictive device, on a daily basis, both for returns and volatility. The method we propose conveys regulation implications in the cryptocurrency markets. Very likely scams come to a play given investors' irrational exuberance and a surge of initial coin offerings (ICOs). However, these challenge the regulators in the presence of bubbles.

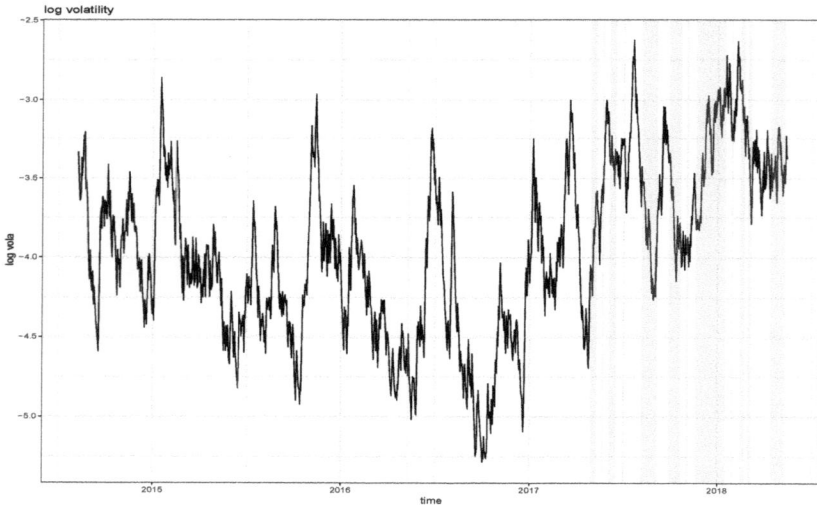

Figure 4. *Cont.*

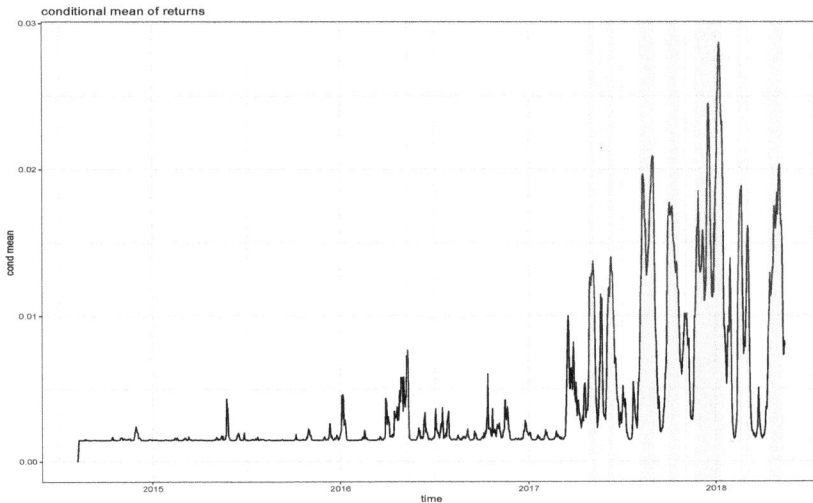

Figure 4. Estimated log volatility (**upper panel**) and conditional mean (**lower panel**). The shaded areas correspond to the estimated bubble periods.

4. Conclusions

Our model allows to test for speculative bubbles in cryptocurrencies using a sentiment index, which drives the transition in a regime switching autoregression. For a popular cryptocurrency index, we find statistically significant regime nonlinearity and identify corresponding bubble periods. Furthermore, volatility is specified as a score-driven EGARCH-type model augmented with the daily changes of the sentiment index. We find that volatility increases as the sentiment index decreases, and vice versa. This is similar to the leverage effect in classical financial markets, where bad news have a stronger effect on volatility than good news, but here this effect is explicitly driven by the sentiment index.

Several extensions of the present analysis are possible. First, it is possible to do forecasting. One-step-ahead forecasting is trivial, but multi-step ahead is not, due to the nonlinearity of the conditional mean function. Several approaches could be employed including bootstrap and Monte Carlo simulation—see, e.g., van Dijk et al. (2002). In addition, the time series properties of the sentiment index would have to be investigated to build a model that explicitly takes the sentiment dynamics into account. Second, we could compare the statistical properties of our testing approach with those of a pure time series based approach such as Phillips et al. (2011). The latter approach uses less information and hence should have less power if the true data generating process is close to a smooth transition autoregression. This is left for future research.

Author Contributions: Both authors contributed equally to all parts of the manuscript.

Funding: This research was funded by grant ARC 18/23-089 of the Belgian government and the Deutsche Forschungsgemeinschaft through IRTG 1792 "High Dimensional Non Stationary Time Series".

Conflicts of Interest: The authors declare no conflict of interest.

References

Avery, Christopher N., Judith A. Chevalier, and Richard J. Zeckhauser. 2016. The "caps" prediction system and stock market returns. *Review of Finance* 20: 1363–81. [CrossRef]

Bauwens, Luc, Christian M Hafner, and Sébastien Laurent. 2012. Volatility models. In *Handbook of Volatility Models and Their Applications*. Edited by Luc Bauwens, Christian M. Hafner and Sébastien Laurent. New York: John Wiley& Sons, chp. 1, pp. 1–50.

Black, Fischer. 1976. Studies in stock price volatility changes. In *Proceedings of the American Statistical Association, Business and Economic Statistics Section*. Washington, DC: American Statistical Association, pp. 177–81.

Cheah, Eng-Tuck, and John Fry. 2015. Speculative bubbles in bitcoin markets? An empirical investigation into the fundamental value of bitcoin. *Economics Letters* 130: 32–36. [CrossRef]

Chen, Cathy Y. H., Romeo Després, Li Guo, and Thomas Renault. 2018. *What Makes Cryptocurrencies Special? Investor Sentiment and Price Predictability in the Absence of Fundamental Value*. Discussion Paper Sfb 649. Unpublished work.

Cheung, Adrian, Eduardo Roca, and Jen-Je Su. 2015. Crypto-currency bubbles: An application of the Phillips-Shi-Yu (2013) methodology on Mt.Gox bitcoin prices. *Applied Economics* 47: 2348–58. [CrossRef]

Christie, Andrew A. 1982. The stochastic behavior of common stock variances: Value, leverage and interest rate effects. *Journal of Financial Economics* 10: 407–32. [CrossRef]

Conrad, Christian, Anessa Custovic, and Eric Ghysels. 2018. Long- and short-term cryptocurrency volatility components: A GARCH-MIDAS analysis. *Journal of Risk and Financial Management* 11: 23. [CrossRef]

Corbet, Shaen, Brian Lucey, and Larisa Yarovaya. 2018. Datestamping the bitcoin and ethereum bubbles. *Finance Research Letters* 26: 81–88. [CrossRef]

Creal, Drew, Siem Jan Koopman, and André Lucas. 2011. A dynamic multivariate heavy-tailed model for time-varying volatilities and correlations. *Journal of Business & Economic Statistics* 29: 552–63.

De Long, J. Bradford, Andrei Shleifer, Lawrence H. Summers, and Robert J. Waldmann. 1990. Positive feedback investment strategies and destabilizing rational speculation. *The Journal of Finance* 45: 379–95. [CrossRef]

Fry, John, and Eng-Tuck Cheah. 2016. Negative bubbles and shocks in cryptocurrency markets. *International Review of Financial Analysis* 47: 343–52. [CrossRef]

Glosten, Lawrence R., and Paul R. Milgrom. 1985. Bid, ask and transaction prices in a specialist market with heterogeneously informed traders. *Journal of Financial Economics* 14: 71–100. [CrossRef]

Granger, Clive W. J., and Timo Teräsvirta. 1993. *Modelling Nonlinear Economic Relationships*. Oxford: Oxford University Press.

Gürkaynak, Refet S. 2008. Econometric tests of asset price bubbles: Taking stock. *Journal of Economic Survey* 22: 166–86. [CrossRef]

Hafner, Christian. 2018. Testing for bubbles in cryptocurrencies with time-varying volatility. *Journal of Financial Econometrics*. [CrossRef]

Harvey, Andrew C. 2013. *Dynamic Models for Volatility and Heavy Tails*. Cambridge: Cambridge University Press.

Kim, Soon-Ho, and Dongcheol Kim. 2014. Investor sentiment from internet message postings and the predictability of stock returns. *Journal of Economic Behavior & Organization* 107: 708–29.

Kjaerland, Frode, Aras Khazal, Erlend A. Krogstad, Frans B. G. Nordstroem, and Are Oust. 2018. An analysis of bitcoin's price dynamics. *Journal of Risk and Financial Management* 11: 63. [CrossRef]

Kruse, Robinson, and Christoph Wegener. 2019. Time-varying persistence in real oil prices and its determinant. *Energy Economics*. [CrossRef]

Luukkonen, Saikkonen, and Teräsvirta. 1988. Testing linearity against smooth transition autoregressive models. *Biometrika* 75: 491–99. [CrossRef]

Nasekin, Sergey, and Cathy Yi-Hsuan Chen. 2018. Deep Learning-Based Cryptocurrency Sentiment Construction. Available at SSRN 3310784. Available online: https://papers.ssrn.com/sol3/papers.cfm?abstract_id=3310784 (accessed on 29 March 2019).

Nelson, Daniel B. 1991. Conditional heteroskedasticity in asset returns: A new approach. *Econometrica* 59: 347–70. [CrossRef]

Pavlidis, Efthymios G., Ivan Paya, and David A. Peel. 2017. Testing for speculative bubbles using spot and forward prices. *International Economic Review* 58: 1191–226. [CrossRef]

Pavlidis, Efthymios G., Ivan Paya, and David A. Peel. 2018. Using market expectations to test for speculative bubbles in the crude oil market. *Journal of Money, Credit and Banking* 50: 833–56. [CrossRef]

Pesaran, M. Hashem, and Ida Johnsson. 2018. Double-question survey measures for the analysis of financial bubbles and crashes. *Journal of Business & Economic Statistics* 1–15. [CrossRef]

Phillips, Peter C. B., Shuping Shi, and Jun Yu. 2015. Testing for multiple bubbles: Historical episodes of exuberance and collapse in the s&p 500. *International Economic Review* 56: 1043–78.

Phillips, Peter C. B., Yangru Wu, and Jun Yu. 2011. Explosive behavior in the 1990s nasdaq: When did exuberance escalate asset values? *International Economic Review* 52: 201–26. [CrossRef]

Teräsvirta, Timo. 1994. Specification, estimation, and evaluation of smooth transition autoregressive models. *Journal of the American Statistical Association* 89: 208–18.

Trimborn, Simon, and Wolfgang Karl Härdle. 2018. Crix an index for cryptocurrencies. *Journal of Empirical Finance* 49: 107–22. [CrossRef]

van Dijk, Dick, Timo Teräsvirta, and Philip Hans Franses. 2002. Smooth transition autoregressive models—A survey of recent developments. *Econometric Reviews* 21: 1–47. [CrossRef]

Yang, Fuyu, and Alasdair Brown. 2016. The Role of Speculative Trade in Market Efficiency: Evidence from a Betting Exchange. *Review of Finance* 21: 583–603.

Journal of
Risk and Financial Management

MDPI

Article

Do Diamond Stocks Shine Brighter than Diamonds?

Vera Jotanovic [1,*] **and Rita Laura D'Ecclesia** [2]

[1]   Louvain Finance and CORE, Center for Research Operations and Econometrics,
      1348 Louvain-la-Neuve, Belgium
[2]   Department of Statistical Sciences, Sapienza University of Rome, 00185 Rome, Italy;
      rita.decclesia@uniroma1.it
*   Correspondence: vera.jotanovic@uclouvain.be

Received: 28 February 2019; Accepted: 24 April 2019; Published: 3 May 2019

Abstract: This paper addresses two practical investment questions: Is investing in the diamond equity market a more feasible and liquid alternative to investing in diamonds? Additionally, is diamond equity affected by polished diamond prices? We assemble an original database of diamond mining stock prices traded on main stock exchanges in order to assess their relationship with diamond prices. Our results show that the market of diamond-mining stocks does not represent a valid investment alternative to the diamond commodity. Diamond equity returns are not driven by diamond price dynamics but rather by local market stock indices.

Keywords: diamond stocks; diamond prices; investment asset; capital asset pricing model

JEL Classification: G10; G11; G15

1. Introduction

Diamonds are emerging as a new investment asset, providing great opportunities for trading, investing and diversification. Hedge funds and financial intermediaries have shown increased interest in the market and recent available data allow us to study its features and dynamics. However, the lack of a standardization system for the diamond commodity prevented the existence of an exchange regulated trading platform for diamonds, leaving diamond-mining companies' stocks as the unique officially tradable asset of the diamond industry. Over the last decade, diamond stocks have been considered as a promising financial asset for investors' portfolios according to finance professionals (Carlin 2017; McKeough 2015; Sizemore 2015; Cameron 2014), though, to our best knowledge, neither academic scholars nor industry professionals have tested this hypothesis.

A diamond-based financial index has not yet emerged as a tradable asset on official exchanges. Commercial experts have been planning to introduce diamond derivatives that could be used to hedge risk in the diamond market; nevertheless, no such product has been launched on official exchanges until the present moment.

In this paper we study the sensitiveness of diamond-mining companies' stocks to diamond prices in order to examine whether they could be a good alternative investment exposure to the diamond market, while still fulfilling the condition of market liquidity. In such a case, the behavior of diamond stock prices would be driven by the diamond market dynamics and would not be influenced by the idiosyncratic risks of the stock markets where they are traded. More precisely we try to give an answer to the following research questions: are diamond mining stocks a good substitute to investing in a diamond-based financial asset? Do they correctly represent the dynamics of the diamond market?

We use the entire set of international diamond stock prices firstly to analyze their statistical features and dynamics and then to test their dependence on diamond prices using the standard CAPM approach (Tufano 1998).

Our results find that diamond stocks should not be considered as a valid tradable substitute for a diamond-based investment tool.

2. Some Recent Research

Literature on the analysis of diamond markets' features and dynamics is quite scarce. Most research primarily tackles the diamond commodity market. Several scholars have studied the dynamics of diamond prices in the last decade (Low et al. 2016; Auer 2014; Auer and Schuhmacher 2013; Vaillant and Wolff 2013; Renneboog and Spaenjers 2012; Scott and Yelowitz 2010; Lu et al. 2010; Cardoso and Chambel 2005; Ariovich 1985), while others analyzed the structure of the diamond market (Spar 2006; Shevelyova 2006; Levenstein and Suslow 2006; Karo 1968).

Commercial reports examining the dynamics of diamond pricing and diamond financial benefits are more common but mostly represent discussions based on general knowledge of the diamond industry (Wieczner 2014; Chesters 2014; Treadgold 2013; Mcgee 2013; Zimnisky 2013; Golan 2012, 2013; Steinberg 2012; Gupta et al. 2010; Adler 2010; Rapaport 2009; Even-Zohar 2012; Turrell 1982; Kempton 1995).

Despite the fact that diamond stocks have attracted interest as financial assets in the commercial financial literature, research studies have remained limited. Bain and Company, Bain and Company and Antwerp World Diamond Center (2011, 2012, 2013, 2018) (AWDC) reports analyzed the overall structure of the mining market and presented the leading companies, without providing any financial analysis of the behavior of the relevant stocks.

Carlin (2017), Sizemore (2015) and Cameron (2014) described diamond stocks as a new investment asset class that could be very beneficial for the financial world. McKeough (2015) and O'Keefe and Bermel (2014) focused on Canadian diamond mining stocks, praising them as financial assets that will hold their value during market setbacks, thus acting as a safe haven. However, apart from O'Keefe and Bermel (2014), no quantitative analysis has been performed in order to test these claims for the overall diamond equity market and the claims are strictly based on the general opinion of the industry's experts.

To authors' best knowledge, no recent research examining the financial potential of diamond stocks and their sensitivity to the price of the diamond commodity has been performed yet. The reason for the absence of research in this scientific domain could be the industry's monopolistic past, as well as the general lack of data transparency.

3. The Market of Diamond Mining Stocks

Diamond mining companies are involved in two major activities of the diamond value chain: exploration and mining. In the exploration phase companies search for diamondiferous kimberlitic rocks, which could represent possible viable sources of diamonds. They do so by testing the ground for changes in the magnetic field. The mining process consists of diamond ore's extraction from kimberlitic pipes using different techniques, such as open-pit mining, underground mining, alluvial mining and marine mining, depending on the origin and location of kimberlites.

Upon mining, diamond ore goes through several stages of crushing and processing in order to extract rough diamonds from it. A very small amount of diamond ore consists of diamonds, as less than 1% of it represents the material with a concentration of diamonds.

The majority of the global diamond reserves[1] are concentrated in Russia, which represents the largest producer of rough diamonds by volume (Figure 1). Russia declared diamonds to be of strategic importance and all mining companies and their exploration processes are, at least partly, state-owned with free access to all country regions. The mining conditions are, however, extremely severe and a large portion of these diamond resources remains unexploited. Africa is the richest world region in

---

[1] Reserves are a part of resources whose extraction is economically justifiable, based on feasibility studies.

terms of estimated diamond resources that could be mined in the future. Nevertheless, their extraction depends on economically feasible processes. In Figure 1 we report annual rough diamond production by country in billions of U.S. dollars during 2013–2018.

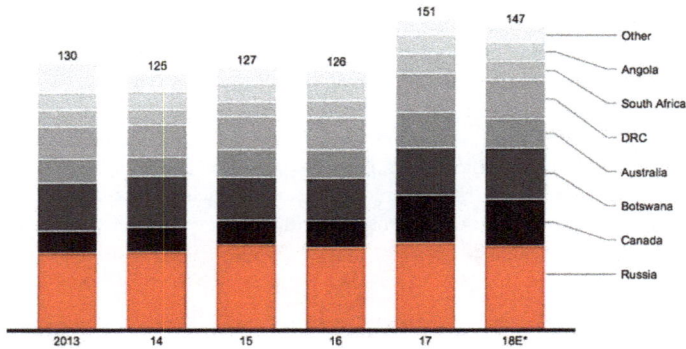

Figure 1. Annual rough diamond production by country in billions of U.S. dollars (2013–2018). Notes: The figure presents annual rough diamond production by country in billions of dollars. Only diamonds tracked by Kimberley Process are included. 2018 data is preliminary estimate. DRC is Democratic Republic of the Congo. *Source*: (Bain and Company and Antwerp World Diamond Center 2018).

Current diamond reserves are divided into projects and mines, owned by different diamond mining companies. The overall diamond mining sector represents the part of the diamond industry value chain that has been achieving the highest profit margins, as reported in Figure 2.

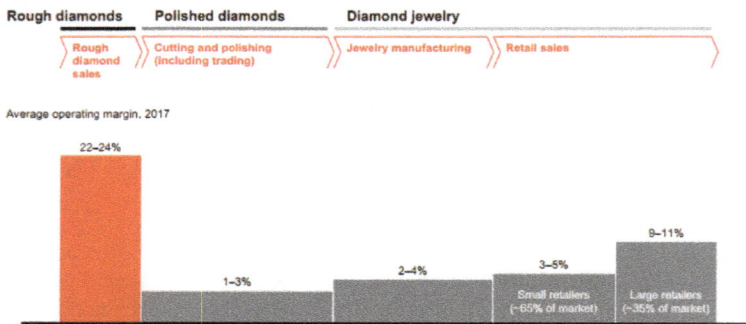

Figure 2. Profit margins of the diamond value chain in 2017. Notes: The figure presents profit margins of the mining value chain in 2017. The analysis of exploration and production is based on data for ALROSA, De Beers Group, Rio Tinto, Dominion Diamond Mines, Petra Diamonds. The analysis of large chains is based on data for Chow Sang Sang, Chow Tai Fook, Gitanjali Jewels, Lukfook, Signet Jewelers, Tiffany & Co., Titan Company. *Source*: (Bain and Company and Antwerp World Diamond Center 2018).

Despite the fact that many international and local companies are involved in the diamond exploration and mining industry, the market is driven by the top five industry players: Alrosa, De Beers, Rio Tinto, BHP Billiton and Dominion Diamond. These five companies accrued 78% of the industry's revenues in 2012 (Bain and Company and Antwerp World Diamond Center 2013). In 2013 BHP Billiton sold its diamond business to Dominion Diamonds, bringing the number of players to four.

Alrosa is the largest diamond volume producer, based on the number of diamond carats produced (Figure 3). De Beers, who had the monopoly of the industry until 2003, is now owned by Anglo

American and remains the largest rough diamond producer in value terms as shown in Figures 3 and 4. This advantage is not unattainable for others, as several competitors are approaching the levels of De Beers' diamond value sales. For instance, while De Beers in 2012 held 37% of the overall rough diamond value sales, while Alrosa's share of the market was 30%.

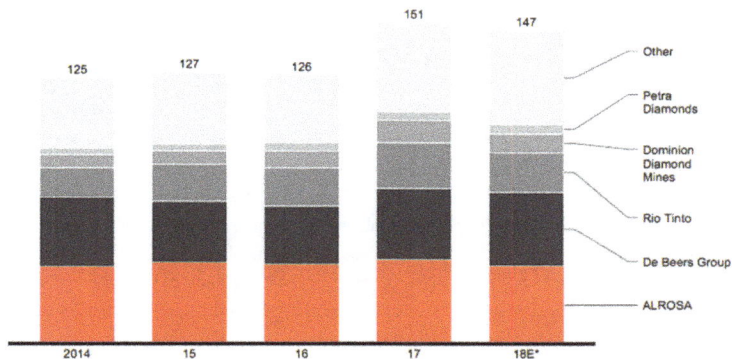

Figure 3. Major producers of rough diamonds in millions of carats (2014–2018). Notes: The figure presents major diamond mining companies and producers of rough diamonds in millions of carats in 2017. *Source*: (Bain and Company and Antwerp World Diamond Center 2018).

World rough diamond sales by producers (including sale of inventories), $ billions

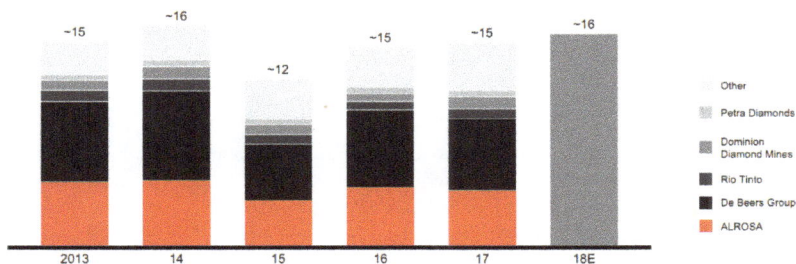

Figure 4. Sales of rough diamonds by producers in billions of dollars, including inventories (2013–2018). Notes: The figure presents major diamond mining companies and producers of rough diamonds in billions of dollars. Estimated realized price is based on an estimate of carats sold if data is published, if not, based on production data. ALROSA revenues represent diamond sales only. Dominion Diamond Mines 2017 results based on H1 2017 as the company was delisted and no longer publishes the data. Petra Diamonds data converted from year ending in June to year ending in December, based on company reports for full year and half year. Only diamonds tracked by Kimberley Process are included. Other is estimated assuming no price change for the players of this segment. E is an estimate. In order to estimate average price per carat sold, total value of diamonds sold is divided by total volume of diamonds sold. *Source*: (Bain and Company and Antwerp World Diamond Center 2018).

4. Methodology

The aim of this work is to investigate the relationship between diamond mining stocks and the price of the diamond commodity. For this purpose, we study statistical features and dynamics of stock prices in levels and log returns by firstly testing for stationarity using the ADF test. We then test the occurrence of structural breaks, using the Bai-Perron (Bai and Perron 1998) test. We further employ the ARCH LM test to examine the presence of heteroscedasticity in log returns. In the case of volatility clustering, we estimate the time-varying conditional variance for each return series by choosing among ARCH, GARCH, TARCH or E-GARCH volatility models (Engle 1982; Nelson 1991). To study the relationship existing between diamond equity prices and diamond prices we use a time varying correlation approach using the DCC-GARCH model (Engle 2002), and the standard CAPM approach presented in Tufano (1998).

5. Data

The database used in this research, composed of price series of diamond mining stocks, has been collected by the authors following thorough background research and represents an original contribution of the paper. It includes daily prices of all companies (21) involved in the diamond-mining sector and traded on different exchanges. It is, to our best knowledge, the only database of diamond-mining companies' stock prices that are traded regularly.

The information on diamond prices are provided by the polished diamond price indices developed in D'Ecclesia and Jotanovic (2018), following a proprietary basket index methodology. In order to account for the different features of diamond prices due to differences in their quality, we use the Mid-range Diamond Index-MDI—corresponding to polished diamonds of mid quality, and the Higher-range Diamond Index-HDI—corresponding to polished diamonds of higher quality. The dynamics of the two indices are reported in Figure 5.

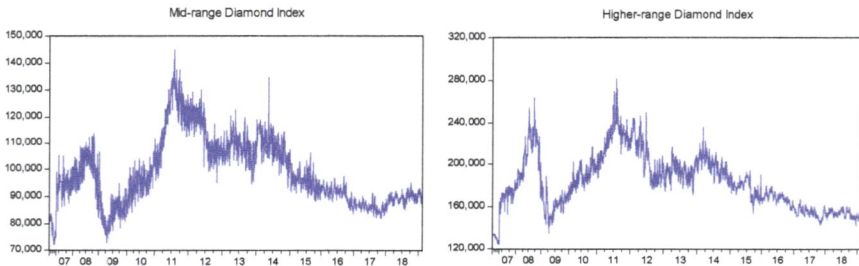

Figure 5. Mid-range and Higher-range diamond indices price dynamics. Notes: Price dynamics of diamond price indices: Mid-range Diamond Index (MDI) and Higher-range Diamond Index (HDI) in their original currencies (USD) for the period 4 June 2007–15 February 2019: *Source*: Polished Prices and D'Ecclesia and Jotanovic (2018).

The list of the stocks included in the database is reported in Table 1. Stock price data were obtained from Bloomberg and Yahoo Finance data platforms. The time interval of the data varies for each stock due to different Initial Public Offering (IPO) dates. All diamond stock prices are daily real traded closing prices from the date of the company's IPO until 15 February 2019.

The selected diamond stocks fulfill the following criteria:

1.   All companies are involved in the process of diamond exploration and mining;
2.   All companies are publicly traded on one or more Stock exchanges.

Some of the diamond mining companies are traded on several exchanges with one of the exchanges serving as the flagship market. In such a case we report only the flagship market of the equity.

The biggest player in the industry today, in terms of billions of carats produced, is Alrosa, listed on the Moscow Stock Exchange-MICEX, followed by Anglo American and Rio Tinto. Another important diamond producer, Dominion Diamond, was acquired in July 2017 by a privately held group of mining businesses, The Washington Companies, and since then has operated as a standalone, private company without being listed on any exchange.

In Table 1 we report all the mining companies traded on exchanges whose main business is related to diamond mining activity. The two exceptions are Anglo American and Rio Tinto that mine a wide range of other metals and minerals as well as diamonds. Nevertheless, these two companies represent important diamond producers and an important part of their revenues is linked to diamond mining, as can be detected by looking at their balance sheets. Moreover, Anglo American owns 85% of De Beers, the previous industry's monopolist and the current leader in diamond production in value (Bain and Company and Antwerp World Diamond Center 2013).

Table 1. Diamond-mining stocks traded at different exchange markets.

No	Company	Ticker	Exchange	Currency	IPO (mm/dd/yy)	Av. Volume
1.	Alrosa *	ALRS.ME	MICEX	RUB	11/29/11	8,468,875
2.	Anglo American	AAAL.L	LSE	GBP	05/24/99	4,551,716
3.	Rio Tinto	RIO.L	LSE	GBP	01/07/88	4,149,613
4.	BlueRock Diamonds *	BRD.L	LSE	GBP	04/09/13	4,021,770
5.	Petra Diamonds *	PDL.L	LSE	GBP	04/01/00	1,963,700
6.	Botswana Diamonds *	BOD.L	LSE	GBP	02/02/11	826,091
7.	Lucara Diamond Corp. *	LUC.TO	TSX	CAD	08/14/07	408,936
8.	Stornoway Diamond Corp. *	SVY.TO	TSX	CAD	08/08/96	349,232
9.	Star Diamond Corp. *	DIAM.TO	TSX	CAD	02/10/87	202,216
10.	Newfield Resources Ltd. *	NWF.AX	ASX	AUD	01/05/11	173,439
11.	Mountain Province Diamonds *	MPVD.TO	TSX	CAD	01/05/96	158,342
12.	Firestone Diamonds *	FDI.L	LSE	GBP	08/14/98	109,490
13.	GEM Diamonds *	GEMD.L	LSE	GBP	02/14/07	84,299
14.	North Arrow Minerals Inc. *	NAR.V	TSXV	CAD	10/25/07	41,904
15.	Pangolin Diamonds Corp. *	PAN.V	TSXV	CAD	08/20/14	37,185
16.	Diamcor Mining *	DMI.V	TSXV	CAD	08/08/96	26,621
17.	Trans Hex Group Ltd. *	TSX.JO	JSE	ZAR	01/08/90	12,312
18.	Tsodilo Resources Ltd.	TSD.V	TSXV	CAD	10/25/07	11,440
19.	Diamond Fields Resources Inc.	DFIFF	TSXV	CAD	01/14/99	611
20.	Archon Minerals Ltd. *	ACS.V	TSXV	CAD	08/16/12	122
21.	Alrosa Nurba *	ALNU.ME	MICEX	RUB	08/12/11	60

Notes: The table presents, to our best knowledge, all diamond-mining companies traded on official stock Exchanges, sorted by the average daily volume during the last 3 months (25 November 2018–25 February 2019). * Companies that are only involved in diamond mining and explorations and no other base or precious metals. *Source*: Elaboration on Bloomberg and Yahoo Finance data.

The companies listed in Table 1 differ substantially based on their dates of initial public offering (IPO) as well as their liquidity (average volume of transactions). In order to have a robust and reliable dataset for our analysis we selected the stocks that satisfy the following criteria:

1. Diamonds as the main activity: The company is involved exclusively in diamond mining activities;
2. Liquidity: The average traded volume of the equity is at least 100,000;
3. Time series length: The company has been listed on an Exchange since 6 April 2007.

In addition to the chosen companies that satisfy the above criteria we include in the research sample the biggest market players traded on official exchanges—Rio Tinto, Alrosa and Anglo American. These three companies do not satisfy the above criteria, as Rio Tinto and Anglo American remain involved in mining and exploration of other metals and minerals as well as diamonds, while Alrosa only became listed on the Moscow Stock Exchange in 2011. Nevertheless, we believe they can provide us with valuable information due to their high stakes in the industry.

Finally, the following 8 diamond stocks were selected for the analysis:

1. Alrosa (ALRS.ME)
2. Anglo American (AAAL.L)   } Biggest players in the market
3. Rio Tinto (RIO.L)
4. Petra Diamonds (PDL.L)
5. Stornoway Diamond Corp. (SVY.TO)
6. Star Diamond Corp. (DIAM.TO)   } Liquid stocks, with diamonds
7. Mountain Province Diamonds (MPVD.TO)
8. Firestone Diamonds (FDI.L)

The 8 selected stocks are traded on Moscow (MICEX), London (LSE) and Toronto Stock Exchanges (TSX). The common time span is 4 June 2007–15 February 2019, while their price dynamics are reported in Figure 6. All 8 companies exhibited a significant price decrease in their values at the time of the Global Financial Crisis of 2008, after which different dynamics for each stock can be observed. Alrosa, Anglo American and Rio Tinto all reported an increasing trend in the last three years while the other five showed a period of high instability (Mountain P. D. and Petra D.), reducing trend (Stornoway D. C.) or constant behavior (Firestone D. and Star D. C.). Firestone Diamonds and Star Diamond Corporation exhibited similar dynamics with no price recovery after the crisis. On the other hand, Mountain Province Diamonds and Petra Diamonds exhibited similar price increases on different occasions, such as during the recovery process in 2010 and then again in 2016.

We further provide additional financial information of the 8 selected companies, reported in Table 2.

Table 2. Financial information of the 8 studied diamond-mining stocks.

Company	Market Value (Millions in USD)	Market to Book Ratio Price/Book	Growth Rate of Sales (%)	Growth Rate of Assets (%)
Alrosa	10,686.00	2.70	8.80	−3.90
Anglo American	34,144.00	1.40	5.21	−4.30
Rio Tinto	97,896.00	2.18	1.20	−5.00
Petra Diamonds	211.00	0.40	25.50	−3.50
Stornoway D. C.	120.00	0.29	0.60	−4.20
Star D. C.	77.00	1.44	no revenues *	−0.03
Mountain P. D.	194.00	0.51	82.80	9.50
Firestone D.	17.00	0.20	1.24	−2.20

Notes: The table presents financial information of the selected 8 diamond-mining stocks. Market value is the market capitalization of a company (number of shares × their current price), expressed in millions of USD. Market to book ratio corresponds to the ratio between market capitalization and company's net asset value. Growth rates correspond to percentage changes between 2017 and 2018, expressed in %. * The company does not currently operate any producing properties and, as such, is dependent upon the issuance of new equity to finance its ongoing obligations. *Source*: Elaboration on Bloomberg and Yahoo Finance data.

As reported in Table 2 we observe that Alrosa operates with the highest market to book ratio, implying that the investors are willing to pay a higher price than its actual net asset value. This could be explained by investors' expectations of future profitability of the company supported by its very high Return on Equity (ROE) of around 36%. Moreover, the management of Alrosa has been very successful in reducing the company's debt and retaining good profits at the same time.

Most of the companies involved solely in diamond mining, with the exception of Stornoway D. C., exhibit market to book ratios that are smaller than 1. This signifies that the investors are skeptical about their profitability and growth, valuing them lower than their net asset values.

Growth rates of sales differ noticeably across diamond mining companies in terms of their values but all result positive, in accordance with the expected increase in diamond sales in 2018 (Bain and Company and Antwerp World Diamond Center 2018). On the other hand, asset growth rate results were mostly negative across diamond–mining companies. The reason for this can be found in increased diamond mining, which reduces the value of diamond mines while no new mines are being acquired. Another possible reason for negative asset growth in balance sheets can be found in the reduction of diamond stock due to the increase in sales.

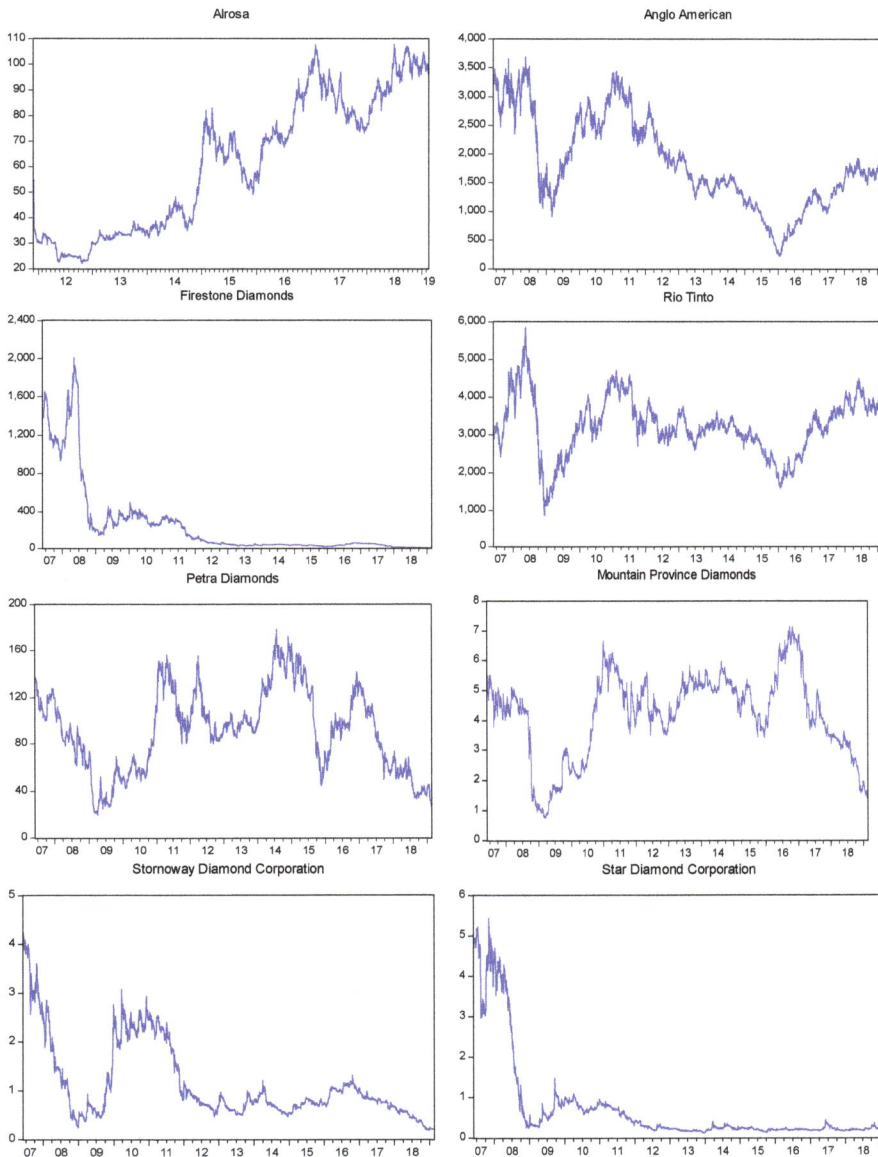

Figure 6. Price dynamics of diamond stocks. Notes: Price dynamics of 8 diamond stocks included in the analysis sub-sample in their original currencies for the period 4 June 2007–15 February 2019: Alrosa (RUB), Anglo American (GBP), Firestone Diamonds (GBP), Rio Tinto (GBP), Petra Diamonds (GBP), Mountain Province Diamonds (CAD), Stornoway Diamond Corporation (CAD) and Star Diamond Corporation (CAD). Alrosa is only listed in 2011. *Source*: Elaboration on Bloomberg and Yahoo Finance data.

6. The Diamond Stock Market

Stock prices are quoted in local currency of the Stock exchange where they are traded. The goal of the paper is not to forecast their dynamics but only to identify whether the drivers of their volatility are governed by the risk factors originating from the global diamond market. We therefore analyze the log returns of each company and study their statistical features.

In Table 3 we firstly report the basic summary statistic for diamond mining stock prices and diamond indices in levels.

Table 3. Summary statistics for diamond stocks and diamond indices in levels (original currencies).

Company		Mean	Min	Max	Prc. 5%	Prc. 95%
		Diamond Stock Prices				
Alrosa	Level	60.48	22.00	107.70	24.66	100.52
	Return	0.00	−0.21	0.34	−0.03	0.03
Anglo American	Level	1807.40	221.10	3680.00	643.09	3227.45
	Return	0.00	−0.24	0.21	−0.05	0.05
Rio Tinto	Level	3198.80	818.70	5847.20	1762.20	4419.01
	Return	0.00	−0.46	0.20	−0.04	0.04
Petra Diamonds	Level	91.68	11.53	178.32	31.77	150.69
	Return	0.00	−0.23	0.29	−0.05	0.05
Stornoway D. C	Level	1.13	0.18	4.32	0.39	2.68
	Return	0.00	−0.22	0.19	−0.05	0.05
Star D. C.	Level	0.67	0.12	5.42	0.17	3.90
	Return	0.00	−0.31	0.43	−0.06	0.06
Mountain P. D.	Level	4.19	0.68	7.15	1.35	6.25
	Return	0.00	−0.33	0.35	−0.04	0.05
Firestone D.	Level	226.03	2.63	2005.00	5.34	1175.00
	Return	0.00	−0.54	0.32	−0.06	0.05
		Diamond Price Indices				
MDI	Level	98,910.00	72,206.00	14,4760.00	83,136.00	122,710.00
	Return	0.00	−0.17	0.22	−0.06	0.06
HDI	Level	18,3023.00	124,472.00	281,240.00	149,519.00	231,381.00
	Return	0.00	−0.15	0.19	−0.04	0.04

Notes: Summary statistics for 8 diamond stocks included in the analysis sub-sample in levels (in their original currencies for the period 4 June 2007–15 February 2019: Alrosa (RUB), Anglo American (GBP), Firestone Diamonds (GBP), Rio Tinto (GBP), Petra Diamonds (GBP), Mountain Province Diamonds (CAD), Stornoway Diamond Corporation (CAD) and Star Diamond Corporation (CAD)). Alrosa is only listed in 2011. *Source*: Elaboration on Bloomberg and Yahoo Finance data.

In Table 4 we report the ADF test statistics for stock price series in levels. In line with the standard features of stock prices, all price series result integrated processes of order 1—$I(1)$, together with the two diamond indices. Following the assumption that stock prices follow a lognormal distribution, we further transform the prices into log-returns and perform the following research studies using this stationary transformation of price data[2].

Bai Perron structural break test results, reported in Table 5, indicate how price dynamics of the various stocks and the two indices are rather different. Several structural breaks occur for each time series in the observed decade but all in quite different dates. Structural breaks in diamond indices seem to be completely unrelated to structural breaks occurring for diamond stock prices. The only

---

[2] The stationarity of log returns has been tested and confirmed and the results can be obtained upon request.

exception may be represented by the structural break of the Mid-range Diamond Index occurring on 10 October 2016, which may have caused breaks in Anglo American and Rio Tinto stock price series that occurred in November and December 2016, respectively.

Table 4. ADF test statistics for diamond stocks and diamond indices in levels.

$\Delta P_t = \alpha + \beta P_{t-1} + \delta t + \sum_{i=1}^{p} \gamma_i \Delta P_{t-i} + \varepsilon_t$				$H_0{:}\beta = 0$	$H_A{:}\beta < 0$		
P_t	α	t_α	β	$t_{\beta(ADF)}$	δ	t_δ	$I(d)$
Diamond Stock Prices							
Alrosa	0.09	1.14	0.00	−0.80	*** 0.01	3.51	$I(1)$
Anglo American	7.59	1.43	0.00	−2.00	0.00	−0.66	$I(1)$
Rio Tinto	16.98	2.37	−0.01	−2.69	0.00	0.23	$I(1)$
Petra Diamonds	0.25	1.53	0.00	−2.02	0.00	−0.22	$I(1)$
Stornoway D. C.	0.01	2.09	* −0.01	−3.15	0.00	−1.18	$I(1)$
Star D. C.	0.00	0.88	* 0.00	−3.27	0.00	−0.57	$I(1)$
Mountain P. D.	0.01	1.42	0.00	−1.73	0.00	−0.11	$I(1)$
Firestone D.	1.18	1.35	−0.01	−2.55	0.00	−1.19	$I(1)$
Diamond Price Indices							
Mid-range D. I.	1238.05	2.33	−0.01	−2.15	−0.11	−1.54	$I(1)$
Higher-range D. I.	*** 2903.46	3.40	−0/01	−3.19	−0.32	−2.58	$I(1)$

Notes: The table presents ADF test statistics of 8 studied diamond stocks in levels in their original currencies for the period 4 June 2007–15 February 2019. The estimated equation includes a constant and a linear trend. Mackinnon critical (asymptotic) values are used for the rejection of the null hypothesis. *** and * indicate 1% and 10% significance levels respectively. *Source*: Elaboration on Bloomberg and Yahoo Finance data.

Table 5. Bai Perron test statistics for diamond stock price series and diamond indices.

Series	No.	F-Stat.	1st Break (mm/dd/yy)	2nd Break (mm/dd/yy)	3rd Break (mm/dd/yy)	4th Break (mm/dd/yy)	5th Break (mm/dd/yy)
Diamond stock prices							
Alrosa	4	36.54	09/18/2013	12/15/2014	01/19/2015	09/05/2016	-
Anglo American	4	92.56	11/13/2009	05/14/2012	12/11/2014	11/22/2016	-
Rio Tinto	4	35.52	08/03/2010	05/04/2012	06/15/2015	12/05/2016	-
Petra Diamonds	5	91.80	03/03/2009	12/02/2010	11/11/2013	08/14/2015	05/18/2017
Stornoway D. C.	4	31.56	12/21/2009	10/20/2011	08/17/2015	05/17/2017	-
Star D. C.	2	283.43	03/05/2009	11/17/2011	-	-	-
Mountain P. D.	3	24.65	09/02/2010	05/13/2013	04/27/2017	-	-
Firestone D.	4	134.49	03/03/2009	09/19/2011	06/26/2013	05/18/2017	-
Diamond price indices							
Mid-range D. I.	4	220.38	12/15/2010	08/13/2012	12/03/2014	10/12/2016	-
Higher-range D.I.	4	134.82	11/03/2010	07/09/2012	08/10/2015	05/30/2017	

Notes: The table presents Bai Perron test statistics for 8 diamond stocks (in their original currencies) and the two Diamond Indices for the period 4 June 2007–15 February 2019. The model tests the null hypothesis of L against $L + 1$ sequentially determined structural breaks. The estimation was performed with 0.15 trimming and maximum breaks set to 5 at 5% significance level. The third column reports F statistics for the selected number of breaks, subject to critical values tabulated by Bai and Perron (2003). *Source*: Elaboration on Bloomberg and Yahoo Finance data.

We also tested the presence of structural breaks by using the improved model suggested by Lee and Strazicich (2003) that allows up to two structural breaks, and obtained similar results[3].

Stock returns and indices returns result heteroskedastic as shown by the ARCH LM test reported in Table 6. We use a GARCH approach to measure the volatility of each series. The estimated GARCH parameters for each stock and the two indices are reported in Table 7, while the single conditional variances are presented in Figure 7. We estimated the most appropriate GARCH model for each individual time series, choosing among ARCH, GARCH, TARCH and E-GARCH. We determined

---

[3] Results can be obtained upon request.

our choice for the most appropriate model for each series by contemplating the values of Akaike and Shwarz information criteria, after estimating all possible models on each series.

Table 6. ARCH LM test statistics for diamond stock prices and diamond indices.

$u_t^2 = \alpha_0 + \alpha_1 u_{t-1}^2 + \ldots + \alpha_p u_{p-1}^2$		$H_0{:}\alpha_0 = \alpha_1 = \ldots = \alpha_p = 0$	$H_A{:}\alpha_0 = \alpha_1 = \ldots = \alpha_p \neq 0$		
P_t	F-Stat.	Prob. (F-Stat.)	Obs.*R^2	Prob. Chi-Square (m)	ARCH Effect
Diamond Stock Prices					
Alrosa	*** 70.28	0.00	*** 67.56	0.00	YES
Anglo American	*** 112.74	0.00	*** 108.32	0.00	YES
Rio Tinto	*** 45.79	0.00	*** 45.06	0.00	YES
Petra Diamonds	*** 3.01	0.01	*** 17.93	0.01	YES
Stornoway D. C.	*** 72.24	0.00	*** 70.36	0.00	YES
Star D. C.	*** 130.26	0.00	*** 124.21	0.00	YES
Mountain P. D.	*** 87.80	0.00	*** 85.03	0.00	YES
Firestone D.	*** 31.67	0.00	*** 31.33	0.00	YES
Diamond Price Indices					
Mid-range D. I.	*** 74.37	0.00	*** 80.86	0.00	YES
Higher-range D. I.	*** 40.07	0/00	*** 39.28	0.00	YES

Notes: the table presents ARCH LM test statistics of 8 diamond stocks in their original currencies for the period 4 June 2007–15 February 2019. The null hypothesis of homoskedasticity is tested against the alternative of heteroskedasticity (ARCH effect). u_t denotes the residual series of the least squares regression on the dependent variable Y_t. Number of lags for the test was chosen based on the AIC. The test is the usual F statistic for the regression on the squared residuals. Obs. *R^2 denotes the LM test statistic for the null hypothesis. The statistic follows a χ^2 distribution with m degrees of freedom. *** indicates 1% significance level. *Source:* Elaboration on Bloomberg and Yahoo Finance data.

Table 7. GARCH parameters for diamond stock prices.

P_t	Model	ω	α	β	γ
Diamond Stock Prices					
Alrosa	E-GARCH (1,1)	*** −1.29 (−11.26)	*** 0.31 (11.44)	*** 0.66 (66.43)	*** −0.06 (3.52)
Anglo American	E-GARCH (1,1)	*** −0.11 (−7.51)	*** 0.09 (9.05)	*** 0.90 (665.09)	*** −0.05 (−7.60)
Rio Tinto	E-GARCH (1,1)	*** −0.14 (−7.67)	*** 0.11 (10.13)	*** 0.86 (645.24)	*** −0.06 (−8.15)
Petra Diamonds	E-GARCH (1,1)	*** −0.17 (−7.89)	*** 0.12 (10.39)	*** 0.78 (406.73)	*** −0.03 (−4.76)
Stornoway D. C	TARCH (1,1)	*** 0.00 (9.85)	*** 0.34 (11.20)	*** 0.51 (14.69)	** 0.08 (0.01)
Star D. C.	TARCH (1,1)	*** 0.00 (7.24)	*** 0.09 (7.33)	*** 0.88 (175.66)	*** 0.05 (5.30)
Mountain P. D.	E-GARCH (1,1)	*** −0.18 (−12.35)	*** 0.14 (17.57)	*** 0.82 621.45	*** −0.04 (−9.23)
Firestone D.	TARCH (1,1)	*** 0.00 (17.87)	*** 0.01 (13.98)	*** 0.96 782.21	*** 0.03 14.99
Diamond Price Indices					
MDI	E-GARCH (1,1)	*** −0.09 (−6.31)	*** 0.12 (8.79)	*** 0.89 (724.59)	** −0.01 (−2.39)
HDI	TARCH (1,1)	*** 0.00 (3.68)	*** 0.01 (10.01)	*** 0.95 (258.45)	** 0.02 (2.44)

Notes: The table presents conditional variances and their parameters of 8 studied diamond stocks in their original currencies for the period 4 June 2007–15 February 2019 estimated by the GARCH family models. α denotes the symmetric ARCH term, β represents the GARCH term measuring the persistence of conditional volatility, while γ measures the leverage effect and asymmetric ARCH term. The leverage affect is confirmed if γ is positive and significant in the case of TARCH. The numbers reported in brackets are z-statistics. *** and ** indicate 1% and 5% significance levels, respectively. *Source:* Elaboration on Bloomberg data. *Source:* Elaboration on Bloomberg and Yahoo Finance data.

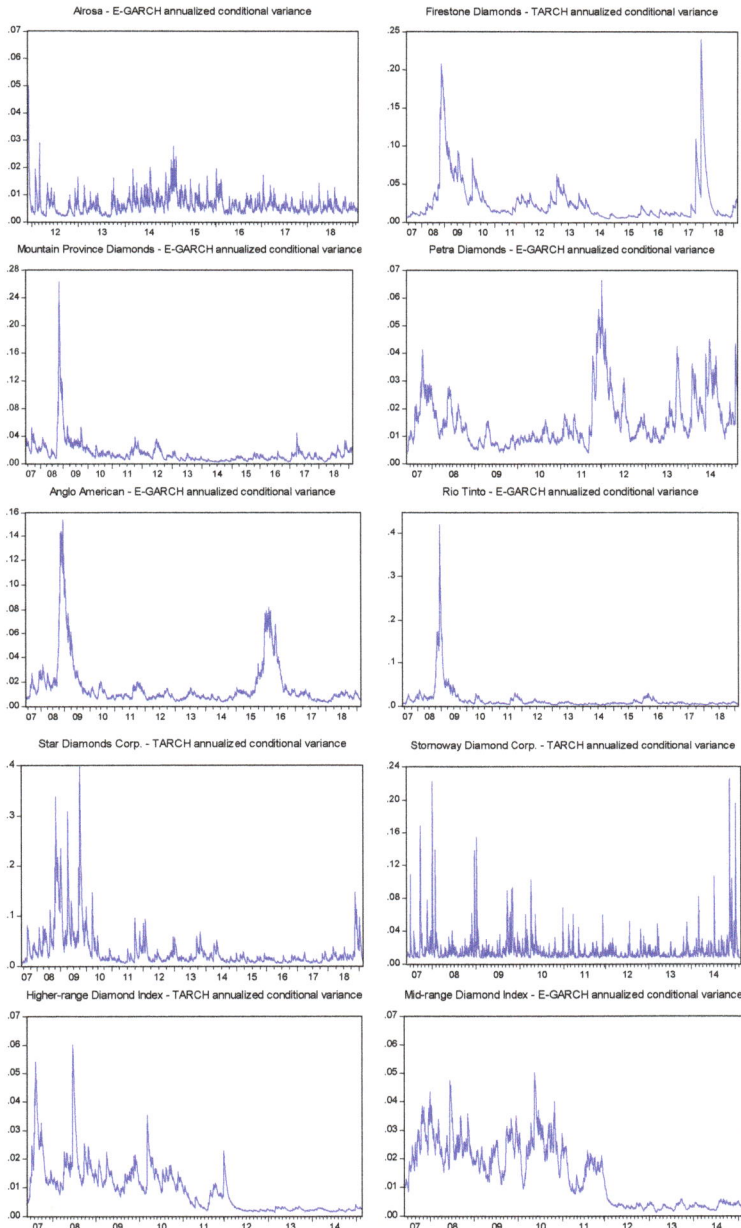

Figure 7. GARCH conditional variances of log returns of diamond stocks and indices. Notes: The figure presents estimated conditional variances (E-GARCH) of log returns of 8 studied diamond stocks (Alrosa, Firestone Diamonds, Mountain Province Diamonds, Petra Diamonds, Anglo American, Rio Tinto, Star Diamond Corporation, Stornoway Diamond Corporation) and 2 diamond indices (Higher-range DI and Mid-range DI) for the period 4 June 2007–15 February 2019. *Source*: Elaboration on Bloomberg and Yahoo Finance data.

Conditional variances show quite different patterns for each stock. Rio Tinto, Mountain Province and Star D. C., after exhibiting an enormous increase in volatility during the GFC, show a pattern of average volatility. Alrosa, Petra D. and Anglo American show several periods in which volatility increases quite aggressively. For instance, the stock Petra D. shows a return to volatility in 2011 that was higher and more erratic than the one that occurred in 2008, and several volatility spikes during the period 2011–2018. Alrosa, on the other hand, shows a very noisy volatility pattern for that entire period.

Diamond Stocks vs. Diamond Prices

Diamond stocks and diamond indices do not show similar dynamics in levels; Moreover, their returns show structural breaks occurring at different dates, not providing evidence that a common driver may explain diamond stocks volatility. We further investigated the relationship between diamond stock returns and the two diamond indices by estimating the Dynamic Conditional Correlation-E-GARCH (1,1) over the studied period. The choice of the model was based on the Akaike information criterion. The DCC-E-GARCH approach allows measuring the short-run correlation existing between the various pairs of securities. A long run relationship may be measured using a cointegration approach.

In Table 8 we firstly report the cross-correlation matrix between the price returns of all studied diamond stocks and the two diamond price indices. We observed very low correlations between diamond stocks and diamonds, with correlation values close to zero. Moreover, the two diamond price indices exhibited a fairly low correlation (0.28), giving further evidence to their different dynamics, as reported in D'Ecclesia and Jotanovic (2018). While the simple correlations among the stock prices of diamond companies result low on average, the stock price returns of Anglo American and Rio Tinto, the two mining giants, were highly correlated (0.80), which could be explained by the common factors affecting the overall mining sector, as well as the fact that both stocks are traded on the London Stock exchange.

Table 8. Cross-correlation matrix among diamond-mining stocks and diamond price indices.

Cross-Correlation Matrix	Alrosa	Anglo A.	Rio Tinto	Petra D.	Stornoway D. C.	Star D. C.	Mountain P. D.	Firestone D.	Mid DI	Higher DI
				Diamond Stock Prices						
Alrosa	1.00	0.11	0.15	0.08	0.02	−0.03	0.05	0.00	0.05	0.04
Anglo A.	0.11	1.00	0.80	0.25	0.08	0.01	0.08	0.02	−0.02	0.04
Rio Tinto	0.15	0.80	1.00	0.25	0.07	0.00	0.08	0.04	−0.01	0.06
Petra D.	0.08	0.25	0.25	1.00	0.04	−0.01	0.12	0.04	0.00	−0.04
Stornoway D. C.	0.02	0.08	0.07	0.04	1.00	0.01	0.04	0.00	−0.01	0.03
Star D. C.	−0.03	0.01	0.00	−0.01	0.01	1.00	0.03	0.01	0.00	0.04
Mountain P. D.	0.05	0.08	0.08	0.12	0.04	0.03	1.00	−0.01	0.04	0.06
Firestone D.	0.00	0.02	0.04	0.04	0.00	0.01	−0.01	1.00	0.01	0.02
				Diamond Price Indices						
Mid-range DI	0.05	−0.01	−0.01	0.00	−0.01	0.00	−0.01	−0.01	1.00	0.28
Higher-range DI	0.04	−0.01	0.01	0.04	0.03	−0.02	0.02	0.00	0.28	1.00

Notes: The table presents cross-correlation matrix of log returns of 8 studied diamond stocks in their original currencies and diamond price indices for the period 4 June 2007–15 February 2019. The series have been individually matched to maintain the maximum number of observations for each pairwise correlation analysis. *Source*: Elaboration on Bloomberg and Yahoo Finance data.

In Figure 8 we further report some of the time-varying DCC-E-GARCH correlations estimated between diamond stocks and the two diamond price indices[4]. The DCC correlation parameters corresponding to all performed estimations are reported in Table 9. The results show that the diamond stock returns are not related to diamond prices given that, on average, each stock shows an average zero correlation with both diamond indices. This might be explained by the fact that stock returns are

---

[4]   The remaining correlation series have not been reported, as they do not differ significantly from those reported in Figure 8. All results are available upon request.

not driven by diamond prices but rather by other factors related to the book values of the companies. In addition, one possible explanation for the lack of correlation found between stock prices and diamond indices may be explained by the fact that polished diamonds are not a direct output of the mining companies. Rough diamonds pass through several value chains before they reach the polished diamond market and the prices for rough diamonds are only available with a monthly frequency. Hence, a different approach must be used to test any possible dependence.

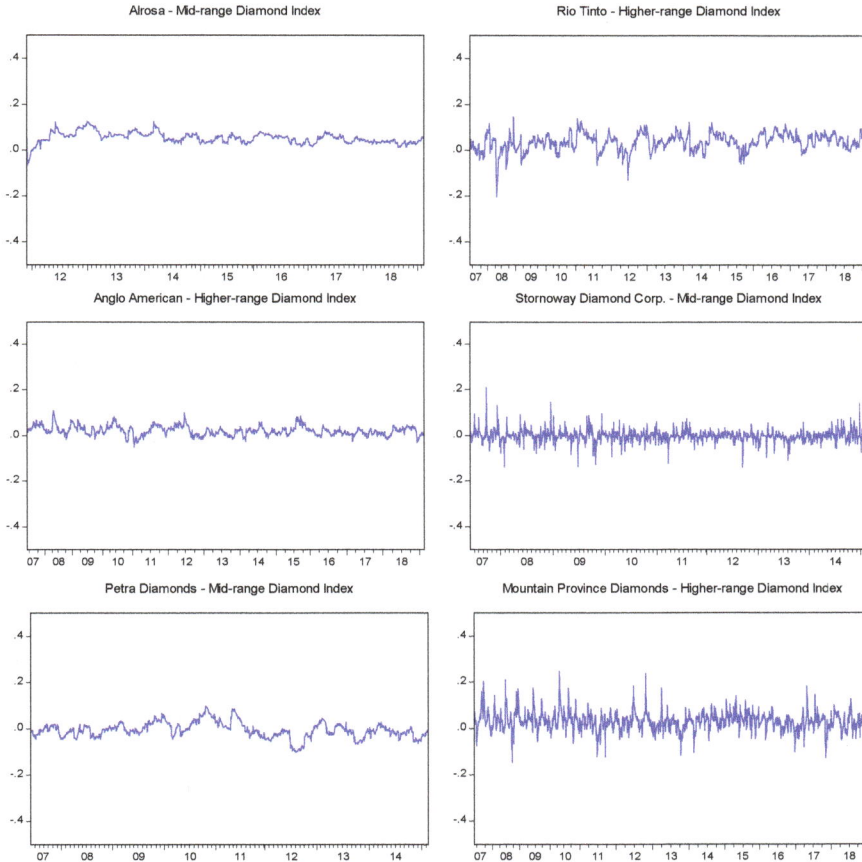

Figure 8. DCC-E-GARCH correlations among diamond stocks and diamond indices. Notes: The figure presents some of the estimated time-varying correlations (DCC-E-GARCHs) between log returns of studied diamond stocks and 2 diamond indices: (Alrosa - Mid-range DI, Rio Tinto - Higher-range DI, Anglo American – Higher-range DI, Stornoway Diamond Corporation – Mid-range DI, Petra Diamonds – Mid-range DI and Mountain Province Diamonds – Higher-range DI) for the period 4 June 2007–15 February 2019. *Source*: Elaboration on Bloomberg and Yahoo Finance data.

Table 9. DCC parameters from the DCC-EGARCH correlation estimations.

Series	Mid-Range Diamond Index				Higher-Range Diamond Index			
	a	z-Stat	b	z-Stat.	a	z-Stat	b	z-Stat
Alrosa	*** 0.99	61.23	** 0.00	2.56	*** 0.78	45.79	*** 0.00	14.35
Anglo A.	*** 0.83	6.82	** 0.02	2.23	*** 0.95	18.48	0.01	0.97
Rio Tinto	*** 0.92	16.89	*** 0.02	10.81	*** 0.98	37.65	* 0.01	1.91
Petra D.	*** 0.98	26.64	0.01	0.75	0.71	0.59	0.52	0.60
Stornoway D. C.	0.64	1.32	* 0.02	1.93	* 0.79	2.19	0.02	0.89
Star D. C.	0.63	1.28	*** 0.02	3.10	0.69	1.37	0.02	1.14
Mountain P. D.	*** 0.76	2.59	0.01	0.95	*** 0.82	7.86	* 0.02	1.72
Firestone D.	0.80	0.38	*** 0.00	2.87	0.80	1.25	*** 0.00	17.94

Notes: The table reports DCC parameters from the DCC-EGARCH correlation estimations of 8 studied diamond stocks and 2 diamond indices for the period 4 June 2007–15 February 2019. ***, ** and * indicate 1%, 5% and 10% significance levels, respectively. *Source*: Elaboration on Bloomberg and Yahoo Finance data.

We further test a possible relationship between the diamond stock prices and the diamond indices using the multifactor approach presented in Tufano (1998), where the author tests how firms engaged in gold mining can be affected by the price of gold. In this paper we analyze the risk exposure of the share returns of the eight firms engaged in diamond mining to changes in the price of diamonds (or their returns).

Managers and investors express share price exposure to the input prices in terms of elasticities; for each percentage change in the input prices they estimate that mining shares would change by 2 to 10 percent, due to financial and operating leverage. These predictions can be confirmed by estimating a multifactor market model, as in Jorion (1990). To estimate the exposure of diamond mining firms to diamond prices, we developed the following market model:

$$R_{s,it} = \alpha_{it} + \beta_1 R_{m,it} + \beta_2 R_{d,it} + \varepsilon_{it}$$

where

$R_{s,it}$—measures the daily return of stock i at time t;

$R_{m,it}$—measures the daily return of regional market stock index i at time t;

$R_{d,it}$—measures the daily return of diamond index i at time t;

For the regional market stock index, we chose the most important market index built in each exchange we analyzed. The coefficients β_1 and β_2 represent the sensitivity of stock i's return for a 1 percent return to holding diamonds, after controlling for movements in broad equity indices that affect the return on these stocks independent of diamond price movements.

In order to obtain unbiased beta estimates, we used the approaches suggested by Dimson (1979), as corrected by Fowler and Rorke (1983), and calculated five sets of diamond and market betas for each diamond mining firm over the entire sample period. These sets of betas differed by the method of adjustment. The adjustments used one lead and one lag term, as adding more than one lead or lag term does not significantly change the measured mean betas. The diamond mining stock returns exhibit the ARCH effect (Table 6) and, hence, we estimated two regressions for each stock using GARCH. The three different stock indices chosen for each of the exchanges we are studying are:

1. MICEX, Russian Stock Index;
2. The S&P/Toronto Stock Exchange 60;
3. FTSE 100 Index, corresponding to London Stock Exchange.

The estimated coefficients from the GARCH mean equations are reported in Table 10. It is interesting to notice that diamond stock returns results were only affected by their respective stock market indices. The Higher-range or the Mid-range diamond indices do not have any role in the

J. Risk Financial Manag. **2019**, *12*, 79

diamond stock returns. This provides further support to the previous result showing that shares of firms engaged in diamond mining cannot be used as an alternative to diamond investments and, therefore, cannot be used as a safe haven.

Table 10. GARCH regression coefficients from the mean equation.

Y_t	MDI ($R_{d,it}$)	Market Index ($R_{m,it}$)	HDI ($R_{d,it}$)	Market Index ($R_{m,it}$)
Alrosa	0.02 (0.22)	*** 0.65 (21.62)	0.00 (0.13)	*** 0.65 (21.75)
Anglo American	0.00 (0.26)	1.63 (64.28)	0.00 (−0.05)	1.63 (63.99)
Rio Tinto	−0.01 (−0.72)	*** 1.52 (66.78)	0.00 (−0.20)	*** 1.52 (67.00)
Petra Diamonds	0.02 (0.46)	*** 0.84 (14.23)	0.03 (1.19)	*** 0.84 (14.14)
Stornoway D. C	−0.02 (0.28)	*** 0.64 (11.88)	0.02 (0.38)	*** 0.63 (11.77)
Star D. C.	−0.01 (0.02)	*** 0.60 (9.36)	−0.06 (−2.34)	*** 0.59 (9.36)
Mountain P. D.	** 0.04 (2.23)	*** 0.71 (14.14)	* 0.07 (3.10)	*** 0.71 (14.07)
Firestone D.	0.01 (0.51)	*** 0.37 (8.32)	−0.01 (−0.33)	*** 0.37 (8.36)

Notes: The table reports estimated betas of diamond mining stocks for the period 4 June 2007–15 February 2019. ***, ** and * indicate 1%, 5% and 10% significance levels, respectively. *Source*: Elaboration on Bloomberg and Yahoo Finance data.

7. Concluding Remarks

Diamonds represent the last hidden commodity that was long neglected by the financial world, given the lack of its fungibility and price transparency. The recent financial crisis encouraged investors to look for alternative assets to protect their portfolios. This brought financial attention to diamonds, which were perceived as a possible new investment asset and eventually viewed as a hedge or a portfolio diversifier. Given that a tradeable diamond financial derivative is still not traded on a regulated exchange, in order to study the potential role of diamonds in the investment context we analyzed the shares of firms engaged in diamond mining. We verified whether they can be a potential liquid substitute to investing in diamonds. We collected a unique dataset of stock prices of all 21 diamond mining companies which are traded on official stock exchanges and studied their price dynamics and possible relationship with diamond prices. For this purpose, we used the Mid-range and Higher-range diamond basket indices built by D'Ecclesia and Jotanovic (2018) as a proxy for the diamond market prices. We then analyzed the relationship between diamond mining stock prices and diamond prices by examining their long-term conditional correlations. Moreover, we also estimated a multifactor market model to verify a possible influence of diamond prices on diamond stock returns. We found that stock returns are only exposed to stock market index returns.

The results show that diamond stocks are not affected by diamonds price dynamics and are not correlated with the diamond market indices.

This paper represents a first step in the scientific analysis of the diamond stock market and leaves plenty of scope for further research. We hope that the original database of diamond mining stocks presented in this article will encourage scholars and facilitate future research in the field.

Author Contributions: V.J. and R.L.D. conceived the presented idea and developed the methodology. V.J. collected the database, performed the computations using the Eviews software and prepared the original draft.

J. Risk Financial Manag. **2019**, *12*, 79

R.L.D. validated the results, reviewed the manuscript and supervised further improvements. V.J. produced the visualizations and further edited the paper.

Funding: This research received no external funding.

Conflicts of Interest: The authors declare no conflict of interest.

References

Adler, Claire. 2010. Martin Rapaport: The Time Has Come for a Mass Market in Sparklers. Financial Times. Available online: https://www.ft.com/content/e72e5078-3155-11df-9741-00144feabdc0 (accessed on 26 February 2014).

Ariovich, G. 1985. The economics of diamond price movements. *MDE Managerial and Decision Economics* 6: 234–40. [CrossRef]

Auer, Benjamin R., and Frank Schuhmacher. 2013. Diamonds—A precious new asset? *International Review of Financial Analysis* 28: 182–89. [CrossRef]

Auer, Benjamin R. 2014. Could diamonds become an investor's best friend? *Review of Managerial Science* 8: 351–83. [CrossRef]

Bai, Jushan, and Pierre Perron. 1998. Estimating and testing linear models with multiple structural changes. *Econometrica* 66: 47–78. [CrossRef]

Bai, Jushan, and Pierre Perron. 2003. Computation and analysis of multiple structural change models. *Journal of Applied Econometrics* 18: 1–22. [CrossRef]

Bain and Company, and Antwerp World Diamond Center. 2011. *The Global Diamond Industry: Lifting the Veil of Mystery*. Antwerp: Bain & Company and Antwerp World Diamond Center Private Foundation.

Bain and Company, and Antwerp World Diamond Center. 2012. *The Global Diamond Industry: Portrait of Growth*. Antwerp: Bain & Company and Antwerp World Diamond Center Private Foundation.

Bain and Company, and Antwerp World Diamond Center. 2013. *The Global Diamond Report 2013. Journey through the Value Chain*. Antwerp: Bain & Company and Antwerp World Diamond Center Private Foundation.

Bain and Company, and Antwerp World Diamond Center. 2018. *The Global Diamond Industry 2018: A Resilient Industry Shines through*. Antwerp: Bain & Company and Antwerp World Diamond Center Private Foundation.

Cameron, Jackie. 2014. Investors Talk up Diamond Mining Stocks. Happily-Ever-After Shares? BizNews. Available online: http://www.biznews.com/global-investing/2014/08/30/investors-talk-up-diamond-mining-stocks-happily-ever-shares/ (accessed on 7 January 2016).

Cardoso, Margarida, and Luis Chambel. 2005. A valuation model for cut diamonds. *International Transactions in Operational Research* 12: 417–36. [CrossRef]

Carlin, Sven. 2017. Two Diamond Stocks to Watch in Upcoming Diamond Supply Gap. Available online: https://seekingalpha.com/article/4112406-two-diamond-stocks-watch-upcoming-diamond-supply-gap (accessed on 15 February 2019).

Chesters, Laura. 2014. Are Diamonds Your New Best Friend? London Evening Standard. Available online: http://www.standard.co.uk/business/business-news/are-diamonds-your-new-best-friend-9168739.html (accessed on 22 November 2014).

D'Ecclesia, Rita Laura, and Vera Jotanovic. 2018. Are Diamonds a safe haven? *Review of Managerial Science* 12: 937–68. [CrossRef]

Dimson, Elroy. 1979. Risk measurement when shares are subject to infrequent trading. *Journal of Financial Economics* 7: 197–226. [CrossRef]

Engle, Robert. 1982. Autoregressive conditional heteroscedasticity with estimates of the variance of United Kingdom inflation. *Econometrica* 50: 987–1007. [CrossRef]

Engle, Robert. 2002. Dynamic conditional correlation—A simple class of multivariate GARCH models. *Journal of Business & Economic Statistics* 20: 339–50. [CrossRef]

Even-Zohar, Chaim. 2012. Diamond Prices Could Fall in 2012 as Supply, Demand in Balance—Tacy Ltd. FORBES. Available online: http://forbes.com/sites/kitconews/2012/03/06/diamond-prices-could-fall-in-2012-as-supply-demand-in-balance-tacy-ltd/#522994d82db8 (accessed on 22 February 2014).

Fowler, David J., and C. Harvey Rorke. 1983. Risk Measurement When Shares Are Subject to Infrequent Trading: Comment. *Journal of Financial Economics* 12: 279–83. [CrossRef]

Golan, E. 2012. The diamond investment promise: Are diamonds finally a commodity? *Idex Magazine* 275: 87–95.

Golan, E. 2013. Diamond prices and the forces that shape them. *Idex Magazine* 268: 90–117.

Gupta, Samir, Michael Polonsky, Arch Woodside, and Cynthia M. Webster. 2010. An impact of external forces on cartel network dynamics: Direct research in the diamond industry. *Industrial Marketing Management* 39: 202–10. [CrossRef]

Jorion, Philippe. 1990. The exchange rate exposure of U.S. multinationals. *Journal of Business* 63: 331–45. [CrossRef]

Karo, Margherita. 1968. The U.S. jewelry industry. *Financial Analysts Journal* 24: 49–56. [CrossRef]

Kempton, Daniel R. 1995. Russian and De Beers: Diamond conflict or cartel? *South African Journal of International Affairs* 3: 94–131. [CrossRef]

Lee, Junsoo, and Mark C. Strazicich. 2003. Minimum Lagrange Multiplier Unit Root Test with Two Structural Breaks. *Review of Economics and Statistics* 85: 1082–89. [CrossRef]

Levenstein, Margaret C., and Valerie Y. Suslow. 2006. What determines cartel success? *Journal of Economic Literature* 44: 43–95. [CrossRef]

Low, Rand Kwong Yew, Yiran Yao, and Robert Faff. 2016. Diamonds vs. precious metals: What shines brightest in your investment portfolio? *International Review of Financial Analysis* 43: 1–14. [CrossRef]

Lu, Chenxi, Terence Tai-Leung Chong, and Wing Hong Chan. 2010. *Long Memory in Diamond Market Returns and Volatility*, Economic Research Paper 2010-2. Laurier Centre for Economic Research and Policy Analysis. The Chinese University of Hong Kong.

Mcgee, S. 2013. Diamonds: A Better Safe Haven than Gold? The Fiscal Times. Available online: http://thefiscaltimes.com/Columns/2013/05/14/Diamonds-A-Better-Safe-Haven-Than-Gold (accessed on 25 February 2014).

McKeough, Pat. 2015. What Is One of the Most Promising Canadian Diamond Stocks? TSI Wealth Daily Advice. Available online: http://www.tsinetwork.ca/daily-advice/mining-stocks/promising-canadian-diamond-stocks/ (accessed on 7 January 2016).

Nelson, Daniel B. 1991. Conditional heteroskedasticity in asset returns: A new approach. *Econometrica* 59: 347–70. [CrossRef]

O'Keefe, Matthew, and Erik Bermel. 2014. Why This Is an Opportune Time to Buy Canadian Diamond Stocks. The Globe and Mail. Research Report. Available online: http://www.theglobeandmail.com/globe-investor/investment-ideas/research-reports/why-canadian-forestry-stocks-are-a-buy-right-now/article18913942/ (accessed on 12 February 2015).

Rapaport, Martin. 2009. Diamonds May Become as Attractive for Investors as Gold. Rough and Polished. Available online: http://rough-polished.com/en/exclusive/26124.html (accessed on 25 February 2013).

Renneboog, Luc, and Christophe Spaenjers. 2012. Hard assets: The returns on rare diamonds and gems. *Finance Research Letters* 9: 220–30. [CrossRef]

Scott, Frank, and Aaron Yelowitz. 2010. Pricing anomalies in the market for diamonds: Evidence of conformist behavior. *Economic Inquiry* 48: 353–68. [CrossRef]

Shevelyova, I. 2006. The world diamond market: Logic of the organization and functioning. *Economics and Management* 2: 79–85.

Sizemore, Charles Lewis. 2015. 5 Cheap "Diamond in the Rough" Stocks to Buy. Available online: https://www.kiplinger.com/slideshow/investing/T052-S001-5-cheap-diamond-in-the-rough-stocks-to-buy/index.html (accessed on 3 March 2019).

Spar, Debora L. 2006. Markets: Continuity and change in the international diamond market. *Journal of Economic Perspectives* 20: 195–208. [CrossRef]

Steinberg, Julie. 2012. Investing in Diamonds: The Clear-Cut Truth. The Wall Street Journal. Available online: http://blogs.wsj.com/totalreturn/2012/10/24/investing-in-diamonds-the-clear-cut-truth/ (accessed on 3 March 2014).

Treadgold, Tim. 2013. Diamonds Could Soon be an Investor's Best Friend as Demand Rises and Supply Falls. Forbes. Available online: http://forbes.com/sites/timtreadgold/2013/10/24/diamonds-could-soon-be-an-investors-best-friend-as-demand-rises-and-supply-falls/ (accessed on 26 February 2014).

Tufano, Peter. 1998. The determinants of stock price exposure: Financial engineering and the gold mining industry. *The Journal of Finance* 53: 1015–52. [CrossRef]

Turrell, Rob. 1982. Rhodes, De Beers and monopoly. *The Journal of Imperial and Commonwealth History* 10: 311–43. [CrossRef]

Vaillant, Nicolas G., and François-Charles Wolff. 2013. Understanding Diamond Pricing Using Unconditional Quantile Regressions. HAL Working Papers. IDEAS halshs-00853384. Available online: https://econpapers. repec.org/paper/halwpaper/halshs-00853384.htm (accessed on 3 March 2015).

Wieczner, Jen. 2014. For Investors, Diamonds Might Be the New Gold. Fortune. Available online: http: //fortune.com/2014/02/19/for-investors-diamonds-might-be-the-new-gold (accessed on 2 March 2015).

Zimnisky, Paul. 2013. Diamonds: Driven by Market Forces for the First Time in 100 Years. Hard Assets. Available online: http://resourceinvestor.com/2013/04/09/diamonds-driven-market-forces-first-time-100-years (accessed on 15 October 2013).

MDPI

St. Alban-Anlage 66

4052 Basel

Switzerland

Tel. +41 61 683 77 34

Fax +41 61 302 89 18

www.mdpi.com

Journal of Risk and Financial Management Editorial Office

E-mail: jrfm@mdpi.com

www.mdpi.com/journal/jrfm

www.ingramcontent.com/pod-product-compliance
Lightning Source LLC
Chambersburg PA
CBHW051843210326
41597CB00033B/5762